37TH CONGRESS, } HOUSE OF REPRESENTATIVES. { Ex. Doc.
3d *Session.* } { No. 81.

REPORT OF MAJOR GENERAL JOHN POPE.

LETTER

FROM

THE SECRETARY OF WAR,

IN ANSWER TO

Resolution of the House of 18th ultimo, transmitting copy of report of Major General John Pope.

MARCH 3, 1863.—Laid on the table, and ordered to be printed.

MARCH 3, 1863.—*Resolved,* That five thousand extra copies of the official report of Major General John Pope's campaign in Virginia be printed for the use of the members of the present House.

WAR DEPARTMENT,
Washington City, March 2, 1863.

SIR: In compliance with the resolution of the House of Representatives of the 18th ultimo, I have the honor to transmit herewith a copy of the report of Major General John Pope, and the accompanying documents, concerning the operations of the army of Virginia, while under his command.

Very respectfully, your obedient servant,

EDWIN M. STANTON,
Secretary of War.

Hon. GALUSHA A. GROW,
Speaker of the House of Representatives.

REPORT

OF

MAJOR GENERAL JOHN POPE, UNITED STATES ARMY

OF HIS

CAMPAIGN IN VIRGINIA.

LIST OF DOCUMENTS.

29. Report of commanding officer 4th New York cavalry.
30. Report of commanding officer 9th New York cavalry.
31. Report of commanding officer 6th Ohio cavalry.
32. Report of commanding officer 1st Maryland cavalry.
33. Report of Brigadier General R. C. Schenck, (by Colonel Cheesebrough, aide-de-camp.)
34. Report of Colonel Krzyzanowski, commanding brigade.
35. Report of Brigadier General George Sykes.
36. Report of G. K. Warren, 5th New York volunteers.
37. Report of Lieutenant Colonel R. C. Buchanan, 4th infantry.
38. Report of Captain S. H. Weed, 5th artillery.
39. Report of First Lieutenant A. M. Randoll, 1st artillery.
40. Report of Second Lieutenant W. E. Van Reed, 5th artillery.
41. Nominal report of casualties of Brigadier General G. Sykes's division.
42. Tabular report of casualties of Brigadier General George Sykes's division.
43. Nominal report of casualties of Brigadier General G. W. Morell's division.
44. Tabular report of casualties of Brigadier General G. W. Morell's division.
45. Report of Brigadier General J. B. Ricketts.
46. Report of Lieutenant Colonel William Chapman, 3d infantry.
47. Report of Colonel William Blaisdell, 11th Massachusetts volunteers.
48. Report of Captain W. M. Graham, 1st artillery.
49. Report of Captain G. E. Randolph, 1st artillery.
50. Report of Brigadier General Milroy. Copies of letters from Lieutenant Colonel R. C. Buchanan.
51. Report of Brigadier General J. P. Hatch.
52. Report of Colonel J. W. Revere, 7th New York volunteers.
53. Report of Lieutenant Colonel R. Thompson, 115th Pennsylvania volunteers.
54. Report of Lieutenant Colonel G. C. Burling, 6th New York volunteers.
55. Report of Captain George Hoffman, 8th New York volunteers.
56. Report of Major G. Banks, 16th Massachusetts volunteers.
57. Report of casualties of the 8th New Jersey volunteers.
58. Report of casualties of the 2d New York volunteers.
59. Report of casualties of the 115th Pennsylvania volunteers.
60. Report of casualties of the 5th New Jersey volunteers.
61. Report of casualties of the 7th New Jersey volunteers.
62. Copies of correspondence between Generals McDowell and Schurz.
63. Appendix "A" to General McDowell's report.
64. Appendix "A" to General Pope's report.
65. Appendix "B" to General Pope's report.

No. 1.

REPORT OF MAJOR GENERAL JOHN POPE OF HIS OPERATIONS IN VIRGINIA.

NEW YORK, *January* 27, 1863.

GENERAL: I have the honor to submit the following report of the operations of the army under my command during the late campaign in Virginia.

Several of the reports of the corps commanders have not yet reached me, but so much time has elapsed since the termination of the campaign that I do not feel at liberty to withhold this report longer.

The strange misapprehension of facts concerning this campaign which, though proceeding from irresponsible sources, has much possessed the public mind, makes it necessary for me to enter more into detail than I should otherwise have done, and to embody in the report such of the despatches and orders sent and received as will make clear every statement which is contained in it.

On the 26th day of June, 1862, by special order of the President of the United States, I was assigned to the command of the army of Virginia. That army was constituted as follows: first corps, under Major General Frémont; second corps, under Major General Banks; third corps, under Major General McDowell. In addition to these three corps, a small and unorganized force, under Brigadier General Sturgis, was posted in the neighborhood of Alexandria, and was then in process of being organized for field service. The forces in the intrenchments around Washington were also placed under my command. All the disposable movable forces consisted of the three corps first named. Their effective strength of infantry and artillery, as reported to me, was as follows: Frémont's corps, eleven thousand five hundred strong; Banks's corps, reported at fourteen thousand five hundred, but in reality only about eight thousand; McDowell's corps eighteen thousand five hundred—making a total of thirty-eight thousand men.

The cavalry numbered about five thousand men for duty, but most of it was badly mounted and armed, and in poor condition for service. These forces were scattered over a wide district of country, not within supporting distance of each other, and many of the brigades and divisions were badly organized and in a demoralized condition. This was particularly the case with the army corps of Major General Frémont, a sad report of which was made to me by General Sigel when he relieved General Frémont in command of the corps.

My first labors were directed to the reorganization of some of the divisions and brigades of that corps, and to supplying the whole force with much of the material absolutely necessary for troops in the field.

The corps of Banks and Frémont were in the valley of the Shenandoah, between Winchester and Middletown, the bulk of the forces being in the vicinity of the latter place.

One division of McDowell's corps was at Manassas Junction, with its advance thrown forward to Catlett's Station. The other division was posted in the vicinity of Falmouth, opposite Fredericksburg. When I first assumed command of these forces the troops under Jackson had retired from the valley of the Shenandoah and were in rapid march toward Richmond; so that at that time there was no force of the enemy of any consequence within a week's march of any of the troops assigned to my command.

It was the wish of the government that I should cover the city of Washington from any attacks from the direction of Richmond, make such dispositions as were necessary to assure the safety of the valley of the Shenandoah, and at the same time so operate upon the enemy's lines of communication in the direction of Gordonsville and Charlottesville as to draw off, if possible, a considerable force of the enemy from Richmond, and thus relieve the operations against that city of the army of the Potomac.

The first object I had in view was to concentrate, as far as possible, all the movable forces under my command, and to establish them in such positions as best to effect the objects set forth. It seemed to me that the security of the Shenandoah valley was not best attained by posting troops within the valley itself, but that the necessary results could be better accomplished, and the other objects with which I was charged best promoted, by concentrating these forces at some point or points from which, if any attempts were made to enter the valley of the Shenandoah from Richmond, I should be able, by rapid marching, to interpose between such force and the main body of the enemy, and cut off its retreat. I felt confident, and this confidence was justified by subsequent results, that no considerable force of the enemy would attempt to enter the valley of the Shenandoah while the forces under my command were so posted as to be able, without difficulty, to intercept its retreat and fall upon its rear. I accordingly sent orders to Major General Sigel, commanding the first corps, to move forward from Middletown, cross the Shenandoah at Front Royal, and, pursuing the west side of the Blue Ridge, to take post at Sperryville by passing through Luray Gap. At the same time I directed Major General Banks, crossing the Shenandoah at the same point, to move forward and take post between six and ten miles east of Sperryville. General McDowell was ordered to move Ricketts's division of his corps from Manassas Junction to Waterloo Bridge, the point where the turnpike from Warrenton to Sperryville crosses the Upper Rappahannock; King's division, of the same corps, it was thought best to leave at Fredericksburg to cover the crossing of the Rappahannock at that point, and to protect the railroad thence to Acquia creek, and the public buildings which had been erected at the latter place. While I yielded to this wish of the War Dapartment, the wide separation of this division from the main body of the army, and the ease with which the enemy would be able to interpose between them, engaged my earnest attention and gave me very serious uneasiness.

Whilst these movements were in progress commenced the series of battles which preceded and attended the retreat of General McClellan from the Chickahominy toward Harrison's Landing. When first General McClellan began to intimate by his despatches that he designed making this movement toward James river, I suggested to the President of the United States the impolicy of such a movement, and the serious consequences which would be likely to result from it, and urged upon him that he should send orders to General McClellan that if he were unable to maintain his position on the Chickahominy, and were pressed by superior forces of the enemy, to mass his whole force on the north side of that stream, even at the risk of losing much materiel of war, and endeavor to make his way in the direction of Hanover Court-House; but in no event to retreat with his army further to the south than the White House or York river. I stated to the President that the retreat to James river was carrying General McClellan away from any re-enforcements that could possibly be sent him within a reasonable time, and was absolutely depriving him of any substantial aid from the forces under my command; that by this movement the whole army of the enemy would be interposed between his army and mine, and that they would then be at liberty to strike in either direction as they might consider it most advantageous; that this movement to James river would leave entirely unprotected, except in so far as the small force under my command was able to protect it, the whole region in front of Washington, and that it would therefore be impossible to send any of the forces under my command to re-enforce General McClellan without rendering it certain that the enemy, even in the worst case for themselves, would have the privilege and power of exchanging Richmond for Washington city; that to them the loss of Richmond would be trifling, whilst the loss of Washington to us would be conclusive, or nearly so, in its results upon this war. I was so deeply impressed with these views that I repeatedly and earnestly urged them upon the President and Secretary of War. After General McClellan had taken up his position at Harrison's Landing, I addressed him a letter stating to him my position and the distribution of the troops under my command, and requesting him in all earnestness and good faith to write me fully and freely his views, and to suggest to me any measures which he thought desirable to enable me to co-operate with him, or to render any assistance in my power in the operations of the army under his command. I stated to him that I had no object except to assist his operations, and that I would undertake any labor and run any risk for that purpose. I therefore desired him to feel no hesitation in communicating freely with me, as he might rest assured that every suggestion that he would make would meet all respect and consideration at my hands, and that, so far as it was in my power to do so, I would carry out his wishes with all energy and with all the means at my command. In reply to this communication I received a letter from General McClellan, very general in its terms, and proposing nothing towards the accomplishment of the purpose I had suggested to him. It became apparent that, considering the situation in which the army of the Potomac and the army of Virginia were placed in relation to each other, and the absolute necessity of harmonious and prompt co-operation between them, some military superior both of General McClellan and myself should be called to Washington and placed in command of all the operations in Virginia.

In accordance with these views Major General Halleck was called to Washington and placed in general command. Many circumstances which it is not necessary here to set forth, induced me to express to the President, to the Secretary of War, and to General Halleck, my desire to be relieved from the command of the army of Virginia, and to be returned to the western country.

My services, however, were considered necessary in the projected campaign, and my wishes were not complied with. I accordingly took the field in Virginia with grave forebodings of the result, but with a determination to carry out the plans of the government with all the energy and with all the ability of which I was master.

Previous to taking the field, I issued the following orders, which set out very fully the policy which I considered advisable, and which at that time received the sanction of the government, and, so far as I know, the approval of the country.

The order requiring the troops to subsist upon the country in which their operations were conducted has, with a wilful disregard of its terms, been construed, greatly to my discredit, as authorizing indiscriminate robbery and plunder; yet the terms of this order are so specific as to the manner and by whom all property or subsistence needed for the use of the army should be seized, and the order is so common in the history of warfare that I have been amazed that it could have been so misinterpreted and misunderstood. It is therefore submitted here for the calm examination of the government and of the public.

I believed then and believe now that the policy there laid down was wise and just, and was well calculated to secure efficient and rapid operations of the army, and, in case of reverse, to leave the enemy without the means of subsisting in the country over which our army had passed, and over which any pursuit must be conducted. The long delay and embarrassment of the army under General Lee, in its subsequent movements towards Washington, occasioned largely by the want of supplies taken from the country under this order, fully justified its wisdom.

It was determined, before I left Washington to take the field in Virginia, that the union of the armies of Virginia and of the Potomac was absolutely essential both to the safety of the national capital and to the further successful prosecution of the operations against Richmond. The mission of the army under my command, therefore, was to cover as far as possible the front of Washington and make secure the valley of the Shenandoah, and so operate upon the enemy's lines of communication to the west and northwest as to force him to make such heavy detachments from his main force at Richmond as would enable the army of the Potomac to withdraw from its position at Harrison's Landing and to take shipping for Acquia creek or for Alexandria. If, as was feared, the enemy should throw his whole force in the direction of Washington, it became my duty to resist his advance at all hazards, and so to delay and embarrass his movements as to gain all the time possible for the arrival of the army of the Potomac behind the Rappahannock. Meantime, before the arrival of General Halleck, I instructed General King, at Fredericksburg, to send forward detachments of his cavalry to operate upon the line of the Virginia Central railroad, and as far as possible to embarrass and destroy communication between Richmond and the valley of the Shenandoah. Several cavalry expeditions which that officer despatched for the purpose were completely successful, and succeeded in breaking up the railroad at several points upon several occasions. At the same time I directed Major General Banks to send forward an infantry brigade with all his cavalry to march rapidly upon Culpeper Court-House, and, after taking possession of that place, to push forward cavalry towards the Rapidan, in the direction of Gordonsville. On the fourteenth of July, after this movement was successfully accomplished, I directed General Banks to push forward during the night of that day the whole of his cavalry force, under Brigadier General Hatch, from Culpeper, with orders to take possession of Gordonsville, and to destroy the railroad for ten or fifteen miles east of that place, with a portion of his forces, whilst all remaining pushed forward in the direction of Charlottesville, destroying the railroad bridges and interrupting that line of communication as far as practicable.

At that time there was no force of the enemy at Gordonsville or in the vicinity, and the whole operation as ordered was not only easily practicable, but would have been attended with serious consequences to the enemy; but, to my surprise and dissatisfaction, I received, on the seventeenth of July, from General Banks, a report that General Hatch had taken with him infantry, artillery, and trains of wagons, and that, in consequence of bad roads, he had, at that date, only succeeded in going as far as Madison Court-House. Meantime, on the sixteenth of July, the advance of Jackson's forces under Ewell had reached Gordonsville, and the proposed movements, as ordered, became impracticable. No satisfactory explanation has ever been made to me of this departure from my orders on the part of General Hatch. Finding it no longer practicable to occupy Gordonsville, as I had designed, I sent orders to General Banks to direct General Hatch to select from his own cavalry and that of General McDowell, which I had sent forward, fifteen hundred to two thousand of the best mounted men, and to proceed from Madison Court-House, around the west side of the Blue Ridge, to a point whence he could make an easy descent upon the railroad west of Gordonsville, and if successful, to push forward to Charlottsville, and, if possible, destroy the railroad between that place and Lynchburg. In compliance with this order, General Hatch commenced to make the movement as directed, but abandoned it very soon after he started, and returned by the way of Sperryville to his post. As soon as I had received the report of this second failure, I relieved General Hatch from the command of the cavalry of General Banks's corps, and sent Brigadier General Buford to report to General Banks as the chief of cavalry of his corps. On the twenty-ninth of July I left Washington, and after reviewing Ricketts's division of McDowell's corps at Waterloo Bridge, repaired to the headquarters of General Banks, a few miles southeast of Little Washington. All preparations having been completed, I instructed General Banks to move forward on the seventh of August and take post at the point where the turnpike from Sperryville to Culpeper crosses Hazel river. General McDowell was ordered on the day previous, to move forward with Ricketts's division from Waterloo Bridge to Culpeper Court-House, so that on the seventh of August all the infantry and artillery forces of the army of Virginia were assembled along the turnpike from Sperryville to Culpeper, and numbered about 28,500 men. King's division, as I have before stated, was left on the Lower Rappahannock, opposite Fredericksburg, and was not then available for active operations in the direction of Gordonsville.

The cavalry forces covering the front of the army on that day were distributed as follows: General Buford, with five regiments, was posted at Madison Court-House, with his pickets along the line of the Rapidan from Burnett's Ford as far west as the Blue Ridge. General Sigel had been directed to post a brigade of infantry and a battery of artillery at the point where the road from Madison Court-House to Sperryville crosses Robertson's river, as a support to the cavalry of General Buford, in front of him. General Bayard, with four regiments of cavalry, was posted near Rapidan Station, the point where the Orange and Alexandria road crosses Rapidan river, with his pickets extended as far to the east as Raccoon Ford, and connecting with General Buford on his right at Burnett's Ford. From Raccon Ford to the forks of the Rappahannock, above Falmouth, the Rapidan was lined with cavalry pickets. On the top of Thoroughfare mountain, about half-way between Generals Bayard and Buford, was established a signal station, which overlooked the whole country as far south as Orange Court-House.

On the seventh I proceeded to Sperryville and inspected the corps of Major General Sigel. I remained at Sperryville until four o'clock on the afternoon of that day, during which time I received several reports from the front that the enemy was crossing the Rapidan at several points between the railroad crossing of that river and Liberty Mills. I reached Culpeper Court-House on the morning of the 8th of August. The town had been occupied for several days by Crawford's brigade of General Banks's corps, and on the 7th Ricketts's division of McDowell's corps had also reached there from Waterloo Bridge. During the whole of the morning of the 8th I continued to receive reports from General Bayard, who was slowly falling back in the direction of Culpeper Court-House from the advance of the enemy, and from General Buford, who also reported the enemy advancing in heavy force upon Madison Court-House. My instructions required me to be careful and keep my communications good with Fredericksburg, and by no means to permit the enemy to interpose between me and that place. Although during the whole of the 8th of August it was very doubtful, from the reports of Generals Bayard and Buford, whether the enemy's movement was in the direction of Madison Court-House or of Culpeper, I considered it advisable, in view of my relations with Fredericksburg, to concentrate my whole force in the direction of Culpeper, so as to keep myself constantly interposed between the main body of the enemy and the lower fords of the Rappahannock. Early in the day I pushed forward Crawford's brigade of Banks's corps, in the direction of Cedar or Slaughter Mountain, to support General Bayard, who was falling slowly back in that direction, and to assist him as far as practicable in determining the movements and the forces of the enemy. I sent orders, also, to General Banks to move forward promptly from Hazel river to Culpeper Court-House, and also to General Sigel to march at once from Sperryville to the same place. To my surprise, I received, after night on the 8th, a note from General Sigel, dated at Sperryville, at half-past six that afternoon, asking me by what road he should march to Culpeper Court-House. As there was but one road between those two points, and that a broad stone turnpike, I was at a loss to understand how General Sigel could entertain any doubt as to the road by which he should march. This doubt, however, delayed the arrival of his corps at Culpeper Court-House several hours, and rendered it impracticable for that corps to be pushed to the point, as I had designed, on the afternoon of the next day.

Early on the morning of the 9th of August I directed General Banks to move forward towards Cedar Mountain with his whole corps, and to join the brigade of that corps, under General Crawford, which had been pushed forward on the day previous. I directed General Banks to take up a strong position at or near the point occupied by that brigade, to check the advance of the enemy, and to determine his forces and the character of his movement as far as practicable. The consolidated report of General Banks's corps, received some days previously, exhibited an effective force of something over fourteen thousand men. Appended to this report will be found the return in question. It appeared subsequently, however, that General Banks's forces at that time did not exceed eight thousand men. But although I several times called General Banks's attention to the discrepancy between this return and the force he afterwards stated to me he had led to the front, that discrepancy has never been explained, and I do not yet understand how General Banks could have been so greatly mistaken as to the forces under his immediate command. I directed him, when he went forward from Culpeper Court-House, that if the enemy advanced to attack him in the strong position which I had instructed him to take up, he should push his skirmishers well to the front and notify me immediately. Three miles in his rear, and within easy supporting distance, Ricketts's division of General McDowell's corps had been posted at the point where the road from Madison Court-House to Culpeper intersects the road from Culpeper to Cedar Mountain. This division was so posted because it was not certain whether a considerable force of the enemy was not advancing on Culpeper from the direction of Madison Court-House. General Buford having reported to me very early on the morning of the 9th, from Madison Court-House, that the enemy was in heavy force on his right, his left, and partly on his rear, and that he was retreating in the direction of Sperryville.

Desultory artillery firing had been kept up all day on the ninth in the direction of General Banks's corps; but I continued to receive during the whole of that day reports from General Banks that no considerable force of the enemy, except cavalry, had come forward, and that though the cavalry had been ostentatiously displayed, he did not believe that the enemy was in sufficient force to make any attack upon him. As late as 5 o'clock in the afternoon General Banks wrote me substantially to the same effect; but before I had received this last note the artillery firing had become so rapid and continuous that I feared a general engagement was going on, or might be brought on at any moment. I therefore instructed General McDowell to move forward Ricketts's division rapidly to the field and accompanied that division myself. At no time during the day did General Banks express any apprehensions of attack in force by the enemy, nor did he ask nor intimate that he needed re-enforcements.

General Sigel's corps began to march into Culpeper Court-House late in the afternoon, and just as I was leaving that place, having been delayed several hours by General Sigel's singular uncertainty as to what road he ought to pursue; I had given orders a number of days previously that all the troops belonging to the army of Virginia should be ready to march at the shortest notice, and should habitually keep two days' cooked rations in their haversacks. Notwithstanding this order, General Sigel's corps arrived in Culpeper without any rations, and was unable to move forward until provisions could be procured from McDowell's train and cooked at Culpeper Court-House.

I have received no report from General Banks of his operations at Cedar Mountain, but I had sent forward Brigadier General Roberts, chief of cavalry of my staff, and had directed him to report to General Banks in the early part of the day of the 9th, and to advise freely with him as to the operations of his corps. General Roberts, as well as General Banks, was fully advised of my wishes, and that I desired General Banks merely to keep the enemy in check by occupying a strong position in his front, until the whole of the disposable forces under my command should be concentrated in the neighborhood. General Roberts reported to me that he had conferred freely with General Banks, and urgently represented to him my purposes; but that General Banks, contrary to his suggestions and to my wishes, had left the strong position which he had taken up and had advanced at least a mile to assault the enemy, believing that they were not in considerable force, and that he would be able to crush their advance before their main body could come up from the direction of the Rapidan. He accordingly threw forward his whole corps into action against superior forces of the enemy strongly posted and sheltered by woods and ridges. His advance led him over the open ground, which was everywhere swept by the fire of the enemy concealed in the woods and ravines beyond. Notwithstanding these disadvantages his corps gallantly responded to his orders and assaulted the enemy with great fury and determination. The action lasted about an hour and a half, and during that time our forces suffered heavy loss, and were gradually driven back to their former position; at which point, just at dusk, Ricketts's division of McDowell's corps, came up and joined in the engagement.

As soon as I arrived on the field, at the head of Ricketts's division, I directed General Banks to draw in his right, which was much extended, and to mass the whole of his right wing at the centre of his line, pushing forward at the same time Ricketts's division to occupy the ground thus vacated. The enemy followed Banks, as he retired, with great caution, and emerging from the wood, which had sheltered him all day, attempted to push forward to the open ground in front of our new line. A sharp artillery engagement immediately commenced, when the enemy was driven back to the woods principally by the batteries of Ricketts's division.

The artillery firing was kept up until near midnight of the 9th. Finding that Banks's corps had been severely cut up and was much fatigued, I drew it back to the rear and pushed forward the corps of Sigel, which had begun to arrive, to occupy the woods on the left of the road, with a wide space of open ground in his front Ricketts's division was also drawn back to the cover of the woods and behind the ridges in the open ground on the right of Sigel. These dispositions were completed about daybreak on the morning of the 10th. Banks's corps, reduced to about five thousand men, was so cut up and worn down with fatigue that I did not consider it capable of rendering any efficient service for several days. I therefore directed General Banks, or, in his absence, General Williams, who succeeded to the command, to assemble his corps on the road to Culpeper Court-House and about two miles in rear of our front; to collect his stragglers, send back his wounded to Culpeper Court-House, and proceed as rapidly as possible to put the corps in condition for service.

In consequence of the vigorous resistance of the night previous, and the severe loss of the enemy in attempting to advance, before daylight of the 10th Jackson drew back his forces towards Cedar Mountain, about two miles from our front. Our pickets were immediately pushed forward, supported by Milroy's brigade, and occupied the ground.

The day of the 10th was intensely hot, and the troops on both sides were too much fatigued to renew the action. My whole effective force on that day, exclusive of Banks's corps, which was in no condition for service, was about 20,000 artillery and infantry, and about 2,000 cavalry. General Buford, with the cavalry force under his command, not yet having been able to join the main body, I had telegraphed General King, at Fredericksburg, to move forward on the 8th by the lower fords of the Rappahannock and Stevensburg to join me. A large part of his command had just returned from a very fatiguing expedition against the Central railroad, but he marched forward promptly and joined the main body late in the evening of the 11th. The whole day was spent by both armies in burying the dead and in bringing off the wounded.

Although, even after King joined me, my whole effective force was barely equal to that of the enemy, I determined, after giving King's division one night's rest, to fall upon him at daylight on the 12th, on his line of communication, and compel him to fight a battle which must have been entirely decisive for one army or the other.

But during the night of the 11th Jackson evacuated his position in front of us and retreated rapidly across the Rapidan, in the direction of Gordonsville, leaving many of his dead and wounded on the field and along the road from Cedar Mountain to Orange Court-House. No materiel of war nor baggage trains were lost on either side, but the loss of life on both sides was severe. Brigadier Generals Geary, Auger, and Carroll were badly wounded, and Brigadier General Prince was captured by accident. Very many of our best field and company officers were killed or wounded. From the verbal reports and statements of General Banks and others, the Massachusetts regiments behaved with especial gallantry and sustained the heaviest losses; but the conduct of the whole corps of General Banks was beyond all praise. Although I regret that General Banks thought it expedient to depart from my instructions, it gives me pleasure to bear testimony to his gallant and intrepid conduct throughout that action. He exposed himself as freely as any one under his command, and his example went far to secure that gallant and noble conduct which has made his corps famous. Generals Geary, Auger, Carroll, Gordon, and Green behaved with distinguished gallantry. General Prince, who had led his brigade throughout the action with coolness and courage, was captured after dark whilst passing from one flank of his command to the other. As I have not received any report from General Banks, it is not in my power to mention the field and company officers who distinguished themselves under his immediate eye in this action; but as soon as his report is received I will transmit it to the government, and endeavor to do justice to every officer and soldier who belonged to his corps. Brigadier General Roberts, chief of cavalry of my staff, accompanied General Banks throughout the day, and rendered most important and gallant service.

No report of killed and wounded has been made to me by General Banks; I can, therefore, only form an approximation of our losses in that battle. Our killed, wounded, and prisoners amounted to about 1,800 men, besides which fully 1,000 men straggled back to Culpeper Court-House and beyond, and never entirely returned to their commands. A strong cavalry force under Generals Buford and Bayard pursued the enemy to the Rapidan and captured many stragglers. The cavalry forces immediately resumed their original positions, and again occupied the Rapidan from Raccoon Ford to the base of the Blue Ridge. On the 14th of August General Reno, with 8,000 men of the forces which had arrived at Falmouth, under General Burnside, joined me. I immediately pushed forward my whole force in the direction of the Rapidan, and occupied a strong position, with my right, under Major Gen. Sigel, resting on Robertson's river, where the road from Cedar Mountain to Orange Court-House crosses that stream; my centre, under General McDowell, occupying both flanks of Cedar Mountain; and my left, under General Reno, a position near Raccoon Ford, and covering the road from that ford to Stevensburg and Culpeper. I began immediately again to operate with my cavalry upon the enemy's communications with Richmond. From the 12th to the 18th of August reports were constantly reaching me of large forces of the enemy re-enforcing Jackson from the direction of Richmond, and by the morning of the 18th I became satisfied that nearly the whole force of the enemy from Richmond was assembling in my front, along the south side of the Rapidan, and extending from Raccoon Ford to Liberty Mills.

The cavalry expeditions sent out on the sixteenth, in the direction of Louisa Court-House, captured the adjutant general of General Stuart, and was very near capturing that officer himself. Among the papers taken was an autograph letter of General Robert Lee to General Stuart, dated Gordonsville, August 15th, which made manifest to me the position and force of the enemy, and their determination to overwhelm the army under my command before it could be re-enforced by any portion of the army of the Potomac. I held on to my position, thus far to the front, for the purpose of affording all time possible for the arrival of the army of the Potomac at Acquia and Alexandria, and to embarrass and delay the movements of the enemy as far as practicable. On the 18th of August it became apparent to me that this advanced position, with the small force under my command, was no longer tenable in the face of the overwhelming forces of the enemy. I determined, accordingly, to withdraw behind the Rappahannock with all speed, and, as I had been instructed, to defend, as far as practicable, the line of that river. I directed Major General Reno to send back his trains, on the morning of the 18th, by the way of Stevensburg, to Kelly's or Burnett's Ford, and, as soon as the trains had gotten several hours in advance, to follow them with his whole corps, and take post behind the Rappahannock, leaving all his cavalry in the neighborhood of Raccoon Ford to cover this movement. General Banks's corps, which had been ordered, on the 12th, to take position at Culpeper Court-House, I directed, with its trains preceding it, to cross the Rappahannock at the point where the Orange and Alexandria railroad crosses that river. General McDowell's train was ordered to pursue the same route, while the train of General Sigel was directed through Jefferson, to cross the Rappahannock at Warrenton Sulphur Springs. So soon as these trains had been sufficiently advanced, McDowell's corps was directed to take the route from Culpeper to Rappahannock Ford, whilst General Sigel, who was on the right and front, was instructed to follow the movements of his train to Sulphur Springs. These movements were executed during the day and night of the 18th, and the day of the 19th, by which time the whole army, with its trains, had safely recrossed the Rappahannock and was posted behind that stream, with its left at Kelly's Ford and its right about three miles above Rappahannock Station, General Sigel having been directed, immediately upon crossing at Sulphur Springs, to march down the left bank of the Rappahannock until he connected closely with General McDowell's right.

Early on the morning of the 20th the enemy drove in our pickets in front of Kelly's Ford and at Rappahannock Station, but finding we had covered those fords, and that it would be impracticable to force the passage of the river without heavy loss, his advance halted and the main body of his army was brought forward from the Rapidan. By the night of the 20th the bulk of his forces confronted us from Kelly's Ford to a point above our extreme right. During the whole of the days of the 21st and 22d efforts were made by the enemy, at various points, to cross the river, but they were repulsed in all cases. The artillery fire was rapid and continuous during the whole of those days, and extended along the line of the river for seven or eight miles. Finding that it was not practicable to force the passage of the river in my front, the enemy began slowly to move up the river for the purpose of turning our right. My orders required me to keep myself closely in communication with Fredericksburg, to which point the army of the Potomac was being brought from the peninsula, with the purpose of re-enforcing me from that place by the line of the Rappahannock. My force was too small to enable me to extend my right further without so weakening my line as to render it easy for the enemy to break through at any point. I telegraphed again and again to Washington, representing this movement of the enemy toward my right and the impossibility of my being able to extend my lines so as to resist it without abandoning my connexions with Fredericksburg.

I was assured, on the 21st, that if I would hold the line of the river two days longer I should be so strongly re-enforced as not only to be secure, but to be able to resume offensive operations; but on the 25th of August the only forces that had joined me, or were in the neighborhood, were two thousand five hundred men of the Pennsylvania reserves, under Brigadier General Reynolds, who had arrived at Kelly's Ford, and the division of General Kearney, four thousand five hundred strong, which had reached Warrenton Junction. The line of the Rappahannock is very weak, and scarce opposes any considerable obstacle to the advance of an army. It is but a small stream above the forks, and can be crossed by good fords every mile or two of its whole length. The movement of the enemy towards my right occasioned me much uneasiness, in consequence of the instructions, which bound me to keep in close communication with Fredericksburg; but I instructed General Sigel, who occupied the right of my line, and who expressed great apprehensions that his flank would be turned, and proposed to withdraw from his position towards the railroad, to stand firm and hold his ground, and to allow the enemy to cross at Sulphur Springs and develop himself on the road toward Warrenton; that, as soon as any considerable force had crossed at that place, I would rapidly mass my army during the night and throw it upon any force of the enemy which attempted to march in the direction of Warrenton. The whole of the cavalry under Brigadier Generals Buford and Bayard was pushed considerably to the right of General Sigel, in the direction of Fayetteville and Sulphur Springs, to watch the movements of the enemy in that direction, and to picket the river as far up as possible. General Sigel was ordered, if any force of the enemy attempted to cross below Sulphur Springs, to march at once against it and to notify me, as I was determined to resist the passage of the river at any point below the springs. Copies of my despatches to the general-in-chief, and of his replies, the despatches from General Sigel, and my orders to him, given during the 20th, 21st, 22d, and 23d of August, are appended, which show completely the condition of things, my understanding of the movements of the enemy, and the dispositions which I made and proposed to make in relation to them.

Finding that the continued movement of the enemy to my right, whilst heavy masses of his force still confronted me at Rappahannock Station, would, within a day, if allowed to continue, either render my position on the Rappahannock wholly untenable, or force me to give battle to the enemy in my front and on my right, I determined, on the afternoon of the 22d, to mass my whole force to recross the Rappahannock by the bridges and fords near Rappahannock Station, and by Kelly's Ford below, and to fall on the flank and rear of the long column of the enemy which was passing up the river towards our right.

I accordingly made the necessary orders on the night of the 22d of August. The attempt would have been dangerous, but no recourse was left me, except to make this attack, to retire to Warrenton Junction and abandon the line of the Rappahannock, or to retire in the direction of Fredericksburg and abandon the Orange and Alexandria railroad and the direct approaches to Washington city. I determined, therefore, to hazard the result, and to fall furiously, with my whole army, upon the flank and rear of the enemy. During the night of the 22d a heavy rain set in, which, before day dawned on the 23d, had caused the river to rise six or eight feet, carried away all our bridges, and destroyed all the fords on the river. To recross the Rappahannock and to make the attack, as proposed, was no longer practicable; but the rise in the river which had prevented the movement I believed also would prevent the retreat of that portion of the enemy which had crossed at Sulphur Springs and Waterloo Bridge, according to the reports which had been sent me by General Sigel.

Early on the morning of the 23d, therefore, I massed my whole force in the neighborhood of Rappahannock Station with the purpose of falling upon that portion of the enemy which had crossed above me, and was then supposed to be between Sulphur Springs, Waterloo Bridge, and the town of Warrenton. As the river was too high to be crossed, and was likely to remain so for at least thirty-six hours, I had no fear that the enemy would be able to interpose between me and Fredericksburg, or to make any attempt upon the Orange and Alexandria railroad north of the Rappahannock. I directed General Sigel to march, with his whole corps, upon Sulphur Springs, supported by Reno's corps and Banks's corps, to fall upon any body of the enemy that he might encounter, and to push forward along the river to Waterloo Bridge. I directed General McDowell to move, at the same time, directly upon the town of Warrenton, so that from that point he would be able, if necessary, to unite with General Sigel on the road from that place to Sulphur Springs or to Waterloo Bridge. To the corps of General McDowell I had attached the Pennsylvania reserves, under Brigadier General Reynolds, the first of the army of the Potomac which had joined my command.

On the night of the 22d of August a small cavalry force of the enemy, crossing at Waterloo Bridge and passing through Warrenton, had made a raid upon our trains at Catlett's Station, and had destroyed four or five wagons in all, belonging to the train of my own headquarters; at the time this cavalry force attacked at Catlett's, and it certainly was not more than three hundred strong, our whole army trains were parked at that place, and were guarded by not less than fifteen hundred infantry and five companies of cavalry. The success of this small cavalry party of the enemy, although very trifling and attended with but little damage, was most disgraceful to the force which had been left in charge of the trains. General Sigel moved, as ordered, slowly up the Rappahannock, in the direction of Sulphur Springs, on the 23d, and first encountered a force of the enemy near the point where a small creek, called Great Run, puts into the Rappahannock, about two miles below the Sulphur Springs; the enemy was driven across the stream, but destroyed the bridges; the heavy rains had caused this small creek to rise so much that it was not then fordable, so that the night of the 23d and part of the morning of the 24th were spent by General Sigel in rebuilding the bridges. On the night of the 23d also the advance of McDowell's corps occupied Warrenton, a cavalry force of the enemy having retreated from there a few hours before.

On the morning of the 24th General Sigel, supported by Generals Reno and Banks, crossed Great Run and occupied the Sulphur Springs, under a heavy fire of artillery from batteries which the enemy had established all along the south side of the Rappahannock. The bridge which had been built at Sulphur Springs, and upon which the forces of the enemy which had crossed a day or two previous escaped from the advance of General Sigel, was destroyed, and General Sigel pushed forward, with the force supporting him, in the direction of Waterloo Bridge. Meantime I had despatched Brigadier General Buford with a heavy cavalry force from Warrenton, on the morning of the 24th, to reconnoitre the country in the vicinity of Waterloo Bridge, and to interrupt the passage of the river at that point as far as practicable. It was then believed by General Sigel, who so reported to me, that a considerable force of the enemy was on the north side of the Rappahannock, and was retiring from his advance in the direction of Waterloo Bridge. By noon of the 24th General Buford reported to me that he had occupied Waterloo Bridge without finding any force of the enemy, and he did not believe that there was any force between that place and Sulphur Springs. I directed him to destroy the bridge at Waterloo and to maintain his position there until the arrival of the advance of General Sigel. I at once informed General Sigel of these facts, and directed him to push forward his advance to Waterloo; Milroy's brigade, constituting the advance of his corps, reached Waterloo late in the afternoon of the 24th. On that afternoon the whole force of the enemy was stretched along the line of the river from Rappahannock station to Waterloo Bridge, with his centre, and I think his main body, in the vicinity of Sulphur Springs.

During the day of the 24th a large detachment of the enemy, numbering thirty-six regiments of infantry with the usual number of batteries of artillery and a considerable cavalry force, marched rapidly towards the north in the direction of Rectortown. They could be plainly seen from our signal stations established on high points along the Rappahannock, and their movements and force were reported to me from time to time by Colonel J. S. Clark, of General Bank's staff, who, both on that day and for many preceding and succeedings day, had given me most valuable and reliable information. I am glad to express here my appreciation of the valuable services of this officer. On the night of the 24th my forces were distributed as follows: Rickett's division, of McDowell's corps, on the road from Warrenton to Waterloo Bridge, and about four miles east of Waterloo; King's division, of the same corps, between Warrenton and the Sulphur Springs; Sigel's corps, near the Rappahannock, with his advance at Waterloo Bridge, and his rear in the direction of the Sulphur Springs; in his rear, and immediately in contact with him, was Banks's corps; while Reno's corps was east, and very near the Sulphur Springs.

I was satisfied that no force of the enemy was on the north side of the Rappahannock, but I feared that during the next day—by which time the river would have fallen sufficiently to be passed at any of the fords—that the enemy would make an attempt to cross at Rappahannock Station, or at the fords between that point and Sulphur Springs; yet, as we were confronted at Waterloo Bridge and Sulphur Springs by the main body of the enemy, still moving towards our right, and as the heavy column mentioned previously was marching with all speed in the direction of White Plains and Salem, and from these points would be able to turn our right by the direction of Thoroughfare Gap, or even north of that place, it was with the greatest reluctance, and only because I felt bound to do so under my instructions, that I took measures again to assure my communications with Fredericksburg. I append herewith orders and despatches sent and received during the 23d and 24th of August, which will of themselves furnish a succinct account of the movements here set forth, and all the information and assurances upon which those movements were made. On the 23d I received a despatch from the general-in-chief, informing me that heavy re-enforcements would begin to arrive at Warrenton Junction the succeeding day, and on the 24th I received despatches from Colonel Haupt, the railroad superintendent at Alexandria, informing me that thirty thousand men, ordered forward to join me, had demanded transportation from him, and that they would all be shipped that afternoon or early the next morning. The force which I thus expected, as reported to me, consisted of the division of General Sturgis, ten thousand strong; the division of General Cox, seven thousand strong; the corps of General Heintzelman, ten thousand strong, and the corps of General Franklin, ten thousand strong. By the night of the 25th it became apparent to me that I could no longer keep open my communications with Fredericksburg and oppose the crossing of the Rappahannock at Rappahannock Station without abandoning the road from Warrenton to Washington, and leaving open to the enemy the route through Thoroughfare Gap, and all other roads north of the Orange and Alexandria railroad; and as the main body of his forces was constantly tending in that direction, I determined no longer to attempt to mask the lower fords of the Rappahannock, but to assemble such forces as I had along the Warrenton turnpike, between Warrenton and Gainesville, and give battle to the enemy on my right or left, as he might choose. I therefore directed General McDowell to occupy Warrenton with his own and Sigel's corps, supporting him by Banks's corps, from the direction of Fayetteville. I pushed Reno forward to occupy a point near the Warrenton turnpike, and about three miles to the east of that town. I sent orders to General Porter, who had reported to me by note from the neighborhood of Bealeton Station, to push forward and join Reno. Heintzelman's corps, which had reached Warrenton Junction, was ordered to remain for the present at that point, it being my purpose to push forward that corps, as soon as practicable, to Greenwich, about half-way between Warrenton and Gainesville. I sent orders to Colonel Haupt to direct one of the strongest divisions being sent forward to take post in the works at Manassas Junction, and requested General Halleck to push Franklin with all speed to Gainesville; that he could march quite as rapidly as he could be transported by rail with the limited means of railroad transportation in our possession, and that his baggage and supplies could be sent forward to Gainesville by rail. I also sent orders to the colonel commanding at Manassas Junction for the first division that reached there from Alexandria to halt and take post in the works at that place, and directed him also to push forward all of his cavalry in the direction of Thoroughfare Gap; to watch any movements the enemy might make from that direction. I had instructed General Sturgis, commanding at Alexandria, on the 23d of August, to post strong guards along the railroad from Manassas Junction to Catlett's Station, and requested him to superintend this in person. I also directed General Kearney, who reached Warrenton Junction on the 23d, to see that sufficient guards were placed all along the railroad in his rear. After these precautions and assurances, I thought, and confidently expected, that by the afternoon of the 26th Franklin would have been at or near Gainesville; one division would have been occupying the works at Manassas Junction, and that the forces under Sturgis and Cox would have been at Warrenton Junction, whence they could have at once been pushed north, in the direction of Warrenton turnpike. The orders for the disposition of the forces then under my command were sent, and the movements made, so far as practicable, during the day of the 26th. About eight o'clock at night, on the 26th, the advance of Jackson's force, having passed through Thoroughfare Gap, cut the railroad in the neighborhood of Kettle Run, about six miles east of Warrenton Junction. The cavalry force which I had sent forward towards Thoroughfare Gap on the morning of the 26th made no report to me.

The moment our communications were interrupted at Kettle Run I was satisfied that the troops which had been promised me from the direction of Washington had made no considerable progress. Had Franklin been even at Centreville on the 26th, or had Cox and Sturgis been as far west as Bull Run on that day, the movement of Jackson through Thoroughfare Gap upon the railroad at Manassas would have been utterly impracticable. So confidently did I expect, from the assurances which I had time and again received, that these troops would be in position, or, at all events, far advanced towards me, that Jackson's movement towards White Plains, and in the direction of Thoroughfare Gap, had caused but little uneasiness; but on the night of the 26th it was very apparent to me that all these expected re-enforcements had utterly failed me, and that upon the small force under my own immediate command I must depend alone for any present operations against the enemy. It was easy for me to retire in the direction of the lower fords of the Rappahannock to Fredericksburg, so as to bring me in immediate contact with the forces there, or arriving there, but by so doing I should have left open the whole front of Washington; and after my own disappointment of the re-enforcements which I had expected I was not sure that there was any sufficient force, in the absence of the army under my command, to cover the capital. I determined, therefore, at once to abandon the line of the Rappahannock, and throw my whole force in the direction of Gainesville and Manassas Junction, to crush the enemy, who had passed through Thoroughfare Gap, and to interpose between the army of General Lee and Bull Run. During the night of the 26th the main body of the enemy still occupied their positions from Sulphur Springs to Waterloo Bridge and above, but towards morning, on the 27th, I think their advance moved off in the direction of White Plains, pursuing the route previously taken by Jackson, and no doubt with a view of uniting with him eastward of the Bull Run range.

From the 18th of August until the morning of the 27th the troops under my command had been continuously marching and fighting night and day, and during the whole of that time there was scarcely an interval of an hour without the roar of artillery. The men had had little sleep, were greatly worn down with fatigue, had had little time to get proper food or to eat it, had been engaged in constant battles and skirmishes, and had performed services laborious, dangerous, and excessive beyond any previous experience in this country. As was to be expected under such circumstances, the numbers of the army under my command had been greatly reduced by deaths, by wounds, by sickness, and by fatigue, so that on the morning of the 27th of August I estimated my whole effective force (and I think the estimate was large) as follows: Sigel's corps, nine thousand men; Banks's corps, five thousand men; McDowell's corps, including Reynolds's division, fifteen thousand five hundred men; Reno's corps, seven thousand men; the corps of Heintzelman and Porter, (the freshest by far in that army,) about eighteen thousand men—making in all fifty-four thousand five hundred men. Our cavalry numbered on paper about four thousand men, but their horses were completely broken down, and there were not five hundred men, all told, capable of doing much service, as should be expected from cavalry. The corps of Heintzelman had reached Warrenton Junction, but it was without wagons, without artillery, with only forty rounds of ammunition to the man, and without even horses for the general and field officers. The corps of Porter had also reached Warrenton Junction with a very small supply of provisions, and but forty rounds of ammunition for each man.

On the morning of the 27th, in accordance with the purpose previously set forth, I directed McDowell to move forward rapidly on Gainesville, by the Warrenton turnpike, with his own corps and Sigel's and the division of Reynolds, so as to reach that point during the night. I directed General Reno, with his corps, followed by Kearney's division of Heintzelman's corps, to move rapidly on Greenwich, so as to reach there that night, to communicate at once with General McDowell, and to support him in any operations against the enemy in the vicinity of Gainesville. I moved forward along the railroad towards Manassas Junction with Hooker's division of Heintzelman's corps, leaving orders for General Porter to remain with his corps at Warrenton Junction until relieved by General Banks, who was marching to that place from Fayetteville; and, as soon as he was relieved, to push forward also in the direction of Gainesville, where, at that time, I expected the main collision with the enemy would occur.

The army trains of all the corps I instructed to take the road to Warrenton Junction, and follow in the rear of Hooker's division towards Manassas Junction, so that the road pursued by the trains was entirely covered from any possible interruption by the enemy.

On the afternoon of the 27th a severe engagement occurred between Hooker's division and Ewell's division of Jackson's forces. The action commenced about four miles west of Bristow Station. Ewell was driven back along the railroad, but still confronted Hooker at dark along the banks of Broad Run, immediately in front of Bristow Station, at which point I arrived at sunset. The loss in this engagement was about three hundred killed and wounded on each side. The enemy left his dead, many of his wounded, and much of his baggage on the field of battle.

The railroad had been torn up and the bridges burned in several places between Bristow Station and Warrenton Junction. I accordingly directed Major General Banks to cover the railroad trains at Warrenton Junction until General Porter's corps had marched from that place, and then to run back the trains as far as practicable, and, covering them with his troops, to repair the bridges as fast as possible. I also directed Captain Merrill, of the engineers, with a considerable force, to repair the railroad track and bridges as far as possible in the direction of Bristow Station. The road was accordingly put in order from

Warrenton Junction to Kettle Run during the 27th, and the trains run back to that point early next day.

At dark on the 27th General Hooker reported to me that his ammunition was nearly exhausted, and that he had but about five rounds to the man left. I had by that time become conscious that the whole force under Jackson, consisting of his own, A. P. Hill's, and Ewell's divisions, was south of the Warrenton turnpike and in the immediate neighborhood of Manassas Junction. McDowell reached his position during the night of the 27th, as did also Kearney and Reno, and it was clear, on that night, that we had interposed completely between Jackson and the main body of the enemy, which was still west of the Bull Run range and in the neighborhood of White Plains. Thinking it altogether likely that Jackson would mass his whole force and attempt to turn our right at Bristow Station, and knowing that Hooker, for want of ammunition, was in little condition to make long resistance, I sent back orders to General Porter, about dark of the 27th, to move forward at one o'clock in the night, and report to me at Bristow by daylight in the morning, leaving instructions in some detail for Banks, who was expected at Warrenton Junction during that night or early in the morning. The orders for all these movements are herewith appended. General Porter failed utterly to obey the orders that were sent him, giving as an excuse that his men were tired, that they would straggle in the night, and that the wagon trains proceeding eastward, in the rear of Hooker's division, would offer obstructions to hism arch. He, however, made no attempt whatever to comply with this order, although it was stated to him in the order itself that his presence was necessary on all accounts at daylight, and that the officer delivering the despatch was instructed to conduct him to the field.

There were but two courses left open to Jackson in consequence of this sudden and unexpected movement of the army: He could not retrace his steps through Gainesville, as it was occupied by McDowell, having at command a force equal, if not superior, to his own, and was either obliged, therefore, to retreat through Centreville, which would carry him still further from the main body of Lee's army, or to mass his force, assault us at Bristow Station, and turn our right. He pursued the former course, and retired through Centreville. This mistake of Jackson's alone saved us from the consequences which would have followed this flagrant and inexcusable disobedience of orders on the part of General Porter.

At nine o'clock on the night of the 27th, satisfied of Jackson's position, I sent orders to General McDowell to push forward at the very earliest dawn of day towards Manassas Junction from Gainesville, resting his right on the Manassas Gap railroad, and throwing his left well to the east. I directed General Reno to march at the same hour from Greenwich direct upon Manassas Junction, and Kearney to march at the same hour upon Bristow. This latter order was sent to Kearney to render my right at Bristow perfectly secure against the probable movement of Jackson in that direction. Kearney arrived at Bristow about eight o'clock in the morning, Reno being on his left and marching direct upon Manassas Junction. I immediately pushed Kearney forward in pursuit of Ewell towards Manassas, followed by Hooker. General Porter's corps did not arrive at Bristow until half-past ten o'clock in the morning, and the moment he found that Jackson had evacuated Manassas Junction he requested permission to halt at Bristow and rest his men. Sykes's division of Porter's corps had spent the whole day of the 27th, from ten o'clock in the morning until daylight of the 28th, in camp at Warrenton Junction. Morell's division of the same corps had arrived at Warrenton Junction during the day of the 27th, and also remained there during the whole of that night. Porter's corps was by far the freshest in the whole army, and should have been, and I believe was, in better condition for service than any troops we had. General McDowell reported to me afterwards that he had given orders for the movement of his command upon Manassas

Junction at two o'clock at night, in accordance with the directions I had sent him, but General Sigel, who commanded his advance, and was at Gainesville, instead of moving forward from Gainesville at daylight, as he was ordered, was absolutely with his advance in that town as late as half-past seven in the morning. Meantime, beginning about three o'clock in the morning of the 28th, Jackson commenced evacuating Manassas Junction, and his troops were marching from that point in the direction of Centreville until ten or eleven o'clock in the day. If the whole force under McDowell had moved forward as directed and at the time specified, they would have intercepted Jackson's retreat toward Centreville by eight o'clock in the morning, and I do not believe it would have been possible for Jackson to have crossed Bull Run, so closely engaged with our forces, without heavy loss.

I reached Manassas Junction with Kearney's division and Reno's corps about twelve o'clock in the day of the 28th, less than an hour after Jackson in person had retired. I immediately pushed forward Hooker, Kearney, and Reno upon Centreville, and sent orders to Fitz John Porter to come forward to Manassas Junction. I also wrote to McDowell and stated the facts, so far as we were then able to ascertain them, and directed him to call back the whole of his force that had come in the direction of Manassas Junction, and to move forward upon Centreville. He had, however, without my knowledge, detached Ricketts's division in the direction of Thoroughfare Gap, and that division was no longer available in his movement towards Centreville. Late on the afternoon of the 28th Kearney drove the enemy's rear guard out of Centreville, and occupied that town, with his advance beyond it, about dark. The enemy retreated through Centreville, one portion of his force taking the road by Sudley Springs, and the other pursuing the Warrenton turnpike towards Gainesville, destroying the bridges on that road over Bull Run and Cub Run. McDowell, with his whole force, consisting of his own corps, except Ricketts's division, Sigel's corps, and the division of Reynolds, marching in the direction of Centreville, encountered the advance of Jackson's force retreating towards Thoroughfare Gap about six o'clock on the evening of the 28th. A severe action took place between King's division of McDowell's corps, and the advance of Jackson, which was terminated by darkness. Each party maintained its ground. Gibbon's brigade of King's division, which was in the advance of that division, sustained the brunt of the action, but was supported handsomely by Doubleday's brigade, which came into action shortly after. This engagement and its result, were reported to me near Centreville about ten o'clock that night.

I felt sure then, and so stated, that there was no escape for Jackson. I accordingly sent orders to General McDowell, as also to General King, several times during the night of 28th, and once by his own staff officer, to hold his ground at all hazards, to prevent the retreat of Jackson to the west, and that at daylight in the morning our whole force from Centreville and Manassas Junction would be up with the enemy, who must be crushed between us. I also sent orders to General Kearney to push forward at one o'clock that night cautiously from Centreville along the Warrenton turnpike; to drive in the pickets of the enemy, and to keep closely in contact with him during the night; to rest his left on the Warrenton turnpike, and throw his right well to the north, if possible, across Little River turnpike; at daylight in the morning to assault vigorously with his right advanced, and that Hooker and Reno would be up with him very shortly after daylight. I sent orders to General Porter, whom I supposed to be at Manassas Junction, where he should have been in compliance with my orders of the day previous, to move upon Centreville at the earliest dawn, and stated to him the position of the forces, and that a severe battle would undoubtedly be fought during the morning of the 29th. The only apprehension I had at that time was that Jackson might attempt to retreat to the north, in the direction of Leesburg, and, for the purpose of preventing this, I directed Kearney to keep closely in contact with him during the whole of the night of the 28th. My forces were so disposed that McDowell, Sigel, and Reynolds, whose joint forces amounted to about twenty-five thousand men, were immediately west of Jackson, and between him and Thoroughfare Gap, whilst Kearney, Hooker, Reno, and Porter, about twenty-five thousand strong, were to fall on him from the east at daylight in the morning, or very shortly after. With this disposition of troops, we were so far in advance of Longstreet that, by using our whole force vigorously, we should be able to crush Jackson before Longstreet could, by any possibility, reach the scene of action. To my great disappointment, however, I learned, towards daylight on the morning of the 29th, that King's division had fallen back in the direction of Manassas Junction, thus leaving open the road to Thoroughfare Gap and making new movements and dispositions of troops immediately necessary.

I submit herewith the reports of Generals King, Gibbon, and Doubleday, of the action of the evening of the 28th, as also a detailed report of General McDowell.

The orders directing all these movements are also appended, and they bring the operations of the army up to the 29th of August. The losses in King's division in the action of the evening of the 28th were principally in Gibbon's brigade of that division, and numbered ———. Gibbon's brigade consisted of some of the best troops in the service, and the conduct of both men and officers was gallant and distinguished. The report of General King, herewith appended, exhibits his high opinion of the conduct of this brigade, and of the officers who distinguished themselves in that action.

The disposition of troops on the west of Jackson having failed through Ricketts's movement towards Thoroughfare Gap, and the consequent withdrawal of King, an immediate change in the disposition and proposed movements of the troops for the succeeding day became necessary, and about daylight on the morning of the 29th, shortly after I received information of the withdrawal of King's division, I sent orders to General Sigel, who was in the neighborhood of Groveton, supported by Reynolds's division, to attack the enemy vigorously as soon as it was light enough to see, and bring him to a stand, if it were possible to do so. I instructed General Heintzelman to push forward from Centreville towards Gainesville at the earliest dawn, with the divisions of Hooker and Kearney, and directed General Reno to follow closely in his rear; to use all speed, and as soon as he came up with the enemy to establish communication with Sigel, and attack with the utmost promptness and vigor. I also sent orders to Major General Fitz John Porter, at Manassas Junction, to move forward with the utmost rapidity with his own corps and King's division of McDowell's corps, which was supposed to be at that point, upon Gainesville, by the direct road from Manassas Junction to that place. I urged him to make all speed, that he might come up with the enemy and be able to turn his flank near where the Warrenton turnpike is intersected by the road from Manassas Junction to Gainesville. Shortly after sending this order I received a note from General McDowell, whom I had not been able to find during the night of the 28th, dated at Manassas Junction, requesting that King's division might not be taken from his command. I immediately sent a joint order to Generals McDowell and Porter, directing them, with their two corps, to march with all speed towards Gainesville, on the direct road from Manassas Junction. This order, which is appended, set forth in detail the movements they were directed to make.

Sigel attacked the enemy about daylight on the morning of the 29th, a mile or two east of Groveton, where he was soon joined by the divisions of Hooker and Kearney. Jackson fell back several miles, but was so closely pressed by these forces that he was compelled to make a stand and to make the best defence possible. He accordingly took up a position with his left in the neighborhood of Sudley Springs, his right a little to the south of Warrenton turnpike, and his line covered by an old railroad grade which leads from Gainesville in the direction of Leesburg. His batteries, which were numerous, and some of them of heavy calibre, were posted behind the ridges, in the open ground on both sides of Warrenton turnpike, whilst the mass of his troops was sheltered in dense woods behind the railroad embankment.

I arrived on the field from Centreville about noon and found the two armies confronting each other, both considerably cut up by the sharp action in which they had been engaged since daylight in the morning. Heintzelman's corps occupied the right of our line, in front or west of the Sudley Springs road. General Sigel was on his left, with his line extended a short distance south of the Warrenton turnpike, the division of General Schenck occupying the high ground to the left of that road. The extreme left was occupied by the division of General Reynolds. General Reno's corps had reached the field, and the most of it had been pushed forward into action, leaving four regiments in reserve and in rear of the centre of our line. Immediately after I reached the ground, General Sigel reported to me that his line was weak; that the divisions of Schurz and Steinwehr were much cut up, and ought to be drawn back from the front. I informed General Sigel that this was utterly impossible, as there were no troops to replace them, and that he must hold his ground; that I would not again push his troops into action, as the corps of Porter and McDowell were moving forward from Manassas Junction on the road to Gainesville, and must very soon be in position to fall upon the enemy's right flank and probably upon his rear. I rode to the front of our line and inspected it from right to left, giving the same information to Generals Heintzelman and Reno. The troops were accordingly suffered to rest in their positions and to resupply themselves with ammunition. From twelve o'clock until four very severe skirmishes occurred constantly at various points on our line, and were brought on at every indication that the enemy made of a disposition to retreat. About two o'clock in the afternoon several pieces of artillery were discharged on the extreme right of the enemy's line, and I fully believed that Generals Porter and McDowell had reached their positions, and had become engaged with the enemy. I did not hear more than three shots fired, and was at a loss to know what had become of these two corps, or what was delaying them; but I received information shortly afterwards that General McDowell was advancing to join the main body by the Sudley Springs road, and would probably be up with us in two hours. At half-past four o'clock I sent a peremptory order to General Porter to push forward at once into action on the enemy's right, and, if possible, to turn his rear, stating to him generally the condition of things on the field in front of me. About half-past five o'clock, when General Porter should have been coming into action in compliance with this order, I directed Generals Heintzelman and Reno to assault the left of the enemy. The attack was made with great gallantry, and the whole of the left of the enemy was doubled back towards his centre, and our forces, after a sharp conflict of an hour and a half, occupied the field of battle, with the dead and wounded of the enemy in our hands. In this attack Grover's brigade of Hooker's division was particularly distinguished by a determined bayonet charge, breaking two of the enemy's lines and penetrating to the third before it could be checked. By this time General McDowell had arrived on the field, and I pushed his corps immediately to the front along the Warrenton turnpike with orders to fall upon the enemy, who was retreating towards the pike from the direction of Sudley Springs.

The attack along the turnpike was made by King's division at about sunset in the evening, but by that time the advance of the main body of the enemy, under Longstreet, had begun to reach the field, and King's division encountered a stubborn and determined resistance at a point about three fourths of a mile in front of our line of battle.

Whilst this attack was going on, the forces under Heintzelman and Reno continued to push back the left of the enemy in the direction of the Warrenton turnpike, so that about eight o'clock in the evening, the greater portion of the field of battle was occupied by our army. Nothing was heard of General Porter up to that time, and his forces took no part whatever in the action, but were suffered by him to lie idle on their arms, within sight and sound of the battle during the whole day. So far as I know, he made no effort whatever to comply with my orders nor to take any part in the action. I do not hesitate to say that if he had discharged his duty as became a soldier under the circumstances, and had made a vigorous attack on the enemy, as he was expected and directed to do, at any time up to eight o'clock that night, we should have utterly crushed or captured the larger portion of Jackson's force before he could have been by any possibility sufficiently re-enforced to have made any effective resistance. I did not myself feel for a moment that it was necessary for me, having given General Porter an order to march towards the enemy in a particular direction, to send him in addition specific orders to attack, it being his clear duty, and in accordance with every military precept, to have brought his forces into action wherever he encountered the enemy, when a furious battle with that enemy was raging during the whole day in his immediate presence. I believe—in fact, I am positive—that at five o'clock in the afternoon of the 29th, General Porter had in his front no considerable body of the enemy. I believed then, as I am very sure now, that it was easily practicable for him to have turned the right flank of Jackson, and to have fallen upon his rear; that if he had done so, we should have gained a decisive victory over the army under Jackson before he could have been joined by any of the forces of Longstreet; and that the army of General Lee would have been so crippled and checked by the destruction of this large force as to have been no longer in condition to prosecute further operations of an aggressive character. I speak thus freely of the strange failure of General Porter, not because I am more convinced of its unfortunate results now than I was at the time, but because a full investigation of the whole subject made by a court-martial has fully justified and confirmed that opinion.

Our losses during the 29th were very heavy, but no separate returns of killed and wounded for that day have been made to me. I believed, from all I could learn from corps commanders, and so reported, that our loss during that day was not less than six or eight thousand killed and wounded, and I think this estimate will be confirmed by the general reports which cover the losses during the battles of the 27th, 28th, 29th, and 30th August, and the 1st of September. My estimate of the loss of the enemy, reported to the department on the morning of the 30th, was based upon the statements made to me by Generals Hooker and Kearney, who had been over the whole field on the left. General Hooker estimated the loss of the enemy as at least two to one, and General Kearney as at least three to one of our own.

Every indication during the night of the 29th, and up to ten o'clock on the morning of the 30th, pointed to the retreat of the enemy from our front. Paroled prisoners of our own, taken on the evening of the 29th, and who came into our lines on the morning of the 30th, reported the enemy retreating during the whole night in the direction of and along the Warrenton turnpike. Generals McDowell and Heintzelman, who reconnoitred the positions held by the enemy's left on the evening of the 29th, confirmed this statement. They reported to me that the positions occupied by the enemy's left had been evacuated, and that there was every indication that he was retreating in the direction of Gainesville.

On the morning of the 30th, as may be supposed, our troops, who had been so continually marching and fighting for so many days, were in a state of great exhaustion. They had had little to eat for two days previous, and the artillery and cavalry horses had been in harness and saddled continually for ten days, and had had no forage for two days previous. It may easily be imagined how little these troops, after such severe labor, and after undergoing such hardship and privation, were in condition for active and efficient service. I had telegraphed to the general-in-chief on the 28th our condition, and had begged of him to have rations and forage sent forward to us from Alexandria with all despatch. I also called his attention to the imminent need of cavalry horses to enable the cavalry belonging to the army to perform any service whatever.

About daylight of the 30th I received a note from General Franklin, herewith appended, written by direction of General McClellan and dated at eight o'clock the evening before, informing me that rations and forage *would* be loaded into the available wagons and cars at Alexandria as soon as I would send back a cavalry escort to bring out the trains. Such a letter, when we were fighting the enemy, and Alexandria was swarming with troops, needs no comment. Bad as was the condition of our cavalry, I was in no situation to spare troops from the front, nor could they have gone to Alexandria and returned within the time by which we must have had provisions or have fallen back in the direction of Washington; nor do I yet see what service cavalry could have rendered in guarding railroad trains.

It was not until I received this letter that I began to feel discouraged and nearly hopeless of any successful issue to the operations with which I was charged; but I felt it to be my duty, notwithstanding the desperate condition of my command, from great fatigue, from want of provisions and forage, and from the small hope that I had of any effective assistance from Alexandria, to hold my position at all hazards and under all privations, unless overwhelmed by the superior forces of the enemy. I had received no sort of information of any troops coming forward to my assistance since the 24th, and did not expect, on the morning of the 30th, that any assistance would reach me from the direction of Washington; but I determined again to give battle to the enemy on the 30th, and at least to lay on such blows as would cripple him as much as possible, and delay as long as practicable any further advance towards the capital. I accordingly prepared to renew the engagement. At that time my effective forces—greatly reduced by losses in killed, wounded, missing, and broken-down men during the severe operations of two or three days and nights previous; the sharp actions of Hooker, King, and Ricketts on the 27th and 28th, and the furious battle on the 29th—were estimated by me and others, as follows:

McDowell's corps, including Reynolds's division, twelve thousand men; Sigel's corps, seven thousand men; Reno's corps, seven thousand; Heintzelman's corps, seven thousand men; Porter's corps, which had been in no engagement, and was, or ought to have been, perfectly fresh, I estimated at about twelve thousand men, including the brigade of Piatt, which formed a part of Sturgis's division, and the only portion that ever joined me. But of this force the brigades of Piatt and of Griffin, numbering, as I understood, about five thousand men, had been suffered to march off at daylight on the 30th to Centreville, and were not available for operations on that day.

This reduced Porter's effective force on the field to about seven thousand men, which gave me a total force of forty thousand men. Banks's corps, about five thousand strong, was at Bristow Station, in charge of the railroad trains and of a portion of the wagon trains of the army still at that place. Between twelve and two o'clock in the day I advanced the corps of Porter, supported by King's division of McDowell's corps, to attack the enemy along the Warrenton turnpike. At the same time I directed Heintzelman and Reno, on our right, to push forward to the left and front towards Warrenton turnpike, and attack the enemy's left in flank, if possible. For a short time Ricketts's division of McDowell's corps was placed in support of this movement on our right.

It was necessary for me to act thus promptly and make an attack, as I had not the time, for want of provisions and forage, to await an attack from the enemy; nor did I think it good policy to do so under the circumstances. During the whole night of the 29th and the morning of the 30th, the advance of the main body under Lee was arriving on the field to re-enforce Jackson, so that by twelve or one o'clock in the day we were confronted by forces greatly superior to our own, and these forces were being every moment largely increased by fresh arrivals of the enemy from the direction of Thoroughfare Gap. Every moment of delay increased the odds against us, and I therefore advanced to the attack as rapidly as I was able to bring my forces into action. Shortly after General Porter moved forward to the attack along the Warrenton turnpike, and the assault on the enemy was made by Heintzelman and Reno on the right, it became apparent that the enemy was massing his troops, as fast as they arrived on the field, on his right, and was moving forward from that direction to turn our left, at which point it was plain he intended to make his main attack. I accordingly directed General McDowell to recall Ricketts's division immediately from our right, and post it on the left of our line with its left refused. The attack of Porter was neither vigorous nor persistent, and his troops soon retired in considerable confusion. As soon as they commenced to fall back, the enemy advanced to the assault, and our whole line, from right to left, was soon furiously engaged. The main attack of the enemy was made upon our left, but was met with stubborn resistance by the divisions of General Schenck, General Milroy, and General Reynolds, who, shortly after the action began, were re-enforced on their left and rear by the division of Ricketts. The action raged furiously for several hours, the enemy bringing up his heavy reserves, and pouring mass after mass of his troops upon our left. So greatly superior in number were his forces that, whilst overpowering us on our left, he was able to assault us also with very superior forces on our right. Porter's forces were rallied and brought to a halt as they were retiring to the rear. As soon as they could be used, I pushed them forward to support our left, and they there rendered most distinguished service, especially the brigade of regulars under Colonel Buchanan.

Tower's brigade of Ricketts's division was pushed forward into action in support of Reynolds's division, and was led forward in person by General Tower with conspicuous skill and gallantry. The conduct of that brigade, in plain view of all the forces on our left, was especially distinguished, and drew forth hearty and enthusiastic cheers.

The example of this brigade was of great service, and infused new spirit into all the troops who witnessed their intrepid conduct. Reno's corps was also withdrawn from its position on our right centre late in the afternoon, and thrown into the action on our left, where it behaved with conspicuous gallantry. Notwithstanding these great disadvantages, our troops held their ground with the utmost firmness and obstinacy, and the losses on both sides were very heavy. By dark our left had been forced back about a half or three-quarters of a mile; but still remained firm and unbroken, and still covered the turnpike in our rear.

About six o'clock in the afternoon I heard, accidentally, that Franklin's corps had arrived at a point about four miles east of Centreville, and twelve miles in our rear, and that it was only about eight thousand strong. The result of the battle of the 30th, the very heavy losses we had suffered, and the complete prostration of our troops from hunger and fatigue, made it plain to me that we were no longer able, in the face of such overwhelming odds, to maintain our position so far to the front; nor would we have been able to do so under any circumstances, suffering as were the men and horses from fatigue and hunger, and weakened by the heavy losses incident to the uncommon hardships which they had suffered.

About eight o'clock at night, therefore, I sent written instructions to the commanders of corps to withdraw leisurely towards Centreville, and stated to them what route each should pursue, and where they should take post. General Reno was instructed with his whole corps to cover the movements of the army towards Centreville. The withdrawal was made slowly, quietly, and in good order, no pursuit whatever having been attempted by the enemy. A division of infantry with its batteries was posted to cover the crossing of Cub Run.

The exact losses in this battle I am unable to give, as the reports received from the corps commanders only exhibit the aggregate losses during the whole of the operations from the 22d of August to the 2d of September. Before leaving the field that night, I sent orders to General Banks, at Bristow Station, to destroy the railroad trains and such of the stores in them as he was unable to carry off, and rejoin me at Centreville. I had previously sent him orders to throw into each wagon of the army trains as much as possible of the stores from the railroad cars, and to be sure and bring off with him from Warrenton Junction and Bristow all the ammunition and all the sick and wounded that could be transported, and for this purpose, if it were necessary, to throw out the personal baggage, tents, &c., from the regimental trains. These several orders are appended. At no time during the 28th, 29th, 30th, and 31st of August was the road between Bristow Station and Centreville interrupted by the enemy. The whole of the trains of the army were on that road in charge of General Banks, and covered and protected by his whole corps. If any of these wagons were lost, as I believe none were, it was wholly without necessity. I enter thus specifically into this matter, and submit the orders sent to General Banks and his subsequent report to me, because no part of the misrepresentation of this campaign has been grosser than the statement of our heavy loss of wagons and supplies. The orders submitted will show conclusively that every arrangement was made, in the utmost detail, for the security of our trains and supplies, and I am quite convinced that General Banks is not the man to neglect the duty with which he was charged.

I arrived at Centreville between 9 and 10 o'clock on the night of the 30th. The same night I sent orders to the corps commanders to report to me in person as early after daylight as possible on the morning of the 31st, and on that morning the troops were directed to be posted as follows: Porter to occupy the intrenchments on the north or right of Centreville; Franklin on his left, in the intrenchments. In rear of Centreville, between Franklin and Porter as a support, was posted the corps of Heintzelman. Sigel occupied the intrenchments on the left and south side of the town, with Reno on his left and rear. Banks was ordered to take post, as soon as he arrived, on the north side of Bull Run, and to cover the bridge on the road from Centreville to Manassas Junction. Sumner, as soon as he arrived, was ordered to take post between Centreville and Chantilly, and to occupy Chantilly in force. McDowell was posted about two miles in the rear of Centreville on the road to Fairfax Court-House. Ammunition trains and some provisions were gotten up on the 31st, and all corps commanders were notified, by special order to each, that the ammunition trains were parked immediately in rear of Centreville, and were directed to send officers to procure such ammunition as was needed in their respective corps. I directed the whole of the trains of the army to be unloaded at Centreville and sent to Fairfax Station to bring up forage and rations.

We remained during the whole day of the 31st resting the men, getting up supplies of provisions, and resupplying the command with ammunition.

The enemy's cavalry appeared in force in front of our advance at Cub Run, during the morning of the 31st, but made no attempt to cross and no attack upon our troops posted there. A few pieces of artillery were fired, but with no result on either side. The whole force that I had at Centreville, as reported to me by the corps commanders on the morning of the 1st of September, after receiving the corps of Sumner and Franklin, was as follows: McDowell's corps, ten thousand men; Sigel's corps, about seven thousand men; Heintzelman's corps, about six thousand; Reno's, six thousand; Banks's, five thousand; Porter's, about nine thousand; Franklin's, eight thousand; Sumner's, eleven thousand—in all, sixty-two thousand men. From these forces two brigades, as I before stated, had been sent to Fairfax Station to guard the trains and the depot at that place, which makes it necessary to deduct four thousand men. It is proper for me to state here, and I do it with regret and reluctance, that at least one-half of this great diminution of our forces was occasioned by skulking and straggling from the army. The troops which were brought into action fought with all gallantry and determination, but thousands of men straggled away from their commands and were not in any action. I had posted several regiments in rear of the field of battle on the 29th of August, and although many thousand stragglers and skulkers were arrested by them, many others passed around through the woods, and did not rejoin their commands during the remainder of the campaign. I had telegraphed to the general-in-chief, from Rappahannock Station, on the 22d, that this practice of straggling was very common, and was reducing our force considerably, even at that time. I also sent orders, on the same day, to General Sturgis to arrest all stragglers arriving at Alexandria, to confine them in military prisons, and to bring them to speedy trial. The active and incessant movements of the army prevented me, during the whole of this campaign, from giving that attention to the subject which ought to be and must be given to it, to preserve efficiency and discipline among any troops. Our cavalry at Centreville was completely broken down, no horses whatever having reached us to remount it. Generals Buford and Bayard, commanding the whole of the cavalry force of the army, reported to me that there were not five horses to the company that could be forced into a trot. It was impossible, therefore, to cover our front with cavalry or to make cavalry reconnoissances, as is usual and necessary in front of an army. I directed General Sumner, on the morning of the 1st of September, to push forward a reconnoissance of two brigades towards the Little River turnpike, to ascertain if the enemy were making any movements in the direction of Germantown or Fairfax Court-House. The enemy was found moving again slowly towards our right, heavy columns of his force being in march towards Fairfax, along Little River turnpike.

The main body of our forces was so much broken down and so completely exhausted that they were in no condition, even on the 1st of September, for any active operations against the enemy, but I determined to attack at daylight on the 2d of September, in front of Chantilly. The movement of the enemy had become so developed by the afternoon of the 1st, and was so evidently directed to Fairfax Court-House, with a view of turning my right, that I made the necessary disposition of my troops to fight a battle between the Little River pike and the road from Centreville to Fairfax Court-House. I sent General Hooker early in the afternoon to Fairfax Court-House, and directed him to assemble all the troops that were in the vicinity, and to push forward to Germantown with his advance.

I directed McDowell to move back along the road to Fairfax Court-House as far as Difficult creek, and to connect, by his right, with Hooker. Reno was to push forward to the north of the road from Centreville to Fairfax, in the direction of Chantilly. Heintzelman's corps was directed to take post on the road between Centreville and Fairfax, immediately in the rear of Reno. Franklin took post on McDowell's left and rear. Sumner was posted on the left of Heintzelman, whilst the corps of Sigel and Porter were directed to unite with the right of Sumner. Banks was instructed, with the wagon trains of the army, to pursue the old Braddock road and come into the Alexandria turnpike in rear of Fairfax Court-House. Just before sunset on the 1st, the enemy attacked us on our right, but was met by Hooker, McDowell, Reno, and Kearney's division of Heintzelman's corps. A very severe action occurred in the midst of a terrific thunder-storm, and was terminated shortly after dark. The enemy was driven back entirely from our front, but during that engagement we lost two of the best and one of the most distinguished of our general officers—Major General Kearney and Brigadier General Stevens—who were both killed while gallantly leading their commands and in front of their line of battle. It is unnecessary for me to say one word of commendation of two officers who were so well and widely known to the country. Words cannot express my sense of the zeal, the gallantry, and the sympathy of that most earnest and accomplished soldier, Major General Kearney. In him the country has suffered a loss which it will be difficult, if not impossible, to repair. He died as he would wish to die, and as became his heroic character.

On the morning of the 2d of September, the enemy still continuing his movement towards our right, my whole force was posted behind Difficult creek, from Flint Hill to the Alexandria turnpike. Although we were quite able to maintain our position at that place until the stragglers could be collected and the army, after its labors and perils, put into condition for effective service, I considered it advisable, for reasons which developed themselves at Centreville, and which I explained to the general-in-chief and set forth herewith in the appendix, that the troops should be drawn back to the intrenchments in front of Washington, and that some reorganization should be made of them, in order that earlier effective service should be secured than was possible in their condition at that time. I received orders about twelve o'clock on the 2d of September, to draw back the forces within the intrenchments, which was done in good order and without any interruption by the enemy. The reasons which induced me, before I took the field in Virginia, to express to the government my desire to be relieved from the command of the army of Virginia and to return to the west, existed in equal, if not greater, force at this time than when I first stated them. I accordingly renewed urgently my application to be relieved. The government assented to it with some reluctance, and I was transferred to the command of the department of the northwest, for which department I left Washington on the 7th of September.

It seems proper for me, since so much misrepresentation has been put into circulation as to the support I received from the army of the Potomac, to state here precisely what forces of that army came under my command and were at any time engaged in the active operations of the campaign. Reynolds's division of Pennsylvania reserves, about two thousand five hundred strong, joined me on the 23d of August, at Rappahannock Station. The corps of Heintzelman and Porter, about eighteen thousand strong, joined me on the 26th and 27th of August, at Warrenton Junction.

The Pennsylvania reserves, under Reynolds, and Heintzelman's corps, consisting of the divisions of Hooker and Kearney, rendered most gallant and efficient service in all the operations which occurred after they had reported to me. Porter's corps, from unnecessary and unusual delays and frequent and flagrant disregard of my orders, took no part whatever except in the action of the 30th of August. This small fraction of twenty thousand five hundred men was all of the ninety-one thousand veteran troops from Harrison's Landing which ever drew trigger under my command, or in any way took part in that campaign. By the time that the corps of Franklin and Sumner, nineteen thousand strong, joined me at Centreville, the original army of Virginia, as well as the corps of Heintzelman and the division of Reynolds, had been so much cut up in the severe actions in which they had been engaged, and were so much broken down and diminished in numbers by the constant and excessive duties they had performed, that they were in little condition for any effective service whatever, and required and should have had some days of rest to put them in anything like condition to perform their duties in the field.

Such is the history of a campaign substantiated by documents written during the operations and herewith appended, which has been misunderstood to an extent perhaps unparalleled in the history of warfare. I submit it here to the public judgment, with all confidence that it will be fairly and deliberately considered and a just verdict pronounced upon it and upon the army engaged in it.

Upon such unbiased judgment I am very willing, setting aside any previous record I have made during this war, to rest my reputation as a soldier. I shall submit cheerfully to the verdict of my countrymen, but I desire that that verdict shall be rendered upon a full knowledge of the facts.

I well understood, as does every military man, how difficult and how thankless was the duty devolved upon me, and I am not ashamed to say that I would gladly have avoided it, if I could have done so consistently with my sense of duty to the government. To confront with a small army vastly superior forces, to fight battles without hope of victory, but only to gain time and to embarrass and delay the forward movements of the enemy, is, of all duties, the most hazardous and the most difficult which can be imposed upon any general or any army. While such operations require the highest courage and endurance on the part of the troops, they are perhaps unlikely to be understood or appreciated, and the results, however successful, have little in them to attract popular attention and applause.

At no time could I have hoped to fight a successful battle with the immensely superior force of the enemy which confronted me, and which was able at any time to outflank me and bear my small army to the dust. It was only by constant movement, by incessant watchfulness, and by hazardous skirmishes and battles that the forces under my command were not overwhelmed, whilst at the same time the enemy was embarrassed and delayed in his advance upon Washington, until the forces from the Peninsula were at length assembled for the defence of that city. I did hope that in the course of these operations the enemy might commit some imprudence or leave some opening of which I could take such advantage as to gain at least a partial victory over his forces. This opportunity was presented by the advance of Jackson upon Manassas Junction; but, although the best dispositions possible under the circumstances were ordered, the object was frustrated in a manner and by causes which are now well understood. I am gratified to know that the conduct of that campaign, every detail of which was communicated day by day to the general-in-chief, was fully approved by him and by the government, and I now gladly submit the subject to the judgment of the country.

General Banks rendered most efficient and faithful service throughout the campaign, and his conduct at the battle of Cedar Mountain and during the operations on the Upper Rappahannock, was marked by great coolness, intrepidity, and zeal. General McDowell led his corps during the whole of the campaign with eminent ability and vigor, and I am greatly indebted to him for zealous and distinguished service both in the battles of the 29th and 30th of August, and in the operations which preceded and succeeded those battles. General Sigel rendered useful service in reorganizing and putting in condition the first army corps of the army of Virginia, and made many valuable and highly important reconnoissances during the operations of the campaign. I cannot express myself too highly of the zealous, gallant, and cheerful manner in which General Reno deported himself from the beginning to the end of the operations. Ever prompt, earnest, and soldierly, he was the model of an accomplished soldier and a gallant gentleman, and his loss has been a heavy blow to the army and to the country. General Heintzelman performed his duty faithfully and honestly, whilst the commanders of the divisions of his corps (Generals Kearney and Hooker) have that place in the public estimation which they have earned by many gallant and heroic actions, and which renders it unnecessary for me to do aught except pay this tribute to the memory of one and to the rising fame of the other. Generals Williams, Auger, Crawford, Green, Geary, Carroll, and Prince, of Banks's corps, have been already noticed for their gallant and distinguished conduct at Cedar Mountain. Generals King and Ricketts, of McDowell's corps, led their divisions throughout the operations with skill and efficiency, and General King, before he marched from Fredericksburg, rendered important service in organizing and despatching the expeditions, which, on several occasions, broke up the line of the Virginia Central railroad. Generals Patrick, Doubleday, Gibbon, Hartsuff, Duryea, and Tower commanded their brigades in the various operations of this campaign with ability and zeal; the latter named officer, especially, was particularly distinguished by the long marches which he made, by his incessant activity, and by the distinguished gallantry he displayed in the action of the 30th of August, in which action he was severely wounded at the head of his brigade. General Hatch, after being relieved from the command of the cavalry of Banks's corps, was assigned to the command of one infantry brigade in King's division of McDowell's corps, and during part of the operations was in command of that division and rendered good service. Generals Schenck and Milroy, of Sigel's corps, exhibited great gallantry and zeal throughout the operations. They were engaged actively in the battles of the 29th and 30th of August, and their commands were among the last to leave the field of battle on the night of the 30th, General Schenck being severely wounded on that day. I must also mention in high terms the conduct of Generals Schurz, Stahel, and Steinwehr during the actions of the 29th and 30th. Generals Birney, Robinson, and Grover, of Heintzelman's corps, commanded their brigades during the action of the 29th and 30th, and Birney during the action of the 1st September, with zeal and gallantry; and General Stevens, of Reno's corps, was zealous and active throughout the operations, and distinguished himself in the most auspicious manner during the battles of the 29th and 30th of August. He was killed at the head of his command, in the battle near Chantilly, on the 1st of September, and his death will be deeply felt by the army and the country. Lieutenant Colonel R. C. Buchanan, commanding a brigade of regulars of Porter's corps, was noticeable for distinguished service on the afternoon of the 30th of August. Of the conduct of the officers commanding divisions and brigades of Porter's corps I know nothing, having received no report from that officer of the operations of his corps. Brigadier General John F. Reynolds, commanding the Pennsylvania reserves, merits the highest commendation at my hands. Prompt, active, and energetic, he commanded his division with distinguished ability throughout the operations, and performed his duties in all situations with zeal and fidelity. Generals Seymour and Meade, of that division, in like manner, performed their duties with ability and gallantry and in all fidelity to the government and to the army.

General Sturgis arrived at Warrenton Junction on the 26th of August with Piatt's brigade of his division, the only portion of that division which joined him. This brigade was temporarily attached to the army corps of Fitz John Porter, and although misled in consequence of orders to follow Griffin's brigade of Porter's corps, which, for some unexplained reason, strayed from its corps to Centreville on the 30th of August, was led forward from that place by Generals Sturgis and Piatt as soon as it was discovered that Griffin did not intend to go forward to the field of battle, and reported to me late in the afternoon of that day. Shortly afterwards the brigade was thrown forward into action on our left, where they acquitted themselves with great courage. Brigadier General Sturgis, as well as General Piatt, deserve especial mention for the soldierly feeling which induced them, after being thus misled and with the bad example of Griffin before their eyes, to push forward with such zeal and alacrity to the field of battle, and for the valuable service which they rendered in the action of the 30th of August. Generals Bayard and Buford commanded the cavalry belonging to the army of Virginia. Their duties were peculiarly arduous and hazardous, and it is not too much to say that, throughout the operations from the first to the last day of the campaign, scarcely a day passed that these officers did not render service which entitles them to the gratitude of the government. The detachments of the signal corps with the various army corps rendered most important service, and I cannot speak too highly of the value of that corps and of the important information which, from time to time, they communicated to me. They were many times in positions of extreme peril, but were always prompt and ready to encounter any danger in the discharge of their duties.

Brigadier General Julius White, with one brigade, was, in the beginning of the campaign, placed in command at Winchester. He was selected for that position because I felt entire confidence in his courage and ability, and during the whole of his service there he performed his duty with the utmost efficiency, and relieved me entirely from any apprehension concerning that region of country. He was withdrawn from his position by orders direct from Washington, and passed from under my command.

I transmit herewith reports of corps, division, and brigade commanders, which will be found to embrace all the details of their respective operations, and which do justice to the officers and soldiers under their command.

To my personal staff I owe much gratitude and many thanks. Their duties were particularly arduous, and at times led them into the midst of the various actions in which we were engaged. It is saying little when I state that they were zealous, untiring, and efficient throughout the campaign. To Brigadier General Roberts, in particular, I am indebted for services marked throughout by skill, courage, and unerring judgment, and worthy of the solid reputation as a soldier he has acquired by many years of previous faithful and distinguished military service I desire, also, specially to mention Brigadier General Elliott, Surgeon McFarlin, Colonel Beckwith, Lieutenant Colonel T. C. H. Smith, Captain Piper, chief of artillery, Captain Merrill, of the engineers, and Lieutenant Skenck, chief of ordnance. I must also honorably mention the following members of my staff, the conduct of all of whom met my hearty approval and merits high commendation: Colonels Macomb, Clary, Marshal, Butler, Morgan, and Welch, Majors Selfridge and Meline, Captains Asch, Douglas, Pope, Haight, Atcheson, De Kay, Piatt, Paine, and Strother. Mr. McCain, confidential telegraph operator at my headquarters, accompanied me throughout the campaign, and was at all times eminently useful and efficient. My personal escort, consisting of two small companies of the first Ohio cavalry, numbering about one hundred men, performed the most arduous service, probably, of any troops in the campaign. As orderlies, messengers, and guards, they passed many sleepless nights and weary days. Their conduct in all the operations, as in every battle, was marked by uncommon activity and gallantry.

The reports of corps, division, and brigade commanders, herewith submitted, exhibit the loss in killed, wounded, and missing in their respective commands. No report of any description has been received from the army corps of Banks and Reno.

I am, general, very respectfully, your obedient servant,

JNO. POPE,
Major General United States Volunteers.

Brigadier General G. W. CULLUM,
Chief of Staff and of Engineers, Headquarters of the Army, Washington, D. C.

No. 2.

REPORT OF MAJOR GENERAL I. McDOWELL.

WASHINGTON, D. C., *November* 6, 1862.

GENERAL: The rapid succession of events, forced marches, separation from books and papers, and other circumstances attending the late campaign of the army of Virginia, were such as made it impracticable for me to make, from time to time, detailed reports of the part taken in it by the third army corps; and as, immediately after the end of the campaign, the corps was sent under another commander on active service into Maryland, and several of the officers commanding divisions and brigades became disabled there, I am still without many of the principal reports and returns which are necessary to make my report as full as it should be. It may, therefore, be found incomplete in some parts, and to comprise much which should have been made the subject of separate reports.

In the movements of the army of Virginia made, I presume, for the purpose of drawing on it the enemy's army from Richmond, and then of holding that army in check till a junction could be effected by our forces with the troops from the Peninsula, the third army corps consisted, in the first place, of King's and Ricketts's divisions and Bayard's cavalry brigade.

On the 7th of August, when we first felt the advance of the enemy, King's division was on the north bank of the Rappahannock at Fredericksburg. Ricketts's division, with the headquarters of the corps, was between the Rappahannock and the Rapidan, about three miles east of the little town of Culpeper Court-House.

Bayard's cavalry brigade was well to the front, in the forks of the Rapidan and its principal northern tributary, (Robertson's river,) with his outposts thrown forward, watching the enemy's line, (which was on the south or right bank of the Rapidan,) from a point some three miles to the east of the crossing of the Orange and Alexandria railroad, to the left of Buford's cavalry, which watched the front from the Rapidan to the Blue Ridge.

The Rapidan, from the left of Bayard's line to the Rappahannock and thence to Fredericksburg, was watched by the 1st Rhode Island, 1st Maine, 5th New York, and Harris's Light Cavalry, making a line of cavalry posts from the Blue Ridge to the Potomac.

The distance between King's division, at Fredericksburg, and Ricketts's, at Culpeper, was too great for either to join the other in case of its being attacked and so far apart as to leave a wide opening for the enemy to get between them by moving down the Rapidan and crossing near its confluence with the Rappahannock.

The weakness of this disposition of the corps early engaged your attention, as it had my own; and you would have remedied it in the beginning by bringing away King's division, but that to do this before the arrival of troops from the Peninsula would cause us to abandon Fredericksburg, and the line from that place to Acquia, which, at the cost of months of labor, had been placed in condition for service, and heavily supplied with railroad rolling stock and other materials for large operations that it was thought might soon have to be undertaken from that point.

General King was, however, held in readiness to leave at the shortest notice, and our cavalry was kept far to the front, so as to give timely warning of the movements of the enemy.

It was at midnight of the 7th of August that the line was broken by the enemy's crossing the Rapidan above the mouth of Robertson's river, driving in Bayard's outposts, and following them, early on the morning of the 8th, on the road leading across Robertson's river, and thence along the northwest base of Cedar Run (or Slaughter's) mountain, towards Culpeper.

Early on the morning of the 8th General Bayard sent Lieutenant Colonel Karge, with a battalion of the 1st New Jersey, to get around the enemy's left flank, whilst the general himself held them in check in front with part of the 1st Pennsylvania, under its colonel, Owen Jones, and part of the 1st New York under Major Beaumont. Slowly falling back towards Robertson's river, he was rejoined by Lieutenant Colonel Karge, (who had been successful in his flank movement—capturing one captain, one lieutenant, and twenty-four privates,) and, after passing his command over the river under a fire of the enemy's artillery, the general destroyed the bridge; thus delaying the enemy's advance, and gaining time to call in all his pickets, and give the notice needed to concentrate the army on the point threatened by the enemy.

This was on the day of your arrival at Culpeper.

The order given by you to King, as soon as news of the enemy's advance became known, found him just returned with a large part of his division (including all of his cavalry) from a demonstration, made in compliance with your orders, on the line of the enemy's railroad communications between Richmond and Gordonsville; and though his men were weary, and would have much liked rest before beginning this march, they set forth at once, and made a forced march of forty miles in thirty-six hours, during oppressively hot weather.

The 1st and 2d corps were between the Blue Ridge and Culpeper, upon which they were directed by your orders.

Crawford's brigade, of Banks's corps, had been occupying the town of Culpepper, and being nearest the enemy was sent by you on the 8th to support Bayard, and joined him that evening at Cedar Run, a small stream running past the eastern base of Cedar Run (or Slaughter's) mountain.

Colonel Duffie's 1st Rhode Island cavalry, and Colonel Allen's 1st Maine cavalry, which had been guarding the fords on the Rapidan below Bayard, also joined him, to aid in holding the enemy in check till the army should be sufficiently massed to offer battle. Thus far this had been done by Bayard's brigade; and now the duty devolved on Crawford, who joined with him infantry and artillery.

General Banks arriving at Culpeper in the evening of the 8th, with the remainder of his corps, was sent by you on the 9th to join his advanced brigade, then operating with the cavalry of my corps holding the enemy in check.

The orders were that General Sigel's corps (the first) should follow and support General Banks; Ricketts's division, of my corps, which had been moved to the southwest of the town, to be in reserve, King's division being more than two days' march distant.

The cannonading of the 8th had been resumed on the 9th, and was kept up more or less throughout the day. The reports from the front sent in to me, and from General Banks to your headquarters, (where, by your direction, I had been throughout the day,) were to the effect that the enemy did not yet seem to be in great force, showing his cavalry somewhat "ostentatiously," and using his artillery only; and these reports continued to be of this character throughout the day, and gave the assurance the enemy would not be able to bring up his main force till our army should have been sufficiently concentrated and got in good condition for battle.

General Sigel's corps having arrived at Culpeper after a forced march, much of it during the night previous, and being reported without provisions and not in a condition to immediately follow General Banks, by your order I directed subsistence to be given General Sigel's men from my supply train, and instantly took Ricketts's division, accompanied by you, to the front to join General Banks without waiting to follow General Sigel, as had been before ordered.

When the order was given me to take Ricketts's division to the front it was not known General Banks had attacked the enemy, or that he purposed doing so, or that the enemy was in sufficient force to attack him; but the cannonading having become more continuous, I was sent forward as a precautionary measure, and to allow General Sigel's men some rest. When between two and three miles from Cedar mountain, we began to meet the evidences of the battle which General Banks had fought at its base—stragglers, singly and in groups, and soon companies, battalions, and batteries, moving to the rear. General Banks had left the position where he had drawn up his troops, and moved them forward to attack the enemy, not believing him to be in any great force, and found him stronger than he had supposed, outnumbering greatly his own corps, and had been driven back after a gallant, severe, and bloody contest.

It was now dark, and under the assurance of General Banks that the remainder of his corps were in the front of a narrow strip of woods which extended across the road, that a brigade was still on a hill to the right of this wood, and that this brigade and the right of his line, which was said to be intact, would be drawn towards and strengthen the centre, which had suffered most, I was ordered to place Ricketts's division to the right and front; this was done by posting Tower's brigade, with two batteries, Shippen's and Thompson's, on the knoll to the right of the wood, Carroll's brigade connecting the left of Tower's line with the woods. Hartsuff's and Druyea's brigades in second line, with Hall's and Thompson's batteries in reserve. But while making these dispositions and moving forward in column to do so, the enemy, following up the retreat of General Banks, established a battery beyond the woods before mentioned and opened on the head of my column, and soon after coming through the woods with infantry, cavalry, and artillery, established another battery on the knoll where you had just before made your headquarters, after your conference with General Banks and others. This battery fired on the second line of Ricketts's division, and until the battalions in mass were placed under the shelter of the rolling ground took effect on Hartsuff's brigade. Quickly the batteries in reserve, under the direction of that most valuable officer Major Tellson, chief of artillery, Hall's 1st Maine and Thompson's 2d Maryland opened on the enemy. It was dark, and only by the flash of the enemy's pieces could they see where to direct their aim, but soon, by a rapid and well-directed fire, they silenced the enemy's batteries and forced them to withdraw, leaving some of their officers and most of their horses dead on the ground. The fire of the enemy's infantry from the woods was mostly at Carroll's brigade, which suffered from it before his men could be got into position in the front line.

The hot reception given the enemy by Ricketts's division caused the enemy to fall back during the night to their former position on and near Cedar Run mountain, some three miles.

Finding Rickett's division too far to the front and right it was drawn over during the night, by your direction, to the right of the position you had directed General Sigel to occupy.

On the morning of the 10th (Sunday) nothing was done by either army beyond a few dropping shots, and we remained in position, under arms, awaiting a renewal of the attack, which was not made, there being only one false alarm of a movement on our right flank.

The 1st Pennsylvania cavalry, under Colonel Owen Jones; the 1st New Jersey cavalry, under Lieutenant Colonel Karge, (Colonel Wyndham being a prisoner of war on parole;) the 1st Rhode Island cavalry, under Colonel Duffie, and the 1st Maine, under Colonel Allen, all under Brigadier General Bayard, had been engaged in the battle before we came up, and I am assured by your chief of cavalry, Brigadier General Roberts, who was present, they performed good service, not only before, but during the action. General Bayard, who had himself rendered most valuable service, speaks warmly of a charge made about 5 o'clock p. m. by that gallant old soldier Major Falls, 1st Pennsylvania cavalry, who led his battalion against the enemy's lines and charged completely through them.

All the regiments above named, and especially the Pennsylvania and New Jersey, had severe duty to perform in holding the enemy in check.

There are two officers of my staff—aides-de-camp—who are deserving of especial mention in connexion, Captain Leslie and Captain Howard Stockton. Having had no officers of topographical engineers, they were placed on this duty, and were constantly in front exerting themselves with a zeal and intelligence that accomplished much for the army, and especially for the advance.

On the 11th nothing in the way of hostilities occurred between the two armies. The burial of the dead and care of the wounded were effected under an informal flag of truce.

On the 12th King's division joined from Fredericksburg, and on the same day the enemy retired from our front across Robertson's river, going, according to the reports of our scouts and the lookouts, from the mountains back to Gordonsville, or, at all events, his main body disappearing from the banks of the Rapidan.

As it was not intended we should go beyond the Rapidan, but to continue to threaten its passage, the strongest defensible position north of that river and east of its northern tributary, Robertson's river, was occupied by the army; Major General Sigel's corps on the right, his right touching Robertson's river; the 3d corps in the centre; Major General Reno, who, at the head of the reinforcements coming up the Potomac to Acquia creek, had followed King's division from Fredericksburg, on the left, his left near the Rapidan; and General Banks in reserve at the little town of Culpeper Court-House. The Orange and Alexandria railroad, which had been repaired, going through the centre of the position The army was in the forks of the Rappahannock and its tributary, the Rapidan. These two streams rise in the Blue Ridge and run through the Bull Run or Piedmont Ridge. Beyond the Rapidan and close to the river the Piedmont Ridge, which disappears at Warrenton, begins again nearly opposite the left of our line, held by Reno, and stretches off to the southwest to Lynchburg.

On the morning of the 18th one of our spies, who had been with the enemy's army, came and reported to you that the enemy had accumulated all his forces, including several divisions just up from Richmond, behind the ridge immediately beyond the river and opposite our extreme left; his artillery horses were all harnessed, and they were expecting orders to march every moment down the river, to cross at Raccoon Ford to get in our rear. This movement, which had been completely hidden from our sight by the ridge, and even from that of our lookouts on the top of Thoroughfare mountain, was one made in the direction which had been expected from the first, and had for its object the interposing of the whole of the enemy's forces between our army and its re-enforcements then coming up from Acquia creek and Fredericksburg, and from Alexandria by way of Manassas Junction.

The information was important, and received in time, provided the enemy gave us that day and night the start.

Your orders for the army to retire forthwith behind the Rappahannock required that the reserve corps (Banks's) should immediately send its baggage to the rear, by way of Brandy Station, to the Orange and Alexandria railroad crossing of the Rappahannock; that the trains of the third army corps should follow those of Banks; that those of Sigel should follow the third corps to Culpeper, and then go by the Warrenton road to the Sulphur Springs crossing of the Rappahannock, some six miles above the railroad crossing; that Reno should take the road by which he came, and which led him back to Kelly's Ford, some six miles below the railroad crossing. The movement of the trains—unfortunately very large—was followed by the march of the troops in the same order, the troops commencing to move after night, so as to allow the trains to get some distance ahead, if possible. The size of the trains, the night march, the corps having, for a large part of the way, to use the same road, made a retreat a very tedious and wearisome one to the troops, although it was entirely successful, and effected without loss or accident, but the troops did not reach the Rappahannock until the evening of the 19th.

Bayard's cavalry, being charged with covering the rear of the column, got no further than Culpeper that night. The next morning, the 20th, agreeably to the instructions given him, he took post at Brandy Station, half way between Culpeper Court-House and the Rappahannock, and sent out strong parties in all the roads coming from the enemy's position. The party sent out on the

Raccoon Ford road soon came upon the head of the enemy's column, which had made the expected movement, but too late to intercept us. The enemy followed up the cavalry to Brandy Station, and thence to the Rappahannock, some skirmishing taking place on the way, and the cavalry retiring across the river.

The entire corps, with the exception of a small party thrown in advance at the head of the bridge, now occupied the left or north bank of the Rappahannock, with General Sigel's corps on the right, General Banks's corps partly in reserve and partly on the left, and Reno's corps below us, at Kelly's Ford, and Reynolds's division, formerly under my command, and which it was soon to rejoin, coming up the river from Fredericksburg.

I understood it was desired the line of the Rappahannock should be held as long as possible, to gain time for the troops coming up the Potomac to join, and particularly those coming by way of Acquia and Fredericksburg, who would be liable to be cut off if we should give up the river before they arrived.

The Rappahannock, above the mouth of the Rapidan, is an inconsiderable stream, and fordable, at most seasons, every few miles. The third corps was posted at and above the railroad bridge, which had been so arranged as to serve for artillery and cavalry.

The advance, a regiment of Hartsuff's brigade, was posted on two small hills on the southern side of the river. The first one was about one hundred and fifty yards from the road and as many from the river; the second some four hundred yards from the road and six hundred from the river. On the first was a small entrenchment thrown up by the enemy at the time of their retreat from Manassas, last spring.

That evening a battery of artillery and a regiment of infantry from Banks's corps, I think, were sent by you to guard a ford to the right of my line.

Early on the morning of the 21st the enemy attempted the ford held by the battery and regiment on my right, and drove them away, dispersing the regiment and disabling the battery. King's division was immediately sent up to retake the position, which it soon did, driving the enemy back with loss, and taking some of the cavalry prisoners. The rifle batteries of both divisions now lined the river bank in such position as commanded the opposite shore, and gave shelter to our troops. The enemy's fire disabled three guns in Naylor's battery, but they themselves were equally damaged, in return, by the accurate fire of Hall's battery, which finally compelled them to retire.

On the 22d, fearing the enemy might gain possession of the most advanced hill, near the bridge, which it was desirable to hold, in the night a trestle-bridge was built by the engineer corps, under Major Huston, of the engineers, about eight hundred yards above the railroad bridge, in a bend of the river, which swept near the further hill, the banks here being covered with woods. This gave us another, and a shorter and hidden, line of communication, and enabled Hartsuff's whole brigade, and Thompson's and Matthews's batteries, to be thrown over to occupy these heights. The firing to-day was very animated between the enemy's batteries and our own.

Since the morning of the 21st the enemy's heavy columns of infantry, artillery, and trains could sometimes be plainly seen passing up to our right, and their course, when behind the woods, was indicated by the lines of dust ascending above the trees. The attack on my front had been followed up by similar ones on the positions held by the other corps above and below me. All the movements of the enemy gave assurances he was moving to turn our right, having failed on the front and left. This was confirmed by the intelligence that he had crossed at Sulphur Springs and was moving on Warrenton.

On the night of the 22d, just as I received your orders for the third corps to cross at the bridge, and, in connexion with the commands of Reno and Reynolds below me, to fall on the rear of that long column which had been passing before us for two days up the south side of the river, an officer came to report to me, in your presence, that the rain which had been falling during the night had so swollen the river that the trestle-bridge had been swept away, and had lodged against the railroad bridge, the centre of which was yielding to the pressure of the flood, and was in imminent danger of being carried off. The river had risen some six feet and all the fords were gone.

Fearing for the safety of Hartsuff's brigade, who were on the opposite bank, I ordered them to be withdrawn. It was now impracticable to cross the river and make the attack you had planned. Your orders then were to move the army against the enemy, who had crossed at Sulphur Springs and gone to Warrenton, whence he had made the attack with his cavalry at Catlett's, and who, it was thought, would be unable, on account of the state of the river, either to recross or be reinforced.

The withdrawal of Hartsuff's brigade from the south side encouraged the enemy to move forward to seize the hills he had abandoned before we could complete the entire destruction of the railroad bridge, which we did not wish to leave for the enemy to repair and use to annoy us on our march to Warrenton. They opened a furious fire upon us, and, moving their infantry down in masses, rushed upon the hill Hartsuff had just left. Matthews's, Thompson's, and Leppier's batteries, and our sharpshooters, returned their fire so vigorously that they were soon driven off. Leppier's especially did them much damage. Further to the right Hall's battery engaged two of the enemy's batteries and drove both of them off, and dispersed a regiment of infantry. The firing of this excellent battery was, as usual, rapid and accurate. Further up the river the batteries of Reynolds and Naylor were also successfully engaged. In the meantime the corps, agreeably to your orders, was on the march to Warrenton, to be on the right of General Sigel, who was to attack the enemy, and who was to have Generals Reno and Banks on his left and rear, General Reno having moved up the river for this purpose. Reynolds's division, following him, rejoined the third corps, and marched after the division of Generals King and Ricketts to Warrenton. The rear guard of the corps was commanded by Brigadier General Tower, who had his brigade and the batteries of artillery holding the river at the bridge, which he was directed to see destroyed before leaving.

In the afternoon, under cover of a thunder storm, which for a while hid all objects at a little distance from view, the enemy again occupied the hill from which they had been driven in the morning, but kept out of sight till after the bridge had been destroyed and the rear guard had taken up its line of march, when, just as the batteries were limbering up to leave, they commenced a rapid fire upon the retiring column. That night the advance of the first division of the corps entered Warrenton, the other divisions being on the road leading there—but from three to five miles from it. The enemy had retreated in the afternoon toward the river. General Sigel, who had been on the right when we were on the river, facing the south, was now, by our change of front, in advance. He was to have intercepted the enemy, but, for some reason, was not able to come up with them before they crossed the river at Sulphur Springs, on a bridge they had built at that place. General Sigel followed up the north bank of the river to Waterloo bridge, on the crossing of Luray turnpike.

On the 24th the whole corps was at Warrenton, and on the road thence to Sulphur Springs.

On the 25th I received your order of that date—

"GENERAL ORDER NO. —.

"HEADQUARTERS ARMY OF VIRGINIA,
"*Warrenton, August* 25, 1862.

"I. The corps of Major General McDowell, to which the division of Brigadier General Reynolds is attached, will occupy Warrenton, with an advance of at least a brigade thrown out toward Waterloo and Sulphur Springs. The cavalry of the corps will be kept along the line of the river.

"II. The first army corps, under Major General Sigel, will occupy Fayetteville, and will there be joined by Brigadier General Cox, whose advance will occupy a strong position in the vicinity of Fayetteville, throwing out an advance of at least a brigade towards the fords in front of the position, and keeping his cavalry along the line of the river.

"III. The corps of Major General Banks, to which will be added ten thousand men under Brigadier General Sturgis, will take post with its right resting on Bealton Station, and its left extended along the north side of Marsh creek. From this corps at least one division will be pushed forward as near as practicable to the railroad crossing of the Rappahannock. If there be any difficulty about water for this corps, wells will be dug immediately.

"IV. The detachment of the ninth army corps, under Major General Reno, will resume its station at Kelly's Ford, putting itself in communication immediately with the forces below it on the river.

"V. The troops of Heintzelman's corps will take post with the centre at Germantown and extended along the Licking river.

"VI. Brigadier General Cox, with the troops under his command, will move forward as soon as possible to Fayetteville and report to Major General Sigel. Those under Brigadier General Sturgis will report to Major General Banks at Bealton Station.

"VII. The headquarters of the army of Virginia will be established at a point near Warrenton Junction, to be hereafter designated.

"By command of Major General Pope.

"Per C. SELFRIDGE,
"*Assistant Adjutant General.*"

directing the 3d corps to occupy Warrenton, &c. This same general order required Major General Sigel's corps to occupy Fayetteville to the left of the 3d corps, General Banks to occupy Bealton's Station to the left of General Sigel, and General Reno to return to Kelly's Ford on the Rappahannock.

The line thus intended to be established would touch the river only on the extreme left at Kelly's Ford, the centre and right being thrown back or refused, and the right held by the 3d corps, resting on the extremity of the Bull Run or Piedmont Ridge at Warrenton.

This order, so far as concerned the 3d corps, was immediately carried out by placing Reno's division on the road to Sulphur Springs, with Meade's brigade thrown forward to within four miles of the springs, which are at the river. Ricketts on the Waterloo road, with Tower's brigade in advance within four miles of the bridge, and King's division near the town, in the forks of the roads abovementioned, which issue from Warrenton at nearly right angles to each other, and are good broad turnpikes; the Waterloo road leading nearly west through the Blue Ridge to Luray, and the Sulphur Springs road nearly south west towards Culpeper.

Buford's cavalry brigade was posted between Tower's advanced brigade and Waterloo bridge, (over the Rappahannock,) and Bayard's brigade was to take post on the Sulphur Springs road between Meade's brigade and the river.

On the night of the 25th I received from you, by telegraph from your headquarters near Warrenton Junction, an order that, leaving Reynolds in reserve, I should make a reconnoissance with my corps across the river at Sulphur Springs, and sending me an open order for General Sigel, which I was to read and send to him, directing him to force the passage of the river at Waterloo. This order was immediately forwarded to General Sigel by the hands of one of my aides-de-camp, Captain F. Haven, and was received at 2 o'clock a. m., whilst the General was on the retreat in the night from Waterloo to Warrenton, through which his troops were moving all night long.

"HEADQUARTERS ARMY OF VIRGINIA,
"*August* 25, 1862—9.30 *p. m.*

"MAJOR GENERAL McDOWELL: I believe that the whole force of the enemy have marched for the Shenandoah valley by the way of Front Royal and Luray. The column which has marched to-day to Gaines's Crossroads has turned north, and when last seen was passing under the east base of Buck mountain towards Salem and Rectorstown. I desire you as early as possible in the morning, holding Reynolds in the reserve at Warrenton or vicinity, to make a reconnoissance with your whole corps and ascertain what is beyond the river at Culpeper Sulphur Springs. There is no force of the enemy between this or Culpeper or at Culpeper.

"I send you a despatch for General Sigel, which please read and send to him immediately.

"Communicate with me fully by telegraph from Warrenton.

"JOHN POPE,
"*Major General Commanding.*

"Received 12 m. August 25, 1862."

Early the next morning, (the 26th,) Ricketts's division, which was on the Waterloo road, was moved across to the Sulphur Springs road to make the attack you had ordered.

In the course of the morning I received your telegram of 5 o'clock a. m.,* and as I was on my way to Sulphur Springs to direct the attack, your telegram of 8.10 o'clock a. m.† These informed me of your order to Reno to make the

---

[Extract.]

*WARRENTON JUNCTION, 5 *a. m.* *August* 26, 1862.

GENERAL McDOWELL: Please ascertain, in some way, whether the enemy be really in force at Waterloo bridge. Sigel insists that he is, while Banks, who was there late yesterday afternoon, asserts positively that there was no enemy during the day there. You will easily see how important it is for us to know positively what has become of the enemy's force, which was in front, and where the column has gone which took yesterday the road towards Salem. Please use every means possible to ascertain this at once. Reno will cross at Rappahannock Station, and push forward a reconnoissance to Culpeper. I wish you would send me a regiment of cavalry. I have not a mounted man here. Send me one of Buford's or Bayard's.

JOHN POPE,
Major General Commanding.

[Extract.]

† WARRENTON JUNCTION, 8.10 *a. m.* *August* 26, 1862.

MAJOR GENERAL McDOWELL: I sent instructions last night to make a strong reconnoissance across to Sulphur Springs, intending that Sigel should do the same thing at Waterloo bridge, and Reno at Rappahannock. Sigel reports himself unable to do anything of the kind, until his men are rested. I directed him to halt them somewhere near Warrenton, and put them in camp for a day. Reno, instead of going to Bealton and then to Kelly's Ford, has come to this place, and is now near here. You must therefore, under these circumstances, exercise your discretion about the reconnoissance to Sulphur Springs; but it will certainly be well for you to ascertain what there is in the direction of Waterloo bridge,

reconnoissance across the river, below Rappahannock Station to Culpeper, and of his failure to do so; and in view of the failure of General Sigel to force the passage of the river above at Waterloo, authorized me to use my discretion as to crossing at Sulphur Springs, and desired me to ascertain, if possible, if the enemy were really in force at Waterloo, and what had become of the head of his column, which yesterday was in front, and had taken the road towards Salem. General Sigel, you informed me, reported his men unable to do anything until they should have some rest. Generals Bayard and Buford reported to me that, owing to the hard, unremitting services performed, their cavalry was broken down—the former, that his would neither charge nor stand a charge; the latter, that his was at that time disorganized.

As the falling back of General Sigel from Waterloo to Warrenton, and the transfer of my troops from the Waterloo road to the Sulphur Springs road, had left the right weakly guarded, and as it was around the right the enemy were then moving, I decided to replace my corps in the position it had occupied the day before.

In order to comply with your wishes to ascertain the force of the enemy at Waterloo and further to the right, agreeably to your instructions of 8.10 a. m., I took command of General Sigel's corps and everything in front, (a copy of my note to General Sigel is below, marked E.)* Brigadier General Buford, with the available cavalry at hand, and some artillery from General Sigel's corps, was sent to turn the head of the enemy's column, which was moving through Salem. This was reported to you and met your approval.

I am obliged here to ask your attention to General Sigel's report, which has been made public. It will be noticed the general gives at some length his reasons for abandoning the position at Waterloo bridge, and falling back under cover of the 25th; a movement with which he seems to wish it to appear I was in some way connected, if, indeed, I was not responsible. He says, first, he had been under my command since his arrival at Waterloo, had sent to me for instructions, &c. It will be seen from your telegram, my letter, and his own report, that he did not come under my orders until the 26th, after he had left his position and fallen behind my command at Warrenton. Second, he says I was to have relieved Milroy's brigade on the bridge. In that he mistakes the general order (which I have quoted) forming the line from Kelly's Ford on the left to Warrenton on the right. The river was to be held, except at Kelly's Ford, by cavalry only, and Buford's brigade was close behind Milroy for this

---

and still further to your right. Send for Milroy; he is a courageous man. * * * If you deem it necessary, assume command also of Sigel's corps. It is essential that we should watch the movements of the enemy towards our right in some manner. Out of Buford's, Bayard's, and Sigel's cavalry enough can certainly be found to perform this service. Troops are accumulating here, but not very fast. Take charge of the front, and use everybody you find there.

JOHN POPE,
Major General Commanding.

P. S.—I will push Reno to Fayetteville. It will be well to have the men cook three days' rations. Please notify Banks and Sigel.

J. P.

*[E.]

HEADQUARTERS THIRD ARMY CORPS,
Army of Virginia, August 26, 1862.

GENERAL: I am instructed by Major General Pope to take command of the troops on the right and front, for the purpose of strengthening some movements I am ordered to make. Please let me know the position and strength of your command, and especially the cavalry. My headquarters are on the hill southwest of Warrenton or Sulphur Springs road.

JAMES McDOWELL,
Major General Commanding.

SIGEL, *Major General Commanding Division.*

purpose. Third, he says, when he fell back he had no support within eight or ten miles of him. It is eight miles, so called, from Waterloo bridge to Warrenton. He had behind and to his right Buford's brigade; behind Buford, Ricketts's division of four brigades and four batteries of artillery, all of which were between four and five miles of the bridge. Fourth, he says matters were confused at receiving a mutilated order or letter from General McDowell, part directed to him, informing him he would meet his bridge train at Fayetteville, and part addressed to General Banks. I did myself know where his bridge train was, and had no right to call on General Banks for any return, for he was my senior. The letter to him, I have been informed by that officer, was from your late chief of staff, and was, I suppose, sent to Warrenton by telegraph from your headquarters, and forwarded thence to its destination by the operator, by means of one of the cavalry of my corps. However this may be, I know nothing of it.

The attack on the enemy beyond Sulphur Springs by my corps was not undertaken, for the reasons I have stated; but before the countermand was given King's division became engaged with the enemy, mostly with artillery, and the firing was kept up during the day. The troops opposed to him, as we learned from a flag of truce sent by the enemy, was a division of Anderson's, formerly Huger's, and, as far as I know, the last of those of which we had any knowledge that had left Richmond. I inferred from this the enemy's rear rested then at Sulphur Springs.

On the supposition the enemy might offer us battle at or near Warrenton, upon which he could now concentrate a large force, you informed me in your telegram of the 26th that the corps on my left and rear would all be pushed forward, so as to be within supporting distance of the 3d corps. The information, however, received in the evening and night from General Buford, from General Sigel's scouts, and from some negroes, was to the effect that the enemy's column, whose rear division we had been fighting at Sulphur Springs, was directed upon Thoroughfare Gap, through which his advance had passed, to attack our communications at Manassas. Copies of the telegrams to and from your headquarters, concerning the supposed designs of the enemy, are herewith marked.*

You then decided to throw the army back on the forces of the enemy which had passed through the Piedmont ridge at Thoroughfare Gap, and agreeably to your order of 8.30 a. m. of the 27th, (and not as stated in General Sigel's proposal,) I gave the latter, who, as we were to march to the rear, was now in front, the following order:

"Push, immediately, a strong advance along the turnpike from Warrenton to Gainesville, for the purpose of taking possession of Buckland Mills, on Broad Run, and get your corps in hand as soon as possible, to follow the advance. No wagons, but for ammunition, will accompany your corps on this road. Your baggage trains will immediately proceed to Catlett's. Detach three batteries from your corps to report to Major General Kearney, commanding division, who will be moving by way of Greenwich to your support. Further instructions will be given as to the route by which the batteries are to join General Kearney, and until they do they will remain with you."

I gave General Sigel the cavalry of my corps in place of his own, which had been detached by your order, and informed him that Reynolds, King, and Ricketts's divisions would immediately follow him,† and that as soon as they closed

---

* See Appendix.

† HEADQUARTERS, THIRD ARMY CORPS,
Army of Virginia, August 27, 1862.

GENERAL: I have just received your note of 12½ p. m. In default of your cavalry, which is not yet returned, I send you this morning General Bayard, with three regiments; when

upon him, he should push his advance to Gainesville, the point where the Warrenton turnpike to Centreville and Alexandria was crossed by the road from Thoroughfare Gap to Manassas Junction.

The divisions of Reynolds, King, and Ricketts, in the order named, followed as soon as they could be brought on. As there was but one road for all these troops to march over, stringent orders were given that all wagons not required for ammunition should be sent to the lower road, so as to leave this one as unencumbered as possible for the passage of the troops. So far as the 3d corps was concerned, this order, with inconsiderable exceptions, mostly in Reynolds's division, was obeyed.

General Sigel succeeded in reaching Buckland Mills in time to save the bridge which I had had made over Broad Run at that place, and had pushed on his advance to Gainesville, as ordered, and that night the three divisions of the corps closed up with him.

Buford, who had been indefatigable on this, as on every other occasion during the campaign, sent in word from our extreme left (our former right) that he had cut the enemy's column and forced Longstreet to deploy between Salem and White Plains. Duffie's Rhode Island cavalry was sent up to watch the road between White Plains and Thoroughfare, to see that the enemy should not fall on the rear of our column unawares.

The night of the 27th I saw General Sigel at Buckland Mills, and informed him that Longstreet would be coming through the Gap next morning, and that, as the head of his corps (Sigel's) was now on the road leading from the Gap to Manassas Junction, I would give him one of my divisions (a third of my force) and charge him with the duty of marching to Haymarket, watching the Gap and engaging the forces when they came through, whilst I would take the remainder of my force and go against those who had already passed. I sent word to you of this, at Bristow. But whilst the preparations were being made to carry it out, I received your order, dated Bristow, August 27, 9 o'clock p. m., as follows:

"At daylight, to-morrow morning, march rapidly on Manassas Junction with your whole force, resting your right on the Manassas Gap railroad, throwing your left well to the east. Jackson, Ewell, and A. P. Hill are between Gainesville and Manassas Junction. We had a severe fight with them to-day, driving them back several miles, along the railroad. If you will march promptly and rapidly at the earliest dawn of day, upon Manassas Junction, we shall bag the whole crowd. I have directed Reno to march from Greenwich at the same time, upon Manassas Junction, and Kearney, who is in his rear, to march on Bristow, at daybreak. Be expeditious, and the day is our own."

I showed this order to General Sigel and sent him a copy of my general order,*

---

yours return, please send him back to me. I will send word to Catlett's about your regimental provision wagons. Brigadier General Reynolds's division is immediately behind you. King and Ricketts follow.

Very respectfully, your obedient servant,

JAMES McDOWELL, *Major General.*

SIGEL, *Major General commanding 1st Corps.*

* HEADQUARTERS THIRD CORPS, REYNOLDS'S CAMP,
August 28, 1862.

GENERAL ORDER, No. 10.]

1. Major General Sigel will immediately march with his whole corps on Manassas Junction; his right resting on the Manassas railroad.

2. Brigadier General Reynolds will march on the turnpike, immediately in the rear of General Sigel, and form his division on the left of General Sigel, and march upon Manassas Junction.

3. Brigadier General King will follow immediately after General Reynolds and form his division on General Reynolds's left, and direct his march on Manassas Junction.

the receipt of which he acknowledged at 2½ a. m. on the 28th. My order required all the forces to march immediately. His advanced division was already at Gainesville, and he had to close his command upon it and march as ordered. I endeavored, by every exertion of myself and staff, to get the force forward as early as you had indicated; and, so far as the 3d corps was concerned, worn as the divisions were by the marching and countermarching of the day previous, up to a late hour in the night, which had prevented many of the regiments from obtaining their supplies, there was no difficulty. They were ready, and marched forward with alacrity, though many of the regiments had barely finished the march of the day before. But General Sigel's rear division was so long getting out of its bivouac that Reynolds's division, after waiting some time, had to pass the larger part of it, and General Sigel's corps, instead of complying fully with my orders, at Warrenton, that all wagons not carrying ammunition should go by the way of Catlett's, had brought with them nearly two hundred, which encumbered the road and embarrassed our movements seriously; and when all the divisions were closed up, instead of a rapid march, everything came to a stand.

At 7½ o'clock I received a message from General Reynolds, who was at the head of the 3d corps, that General Sigel was halting on the road, at the junction of the railroad, (Gainesville,) and was making no preparations to advance or to organize, or form his line, and that his men had built fires to cook their breakfast, and had blocked up the road so that he could not get forward. I sent my assistant adjutant general to the head of the column to urge General Sigel to march immediately on Manassas Junction, as ordered, but it was too late in the forenoon before the head of the corps passed him.

All the forces of the army were now, by your orders, converging on Manassas, and had been moving, till we crossed the railroad at Gainesville, in the angle comprised between the Orange and Alexandria railroad, and the Manassas railroad, which unite at Manassas Junction.

The troops under my command, the first and third corps, were to cross the Manassas road at Gainesville, and move with the right on that road, the left well to the east.

General Sigle says, in his report, that he understood he was to have his right on the railroad leading from Warrenton Junction to Manassas Junction, the Orange and Alexandria railroad, some six miles to the south of us. He saw your order to move with his right on the Manassas railroad, and had my general order, in writing, to the same effect. When I arrived at Gainesville, I found he had moved to the right, or south side, instead of to the left, or north side, of the Manassas road.

I varied from your orders to march with "my whole force" only so far as concerned General Ricketts's division, and the cavalry of Buford and Bayard. Knowing that Longstreet would be coming through Thoroughfare, I sent, early in the morning, Colonel Wyndham's First New Jersey regiment of cavalry to the Gap, and sent up other cavalry as fast as I could get hold of it; and on receiving word the enemy was coming through, I detached Ricketts's division to hold him in check.

This departure from your orders, to move with "my whole force" on Manassas, I felt called upon to make, to carry out the *spirit* of your plan of crushing

---

4. Brigadier General Ricketts will follow Brigadier General King and march to Gainesville; and if, on arriving there, no indication shall appear of the approach of the enemy from Thoroughfare Gap, he will continue his march along the turnpike, form on the left of General King, and march on Manassas Junction. He will be constantly on the lookout for an attack from the direction of Thoroughfare Gap, and in case one is threatened, he will form his division to the left and march to resist it.

The headquarters of the corps will be at King's division.

By command of MAJOR GENERAL McDOWELL.

the enemy at that place before his re-enforcements, of whose position I had just received positive intelligence, could join, as those re-enforcements, I thought, could be better held in check at the Gap than this side of it.

As soon as the Warrenton road was free, Reynolds's division pushed forward across the railroad, and after a short march the head of his column found itself opposed by the enemy, with a battery of artillery posted on a hill. The attack, commenced by the enemy as soon as we came in view, caused Reynolds to deploy his column; to bring up his artillery, and sent out his skirmishers. After a short engagement the enemy retired, so that when our skirmishers occupied the hill he left; he was nowhere to be seen. Supposing, from the movements of this force, that it was some rear guard or cavalry party, with artillery, sent out to reconnoitre, the march of the division, after caring for the killed and wounded, was resumed, and it turned off to the south of the road to go to Manassas. General Sigel's, getting so far to the south of Manassas railroad, left so wide a distance between him and the leading division of the corps—Reynolds's—that King's division, which was to have gone to the left of Reynolds's, was now brought between it and General Sigel's corps, and the march on Manassas resumed.

The country between the Warrenton turnpike and the Manassas railroad, on which we were now marching, was unknown to us. It was partly in fields, but mostly in woods, across and through which we were going in the general direction ordered. It was now late in the afternoon, and I ascertained that the enemy were no longer at Manassas Junction; and soon after I received your despatch* of 1.20, from that place, which must have been delayed on the way—for after giving the necessary orders to carry out your instructions, but before the troops had received them, your second despatch,† from Manassas, was received, informing me that the enemy were on the other side of Bull Run on the Orange and Alexandria railroad, as also near Centreville, and directing me to march with my command upon the latter place. King's division, which was nearest the Warrenton and Centreville turnpike, was ordered to march by that road, and Reynolds's division, which was near the Sudley Springs and Manassas road, was ordered to move by that road and thence by the Warrenton turnpike. After putting these divisions in motion and going with Reynolds's division to near Manassas, I proceeded to that place to confer personally with you. King's division moved along the Warrenton road and became engaged with the enemy, and at the same time Ricketts's, some six or eight miles further to the west, became

---

* HEADQUARTERS ARMY OF VIRGINIA,
Manassas Junction, August 28, 1862, 1.20 *p. m.*

MAJOR GENERAL McDOWELL: I sent you a despatch a few minutes ago directing you to move on Gum Spring to intercept Jackson. Since then I have received your note of this morning. I will, this evening, push forward Reno to Gainesville, and follow with Heintzelman, unless there is a large force of the enemy at Centreville, which I do not believe. Ascertain, if you can, about this. I do not wish you to carry out the order to proceed to Gum Spring if you consider it too hazardous, but I will support you in any way you suggest, by pushing forward from Manassas Junction across the turnpike. Jackson has a large train, which should certainly be captured. Give me your views fully; you know the country much better than I do. Come no further in this direction with your command, but call back what has advanced thus far.

JOHN POPE, *Major General Commanding.*

† HEADQUARTERS, *Manassas Junction, August* 28, 4.15 *p. m.*

MAJOR GENERAL McDOWELL: The enemy is reported in force on the other side of Bull Run on the Orange and Alexandria railroad, as also near Centreville. I have ordered Sigel to march on Centreville immediately, as also Kearney and Reno. I will advance Hooker as reserve. Please march immediately with your command upon Centreville from where you are.

JOHN POPE, *Major General Commanding.*

engaged with Longstreet's corps as it attempted the passage of the defile at Thoroughfare Gap. I have, as yet, received no reports from King's division, or from any of the brigade commanders. I cannot say, therefore, as to the engagement of Thursday, the 29th; but from verbal reports, I understand it to have been mostly an affair of General Gibbon's brigade—one of the finest in the army, and part of Doubleday's brigade, with some two brigades of the enemy, and that the troops behaved most creditably. The loss in Gibbons's brigade was severe—in both men and officers. The gallant Colonel O'Connor, 2d Wisconsin, and Major May, 19th Indiana, killed; Colonel Cutler, 6th Wisconsin—one of the best officers we have—badly wounded, and at the time reported dead; the gallant Colonel Robertson, 7th Wisconsin, Major Allen, 2d Wisconsin, Lieutenant Colonel Charles Hamilton, 7th Wisconsin, and Major Bells, 7th Wisconsin, wounded.

General Ricketts engaged the enemy until dark, holding him in check and forcing him back; but finding him crossing at Hopewell Gap, above and on his right, and threatened with being turned on his left, he withdrew at nightfall to Gainesville; and here learning from General King that he intended to fall back to Manassas at one o'clock a. m. from the Warrenton road, General Ricketts did the same by the way of Bristow, which gave him a long and fatiguing march. Finding on my arrival there that you had left Manassas, I turned towards Reynolds's division, but did not succeed in finding it—it being now dark—until daybreak next morning, on the hill by the Warrenton road, near Groveton. It was here I learned of the movements of King's and Ricketts's divisions of the night before.

Early in the morning of the 29th General Sigel, who had come up the night before from near Manassas, and who was on Reynolds's right, made demonstrations against the enemy, who seemed to be on the north of us. I directed Reynolds to support General Sigel on the left in the movements he might make, and then proceed to join General King's and Ricketts's divisions.

At Manassas I found Major General Fitz John Porter's corps coming up, and soon after, in answer partly to a message of mine, I received your order* of the 29th, from Centerville, addressed, jointly, to General Porter and myself.

In compliance with it, King's and Ricketts's divisions were directed, as soon as they could be placed on the road from Manassas Junction to Gainesville, which runs nearly west, to follow in the rear and close to General Porter's corps.

---

* HEADQUARTERS ARMY OF VIRGINIA,
Centreville, August 29, 1862.

GENERALS McDOWELL AND PORTER: You will please move forward with your joint commands towards Gainesville. I sent General Porter written orders to that effect an hour and a half ago Heintzelman, Sigel, and Reno are now moving at Warrenton turnpike, and must now be not far from Gainesville. I desire that as soon as communication is established between this force and your own, the whole command shall halt. It may be necessary to fall back behind Bull Run, at Centreville, to-night. I presume it will be so on account of our supplies I have sent no orders of any description to Ricketts, and none to interfere in any way with the movement of McDowell's troops, except what I sent by his aide-de-camp last, which were to hold his position on the Warrenton 'pike until the troops from here should fall on the enemy's flank and rear. I do not even know Ricketts's position, and I have not been able to find out where General McDowell was until a late hour this morning. General McDowell will take immediate steps to communicate with General Ricketts, and instruct him to rejoin the other divisions of his corps as soon as practicable. If any considerable advantage is to be gained by departing from this order, it will not be strictly carried out; one thing must be held in view, that the troops must occupy a position from which they can reach Bull Run by to night or by morning. The indications are that the whole force of the enemy is moving in this direction, at a pace that will bring them here by to-morrow night or next day. My own headquarters will be, for the present, with Heintzelman's corps, at this place.

JOHN POPE, *Major General Commanding.*

Both these divisions had been on foot night and day for several days past, had marched the most of the night before, and were separated from their baggage and subsistence. They moved forward, however, cheerfully. The column coming to a halt, I rode forward and found General Porter at the head of his corps, on a slight eminence; in front was an open piece of ground, and beyond it the woods skirting the Warrenton road, down which, as we could see from the dust above the trees, the enemy was moving from Gainesville upon Groveton, where the battle was now going on.

Just before reaching General Porter I received a note from General Buford, commanding cavalry brigade, who was on our then left and front, acquainting me with the strength of the enemy, which he had seen as they passed through Gainesville, then moving down the road. It consisted of seventeen regiments, one battery, and five hundred cavalry. As this was an inferior force to General Porter's, I decided for him to throw himself at once on the enemy's flank, and as the head of my column was sure three miles back, near the Sudley Springs road, I would move it directly north on that road, upon the field, where the battle was then at its height. Under the authority they gave me I deviated from the letter of your instructions, for I thought in this way the forces could be soonest and best applied, and that by coming up on the left of the line, then actually engaged with the enemy, the best disposition would be effected, and the fixed point in your instructions, which was "that the troops should occupy a position from which they could reach Bull Run that night, or the next morning," would be still fulfilled.

Leaving General Porter, I returned to the head of my two divisions, and turned them immediately north, on the Sudley Springs road, to the battle-ground, and, after seeing most of them off, I rode forward to the head of King's division, now commanded by Brigadier General Hatch, General King, who had the misfortune to be struck down by a severe illness on the Rappahannock, but who had since tried to return to duty, being at last forced to relinquish the command. I found General Hatch absent. He had gone, as I was told, to see General Sigel.

Gneral Reynolds reports that in the meantime, after I had left him in the morning, he had, agreebly to my orders to support General Sigel in any movement the latter might make, formed his division on the left of General Schenk's, but the right of the enemy's position being discovered upon the heights above Groveton, on the right of the Warrenton turnpike, the division advanced in that direction, Cooper's battery, supported by Meade's brigade, coming gallantly into action on the same ridge on which the enemy's right was posted. By some movement in General Sigel's corps, Reynolds's right becoming unsupported, and the enemy's whole fire being concentrated upon it, he was obliged to fall back.

Later in the day General Pope, arriving on the right of the line from Centreville, renewed the attack on the enemy, and drove him back some distance. General Reynolds was then directed to threaten the enemy's right and rear, which he proceeded to do, under a heavy fire of artillery from the ridge to the left of the pike. Generals Seymour and Jackson led their brigades in advance, but, notwithstanding all the steadiness and courage of the men, they were compelled, by the fire of the enemy's artillery and infantry on their front and left, to resume their former position.

Immediately on my arrival with King's division, I directed it to move forward, and take place on the left of Reynolds, then still engaged on the left of Sigel's corps, and some of the brigades went forward to do so, when I received your instructions to order the division over to the north of the turnpike, to support the line held by Reno, which had been hotly engaged all day, and the division was recalled, and brought back to the Sudley Springs road, for this purpose.

One of the brigades—Patrick's—having received an order, as he informed me, direct from your headquarters, to move across the field, became separated from the division, and, though he moved at the quickest pace, was not able to rejoin till late that evening.

About the time the division arrived at the crossing of the Sudley Springs and Warrenton turnpike I received word from you that the enemy were falling back, and to send the division right up the turnpike after them. It was now near dusk, and though the men had been on foot since one o'clock in the morning, they moved forward with the greatest enthusiasm. They were led gallantly up the road by Brigadier General Hatch, who, trusting to find the enemy in retreat, as he was told, and hoping to turn their retreat into a flight, took the men forward, his own and Doubleday's brigades, and Gerrish's battery of howitzers, with Patrick's brigade in reserve, with an impetuosity akin to rashness.

The attack was severe, both on the enemy and our men.

About the same time an attack was made by Bayard's cavalry, on the left of Hatch, on the enemy south of the road, in which Seymour's squadron suffered severely. These were the finishing strokes of the day, which we could now safely claim as ours.

The batteries of King's division, except Gerrish's, supported by Gibbon's brigade, had been sent to reinforce and relieve those on the ridge near Groveton. Ricketts's division, coming on in the rear of King's, was taken up the Sudley Springs road, north of the Warrenton pike, and held as a reserve, for the time, in front.

On the morning of Saturday, the 30th, Major General Fitz John Porter's corps came on the ground, by the same road that had been taken by the divisions of King and Ricketts—the Sudley Springs road—and turned up the Warrenton turnpike, following the course of King's division.

The order you just gave was, that we should hold the centre and left, and mass our troops on the right to attack the enemy's left; and as you ordered me to make this attack with the 3d corps, added to the corps of Porter and Heintzelman, I asked to make a reconnoissance in person before sending the troops in, and requested General Hintzelman to accompany me.

The Sudley Springs road is nearly north and south, and the Warrenton turnpike is nearly east and west, crossing each other near where you established your headquarters.

I found the enemy had, the day before, occupied nearly the half of a circle, commencing at a point beyond Bull Run on the northeast angle made by those roads, and sweeping around irregularly through Sudley Springs to the west, and then south to a point in the southwest angle. Our line, opposing them, had on the right Hintzelman's corps; in the centre, first, Reno's and then Sigel's corps, and on the left, King's division and Bayard's cavalry; Ricketts, in an interior position, in reserve. Porter's corps, which on the day before had been detached and been on the extreme left, hanging on the enemy's right and rear, was now on the left, up the Warrenton road.

On going with General Heintzelman over the position held by his troops, we found all the points held by the enemy the day before, beyond Bull Run, abandoned; and in going over to the Sudley Springs road and west of it, we saw no evidences of the enemy in force, some skirmishers and advanced posts or rear guards, as the case might be, being all that we found.

On returning to headquarters and reporting these facts, we found that word had been sent in from the front that the enemy was moving back on the road to Gaines's Mill; similar word was given by General Patrick. On the suppo sition that the enemy was falling back, I received your orders* to take command of the corps above named and pursue the enemy; I accordingly gave orders that Ricketts's division should report to General Heintzelman, who was to have charge of the right of the advance, and was to move on the enemy by the road from Sudley Springs to Hay-market, a road running west nearly parallel with the Warrenton turnpike and the north side of it, and placed the other divisions, Reynolds's and King's, which were to the front, on the Warrenton turnpike and near General Porter's corps, under that general, to support him in his advance on that road; but just as these† orders were issued General Reynolds rode up to my headquarters and reported, of his own personal knowledge, that the enemy were not falling back; on the contrary, that he was passing his troops to the south of Warrenton turnpike, and massing them behind the woods, to turn our left and make an attack on the southwest angle of the two roads, and thence across the Sudley Springs road to the southeast angles. It may be well to state here, what, however, is well known to you, that the country around the field of battle is, much of it, thickly wooded, and that the march of large bodies on the side of the enemy could only be seen at intervals, and can be easily hidden from view.

---

*HEADQUARTERS NEAR GROVETON,
August 30th, 1862, 12 *o'clock m.*

Special order No. .]

The following forces will be immediately thrown forward and in pursuit of the enemy, and press him vigorously during the whole day. Major General McDowell is assigned to the command of the pursuit. Major General Porter's corps will push forward on the Warrenton turnpike, followed by the divisions of Brigadier Generals King and Reynolds.

The division of Brigadier General Ricketts will pursue the Hay-market road, followed by the corps of Major General Heintzelman; the necessary cavalry will be assigned to these columns by Major General McDowell, to whom regular and frequent reports will be made. The general headquarters will be somewhere on the Warrenton turnpike.

By command of Major General Pope.

GEO. D. RUGGLES,
Colonel and Chief of Staff.

†HEADQUARTERS 3D CORPS ARMY OF VIRGINIA,
August 30th, 1862.

Major General McDowell being charged with the advanced forces ordered to pursue the enemy, directs me to inform you that your corps will be followed immediately by King's division, supported by Reynolds; Heintzleman, with his corps, preceded by Reynolds's division, will move on your right, on the road from Sudly Springs to Haymarket. He is instructed to throw out skirmishers to the left, which it is desirable you should join with your right. General McDowell's headquarters will be at the head of Reynolds's division on the Warrenton road. Organize a strong advance to precede your command and push on rapidly in pursuit of the enemy until you come in contact with him. Report frequently. Bayard's brigade will be ordered to report to you; push it well to the left as you advance.

Very respectfully, your obedient servant,

ED. SCHRIVER,
Colonel and Chief of Staff.

Major General PORTER, *Commanding, &c., &c.*

HEADQUARTERS 3D ARMY CORPS, ARMY OF VIRGINIA,
August 30th, 1862.

GENERAL: Major General McDowell directs that you push on the movement, suggested in your note to him, to the left, and General Heintzelman, now here, will attend to the front and right. You have at you disposal, to reinforce you, King's division and Reynolds's.

Very respectfully, your obedient servant,

ED. SCHRIVER,
Colonel and Chief of Staff.

Major General FITZ JOHN PORTER, *Commanding, &c., &c.*

On General Reynolds's information, seeing no time was to be lost, and that instant measures were to be taken to meet this unexpected movement, I gave him orders to take his division immediately over to provide for this threatened attack, and occupy the hill south of the turnpike, he knowing the ground well, having been over it in the course of the battle the day before. You, at the same time, gave orders that some of General Sigel's corps should also move to the south of the turnpike, on the Bald Hill, so called, near Groveton. I immediately wrote to General Porter that he must exercise his discretion as to the use of King's division in the movement. He suggested, in his front, that I had been obliged to take Reynolds's division from him to guard the left, and had to go there in person to see to it; that you said if he should need more force, you would send him General Sigel. I sent word, also, to General Heintzelman of the change, and that I was obliged to take from him two brigades and two batteries of artillery, of Ricketts's division, to aid in improving the defence of the left, south of the turnpike, where I immediately repaired and remained throughout the battle, having no further communication either with General Ricketts's division, under General Heintzelman, or General King's division, under General Porter.

The Warrenton turnpike goes west, up the valley of the little rivulet of Young's Branch, and through the battle-field—is mostly close to the stream. The ground rises from the stream on both sides; in some places quite into hills. The Sudley Springs road, in crossing the stream at right angles, passes directly over one of these hills, just south of the Warrenton turnpike, and this hill has on it a detached road, with fields stretching back, away from it, some hundreds of yards to the forest. This is the hill on which the Henry House stood. To the west of it is another hill—the Bald Hill, so called—which is, in fact, a rise lying between the roads, and making about the same angle with each, and running back to the forest. Between the two hills is a small stream, a tributary, I think, of Young's Branch.

The two brigades under Brigadier General Tower, and the two batteries from Ricketts's division, were taken from north of the Warrenton turnpike, on the Sudley Springs road, to the hill just above mentioned, to the further side of the first woods. Whilst reconnoitering in advance of these woods—the positions which the enemy would be likely to occupy in the direction indicated by General Reynolds—I was joined by that officer, and, seeing evidence at that time of the enemy to the left, I accompanied him across to the Bald Hill ridge, on which, next to the main woods, his division was taking up its position, and on which, next to General Reynolds, General Schenck was coming up from the Warrenton road. Whilst these troops were forming on this ridge, which commanded a view of the enemy in the northwest angle of the two roads before mentioned, and which overlooked the Warrenton road, we saw the effects of the attack which had been made by Major General Porter in front, with his own troops and King's division of my corps. Seeing that it was resulting disas-

---

NOTE.—The enemy having shown indications of advancing by the right, Reynolds has been withdrawn from your column and put over on our left; it is still thought you will be strong enough to effect your purpose with King; if not, General Pope will send you Sigel.

HEADQUARTERS 3D ARMY CORPS, ARMY OF VIRGINIA,
August 30th, 1862.

Major General McDowell is now busy attending to our left; he directs me to inform you that you must use your discretion in reference to the employment of King's division in connexion with the service you are to perform.

Very respectfully, your obedient servant,

ED. SCHRIVER,
Colonel and Chief of Staff.

Major General PORTER, *Commanding, &c., &c.*

trously for us, and that our troops were falling back, I returned immediately to the Henry House Hill, to see to the placing of Tower's two brigades and the two batteries. On my way I met one of your staff with your message, asking if, on ordering over this force, I had not taken too much from the right. But soon after meeting you, as you came up the Henry House Hill from the right, and representing the state of affairs in front, with your sanction I sent Tower's command over to the Bald Hill, to the right of General Schenck. The line thus formed, in connexion with that on the north of the turnpike, held by Reno, Sigel, and others, commanded the Warrenton road and protected the retreat of Porter's command, then moving down from the front. The line had not been formed any too soon, for the enemy, after our troops in front had retreated, made the expected attack, and assailed the troops on the ridge both in front and on their left flank. Those of the enemy who had passed to the south of the Warrenton turnpike, as represented by General Reynolds, soon after opened a severe fire from the southwest of the Henry House Hill, on the Bald Ridge, and at the same time prepared to move down to take the woods on the Henry House Hill itself. The next step was to provide, in some way, for the defence of this hill, and as at this time some battalions of regulars, of Sykes's division, came up the hill, they were sent to the left to occupy the woods which covered it. The Rhode Island battery, under Captain Munroe, and some time after two brigades of Reynolds's division, under Generals Meade and Seymour, which had been withdrawn from the extreme left of the front to form a line across the road, behind which General Porter's troops might rally, were brought over from the right and relieved the regular battalions. The latter rejoined their division, which formed another line on the hill to the east, in rear of the Henry House Hill, and at a few hundred yards distant from it.

Reno's corps was also withdrawn, by your order, from the north of the turnpike to the Henry House Hill.

The attack on the Bald Ridge line had been too severe for the troops to hold it long under the hot fire the enemy maintained upon it. Jackson's brigade, of Reynolds's division; McLean's, of Schenck's, and Tower's two brigades, of Ricketts's division, were, after heavy losses, little by little compelled to yield it, General Schenck and General Tower receiving severe wounds, the former in the arm, the latter in the left knee, as they were encouraging and leading on their men. Colonel Fletcher Webster, 12th Massachusetts, and Captain Fessenden, aide to General Tower, were mortally wounded.

Though we lost this position, it had been held long enough to aid in protecting the retreat of our men from the front, who, as they came in, either formed behind it, or in rear of the line on the north of the turnpike. It was the only position on the left, from which we were forced, and its loss reflects no discredit on those who held it, for they yielded to the overwhelming force of the whole right of the enemy's army, which was concentrated on them, after our advance had been driven back.

The troops immediately north of the Warrenton turnpike then commenced falling back.

On going to the turnpike, where it ascended from the bridge over Young's branch to the top of the hill, to the right and rear of the Henry House Hill, to see to the placing of some troops, which I thought might be of King's division of my corps, coming there from the front, I found Brigadier General Carl Schurz, with some of General Sigel's corps drawn up by the road. The general spoke to me concerning the posting of a battery, then out of position, which I caused to be placed so as to be of use, in case we should be forced from the Henry House Hill, as we had been from the Bald Hill; but with warning they were not to fire till after our men should have left the position in front. Seeing them commence loading, I sent a captain on my staff to warn the battery not to fire, except on the contingency mentioned. I refer to this incident, as it may have served as foundation for one of the strange stories that soon after became prevalent as to this battle.

I annex hereto an extract from General Schurz's report, and a correspondence which grew out of it, from which it will be seen that the general says "he did not mean what he seems to have said."*

Leaving General Schurz drawn up on the hill, I went to the left where the corps of General Porter or the larger part of it, that came out of the fight in front, had been formed in double line, and when near Sykes's divivision of regulars, Brigadier General Milroy, a gallant officer of General Sigel's corps, came riding up in a state of absolute frenzy, with his sword drawn, and gesticulating at some distance off, shouting to send forward re-enforcements, to save the day, to save the country, &c. His manner, his dealing in generalities, which gave no information whatever, and which, in the way he uttered them, only showed him as being in a state of mind as unfit to judge of events as to command men, and as being away from his command, caused me to receive him coldly.

It was a question with me whether we could hold the Henry House Hill, whether to break the line of reserve at this time, or hold the position that they occupied.

It was a question of importance, on which I should have liked to consult you, the general-in-chief, before deciding—the more so, as I had reason to think this line had been established under your own orders given direct. But you were further over to the left, and the case had to be determined at once.

But whilst General Milroy gave me nothing whatever on which I could be justified in acting, and whilst in doubt, for the moment, in view of the circumstances as to the course to be taken, I received a clear message from that intelligent as well as gallant officer, Brigadier General Meade, through one of his aides-de-camp, to the effect that if he could have some re-enforcements sent to him, in the woods on the Henry House Hill, he could not only hold them, but drive out the enemy, who were not there in great force. Relieved from all doubt by this message, I exclaimed, "Meade shall have re-enforcements," and immediately gave General Porter orders to send them forward.

I send herewith an extract† from General Milroy's report, to which I regret I have to refer to say that his statement, that I refused to send re-enforcements to General Sigel is without foundation in anything that I said or thought. I had just come from a large part of General Sigel's corps. I had received no intelligence from General Sigel that he needed re-enforcements.

* "I found Major General McDowell with his staff, and around him troops of different corps, and of all arms, in full retreat."

† "At one time, not receiving assistance from the rear, as I had a right to expect after having sent for it, and our struggling batteries being nearly overcome by the weight and persistence of the enemy's attack, I flew back about half a mile to where I understood General McDowell was with a large part of his corps. I found him and appealed to him in the most earnest manner to send a brigade forward at once to save the day, or all would be lost. He answered coldly, in substance, that it was not his business to help everybody, and he was not going to help General Sigel. I told him that I was not fighting with General Sigel's corps; that my brigade had got out of ammunition some time before, and had gone to the rear, and that I had been fighting with half a dozen different brigades, and that I had not inquired where or to what particular corps they belonged. He inquired of one of his aides if General —— was fighting over there on the left. His aide said he thought he was. McDowell replied, that he would soon help him, for he was a good fellow. He then gave the order for a brigade to start; this was all I desired. I dashed in front of them, waved my sword, and cheered them forward. They raised the cheer, and came on at a double quick. I soon led them to where they were most needed, and the gallant manner in which they entered the fight, and the rapidity of their fire soon turned back the tide of battle. But this gallant brigade, like many others that had preceded it, found the enemy too strong for them, as they advanced into the forest, and were forced back by the tremendous fire that met them."

He was in reserve and mostly in a different part of the field than that in which I had been operating. On Friday, I had re-enforced him with Reynolds's whole division, and on Saturday the only part of his corps with which I had had anything to do, up to the time of my seeing General Schurz, was General Schenck's division, which I had re-enforced, without being asked, with every man I had at the time under my control.

I send herewith a copy of my correspondence with Colonel Buchanan, commanding the brigade of regulars I sent forward at the time in question, and with other officers present on the occasion, from which you see the condition of mind General Milroy was in, and how little his impressions at the time are to be relied on either as to what he did or what I said.

To General Sigel, personally, I bore no ill-will, but had he been my enemy, and had I desired to see him harmed—"General Sigel" here represented several thousand men, many of them from my own State, and, aside from the great question of the loss of the battle, the fate of the campaign, and the ruin of the country, which might all have been involved—I could not be so stupidly bad, so utterly false to the simplest form of duty, as to refuse aid to my brother soldiers, when I had the power to give it, only because they were under an officer I did not like.

As it seems to have been the impression not only that I was unfriendly to General Sigel, but that we had bitter altercations and even personal conflicts, on the field itself, I take the occasion to state that during the whole course of the operations from Thursday morniug, at Buckland Mills, to the next Monday evening, at Fairfax Court-House, not only I did not exchange a word with General Sigel, but I did not see him, and I do not think he saw me.

The re-enforcements taken forward by Colonel Buchanan and the troops brought by your orders from the north of the turnpike held the position on the Henry House Hill until they were withdrawn long after dark.

It was about seven o'clock when I received your order to take such portions of my corps as I might find in tact, and proceed with them to take a position covering the bridge over Bull Run and Cub Run.

Proceeding to the place where I had left General Schurz, I found he had withdrawn, but General Gibbon's brigade, of King's division, was just coming up the hill, and seeing it would not be well to leave the position as unsupported as it then was, I told General Gibbon to take post there and hold it till everything should have passed him. He remained there, I am told by one of the colonels of his brigade, till some two hours after dark, when he withdrew.

Learning at this place that Patrick's brigade, of King's division, had just passed towards the bridge, I followed it there. Seeing the road much blocked up with wagons, I endeavored to find the ford, a couple of hundred yards below the bridge, but it was so dark I could not see the way, and returned to the road and crossed over. I left here two officers of my staff and a guard of Pennsylvania Bucktail battalion, belonging to the 3d corps, under the gallant Colonel Kane, and directed some pieces of artillery that were passing by to be placed in position on the left bank. All contest, however, save a shot now and then from one of our pieces on the Henry House Hill; had ceased for some time.

This brave little battalion remained here until everybody had passed, when they destroyed the bridge and brought up the rear.

The troops, in passing over the bridges and in moving to the rear, did so in good order. Stragglers there were, of course—a march, either in advance or retreat, is seldom without them—but the mass of the men preserved their organization and moved by battalions and batteries. At Cub Run bridge I left, with Major Houston, United States engineers, who had constructed the bridge over Bull Run, and rendered valuable service throughout the campaign, a regiment to keep the troops in the proper order in passing to the rear.

I have no reports from King's division, and, as its operations were under direc tion of another commander, I am unable to speak as I would like to do concerning it. It was, I know, driven back in the engagement in front, but I know it to be one of the finest, best-drilled, best-disciplined bodies of troops in the service, and in the main ably commanded; and if it could not accomplish its task, it must have been an excessively hard one it was called on to perform.

The two brigades of Ricketts's division, engaged over in the extreme right, under General Heintzelman, were under General Ricketts, whose report is herewith.

On the morning of the 31st the corps was united, and, by your order, placed in reserve behind Centreville, the cavalry, under Bayard, being detached and operating to the right of that place.

On the 1st of September I received your order, herewith,* to move immediately to Germantown to intercept the march of the enemy then moving down the Little River (or Aldie) turnpike to Fairfax Court-House. This was complied with within a few minutes after its receipt, and the corps was in position at Germantown in time to receive the enemy at the crossing of the Difficult. Here Ricketts's division was drawn up, under the direction of Major General Hooker, with a battalion thrown across the valley of the stream, and, opening on the enemy's advance, held it in check at the time Reno's corps attacked him in flank and repulsed him.

September 2, in compliance with general orders, the corps fell back to Hall's and Upton's Hills, in front of Washington.

Here the campaign ended. If it had been short, it had been severe. Beginning with the retreat from Cedar Mountain, seldom has one army been asked to undergo more than our men performed. With scarcely a half-day's intermission, the 3d corps was either making forced marches, many times through the night, and many times without food, &c., or were engaged in battle. These fatigues were most severe towards the last, when, on account of the movements of the enemy, we had to separate from our supplies, and many generals, as well as privates, had no food, or only such as could be picked up in the orchards or cornfields along the road. In all this the patience and endurance and general good conduct of the men were admirable. To fight and retreat, and retreat and fight, in the face of a superior force, is a severe test of soldiership. This they did for fifteen days; and, though many broke down under the fatigue and exposures, and many straggled from the ranks, the troops, as a general thing, behaved most creditably, and, even to their return to the lines in front of this place, though they were sad at seeing their numbers so much diminished by hardships and battles, which had availed them nothing, and were tired and reduced from marching and fasting, they preserved their discipline, and it is an abuse of words to say they were either demoralized or disorganized.

This report has been delayed so long, for the reasons mentioned at the commencement, that I now forward it without returns of the killed, wounded, and missing. I will supply this deficiency when all the returns are received.

General Ricketts, who, at Cedar Mountain and at Rappahannock, was under my immediate command, and rendered valuable service with his division, speaks in high terms of the gallantry of Brigadier Generals Duryea and Tower, both at Thoroughfare Gap and in the battle of the thirtieth (30,) in which the former was slightly and the latter severely wounded.

---

* CENTREVILLE, *September* 1, 1862—12 *m.*

You will march rapidly back to Fairfax Court-House with your whole division. Assume command of the two brigades now there, and immediately occupy Germantown with your whole force, so as to cover the turnpikes from this place to Alexandria. Jackson is reported advancing on Fairfax with twenty thousand men. Move rapidly.

JOHN POPE,
Major General Commanding.

Major General McDOWELL.

The services of Tower's brigade were especially arduous, forming the rear guard on almost every occasion. On the retreat from Cedar Mountain, from the Rappahannock Station, from the Waterloo road, and from Thoroughfare Gap, it had an undue share of the severities of this campaign. The general was detached from the division with his own, Hartsuff's brigade, and posted on the Bald Hill ridge, where he remained till a severe wound forced him to retire.

Brigadier General Hartsuff was so ill and weak from overwork as to have to move from place to place in an ambulance. He had rendered valuable service both at Cedar Mountain and at Rappahannock, where he occupied the advanced position beyond the river. He would not leave his brigade, though unable to get on his horse, and to save his life I was obliged to interfere and have him quit us at Warrenton, and thus lost him in the battles which followed.

Colonel Carroll, and acting brigadier general, commanding brigade, was wounded beyond Cedar Mountain in visiting the outposts, and left before we began the retreat. He had done good service at Cedar Mountain, and by his wound was lost to us in the succeeding battles.

Thus Rickett's division lost all of its brigadiers.

Amongst others, General Ricketts makes especial mention of those excellent volunteers—Colonel Root, 94th New York volunteers, who, although painfully wounded, continued on duty; of Colonel Coulter, 11th Pennsylvania volunteers, whose regiment bore the brunt of the action at Thoroughfare Gap; and of Colonel Thorburne, 1st Virginia, commanding Carroll's brigade after the latter was wounded.

Brigadier General Reynolds, always active himself, and whose division did good service in the campaign, makes especial mention of the services of Brigadier Generals Meade, Seymour, and Jackson, commanding brigades; also of Surgeons King and Read, who remained on the field to attend to the wounded, there being no ambulances with the division to bring them away. General Reynolds mentions the 1st rifles, under Colonel McNeil, to whose lot the advance skirmishing principally fell; the 1st infantry, Colonel Roberts; the 2d infantry, Colonel McCandless; the 6th infantry, Colonel Sinclair; the 7th, Lieutenant Colonel Henderson; and the 12th, Colonel Hardin.

Of General King's division, I have but the report of Brigadier General Hatch, (which had been received since the foregoing report was written,) who commanded the division after Brigadier General King left. From it, and what I know from the verbal reports of others, I am justified in mentioning favorably the conduct of Brigadier Generals Doubleday, Patrick, and Gibbon, the last having sustained the weight of the action of Thursday evening, and the first especially commanded by General Hatch for his gallantry on the 29th and 30th. General Hatch was himself slightly wounded in the early part of the engagement of Saturday.

Colonel Post, commanding 2d sharpshooters, a valuable regiment, much exposed, and which rendered most excellent service, is deserving of especial mention for his conduct, amongst others, in the battle of the 30th.

The accomplished and gallant Colonel Pratt, commanding the 20th New York militia, was mortally wounded. The brave Colonel Frisby, 30th New York, killed.

Lieutenant Colonel Fowler, commanding the gallant 14th (Brooklyn) New York militia, was severely wounded on the 29th whilst leading his regiment into battle.

My staff were always faithful, zealous, active and fearless in the discharge of their duties, which were incessant and exhausting, and under which many of them broke down in health, some being still unable to leave their beds. I desire to record their names, with my best thanks for the support they gave. They were: Colonel Edward Schriver, chief of staff; Lieutenant Colonel Myers, chief quartermaster; Major Daniel Tillson, chief of artillery; Major S. F.

Barston, assistant adjutant general; Major D. C. Houston, chief of engineers; Major J. M. Sanderson, commissary; Surgeon D. L. Magruder, medical director; Majors C. S. Brown and Joseph C. Williard, and Captains F. Haven, G. H. Abbe, W. Leski, W. H. W. Krebs, J. E. Jewett, J. P. Droulliard, J. D. W. Cutting, C. W. Wadsworth, Howard Stockton, and F. Ball, aides-de-camp. Captains Merritt, Hughes, and Slossum, and 1st Lieutenant Thomas Williams, 5th artillery, who had been assigned to my staff, were on duty with Brigadier Generals King and Tower.

Brigadier General John Buford, commanding the cavalry of the 2d corps, was several times under my orders on the retreat from Warrenton, &c., and was actively engaged on the extreme left on the 30th I beg leave, therefore, to add his name with that of Brigadier General Bayard, commanding cavalry of the 3d corps, to those deserving especial mention.

I have the honor to be, very respectfully, your most obedient servant,

JAMES McDOWELL,

Major General, Commanding 3d Corps Army of Virginia.

Major General JOHN POPE,

Commander of the late Army of Virginia.

HEADQUARTERS DEFENCES OF WASHINGTON SOUTH OF THE POTOMAC,
Arlington, Virginia, October 21, 1862.

COLONEL: I have the honor to make the following report of the operations of the 3d army corps immediately previous to and in the recent battles in the vicinity of Centreville.

On the 14th of August, at 9 o'clock p. m., I received orders to retreat with my corps from Harrison's Bar, on James river. The next morning General Birney's brigade, of General Kearney's division, marched for Jones's (Soan's) bridge, on the Chickahominy, which we were to hold till the troops had well started from our old camp at Harrison's Bar. On the 16th I fell back to Barhamsville; the next day to Williamsburg, and the day after to Yorktown. This movement was covered by Colonel Averill's cavalry thrown out towards Richmond and the White House. At Williamsburg we united with the main body of the army.

On the 20th the advance of the corps of General Kearney's division commenced to embark for Acquia creek, rapidly followed by the rest of my troops. Off Acquia creek I received orders changing my destination to Alexandria. I arrived at Alexandria at 1.30 p. m. on the 22d, and met, on the wharf, Major Key, of General Halleck's staff, with orders to hurry forward my corps to the support of General Pope. Part of General Kearney's division left in the cars that afternoon, soon followed by my whole force. On the 26th my troops were all in the vicinity of Warrenton Junction. At dark I received orders to occupy Weaversville and vicinity, and also learned that the enemy had possession of the railroad in our rear. General Pope directed me to send a regiment and drive them back. This regiment found the enemy in force and fell back.

The next morning (the 27th) General Hooker was ordered as far as Bristow Station, and to advance the day after that to Greenwich; General Kearney's division to take a left-hand road and follow General Reno's division towards Greenwich.

I was detained at Warrenton Junction till 3 p. m. to accompany General Pope. When we reached Bristow Station the enemy had, after a sharp engagement, retreated toward Manassas Junction. They belonged to General Ewell's division.

Our troops behaved with their usual gallantry. Our loss was some 300 men, mostly of the Excelsior brigade. At Bristow Station we found the remains of two locomotives and trains of cars that the enemy had burned. In places the rails and cross-ties had been torn up, culverts destroyed, and bridges burned. I am still without General Hooker's report and that of the 2d brigade.

The next morning (August 28) General Kearney's division advanced on Manassas Junction, followed by General Hooker's as a reserve. About noon General Kearney reached the Junction. Our railroad trains, fired by the enemy, were still burning. We here learned that he had retreated on Centreville, and was 30,000 strong. The pursuit was continued. The advance of General Kearney's division found but one regiment of rebel cavalry at Centreville, which fell back at his approach. We now learned that the enemy had fallen back on the Warrenton turnpike. General Kearney's division encamped near Centreville, between there and Bull Run. General Hooker's division encamped on the south side of Bull Run.

At 11 p. m. I received instructions that General McDowell had intercepted the retreat of the enemy, and that General Kearney's division was ordered to advance at 1 a. m. until he met the enemy's pickets, there to await daylight, and for me to follow at daylight with General Hooker's division. From some cause, to me unknown, General Kearney's division had not moved at daylight. I ordered it forward and he soon joined it.

At 10 a. m. I reached the field of battle, a mile from Stone Bridge, on the Warrenton turnpike. General Kearney's division had proceeded to the right and front. I learned that General Sigel was in command of the troops then engaged.

At 11 a. m. the head of Hooker's division arrived; General Reno an hour later. At the request of General Sigel I ordered General Hooker to place one of his brigades at General Sigel's disposal to re-enforce a portion of his line then hard pressed. General Grover reported, and before long became engaged, and was afterwards supported by the whole division. General Pope arrived between one and two p. m. The enemy were driven back a short distance towards Sudley's Church, where they made another stand, and again pressed a portion of our line back. All this time General Kearney's division held its position on our extreme right. Several orders were sent to him to advance, but he did not move until after the troops on his left had been forced back, which was near 6 p. m. He now advanced and reported that he was driving the enemy. This was not, however, until after the renewed heavy musketry fire on our centre had driven General Hooker's troops, and those he was sent to support, back. They were greatly outnumbered, and had behaved with exceeding gallantry.

It was on this occasion that General Grover's brigade made the most gallant and determined bayonet charge of the war. He broke two of the enemy's lines, but was finally repulsed by the overwhelming numbers in the rebel third line. It was a hand-to-hand conflict, using the bayonet and the butt of the musket. In this fierce encounter of not over twenty minutes' duration, the 2d New Hampshire, Colonel Marston, suffered the most. The 1st, 11th, and 16th Massachusetts, and 26th Pennsylvania were engaged. The loss of this brigade, numbering less than 2,000 present, was a total of 484, nearly all killed and wounded. I refer you to General Grover's accompanying report.

Had General Kearney pushed the enemy earlier it might have enabled us to have held our centre and have saved some of this heavy loss. Kearney on the right, with General Stevens and our artillery, drove the enemy out of the woods they had temporarily occupied. The firing continued until some time after dark, and when it ceased we remained in possesion of the battle-field. During the night, however, our troops again fell back from the woods that had been so obstinately disputed all the afternoon. At 5.30 a. m., August 30, a few shots were fired on my front. The morning was spent in procuring rations from General Sigel's train, our own having been left, from necessity, in our last camp on Bull

Run. After holding a short conference and making reconnoissances, it was decided that General McDowell should take his corps, mine, and General Porter's, to make an attack on the enemy's left. At 12 m. General McDowell and myself went to our right to reconnoitre more clearly the enemy's position, preparatory to moving. We saw but few of the enemy, and appearances were that they were retreating. On our return we met General Sigel, who expressed, as the result of his observations, the same opinion. At general headquarters the impression was that the enemy was retreating during the night. It was then determined that I should advance with General Rickett's troops and my corps, on the road leading to Sudley Spring, and thence towards Haymarket. The first step in advance brought us in contact with the enemy's skirmishers. These were driven out of the woods, but our further advance was resisted by the rebel artillery commanding the road. The enemy was evidently still in force. Soon after (at 2 p. m.) General Porter became engaged with the enemy on our left, and at 4 p. m. this attack extended to our centre. We then learned that the withdrawal of troops from opposite our right was to mass them on our centre and left. General Hooker's division now advanced into the woods near our right and drove the enemy back a short distance. At 5.30 our troops on the left, and then the centre, began to give way. Shortly before night, on the falling back of the troops on the left and centre, I was directed to retire and hold successive positions. General Hooker's division was ordered by General Pope to the left about dark, and I lost sight of it until after the whole army was in retreat, when I overtook it on the road beyond the stone bridge. We fell back to the Wier House (I believe,) used as a hospital, and there established a new line of battle. I sent General Kearney's division to the left to close a gap between my left and the main body of the army, keeping Generals Stevens and Ricketts's troop to hold the right. After dark I sent my artillery to the rear by a road I had sent Major Hunt and Dr. Milhau, of my staff, to examine, as it was too dark to use it with effect. Somewhat later the enemy attacked General Ricketts's troops, and they gave way. A mile further to the rear Colonel McLean's brigade was drawn up and covered the retreat across Bull Run. Part of these troops forded Bull Run a short distance above the stone bridge, and the others crossed the bridge, which had been repaired the night before. Where the Sudley Church road joins the Warrenton turnpike, near Cub Run, I halted some cavalry and sent it out to obstruct this road and hold it until all our troops had passed. Late in the afternoon some cavalry and artillery were seen on this road, and a few shots were exchanged with my extreme right.

At about 11 p. m. we reached Centreville, and, in obedience to orders from general headquarters, took post at the north of the town. The next day my corps was directed to form a reserve in rear of General Franklin's corps, which we found at Centreville. On the 1st of September, at 1 p. m., I learned from General Pope that the enemy was threatening our rear, and he detached General Hooker from his division to take command of some troops near Germantown to hold the enemy in check, advancing on the Little River turnpike.

General Sumner and I were ordered to march at daylight the next norning across the Little River turnpike, in the direction of Chantilly, to aid in this movement. I had scarcely returned to my headquarters and given the necessary orders before I received notice from the commanding general that the enemy were about to attack us, and to get my corps under arms.

I was next sent for to general headquarters, and at 3.30 p. m. ordered to fall back on the road to Fairfax Court-House two and one-half miles, and face to the left to aid General Reno in driving back the enemy, then threatening from the Little River turnpike our right flank and line of retreat. At 4 p. m. General Kearney's troops were in motion, followed by General Grover, now in command of General Hooker's division. At 5.50 firing commenced by General Reno on the enemy between the Little River and Warrenton turnpikes. The enemy were within half a mile of the latter when they attacked him. A portion of General Reno's troops gave way, but General Birney's brigade, of General Kearney's division, gallantly supported them. General Kearney rode forward, alone, to reconnoitre, in his usual gallant, not to say reckless, manner, and came upon a rebel regiment; in attempting to escape he was killed. The country has to mourn one of her most gallant defenders. At the close of the seige of Yorktown he relieved General Hamilton in the command of the division, and led it in the various battles on the peninsula, commencing with Williamsburg. His name is identified with its glory.

Our troops held the battle-field till near daylight, when they received orders to retire to Fairfax Court-House. Soon after daylight I reported to the commanding general, who directed me to take post with my corps on the left of the town. At 9.30 (September 2) I was informed that General Sumner's corps would occupy Flint Hill, and that I should with my corps take post on his right, on the road to Vienna, as the enemy were moving to or beyond our right. At 11 a. m. I received orders directing the whole army to fall back to the lines in front of Washington, my corps to Fort Lyons. Left Fairfax Court-House at 11.40 a. m., and the troops reoccupied their old lines the next day.

In the encounters with the enemy at Bristow Station General Hooker's division suffered severely, and again on the 29th of August; also General Kearney's on the afternoon of the 1st September, near Chantilly.

On our arrival from the peninsula at Alexandria we were hurried forward, without artillery or wagons, and many of the field-officers without their horses. This, in connexion with overcrowding on the transports, hard marching, and hard fare, caused a large amount of straggling, both at Alexandria and during the various battles, till, at Fairfax Station, on the 2d September, I had but 5,000 men left in my two divisions to draw rations. I am, however, happy to add that returning stragglers and convalescents have since much increased this force.

General Hooker's division had above 10,000 men when it landed near Yorktown last April, and after the battle of Fair Oaks was re-enforced by about 3,000 more. At Fairfax Station it drew rations for 2,600 men. General Kearney's division suffered as much.

Although we were driven back, and finally to the defences of Washington, I do not feel that the gallant veterans of the 3d corps have lost any of their well-earned reputation from the battles on the peninsula. My staff performed their appropriate duties with their usual assiduity. Not having been able to obtain all the brigade reports, the lists annexed are incomplete. In General Hooker's division I have no report of the losses of the 2d brigade, nor is there any report of the losses of General Kearney's division at Chantilly. Imperfect as they are, they sum up an aggregate of 1,491.

All of which is respectfully submitted.

S. P. HEINTZELMAN,
Major General Commanding.

Colonel GEORGE D. RUGGLES,
Assistant Adjutant General, Army of Virginia.

Consolidated list of killed, wounded, and missing in actions of the 29*th and* 30*th August,* 1862.

IN 1ST BRIGADE, 1ST DIVISION, 3D CORPS.

Regiments.	KILLED.		WOUNDED.		MISSING.		Aggregate.
	Officers.	Enlisted men.	Officers.	Enlisted men.	Officers.	Enlisted men.	
20th Indiana vols..	1	3	--------	35	--------	6	45
63d Penn. vols	--------	15	6	88	--------	11	120
105th Penn. vols...	1	6	5	32	--------	8	52
	2	24	11	155	--------	25	217

IN 2D BRIGADE, 1ST DIVISION, 3D CORPS.

Regiments.	KILLED.		WOUNDED.		MISSING.		Aggregate.
	Officers.	Enlisted men.	Officers.	Enlisted men.	Officers.	Enlisted men.	
38th N. Y. vols....	--------	--------	3	6	2	--------	11
3d Maine vols	--------	--------	--------	11	1	22	34
4th Maine vols	--------	7	--------	30	--------	12	49
40th N. Y. vols....	--------	5	6	54	--------	18	83
101st N. Y. vols ...	--------	6	3	47	--------	13	69
57th Penn. vols....	--------	--------	--------	3	--------	--------	3
	--------	18	12	151	3	65	249

IN 3D BRIGADE, 2D DIVISION, 3D CORPS.

Regiments.	KILLED.		WOUNDED.		MISSING.		Aggregate.
	Officers.	Enlisted men.	Officers.	Enlisted men.	Officers.	Enlisted men.	
37th N. Y. vols ...	--------	--------	--------	3	--------	--------	3
2d Michigan vols...	--------	--------	1	2	--------	6	9
3d Michigan vols...	2	22	7	93	--------	15	139
5th Michigan vols..	--------	--------	--------	6	--------	--------	6
99th Penn. vols....	--------	--------	--------	2	--------	15	17
	2	22	8	106	--------	36	174

IN 1ST DIVISION, 3D CORPS.

Brigades.	KILLED.		WOUNDED.		MISSING.		Aggregate.
	Officers.	Enlisted men.	Officers.	Enlisted men.	Officers.	Enlisted men.	
1st brigade	2	24	11	155	....	25	217
2d brigade	....	18	12	151	3	65	249
3d brigade	2	22	8	106	....	36	174
	4	64	31	412	3	126	640

IN 1ST BRIGADE, 2D DIVISION, 3D CORPS.*

Regiments.	Killed.	Wounded.	Missing.	Aggregate.
1st Massachusetts volunteers	5	66	7	78
2d New Hampshire volunteers	16	87	30	133
11th Massachusetts volunteers	10	77	25	112
16th Massachusetts volunteers	4	64	42	110
26th Pennsylvania volunteers	6	33	14	53
	41	327	116	484

NOTE.—No reports of the killed, wounded, and missing, in 2d brigade, 2d division, 3d corps, in actions of the 29th and 30th August, 1862, have been furnished to these headquarters. They were forwarded direct to Major General Hooker. A consolidated list of this brigade and 2d division cannot therefore be completed.

IN 3D BRIGADE, 2D DIVISION, 3D CORPS.

Regiments.	KILLED.		WOUNDED.		MISSING.		Aggregate.
	Officers.	Enlisted men.	Officers.	Enlisted men.	Officers.	Enlisted men.	
2d N. Y. vols	....	11	6	55	....	9	81
5th N. J. vols	2	4	2	33	1	10	52
6th N. J. vols	....	18	2	50	....	38	108
7th N. J. vols	1	2	....	19	1	10	33
8th N. J. vols	1	4	2	52	....	....	59
115th Penn. vols	....	4	4	14	....	12	34
	4	43	16	223	2	79	367

S. P. HEINTZELMAN,
Major General Commanding.

HEADQUARTERS WASHINGTON, *December* 17, 1862.

* No list furnished. The above taken from General Grover's report.

No. 4.

REPORT OF BRIGADIER GENERAL D. B. BIRNEY.

HEADQUARTERS FIRST DIVISION, THIRD CORPS,
Camp Fort Lyon, Va., September 4, 1862.

SIR: I have the honor to report the part taken by this division in the battle at Chantilly, between Centreville and Fairfax Court-House, on Monday, September 1.

The division reached Chantilly at about five o'clock p. m., under orders from Major General Heintzelman to support General Reno, and found him actively engaged with the enemy.

Under orders from Major General Kearny, I reported my brigade to General Reno, and was ordered by him to the front. On reaching that point I found the division of General Stevens retiring in some disorder before the enemy; the officers in command of regiments stating that their ammunition had been exhausted.

I immediately ordered forward the 4th Maine regiment, and it gallantly advanced and was soon in active conflict. I successively took forward the 101st New York, 3d Maine, 40th and 1st New York. These regiments held the enemy, and sustained unflinchingly the most murderous fire from a superior force.

At this juncture General Kearny reached the field with Randolph's battery, and placing it in position, aided my brigade by a well-directed fire. I pointed out to the general a gap on my right, caused by the retiring of Stevens's division, and asked for Berry's brigade to fill it. He rode from me to examine the ground, and, dashing past our lines into those of the enemy, fell a victim to his gallant daring.

I sent forward the 38th New York and 57th Pennsylvania to complete our victory. They advanced gallantly, and night closed in, leaving my brigade in full possession of that portion of the battle-field in which we were engaged.

General Kearny not returning, and supposing that he had been taken prisoner, I assumed command of division, and ordering forward Robinson's and Berry's brigades, relieved my tired regiments, and held until three o'clock a. m., September 2, the battle-ground, at which time I followed with the division, the corps of General Reno, to Fairfax Court-House.

During the night we removed our wounded. Our loss has been heavy, a detailed statement of which, with reports of regimental and brigade commanders, will be shortly forthcoming.

I was ably supported by the commanding officers of my regiments; all of whom sustained the high character accorded to them by our late lamented commander in his report of Friday's engagement.

Lieutenants Lee and Phillips, of my staff, deserve especial mention for their untiring efforts to carry my orders to all parts of the field. I have mentioned Lieutenant Lee in previous reports for gallantry.

Robinson's brigade had been placed on my left, by General Kearny, to support Graham's battery, but were, unfortunately, not called upon to engage the enemy; but assisted greatly, with Berry's brigade, during the night, in holding the battle-field, in front of the vastly superior force of the enemy. I was much indebted to General Robinson and Colonel Poe commanding Berry's brigade, for their prompt, ready assistance, and the gallant bearing of their tired commands.

I am, colonel, your obedient servant,

D. B. BIRNEY,
Brigadier General, Commanding First Division.

Lieutenant Colonel CHAUNCEY MCKEEVER,
A. A. G., Third Corps,

Consolidated list of killed, wounded, and missing in the first division, third corps, army of the Potomac, in the actions of 27th, 29th, and 30th August, 1862.

FIRST BRIGADE.

Twentieth Indiana volunteers.

Killed.—Colonel Wm. L. Browne; Privates V. M. Chesnut and Dan'l Hernmiller, company G; Private Edgar Furgusson, company K. Total, 4.

Wounded.—Sergeant Chas. R. Peno, Privates Phil. H. Larkin and John M. Tucker, company A; Sergeant Jares Johnes, Corporal A. V. Chapman, Privates C. Hollyworth and Melvin Glazin, company B; Sergeant E. B. Robins, Corporals Wm. Hall and Joseph Inks, and Private Jesse Woodruff, company C; Corporal Geo. W. Peirce, company D; Corporal Stephen Smith, Privates Wm. Muir, Jacob Everly, John D. Taylor, and Lewis Novil, company E; Privates Frank Knowl, Charles Wheeler, Jas. W. Redfere, and Chas. Moon, company F; Privates R. T. Foster, Henry Jett, J. J. Genions, W. M. Rooker, Henry Becker, Wm. L. Milford, and Andrew J. Costater, company G; Privates Thos. Vore, and Wm. Goldesbury, company I; Privates J. B. Harbett, Wm. Vanaats, Elias Bowers, Nathan White, and Theodore Slyres, company K. Total, 35.

Missing.—Private Aaron Pickerel, company C; Privates Nathan Caney and John Hanes, company E; Privates Wm. H. Hughey and Frank Barrioch, company G; Private Joseph Rogers, company I. Total, 6.

Sixty-third Pennsylvania volunteers.

Killed.—Corporal John Stone and Private J. M. Williams, company C; Privates Jas. McLain and M. Purcell, company D; Sergeant Sam'l R. Guthrie, company F; Privates Dan'l Cannon, S. R. Wood, John McCollough, and Ed. Maginis, company H; Sergeant Wm. Story, Privates Sam. Ginbaugh and Rob't F. Gould, company I; Privates Rob't Westerman, Dan'l B. Young, and Jacob Keith, company K. Total, 15.

Wounded.—Colonel Alex. Hays and Captain W. S. Kirkwood, acting major; Privates John Lernier, W. W. Morris, Geo. Gibson, Dan'l Fee, James Miller, Jas. McAtoo, Wm. Depont, John Ward, and Lewis A. West, company A; Sergeant Ed. Saint, Privates Klinefalter, W. Clarke, John Frax, and Cyrus Wills, company B; Lieutenant Geo. Weaver, Corporal Daniel Stone, Privates John Watterson and John Woods, company C; Sergeant W. J. Thompson, Corporal D. Glass, Privates Thos. Glass, W. J. Robinson, Jas. McAdams, J. C. Trimble, D. McCreany, and John Moore, company D; Sergeant Wm. J. Marks, commanding, Privates Jas. A. Bateman, Sam'l R. Balchori, John Cooper, Ralph H. Dawson, Jas. W. Galbraith, A. H. Johnes, B. Barton, J. A. Powers, and Sam'l Porter, company E; Lieutenant Geo. W. Fox, commanding, Sergeant Jas. Waly, Corporal T. H. Martin, Privates Alfred T. Rance, Joseph S. Elder, Martin Castern, E. Highburgher, Jas. Sample, and Dan'l O. Neil, company F; Captain W. McHenry, Privates A. O. Douglass, W. H. Gum, and A. W. Gilman, company G; Sergeant Mathes Kane, Color-sergeant W. W. Weeks, Corporals W. W. Wample and Joseph H. Weeks, Privates Pat. Collins, Thos. Crampton, John Cannon, Sam'l P. Dillman, Pat. Duggery, Jas. Dowling, Pat. Gallaher, David Griffith, Mich's Kelly, W. H. Marshall, Jas. Redmond, John Woods, Jas. Friel, and John Hill, company H; Captain Jas. W. Ryan, Corporal Wm. Semple, Privates J. W. Gamble, Geo. Solis, John Hoffman, Joseph Evans, Peter Lafferty, Peter Wray, Robt. Wiper, Thos. L. Hunter, John Krough, Wm. Wigham, John Wolf, Tantilius Muse, James Irwin, and Wm. Brown, company I; Sergeant Thos W. Boggs, Corporals James M. Minold and Ed. Brundley, Privates John G. Green, Robt. Orr, G. W. Helderbroul, Robt. Dunham, Thos. Sculley, Henry Hursch, company K. Total, 94.

Missing.—Private Mat. Hessy, company A; Private W. Bliss, company C; Privates C. Tishner and Thos. A. Miller, company E; Privates Henry Shoup and John Thompson, company F; Private Wm. J. Graham, company G; Private John Johnson, company H; Privates Reuben George, — Moots, and Rob't Hodge, company K. Total, 11.

One hundred and fifth Pennsylvania volunteers.

Killed.—Privates John E. Saddler, Wm. McHenry, and John P. Imler, company A; Private Henry W. McCormick, company C; Privates Thos. Orr and David Johnston, company F; Second Lieutenant J. L. Gilbert, company I. Total, 7.

Wounded.—Captain C. A. Craig, commanding regiment; Captain John Hastings, Lieutenant Neel, Sergeant Arthur H. Murray, Privates Geo. Gohen, Geo. M. Johnston, John Means, and Augustus C. Nolf, company A; Privates Wm. Alshouse, Francis O. Brookwater, George Drigard, Ross McCoy, John Mayo, and David Mitchell, company C; Private Elias Wilson and Corporal Perry Smith, company D; Privates L. G. Dom, Fred Mysick, and Andrew Wish, company E; Captain Robt. Kirk, Corporals Geo. W. Randolph and Gew. W. Campbell, Privates James Pounds, Saml. Fulman, Jas. Awl, Saml. Fry, James Drum, Charles Gill, Geo. W. Maynard, and Saml. Cochian, company F; Privates John Blouser and Chapman Rose, company I; Captain A. C. Thompson, Privates Saml. Lydick, James Taylor, Isaac Henis, and M. Nudo, company K. Total, 37.

Missing.—Privates David Y. Sattgwin and Jas. W. Broch, company A; Private Geo. Reiche, company C; Privates Wm. B. Hoel and Geo. Wilson, company D; Private Frank Dunbar, company E; Private G. B. Hall, company F; Private Oliver Graham, company I. Total, 8.

RECAPITULATION.

Regiments.	KILLED.		WOUNDED.		MISSING.		Aggregate.
	Officers.	Enlisted men.	Officers.	Enlisted men.	Officers.	Enlisted men	
20th reg't Ind. vol's	1	3	....	35	....	6	45
63d reg't Penn. vol's	....	15	6	88	....	11	120
105th reg't Penn. vol's	1	6	5	32	....	8	52
	2	24	11	155	....	25	217

SECOND BRIGADE.

Thirty-eighth New York volunteers.

Wounded.—Private Matthew McEllany, company A; Privates George Hannah and Danl. Hoffer, company D; Captain Aug. Funk and Lieutenant H. C. Pratt, company F; Lieutenant John M. Hyde, company G; Privates Luther L. Mills, Wm. Barker, Hugh Darmyan, company H. Total, 9.

Missing.—Second Lieutenant Sam. Johnson, company B; Second Lieutenant H. Pendergrast, company D. Total, 2.

Third Maine volunteers.

Wounded.—Privates G. W. Thompson and Leurs Selbing, company B; Sergeant G. E. Gower and Private S. S. Fall, company C; Private J. E. Purrington, company D; Sergeant G. O. Russell and Private H. C. Castor, company E; Privates S. S. McDermid and Perley Smith, company F; Private A. P. Herrick, company G; Private Joseph Perry, company H. Total, 11.

Missing.—Corporal F. R. Blasland and Private G. A. Glazier, company A; Lieutenant W. Cox, Corporals Ed. Smith, Wm. M. Davitt, and Wm. McDonald, company B; Sergeant H. W. Jarvis and Private J. W. Kimball, company C; Corporal Turner Farnam, company D; Sergeant C. M. Bursley, Privates W. F. Bragg, E. A. Calcott, C. M. Dodge, and C. E. Morrill, company E; Privates G. W. Stewart, Jas. Lambert, and Luther Williamson, company F; Private C. C. Griffin, company G; Privates Saml. Austin and Lewis Bragg, company H; Corporal F. M. Boyerton, Privates Briggs Turner, Geo. L. Fellows, and James Orrick, company I; Sergeant J. C. Richer, Corporal B. W. Smart, Privates A. P. Bachelder, Andrew Butler, Geo. A. Butler, Jas. O. Carroll, A. H. Frost, Chas. H. Smiley, and Wm. G. Wilson, company K. Total, 33.

Fourth Maine volunteers.

Killed.—First Sergeant Franklin Achorn, company C; Private Chas. Clark, company D; Corporal Jas. A. Hatch, company E; Private G. W. Robinson, company F; Private Moses A. Debeck, company H; Sergeant Chas. Brown and Private Wm. King, company K. Total, 7.

Wounded.—Privates Marion McManus and Anson Trussel, company A; Privates Patrick Black, D. C. Norris, Edmund Cowan and F. J. Dow, company B; Privates Saml. N. Cain, Philander Proctor, C. A. Libbey, F. E. Snowdeal and C. H. Miller, company C; Private Josh. Clark, company D; Sergeant Z. C. Gowan and Corporal Jas. G. Rhodes, company E; First Sergeant G. M. Bragg, Sergeant H. Leach, Corporal W. H. Chick, Privates W. A. Dollis, C. H. Elwell, and J. J. Shepard, company F; Corporal Hiram Hackett, Privates John Carlton, Sewell Seary, and Albion Lowell, company G; Private Geo. Cox, company H; First Sergeant F. P. Eames, Privates M. H. William and Rufus Sidelinker, company I; Private Willard R. Fowler, company K. Total, 29.

Missing.—Sergeant G. R. Greer, company A; Privates Ellis Bigdale and C. O. Murray, company B; Corporal R. O. Fales, Privates A. Pottle and J. H. Thomas, company C; Private H. C. Davis, company D; Privates S. B. Holgan, Nick Butler, and Timothy Bragg, company E; Private E. D. Tasker, company F; Private John ——, company G; Private Thos. Doyle, company I. Total 13.

Fortieth New York volunteers.

Killed.—Color-corporal J. W. Brundage, company F; Private Horace Wilson, company G; Sergeant John Hickey, Privates Pat. Welch and John Shehan, company K. Total, 5.

Wounded.—Adjutant Wm. H. Warner; Captain F. A. Johnson, Corporal Wm. Clarke, Privates John Steiger, Jas. Dunn, Saml. Morrison, and Joseph Schofield, company A; Sergeant John Pender, Corporal Geo. A. Morrell, Privates Danl. E. Blackstock, Asa Jentice, John Allen, and Jas. W. Dockhand, company B; Sergeant John H. Taylor, Corporal Henry Openshaw, Privates

Jas. O. Brine, Jas. Armstrong, Edwin Rogers, Wm. Carlan, Thos. Cunningham, Jonathan Mills, Thos. Boyce, and John Coley, company C; First Lieutenant Chas. H. Gesner, Second Lieutenant Wm. H. Plumly, Privates Peter Khor, Henry Sinclair, Jas. Anyling, John Burns, John Shuster, Theo. Mount, Francis Sweeny, and —— Suarr, company D; Privates John King, Mathew Lynch, and John Schiffer, company E; Corporal John Sullivan, Privates Wm. Purton, Michl. Cosgriff, Alex. Rooney, and John Britton, company F; Lieutenant Alfred Malpas, Corporal H. B. Goodnow, and Private George H. Fisk, company G; Sergeants F. McLain and John Hannah, Privates John Michan, Thos. McCarty, Geo. W. Russell, and Chas. Angell, company H; First Sergeant Adam Goss, company I; First Lieutenant Jas. R. Stevens, Sergeants Jerome Sullivan and Jerema Slattery, Privates Pat. Burns, Jas. McDonnell, Chas Riley, Thomas McGloud, Michl. Walsh, James Vallery, and Wm. Hamilton, company K. Total, 60.

Missing.—Corporal Geo. Fink and Private Joseph Maddin, company F; Privates C. O. Fairbanks and G. O. Hutchings, company G; Privates Harrison Booth, Chas. Earnst, Dennis Conway, H. C. Cobb, Danl. Barnett, and J. G. Morrill, company H; Privates H. Smith (wounded,) Jas. Lowry, P. Leahy, Saml. Shute, John Airey, Philip Fritag, and John Kenney, company I. Total, 18.

One hundred and first New York volunteers.

Killed.—Corporal O. Nell, company A; Corporal O. V. Carne, company B; Privates W. Donlin and W. Ryan, company D; Corporal G. Eastwood, company I; Corporal D. Hill, company K. Total, 6.

Wounded.—Captain W. C. Allen, Corporal J. K. Jonston, Privates E. Sweeny and J. Mahay, company A; Sergeant O. R. Patterson, Privates L. Colburn, W. Hund, G. M. Strawbridge, L. Downer, and J. Brennan, company B; Lieutenant Warner, Sergeant C. E. Sheppard, Privates M. Thomas, W. Ringault, C. Malory, and J. Wilson, company C; Privates —— Goodwin, —— Lockwood, —— Neeclin, —— Leyman, and —— Alberts, company D; Captain D. L. Beckwith, Corporal A. Walters, Privates A. Anderson, W. Snyder, W. Brower, and C. Porter, company E; Privates Harvey Strait, N. Stevens, W. Tucker, and W. Fransien, company F; Sergeants Anderson and Coburn, Privates Clue and Ridman, company G; Corporal Miller, Privates H. Suther, J. Waggman, S. Reid, F. Bapst, H. Hochstraser, F. Hutin, D. Allen and C. Hufer, company H; Corporal H. O. Woods, Privates Geo. Vranklen and W. E. White, company I; Sergeant Hardenburg, Privates Fillmore and Newton, company K. Total 50.

Missing.—Privates S. Bowles and O. Bulges, company A; Private Wm. Howland, company B; Privates H. Morgan and C. Harwood, company C; Private —— Smith, company D; Sergeant R. Gray and Private C. Keith, company F; Sergeant Dow and Private Race, company G; Sergeant Jas. Vail and Private John Saunders, company I; Private Bowerman, company K. Total 13.

Fifty-seventh Pennsylvania volunteers.

Wounded.—Privates S. M. Osborn and J. Fitzgerald, company A; Private R. C. Harrison, company K. Total 3.

RECAPITULATION.

REGIMENTS.	KILLED.		WOUNDED.		MISSING.		Aggregate.
	Officers.	Enlisted men.	Officers.	Enlisted men.	Officers.	Enlisted men.	
38th reg't N. Y. vol's	....	....	3	6	2	....	11
3d reg't Maine vol's	....	....	....	11	1	22	34
4th reg't Maine vol's	....	7	....	30	....	12	49
40th reg't N. Y vol's	....	5	6	54	....	18	83
101st reg't N. Y. vol's	....	6	3	47	....	13	69
57th reg't Penn. vol's	....	....	....	3	....	....	3
	....	18	12	151	3	65	249

THIRD BRIGADE.

Thirty-seventh New York volunteers.

Wounded.—Private Wm. Mooney, company C; Private Thomas Lowler, company D; Private Pat. Flannagan, company G. Total 3.

Second Michigan volunteers.

Wounded.—Second Lieutenant Wm. Plumb, company D; Private John Deeg, company A; Private Geo. Walter, company F. Total 3.

Missing.—Private C. Eiker, company C; Corporals S. D. Southworth, Chas. Dryer, and Clinton Snyder, and Private Silas T. Abbott, company G; Private Hen. Smith, company I. Total 6.

Third Michigan volunteers.

Killed.—Privates John Reichberg and Fred. Shriver, company B; Private Andrew Santer, company C; Lieutenant Byron E. Hess, Corporals C. Berrenger, P. Vandenson, and S. Traverse, and Private James Dailey, company D; Sergeant Danl. Bugle, Corporals E. Bell and Joseph N. Jacobs, Privates Ed. Rierdon, Levi E. Metcalf, Willard Washburn, and Elijah Fish, company F; Corporal Wm. F. Hogan and Private Albert Lewis, company G; Privates P. S. Archer and Dennis Conway, company H; Privates Joseph Brown and George Chryesler, company I; Corporal H. H. Mead, Privates Cyrus W. Bullen and Henry P. Beckwith, company K. Total, 24.

Wounded.—Sergeant D. G. Lovell, Corporal A. C. Parker, Privates Thos. Putnam and D. Hierds, company A; Captain Fred. Shriver, Corporals Jos. B. Wood and W. W. Wilder, Privates M. S. Bacon, H. P. Bateman, S. C. Brigham, and Geo. W. Gates, company B; Sergeant Augt. Smidt, Corporal Augt. Hoyer, Privates Danl. Moe, G. Schwartyler, Henry Dykeman, Lewis Hartman, and Peter Myers, company C; Sergeant H. S. Mather, Corporal D. Lock, Privates B. T. Call, Wm. Wright, Geo. Hammond, I. Francis, Jas. Renwick, A. Barber, M. Barber, P. Grooms, M. McGrath, and David Benton, company D; Sergeant C. M. Finch, Corporals E. A. Synold and M. P. Long, Privates J. M. Call, E. Van Wert, J. W. Salter, S. Dalrample, Job Scott, A. G. Kilpatrick, C. B. Soveim, and Geo. Armes, company E; Captain I. C. Smith, Sergeants Thos. Conger and Jas. E. Vandam, Corporals Ste. D. Thompson and

Berry F. Gooch, Privates John August, Eli Hamblin, Wm. P. Wilson, Andrew Duran, and P. H. Doran, company F; Sergeants Geo. Ellis and Artemus Newman, Corporal Allen S. Shattuck, Privates Ben. F. Hammond, Wm. Bryce, Ira M. D. Crame, Andrew J. Hath, Alex. Ross, Alva W. Weller, John Stanton, and Oliver Richards, company G; First Lieutenant W. S. Ryan, Second Lieutenant Thos. J. Waters, Sergeant P. P. Bergevin, Corporals Fred. Higbee, Wm. Millney, Saml. Jenner, Chas. Althouse, and Walter Jones, Privates Wm. Furguson, A. A. Shelley, John Smith, Judson Smoke, Chas. Henderson, and Chas. Rose, company H; First Lieutenant Simeon Brennan, Second Lieutenant Thos. Tate, Sergeant J. F. McGinley, Corporal Oscar Foster, Privates Ben. Austin, B. E. Baker, Harley Bennet, E. S. Cole, Perry Goshon, Albert Hanlin, and H. Heindermier, company I; Second Lieutenant Dan. S. Root, Sergeant Jas. O. Donahue, Corporals Alex. McIntire and Robt. Misener, Privates Geo. Cochran, Alex. French, Chas. W. Furber, Harmon Kusig, Elias H. Judd, Chas. Henry, Orrin K. Newton, Martin Neilson, and Alfred Pelton, company K. Total, 100.

Missing.—Privates Jas. Congdon, Jas. H. While, and B. Charmschad, company B; Privates G. H. March, Jas. P. Drake. Geo. P. Scranton, and E. A. Hamilton, company E; Privates Peter Clays and Americus Miller, company G; Privates Horatio Barnham, John George, and Zeph. Jeffer, company H; Private Chas. A. Morgan, company I; Privates Wm. Halsey and John J. Rowley, company K. Total 15.

Fifth Michigan volunteers.

Wounded.—Privates Danl. Millspaugh and Allen E. Hicks, company B; Private John Winslow, company D; Private Othello Phelps, company E; Private Saml. Murrall, company G; Corporal Chas. McNaughton, company I. Total, 6.

Ninety-ninth Pennsylvania volunteers.

Wounded.—Private Thos. Blankarm, company G; Private Pat. Branagen, company H. Total 2.

Missing.—Privates John Germon and Dennis Buckley, company E; Privates J. S. Smith, Benj. Eldridge, and Z. Powell, company F; Privates Thos. Stackhouse and E. Wilder, company G; Privates Phil. Murray and Martin Kelly, company H; Privates John Adams and John Rodgers, company I; Privates L. Martin, A. Krier, Danl. McDevitt, and P. Clause, company K. Total, 15.

RECAPITULATION.

REGIMENTS.	KILLED.		WOUNDED.		MISSING.		AGGREGATE.
	Officers.	Enlisted men.	Officers.	Enlisted men.	Officers.	Enlisted men.	
37th reg't N. Y. vol's				3			3
2d reg't Mich. vol's			1	2		6	9
3d reg't Mich. vol's	2	22	7	93		15	139
5th reg't Mich. vol's				6			6
99th reg't Penn. vol's				2		15	17
	2	22	8	106		36	174

Recapitulation of killed, wounded, and missing in the first division of the third army corps.

BRIGADES.	KILLED.		WOUNDED.		MISSING.		Aggregate.
	Officers.	Enlisted men.	Officers.	Enlisted men.	Officers.	Enlisted men.	
1st brigade	2	24	11	155	....	25	217
2d brigade	....	18	12	151	3	65	249
3d brigade	2	22	8	106	....	36	174
	4	64	31	412	3	126	640

Respectfully transmitted,

D. B. BIRNEY,
Brigadier General, Commanding Division.

No. 5.

REPORT OF BRIGADIER GENERAL J. F. REYNOLDS.

HEADQUARTERS REYNOLDS'S DIVISION,
Camp near Munson's Hill, Va., September 5, 1862.

COLONEL: I have the honor to report the operations of this division since leaving Fredericksburg, on the 21st of August last, under orders from Major General Burnside, to proceed to Kelly's Ford, on the Rappahannock river.

The division having been united at Fredericksburg, with the exception of the 2d regiment, Colonel McCandless, not yet debarked at Acquia Creek, accompanied by an ammunition train supplied by General Burnside, proceeded to Kelly's Ford, where it arrived, after a severe and arduous march, on the evening of the 22d ultimo, and relieved a brigade of Reno's division under Colonel Farnsworth, of the 79th New York.

On the morning of the 23d the division joined the army of Virginia under General Pope, then on its march to Warrenton from Rappahannock Station, and on arriving at Warrenton was attached, temporarily, to McDowell's army corps. On the 24th the division encamped on the Sulphur Springs road, one mile south of Warrenton, with Meade's brigade advanced two miles on that road. On the 26th we moved to the Waterloo road. On the 27th it marched with the army, on the Alexandria and Warrenton turnpike, and encamped at Broad Run. On the 27th marched to Manassas, by way of Gainesville; on the supposition that the enemy was at the former place, I was directed to follow General Sigel's corps until our arrival at Gainesville, where I was to form in columns of echelons on his left—King's division to form in like manner on my left—in which order we were to move on Manassas. On arriving at Gainesville the head of my column was fired upon by two pieces of the enemy, in position on the heights above Groveton and to the left of the turnpike, which were immediately replied to by Ransom's battery, and Meade's brigade rapidly thrown into line of battle by that general. The range being too great for Ransom's guns, his battery was replaced by the rifled guns of Captain Cooper, when the enemy withdrew, not, however, before some loss had been sustained by Meade. Some force was displayed and skirmishers sent forward along the pike and through the woods on the right of the road. On the opening of fire upon the enemy from our rifled guns he retired from our front. This was supposed to be merely a demonstration by the enemy to save a wagon train, which was seen moving off on the Sudley Springs road, and the column continued its march towards Manassas.

About five o'clock I received orders to march upon Centreville, and the column turned off at Bethlehem church and took the Sudley Springs road towards the Warrenton pike. About this time heavy cannonading was heard both to our front and left, the former supposed to be from Sigel's corps, and the latter from King's division, which had taken the Warrenton pike from Gainesville. I sent word to the column to hasten its march, and proceeded to the left at once, myself, in the direction of the firing, arriving on the field just before dark, and found that Gibbon's brigade of King's division was engaged with the enemy, with Doubleday's and Patrick's brigades in the vicinity. After the firing ceased I saw General King, who, determining to maintain his position, I left about 9 o'clock p. m. to return to my division, promising to bring it up early in the morning to his support.

Before leaving, however, I heard the division moving off, and I learned from General Hatch that it was moving by Gainesville towards Manassas. I then returned to my own division, which I reached at daylight on the morning of the 28th; closed up with General Sigel's command on the old battle-field of Bull Run. General Sigel reported the enemy in his immediate front, and requested my co-operation with him in an attack upon his position. I accordingly formed my division on the left of General Sigel's corps, next to the division of General Schenck. General McDowell joined the command at daylight, and directed my co-operation with General Siegel.

The right of the enemy's position could be discerned upon the heights above Groveton, on the right of the pike. The division advanced over the ground to the heights above Groveton, crossed the pike, and Cooper's battery came gallantly into action on the same ridge on which the enemy's right was, supported by Meade's brigade; while pressing forward our extreme left across the pike, re-enforcements were sent for by General Sigel for the right of his line under General Milroy, now hardly pressed by the enemy, and a brigade was taken from Schenck's command on my right. The whole fire of the enemy was now concentrated on the extreme right of my division, and unsupported there the battery was obliged to retire with considerable loss in both men and horses; and the division fell back to connect with Schenck.

Later in the day, General Pope, arriving on the right from Centreville, renewed the attack on the enemy and drove him some distance. My division was directed to threaten the enemy's right and rear, which it proceeded to do under a heavy fire of artillery from the ridge to the left of the pike. Generals Seymour and Jackson led their brigades in advance, but notwithstanding all the steadiness and courage shown by the men they were compelled to fall back before the heavy fire of artillery and musketry which met them both on the front and left flank; and the division resumed its original position. King's division engaged the enemy along the pike on our right, and the action was continued with it until dark by Meade's brigade.

On the morning of the 30th I was directed to take post with my division on the left of the pike near the Henry House, and ordered by Major General Pope to form my division in column by company at full distance, with the whole of my artillery on the left; that I would be the pivot in the attack which Porter's corps was to make on the enemy's right, then supposed to be on the pike and in retreat. Having formed my division in the position indicated, and opened with my rifled batteries to drive the enemy from the first ridge, the skirmishers advanced and the attack by Porter's corps commenced. When the skirmishers arrived in the thick woods opposite Groveton, I found the resistance so great that another regiment was deployed to support them, and finally a second; in all, three regiments.

The advanced skirmishers were the 1st rifles, Colonel McNeil, and the 1st infantry, Colonel Roberts, supported by the 7th infantry, Lieutenant Colonel Henderson. The 6th regiment, Colonel Sinclair, was thrown through the woods on our left flank. Becoming convinced that the enemy were not in retreat, but were posted in force on our left flank, I pushed through the skirmishers to the edge of the woods on the left, gaining sight of the open ground beyond; and advancing myself into the open ground, I found a line of skirmishers of the enemy nearly parallel to the line of skirmishers covering my left flank, with cavalry formed behind them, perfectly stationary, evidently masking a column of the enemy, formed for attack on my left flank when our line should be sufficiently advanced. The skirmishers opened fire upon me, and I was obliged to run the gauntlet of a heavy fire to gain the rear of my division, losing one of my orderlies who had followed me through the woods. I immediately communicated this to the commanding general of the corps, who came upon the ground, and directed me to form my division to resist this attack, the dispositions for which were rapidly completed. Other troops were to be sent to my support, when the commanding general, observing the attack of Porter to have been repulsed, ordered me with my division across the field to the rear of Porter, to form a line behind which the troops might be rallied. I immediately started my division in the direction indicated; but before the rear of my column had left the position the threatened attack by the enemy's right began to be felt, and the rear brigade, under Colonel Anderson, with three batteries of artillery, were obliged to form on the ground on which they found themselves to oppose it. Passing across the field to the right, with Meade's and Seymour's brigades and Ransom's battery, my course was diverted by the difficult nature of the ground, and the retreating masses of the broken columns, among troops of Heintzelman's corps, already formed, by which much time was lost and confusion created, which allowed the enemy to sweep up with his right, so far as almost to cut us off from the pike, leaving nothing but the rear brigade and the three batteries of artillery of my division and scattered troops of other commands to resist the advance of the enemy upon our left. It was here that the most severe loss of the division was sustained, both in men and material, Kerns losing his four guns, but not until wounded and left on the field; Cooper, his caisson.

Colonel Harden, commanding 12th regiment, was here severely wounded. The brigade under command of Colonel Anderson sustained itself most gallantly, and though severely pushed on both front and flank maintained its position until overwhelmed by numbers, when it fell back, taking up new positions wherever the advantages of ground permitted. The two brigades and battery of artillery under my immediate command, finding ourselves perfectly out of place, moved, by the direction of an officer of General Pope's staff, to a position to the right of the Henry House, which position was most gallantly maintained by the commands of Meade and Seymour and Ransom's battery for nearly two hours, when they were relieved by the division of regular troops under Colonel Buchanan.

My division was then united and marched during the early part of the night towards Centreville, and bivouacked with Syke's division upon the east bank of Cub Run. On the following morning it proceeded to Centreville.

On the afternoon of the 31st my division was directed to relieve the command of General Reno, (Stevens's brigade,) occupying the position of Cub Run, where it remained during the night. On the 1st instant the division marched with the army from Centreville, and encamped near Fairfax Court-House. On the 2d it proceeded by the Alexandria and Columbia turnpike to the vicinity of

Hunter's chapel and Arlington. On the afternoon of the 4th the division arrived at this place, and encamped in position to the rear of Munson's hill.

The conduct of the officers and men during the several actions, and the arduous marches they were subjected to since leaving Fredericksburg, was generally good and commendable. Many straggled from the ranks, unable to keep up, and some few left the ranks on the field, but rejoining their commands at Centreville it is impossible to ascertain who were censurable. General Meade mentions the 1st rifles, under Colonel McNeil, to whose lot the advance skirmishing principally fell, as deserving particular notice. The 1st infantry, under Colonel Roberts, the 2d, Colonel McCandless, the 6th, Colonel Sinclair, the 7th, Lieutenant Colonel Henderson, and the 12th, Colonel Hardin, are also particularly mentioned.

Generals Meade and Seymour, as heretofore, led and conducted their brigades in the most skillful manner throughout the entire marches and actions; also General Jackson, commanding 3d brigade, up to the time that he was taken sick on the field and obliged to retire on the 30th. His command devolved upon Colonel Anderson, who conducted the brigade through that day. To the officers of my small staff, consisting of Captain Kingsbury, assistant adjutant general, Lieutenant Lamborn, aide-de-camp, and Lieutenant Snyder, of the 7th regiment, acting aide-de-camp, I am greatly indebted for their indefatigable efforts to execute my orders, rendered more arduous by the incompleteness of the division as well as brigade staffs, having neither quartermaster nor commissary with the division.

Division Surgeon King remained upon the field with Surgeon Read, of the 1st infantry, to attend to our wounded. Not having a single ambulance with the division, it was impossible to bear our wounded any distance from the field.

I enclose a return of the killed, wounded, and missing in the several actions; also a list by name.

I neglected to mention that the 2d regiment, under Colonel McCandless, joined the division at Warrenton, and that Colonel McCandless was severely wounded in the action of the 30th.

Respectfully submitted,

JOHN F. REYNOLDS,
Brigadier General of Volunteers, Commanding Division.

Col. SCHRIVER, *Chief of Staff,*
3d Army corps.

Return of killed, wounded and missing, in Reynolds' Division during the actions of the 28th, 29th, and 30th of August, 1863.

	Killed.	Wounded.	Missing.	Total.
1st brigade, (Meade.)				
1st rifles, Colonel McNeil	5	19	3	27
3d infantry, Colonel Sickles	2	21	27	50
4th infantry, Colonel Magillon		12	2	14
7th infantry, Lieut. Col. Henderson		23	13	36
8th infantry, Captain Lemon	5	21	32	58
Total	12	96	77	185
2d brigade, (Seymour.)				
1st infantry, Colonel Roberts	6	23		29
2d infantry, Colonel McCandless	1	15		16
5th infantry, Major Fentmyer	1	9		10
6th infantry, Colonel Sinclair	5	36	20	61
Total	13	83	20	116
3d brigade, (Jackson.)				
9th infantry, Colonel Anderson				
10th infantry, Colonel Kirk	12	52	35	99
11th infantry, Lieutenant Colonel Jackson	12	34	19	65
12th infantry, Colonel Hardin	5	47	5	57
	5	38	23	66
Total	34	171	82	287
Artillery.				
Battery C, 5th artillery, Capt. D. R. Ransom		1	1	2
Battery A, 1st Pennsylvania artillery	1	5	1	7
Battery B, 1st Pennsylvania artillery	4	19		23
Battery G, 1st Pennsylvania artillery	3	22	8	33
Total	8	47	10	65
Total of the division	67	397	189	653

Respectfully submitted.

JOHN F. REYNOLDS,
Brigadier General Volunteers, Commanding.

CAMP NEAR UPTON HILL, *September* 5, 1862.

HEADQUARTERS FIRST ARMY CORPS,
October 9, 1862.

GENERAL: I observe in the report by General Schenck's acting assistant adjutant general, published in the Philadelphia Inquirer of to-day, of the operations of that general's division when General Sigel advanced to attack the enemy on the morning of the *29th of August* last, (you will yourself observe the error in the dates,) several misstatements, unintentional, no doubt, when referring to the movements of my division. My division manœuvred on his left from early in the morning until he gained the position alluded to on the pike near Gibbon's battle-ground of the evening previous. It was here that General Schenck asked me for a battery. Cooper's battery, with Meade's brigade as a support, was immediately placed in position on the ridge to the right of the pike and on the left of the woods where Gibbon's brigade had been in action, by General Meade and myself. In returning from this position, to bring up the other battery and Seymour's brigade, I passed through Schenck's troops, drawn up on the *right* of the woods before alluded to, in which Gibbon had been engaged. But, in bringing up Ransom's battery and Seymour's brigade along the pike, I noticed that Schenck's troops had disappeared from this position and were nowhere in sight. I understood that Schenck had detached a brigade to the right to the support of Milroy, and that I was therefore left alone, as far as I knew. I immediately arrested Seymour's movement, and directed the division to occupy the position across the pike from which it had moved, in doing which McLean's brigade was discovered occupying a piece of woods just on the left of the pike, and, as soon as could be, this movement was arrested and made to correspond with his position. It was subsequently ascertained that he was disconnected from the rest of Sigel's troops, and the position was again changed to make them correct.

I sent no word to General Schenck of the kind indicated in this paper of the movement of the enemy, at the time this change of position was made, nor at any time. There was a report came later in the evening that the enemy were moving over the pike, but I am not aware that I communicated it to General Schenck, as at that time I had no connexion with him.

I am, general, very respectfully, your obedient servant,

JOHN F. REYNOhDS,
Brigadier General Volunteers, Commanding.

Major General MCDOWELL, *Washington, D. C.*

I make this correction to you and without any desire to enter into a controversy in the paper on official matters.

J. F. R.

No. 6.

REPORT OF BRIGADIER GENERAL J. C. ROBINSON.

HEADQUARTERS ROBINSON'S BRIGADE,
Centreville, Virginia, August 31, 1862.

CAPTAIN: I have the honor to submit the following report of the operations of my brigade yesterday and day before: On Friday morning I was ordered to "support Colonel Poe's brigade and to develop his line of battle to the right." After crossing Bull Run, I moved forward in two lines, the first composed of the 20th Indiana and 105th Pennsylvania, and the second of the 63d Pennsylvania and five companies of the 30th Ohio, which were temporarily attached to my command. Arriving on the ground assigned me, I remained for a considerable time exposed to a heavy artillery fire, after which I took up my position on high ground further to the right. I was soon after directed by Major General Kearney, commanding division, to move to the support of Poe's left, when I formed the 63d and 105th Pennsylvania in line of battle on the Leesburg road, holding the 20th Indiana and Ohio battalion in reserve. At this time there was a heavy musketry fire to our left and front, and I was directed to move forward through the woods to turn the enemy and cut off his retreat through the railroad cut. On arriving on the ground with the 63d and 105th Pennsylvania, 20th Indiana, and 3d Michigan, I found the railroad already occupied by our own troops, and the cornfield in front filled with the enemy. I then deployed the 63d and 105th Pennsylvania along the railroad to the right of the troops in position, directing the 3d Michigan to protect my right flank, placing the 20th Indiana in reserve, and throwing skirmishers to the front. Soon after taking this position the regiments on my left gave way and passed rapidly to the rear, out of the woods, leaving my left flank entirely exposed. As rapidly as possible I moved my command to the left to occupy the deserted ground, but before my troops could get fairly into position I was fiercely attacked by a superior force that had succeeded in crossing the road. I then threw forward my right wing, forming my line of battle at right angles to the original position, and checked the progress of the enemy. At this time General Birney brought up and turned over to me his 4th Maine. He afterwards sent me his 1st, 40th, and 101st New York regiments. These troops were deployed to the right and left of the railroad, and pushed forward to the support of my regiments in front, which were suffering severely from a terrific fire of musketry and the enemy's artillery posted on a hill to our right and rear. Our men now gained steadily on the enemy, and were driving him before them until he brought up fresh masses of troops, (supposed to be two brigades,) when, with ammunition nearly expended, we withdrew to our second position. Our loss in this action was severe, embracing some of our best officers. It was here that my 20th Indiana lost their brave colonel, William L. Brown, who fell while gallantly leading his regiment. The loss of this gallant officer and true patriot is irreparable. With him fell other brave officers and men, who will ever be remembered as among our country's heroes and martyrs. The enemy's loss must have been very great.

On Saturday morning I was ordered with my brigade to support the right of our line, and took my position in front of one of the fords of Bull Run, placing two regiments in line and one in reserve. The left wing of the 30th Ohio regiment, which afterwards reported to me for duty, was placed on the left of my line. I remained in this position, exposed part of the time to the fire of artillery, until, it becoming evident that the enemy was turning the left flank of the army, I was directed by the major general commanding division to take position on the hill by the Brown House. I moved to this point in column, and so remained, ready to take any position necessary; when, on appearance of the enemy, I deployed into line of battle, facing towards our original front. Soon after, by order of General Heintzelman, I moved in column of regiments to the hollow in front, ready to push forward to the support of Birney's brigade, which was now threatened by masses of the enemy, and my first position on the hill was occupied by troops of Ricketts's division. Soon a straggling musketry fire was heard from there, and I supposed the enemy was repulsed. It was now dark, and I was surprised to learn soon after that our troops had left the hill in possession of the enemy. I used every precaution to conceal from him the knowledge of my position, and, although within speaking distance, I remained there until about ten o'clock, when I withdrew my brigade silently and in perfect order. I cannot speak too highly of the conduct of officers and men during the whole of the two days' conflict; all seemed to be animated by the same spirit, and the evolutions in face of the enemy were performed with the same coolness and precision as on drill. I leave it for the regimental commanders to mention those of their commands most deserving of notice. I received much assistance from the lamented Colonel Brown, of the 20th Indiana, and from Colonel Hays, of the 63d Pennsylvania, who led his regiment in his usual gallant manner on the 29th until wounded and taken from the field. Captain Craig, 105th Pennsylvania, gallantly led his regiment and was also wounded. My thanks are due to Colonel Champlin, 3d Michigan; Colonel Egan, 40th New York; Colonel Gesner and Lieutenant Colonel Brown, 101st New York; and Colonel Walker, 4th Maine, for valuable services.

The officers of my staff, Captain Kidder, assistant adjutant general; Lieutenant Robinson, aide-de-camp; and Colonel Chester and Lieutenant Sweet, acting aids, were zealous and active, performing their duties gallantly under severe musketry and artillery fire.

The regiments engaged suffered the loss of 3 officers killed, 25 officers wounded; 69 enlisted men killed, 375 wounded; 106 missing. Aggregate loss, 578.

Very respectfully, your obedient servant,

JOHN C. ROBINSON,
Brigadier General.

Captain G. H. MENDILL,
Acting Assistant Adjutant General,
First Division, Third Corps, Army of Potomac.

HEADQUARTERS ROBINSON'S BRIGADE,
Camp near Fort Lyon, Virginia, September 8, 1862.

MAJOR: I have the honor to report that in the affair of Chantilly, on the 1st instant, this brigade, with Graham's battery, was placed in line of battle on rolling ground to the left of the Centreville road. The 20th regiment of Indiana volunteers was directed to hold the woods on our right. The brigade was, by order of the division commander, held in this position until near night, when I advanced about half a mile. Soon after I received orders from Brigadier General Birney, who had succeeded to the command of the division, to move to the right and front, when I formed the brigade in columns of regiments on his right, and there remained until the division was withdrawn at an early hour the next morning, In this engagement the brigade suffered no loss.

Very respectfully, your obedient servant,

JNO. C. ROBINSON,
Brigadier General.

Major BREVOORT, *Assistant Adjutant General,*
First Division, Third Corps, Army of the Potomac.

HEADQUARTERS FIRST BRIGADE,
Centreville, Virginia, August 31, 1862.

Respectfully forwarded.

D. B. BIRNEY,
Brigadier General, Commanding Division.

No. 7.

REPORT OF COLONEL ORLANDO M. POE, SECOND MICHIGAN VOLUNTEERS.

CAMP WILTON, VIRGINIA, *September* 9, 1862.

SIR: I have the honor of reporting, for the information of the brigadier general commanding division, that on Monday afternoon, September 1st, the third brigade of this division, of which I was then in command, moved from its camp at Centreville, taking the road to Fairfax Court-House. Some three or four miles out on this road, I received orders from General Kearney to form the brigade in line of battle on the road, and move forward in the direction of the firing, then going on between Reno's division and the enemy, until our left connected with General Robinson's right. We did so, and halted for a few minutes, when Lieutenant Colonel Brown, aide-de-camp, brought me an order to move forward by a road which he would point out, and support Reno's left flank. We did so, until arriving a short distance in the rear of where Randolph's battery had been at work, where we halted; and in the absence of other officers, who could not at the moment be found, (General Kearney was not then known to have been killed,) I reported to General Reno, who directed me to remain where I was until further orders, at the same time telling me to detach one regiment in support of a battery upon our left. The 5th Michigan was sent to perform this duty. It was now dark, when an order came from General Birney, who had assumed command of the division in the prolonged absence of General Kearney, to move to the front and relieve the first brigade, which had expended its ammunition in the fight. We did so at once; relieving the 38th New York with the 2d Michigan, the 40th New York with the 99th Pennsylvania, and with the 3d Michigan and 37th New York in support. These arrangements had scarcely been made when I was ordered to leave one regiment on picket in the advanced position, and form the other three in column of regiments at a point indicated. While executing this movement some firing took place between the pickets, and whatever loss (see list appended) we suffered occurred at this time. The firing soon stopped. At 2.30 a. m. I was directed to withdraw in the direction of Fairfax Court-House, following the second brigade. We moved in the indicated direction, leaving the 2d Michigan on picket until the brigade was fairly in motion, when it was withdrawn, acting as the rear guard until we struck the main road, where we met and passed General Hooker's division, reaching Fairfax Court-House at an early hour in the morning.

CASUALTIES.

Second Michigan Volunteers.

Killed, Private John B. Miller, company F. Wounded, Corporal A. B. Simpson, company C.

Ninety-ninth Pennsylvania Volunteers.

Killed, Private William H. Anderson, company C. Missing, Private George A. Logan, company F.

RECAPITULATION.

Second Michigan volunteers: Killed, 1; wounded, 1. Ninety-ninth Pennsylvania volunteers: Killed, 1; missing, 1.

Total: Killed, 2; wounded, 1; missing, 1.

I am, sir, very respectfully, your obedient servant,

ORLANDO M. POE,
Colonel 2d Michigan volunteers, (late) Commanding Brigade.

Major HENRY W. BREVOORT,
Assistant Adjutant General, &c.

No. 8.

REPORT OF BRIGADIER GENERAL C. GROVER.

HEADQUARTERS SECOND DIVISION, THIRD CORPS,
September 26, 1862.

SIR: I have the honor herewith to enclose the official reports of the first and third brigades of this division, and to state that the report of the second brigade and of the batteries were forwarded to General Hooker soon after our arrival here, at his request. I have also, at General Hooker's request, forwarded to him copies of the within reports.

I am, sir, very respectfully, your obedient servant,

C. GROVER,
Brigadier General, Commanding Division

The ASSISTANT ADJUTANT GENERAL, *third corps.*

HEAD QUARTERS FIRST BRIGADE HOOKER'S DIVISION.

SIR: I have the honor to report that on the 25th day of August the 1st brigade of Hooker's division left its camp in the vicinity of Alexandria, Virginia, and by rail proceeded to Warrenton Junction, to the left and front of which on the following day it took position.

Early on the following day it moved to Bristow Station, preceded by the 2d and 3d brigades, which soon became hotly engaged with the enemy on the line of the railroad. Under the orders of Major General Hooker, I formed line of battle, throwing out skirmishers to the front and on the right, and advanced; but the enemy, having once broken before the preceding brigades, fell back without making a stand until reaching a high bluff north of Cedar Run, where, in strong position, supported by artillery, he awaited an advance. At this time, about sundown, I received an order to move to the left of the road and take position on the high ground, and to hold with three regiments of my command a position on our front and flank, where a road from Richmond intersected the main road, while the remaining two guarded the approaches to our position on the right. Here we rested on our arms for the night. My command had not been under musketry fire during the day, and had been but little annoyed by the enemy's shells, one man of the 11th Massachusetts volunteers only having been wounded.

On the following day we recontinued our march for the plains of Manassas by the way of Centreville, and arrived upon the battle-field about 9 a. m. The battle had already commenced, and as my column moved to the front the shells fell with remarkable precision along the line of the road, but fortunately did no damage.

My brigade was temporarily placed under the orders of Major General Sigel, whose troops were then engaging the enemy in the centre. Under instructions received from him, I threw forward the 1st Massachusetts volunteers to support his line, while my remaining four regiments were drawn up in two lines, sheltered from the enemy's fire by a roll of the field in front. This position was occupied until about 2.30 p. m.

In the meantime I rode over the field in front as far as the position of the enemy would admit. After rising the hill under which my command lay, an open field was entered, and from one edge of it gradually fell off in a slope to a valley, through which ran a railroad embankment. Beyond this embankment the forest continued, and the corresponding heights beyond were held by the enemy in force, supported by artillery.

At 3 p. m. I received an order to advance in line of battle over this ground, pass the embankment, enter the edge of the woods beyond and hold it. Dispositions for carrying out such orders were immediately made; pieces were loaded, bayonets fixed, and instructions given for the line to move slowly upon the enemy until it felt his fire, then close upon him rapidly, fire one well directed volley, and rely upon the bayonet to secure the position on the other side.

We rapidly and firmly pressed upon the embankment, and here occurred a short, sharp, and obstinate hand to hand conflict with bayonets and clubbed muskets. Many of the enemy were bayonetted in their tracks, others struck down with the butts of pieces, and onward pressed our line. In a few yards more it met a terrible fire from a second line, which, in its turn, broke. The enemy's third line now bore down upon our thinned ranks in close order, and swept back the right centre and a portion of our left. With the gallant 16th Massachusetts on our left, I tried to turn his flank, but the breaking of our right and centre and the weight of the enemy's lines caused the necessity of falling back, first to the embankment, and then to our first position, behind which we rallied to our colors.

In this fierce encounter, of not more than twenty minutes' duration, our loss was as follows:

	Killed.	Wounded.	Missing.	Total
First Massachusetts volunteers	5	66	7	78
Second New Hampshire volunteers	16	87	30	133
Eleventh Massachusetts volunteers	10	77	25	112
Sixteenth Massachusetts volunteers	4	64	42	110
Twenty-sixth Pennsylvania volunteers	6	33	14	53
	41	326	116	484

Though forced to retire from the field by the immensely superior numbers of the enemy, supported by artillery, and by the natural strength of his position, men never fought more gallantly or efficiently.

I must make special mention of my personal observation of the 2d New Hampshire, and 11th and 16th Massachusetts regiments, that, under every trial, have won new distinctions. The well-known first Massachusetts, though not under my personal observation, was, as usual, in the van. The 26th Pennsylvania, which supported the left, did not have that opportunity of showing its metal that I could have desired, owing to the nature of the ground.

Striking examples of personal gallantry were unusually numerous. The gallant Lieutenant Colonel Tileston, of the 11th Massachusetts; Captains Littlefield, of the 2d New Hampshire, and Stone, of the 11th; Lieutenant Roberts, of the 1st Massachusetts; Lieutenants Rogers and Moore, of the 2d New Hampshire; Lieutenant Porter, of the 11th, and Lieutenant Banks, of the 16th, were either killed upon the field or died from the effects of wounds soon after the battle.

Among those that in the short duration of the engagement I especially noticed were Captains McDonald, of the 11th; O'Hara, of the 16th, (wounded;) Lieutenant Merriam and Lieutenant Banks, (killed.) I had not the opportunity to observe but few cases of signal daring; but, with few exceptions, all officers and men there engaged can look back with just pride to their conduct on that day.

After the battle we bivouacked on the field about a mile to the rear. At about 6 p. m. on the 30th, under orders from the major general commanding the division, my command retired from the field and marched to Centreville, where it encamped at about 11 p. m. Since the latter date it has been engaged in no operations worthy of note.

In closing, I must acknowledge my great indebtedness to my staff officers, Captain Hibbert, A. A. G.; Captain Perkins, A. Q. M.; Captain Corvie, C. S.; Lieutenants Hubbard and Brown, aides-de-camp, for meritorious and efficient services in their especial lines of duty during the period embraced in this report.

Very respectfully, your obedient servant,

C. GROVER,
Brigadier General, Commanding First brigade.

Captain JOSEPH DICKINSON,
Assistant Adjutant General Hooker's Division.

REPORT OF MAJOR GENERAL P. KEARNEY (BY GENERAL BIRNEY.)

HEADQUARTERS FIRST DIVISION, THIRD CORPS, A. P.,
Fort Lyon, September 4, 1862.

Respectfully forwarded as the official report drawn up by the late Major General Philip Kearney and intended to have been signed by him the day of his death.

D. B. BIRNEY,
Brigadier General, Commanding Division.

No. 9.

REPORT OF MAJOR GENERAL P. KEARNEY, (BY GENERAL BIRNEY.)

HEADQUARTERS 1ST DIVISION, 3D CORPS, ARMY OF THE POTOMAC,
Centreville, Va., August 31, 1862.

COLONEL: I report the part taken by my division in the battles of the two previous days. On the 29th, on my arrival, I was assigned to the holding of the right wing, my left on Leesburg road. I posted Colonel Poe, with Berry's brigade, in first line; General Robinson, 1st brigade, on his right, partly in line and partly in support, and kept Birney's most disciplined regiments reserved and ready for emergencies. Towards noon I was obliged to occupy a quarter of a mile additional on left of said road, from Schurz's troops being taken elsewhere.

During the first hours of combat General Birney, on tired regiments in the centre falling back, of his own accord rapidly pushed across to give them a hand to raise themselves to a renewed fight.

In early afternoon General Pope's order to General Roberts was, to send a pretty strong force diagonally to the front to relieve the centre in woods from pressure. Accordingly, I detached on that purpose General Robinson, with his brigade, the 63d Pennsylvania volunteers, Colonel Hays, the 105th Pennsylvania volunteers, Captain Craig, the 20th Indiana, Colonel Brown, and additionally, the 3d Michigan marksmen, under Colonel Champlin. General Robinson drove forward for several hundred yards, but the centre of the main battle being shortly after driven back and out of the woods, my detachment, thus exposed so considerably in front of all others, both flanks in air, was obliged to cease to advance, and confine themselves to holding their own. At 5 o'clock, thinking—though at the risk of exposing my fighting line to being enfiladed—that I might drive the enemy by an unexpected attack, through the woods, I brought up additionally the most of Birney's regiments, the 4th Maine, Colonel Walker and Lieutenant Colonel Carver, the 40th New York, Colonel Egan, 1st New York,

Major Burt, and 101st New York, Lieutenant Colonel Gesner, and changed front to the left, to sweep, with a rush, the first line of the enemy. This was most successful. The enemy rolled up on his own right. It presaged a victory for us all. Still, our force was too light. The enemy brought up rapidly heavy reserves, so that our further progress was impeded. General Stevens came up gallantly in action to support us, but did not have the numbers.

On the morning of the 30th, General Ricketts, with two brigades, relieved me of my extra charge of the left of the road, and I again concentrated my command. We took no part in the fighting of the morning, although we lost men by an enfilading fire of the enemy's batteries. A sudden and unaccountable evacuation of the field, by the left and centre, occurring about 5 p. m., on orders from General Pope, I massed my troops at the indicated point, but soon reoccupied with Birney's brigade, supported by Robinson's, a very advanced block of woods. The key point of this new line rested on the Brown House towards creek. This was held by regiments of other brigades. Soon, however, themselves attacked, they ceded ground and retired without warning us. I maintained my position until 10 p. m., when, in connexion with General Reno and General Gibbon—assigned to the rear guard—I retired my brigades.

My command arrived at Centreville, in good order, at 2 a. m. this morning, and encamped in front of the Centreville forts. My loss in killed and wounded is over 750, about one in three; in some regiments engaged a great deal severer; in the 3d Michigan, 140 out of 260; none taken prisoners, except my engineer officer, who returned to the house supposed to be held by the troops alluded to.

It makes me proud to dwell on the renewed efforts of my generals of brigade, Birney and Robinson. My regiments all did well, and the remiss in camp seemed as brightest in the field. Besides my old tried regiments, who have been previously noted in former actions, and maintained their prestige, I have to mark the 101st New York volunteers and 57th Pennsylvania volunteers, as equalling all that their comrades have done before. Their commanders, Lieutenant Colonel Gesner, of the 101st New York volunteers, and Major Birney, with the 57th Pennsylvania volunteers, have imparted to them the stamp of their own high character. The 63d Pennsylvania, and 40th New York volunteers, under the brave Colonel Egan, suffered the most. The gallant Hays is badly wounded.

The loss of officers has been great; that of Colonel Brown can hardly be replaced. Brave, skillful, a disciplinarian, full of energy, and a charming gentleman, his 20th Indiana must miss him. The country loses, in him, one who promised to fill worthily high trust.

The 3d Michigan, ever faithful to their name, under Colonel Champlin and Major Pierce, lose 140 out of 260 combatants.

Colonel Champlin is again disabled. The staunch 4th Maine, under Walker, true men of a rare type, drove on through the stream of battle irresistibly. The 105th Pennsylvania volunteers was not wanting. They are Pennsylvania's mountain men. Again have they been fearfully decimated. The desperate charge of these regiments sustain the past history of this division.

The lists of killed and wounded, and reports of brigades and regiments, will be shortly furnished.

Randolph's battery of light twelves was worked with boldness and address. Though narrowly watched by three long-reaching enfilading batteries of the enemy, it constantly silenced one of theirs in its front, and shelled and richochetted its shot into the re-enforcements moving from the enemy's heights down into the woods. On the 27th, with two sections and Robinson's 1st brigade, Captain Randolph had powerfully contributed to General Hooker's success at Bristow Station.

Captain Graham, 1st United States artillery, put at General Sigel's disposition, as repeatedly drove the enemy back into the woods as the giving way of that infantry left the front unobstructed. His practice was beautifully correct, and proved irresistible. On the 31st, Captain Graham, not being required on the right, was sent to the extreme left, and rendered important service with General Reno, firing until late in the night.

Lieutenant * * * *, a German officer of distinction, put at my disposal by General Sigel, with two long range Parrotts, covered our right flank and drove off an enemy's battery and regiments. I name these gentlemen as ornaments to their branch of the service.

I must refer to General Hooker to render justice to the part taken by my 1st brigade under General Robinson, and Randolph's battery, in the affair of the 27th, at Bristow Station.

Again am I called on to name the efficiency of my staff. Captain Mindil, often cited, brave and intelligent, was the only military aide present to assist me; but Doctor Pancoast, division surgeon general, not only insured the promptness of his department, but with heroism and aptitude carried for me my orders.

Very respectfully, your obedient servant.

Commanding 1st Division.

Col. GEO. D. RUGGLES,
Chief of Staff to Major General John Pope.

No. 10.

REPORT OF GENERAL FRANZ SIGEL.

HEADQUARTERS FIRST CORPS, ARMY OF VIRGINIA,
Near Fort De Kalb, Virginia, September 16, 1862.

COLONEL: I have the honor to submit the following reports:

I. *Operations previous to the battles of the 29th and 30th August.*

After the battle of Cedar Mountain, the retreat of the first corps from the Rapidan behind the Rappahannock, and the several engagements of that corps near Rappahannock Station, Freeman's Ford, and Sulphur Springs, we advanced to Waterloo bridge on the same day. We had taken possession of Sulphur Springs on the 24th August. The brigade of General Milroy occupied a position on the north side of the bridge, extending his line of sharpshooters along the shore of the river. The main body of the corps was encamped between the bridge and Sulphur Springs, and behind it the corps of Major General Banks and General Reno's division.

The enemy had advanced from Rappahannock Station along the south side of the river, in a line parallel with the route taken by our troops, and was trying to cross at the above-named ford, (Freeman's,) and the bridges at Sulphur Springs and Waterloo. On the night of the 24th of August his camp fires extended from Waterloo bridge to Jefferson village, a distance of four or five miles—his main force of about 30,000 men occupying the latter point.

Early on the morning of the 25th a sharp skirmish commenced at the (Waterloo) bridge, which was reported to me by General Pope to have been destroyed by General Buford, but which we found on our arrival in good order and strongly defended by the enemy. While we were taking position on the north side the enemy began to break up his camp at Jefferson and to mass his troops on the south side of the bridge. By noon 28 regiments of infantry, 6 batteries, and several regiments of cavalry of the enemy had arrived and taken their position. I had, the night before, given notice of the enemy's strength and movements to Major General Pope, and now again informed him of the position of affairs; as the disposition he had made of our forces was evidently based on the supposition that the enemy would force the passage of the river between Bealeton and Waterloo Bridge. In the mean time I had been directed to march to Fayetteville, and form part of the centre of the army to be arrayed in a line extending from Waterloo Bridge to Bealeton Station.

In accordance with this order, General Milroy should have been relieved in the morning by a brigade of General McDowell; another brigade of the 3d corps (McDowell's) had to march to Sulphur Springs. In the forenoon of the same day General Roberts, of Major General Pope's staff, delivered to me a verbal order to hold my position at Waterloo Bridge under all circumstances, and to meet the enemy if he should try to force the passage of the river, and that General McDowell would be on my right, with the cavalry brigade of General Buford, and General Banks on my left.*

Soon afterwards I received intelligence that a large force of the enemy's cavalry had crossed on my right and was moving towards Orleans, and that another force had crossed on my left, at Sulphur Springs, and taken possession of that place. I immediately ordered General Beardsley, with the 9th New York cavalry and four mountain howitzers, to Sulphur Springs, to shell the enemy out of the place, which he did. The rest of my cavalry, consisting of three companies of the 1st Virginia and two of the 1st Maryland, I ordered towards Orleans, for the purpose of protecting my right flank. Meanwhile, cannonading was kept up near the bridge, and from all indications I supposed that the enemy would avail himself of the opportunity to make a combined attack against my position. I therefore sent to the left to find Generals Banks and Reno, and to the right to look after General McDowell's troops, especially the cavalry brigade, and was not a little astonished to learn that Generals Banks and Reno were, by orders of General Pope, on their march to Bealeton, and that no troops could be found on my right except the cavalry brigade of General Buford, which was encamped four miles behind us on the Warrenton road. To confuse† matters still more, I received a despatch from General McDowell, one section of it directed to Major General Banks, asking for news from his corps, and the other directed to myself, informing me that I would join my pontoon train at Fayetteville. I sent this despatch to General Banks, and requested him to furnish me with what information he could, so that, in the absence of instructions, I might be enabled to direct my movements properly. I also sent to Generals Pope and McDowell, at Warrenton, for an explanation and for orders; but General Pope had left for Warrenton Junction, and General McDowell did not furnish me with any instructions.‡

It was now nearly sunset, and my situation exceedingly critical. Threatened on my right and left flank, an army of 30,000 menacing my front, and separated from me only by a shallow river, fordable at many points for infantry as well as cavalry and artillery, no supporting force within eight or ten miles, I supposed that it was not really the intention of the commanding general to leave me in this position. I was corroborated in my opinion by the answer of General Banks, who advised me to march to Fayetteville, and by the fragmentary paper saying that I would find my pontoon train at that point.§ Considering all this, I resolved to march to Fayetteville at night, and made my preparations accordingly, although I did not believe in the correctness of the whole plan.

Just at the moment when my troops were about to move, one of my officers returned with an order of General Pope, directing me to march to Warrenton

*General Buford's whole cavalry force was on Sigel's right, picketing the river for several miles above.

†The confusion was entirely in General Sigel's own mind.

‡Sigel at this time was not under McDowell's orders at all.

§Entirely unfounded. General Sigel's opinion, formed in ignorance of our condition, is, perhaps, not valuable, and certainly out of place in this report.

and to encamp there. I put my troops in motion in compliance with this order, and cautiously withdrew from Waterloo Bridge, as I had not a single company of cavalry to cover my retreat.* Before withdrawing, however, I ordered the destruction of the bridge, which was accomplished under the direction of General Milroy, after much exertion and some loss of life.

At two o'clock next morning, (August 26,) as I was entering Warrenton with my rear guard, I received another order from General Pope, through General McDowell, directing me to "force the passage of the Waterloo Bridge at daylight." As this was a matter of impossibility, the troops having marched the whole night on a very inconvenient road, I reported Major General Pope this fact, and received orders to stay at Warrenton.

During the day I ascertained that the enemy was marching by Thoroughfare Gap to Manassas, and on the following night that his main army was encamped at White Plains, the advance guard east of Thoroughfare Gap, and the rear at Orleans.† This news was brought in by all the scouts sent out by me, with some cavalry, to Sperryville, Salem, and Gainesville, and was immediately communicated by telegraph to Major General Pope. It was also reported to me that the enemy was moving during the night, (Tuesday;) that Jackson would be in Manassas next day, (Wednesday;) and that Longstreet had not yet joined him, but was two miles from Salem at noon on Wednesday, the 27th.

In view of these facts, I proposed to General McDowell, to whose command the first corps had been attached since its arrival at Waterloo Bridge, to concentrate our forces at Gainesville, and thereby separate Longstreet's troops from those of Jackson, taking the enemy at Manassas in the rear, and by forcing him to evacuate Manassas effect a junction with the army of General McClellan.‡ This movement was executed.

On the morning of the 27th the first corps left Warrenton for Buckland Bridge on the road to Gainesville, with directions to take possession of the bridge, and thereby open the road to Gainesville. The brigade of Brigadier General Milroy advanced rapidly towards the bridge, and drove the enemy, who was stationed there with some cavalry and artillery, back towards Gainesville, while the pioneers repaired the bridge, which had been set on fire and partially destroyed by the enemy. In a short time the whole of General Milroy's brigade had passed the river and pressed forward against Gainesville, making on their way about one hundred and fifty prisoners. I now ordered General Schurz to pass the river and follow General Milroy, and to take position behind him. The division of General Schenck also crossed the river, and the infantry brigade of General Steinwehr remained in reserve at the bridge. Such was the position of the first corps on the evening of the 27th.

During the night General McDowell's corps arrived at Buckland Mills, and I received orders, at three o'clock in the morning, to march to Manassas and to take a position, with my right resting on the railroad leading from Warrenton Junction to Manassas Junction; so, at least, I understood the order.§

On this march our cavalry, sent out to the left in the direction of Groveton, was shelled by the enemy, about one and a half mile distant from the road on which we marched; and, besides this, an artillery engagement began between the corps of General McDowell and the enemy. I immediately halted, ordered the whole corps to countermarch, and formed in order of battle on the heights

*Where were Sigel's and Buford's cavalry?

†General Sigel has just before stated the extreme peril of his command at midnight on the 25th from the main force of the enemy at Waterloo Bridge. How could they have been at White Plains so soon?

‡General Pope never heard of such a proposition, and General McDowell says in his report General Sigel never made it.

§No such order given. See the orders in McDowell's report, and General Pope's.

parallel with the Centreville-Gainesville road. The enemy's infantry and cavalry pickets were about three hundred yards from our line, and our skirmishers had already advanced against them, when, on a report made to General McDowell, I received orders to march forthwith to Manassas Junction. I reluctantly obeyed this order, marched off from the right, and was within two and a half miles from Manassas when our cavalry reported that Manassas was evacuated by the enemy, and that General Kearney was in possession of that point. As I was sure that the enemy must be somewhere between Centerville and Gainesville, I asked permission to march to New Market, whereupon I was directed to march to Centerville.* This order was in execution, and the troops prepared to cross the fords of Bull Run, when our advance met the enemy on the road leading from New Market to Groveton and Sudley's Ford, this side of Bull Run; about the same time I received a report from General Pope that the enemy was concentrating at Centreville. Supposing that this was correct, I directed the brigades of General Milroy and Colonel McLean to advance against the enemy this side of Bull Run, on the road to Sudley Springs, and left General Stahel's brigade and General Schurz's division near the fords, the latter division facing towards Centreville.

As soon, however, as I had ascertained that Centreville was evacuated by the enemy, I followed with these troops to assist Brigadier General Milroy and Colonel McLean, who, under the direction of Brigadier General Schenck, were briskly engaged with the left of the enemy's forces, whose right had engaged a brigade of the third corps. Our artillery advanced steadily until the darkness of night interrupted their movements; they encamped for the night near Mrs. Henry's farm, one regiment having taken position on the Centreville-Gainesville turnpike, the main force fronting towards Sudley Springs and Groveton.

II.—*Battle of Groveton, near Bull Run, on Friday, August* 29 1862.

On Thursday night, August 28, when the first corps was encamped on the heights south of Young's branch, near Bull Run, I received orders from General Pope to "attack the enemy vigorously" the next morning. I accordingly made the necessary preparations at night and formed in order of battle at daybreak, having ascertained that the enemy was in considerable force beyond Young's branch, in sight of the hills we occupied. His left wing rested on Catharpin creek, front towards Centreville; with his centre he occupied a long stretch of woods parallel with the Sudley Springs (New Market) road; and his right was posted on the hills on both sides of the Centreville-Gainesville road. I therefore directed General Schurz to deploy his division on the right of the Gainesville road, and by a change of direction to the left to come into position parallel with the Sudley Springs road. General Milroy, with his brigade and one battery, was directed to form the centre, and to take possession of an elevation in front of the so-called "stone house," at the junction of the Gainesville and Sudley Spring roads. General Schenck, with his division forming our left, was ordered to advance quickly to an adjoining range of hills, and to plant his batteries on these hills—at an excellent range from the enemy's position.

In this order our whole line advanced from point to point, taking advantage of the ground before us, until our whole line was involved in a most vehement artillery and infantry contest. In the course of about four hours, from half-past six to half-past ten o'clock in the morning, our whole infantry force and nearly all our batteries were engaged with the enemy, Generals Milroy and Schurz advancing one mile, and General Schenck two miles, from their original positions. At this time (10.30 o'clock) the enemy threw forward large masses of infantry

*Altogether incorrect. See reports of Generals Pope, McDowell, Reynolds, and Sigel's own despatches to General Pope.

against our right, but was resisted firmly and driven back three times by the troops of Generals Milroy and Schurz. To assist these troops, so hard pressed by overpowering numbers, exhausted by fatigue, and weakened by losses, I ordered one battery of reserve to take position on their left, and posted two pieces of artillery, under Lieutenant Blum, of Schirmer's battery, supported by the 41st New York volunteer infantry, beyond their line, and opposite the right flank of the enemy, who was advancing in the woods. These pieces opened fire with canister most effectively, and checked the enemy's advance on that point. I now directed General Schenck to draw his lines nearer to us, and to attack the enemy's right flank and rear by a change of front to the right, thereby assisting our troops in the centre. This movement could not be executed by General Schenck with his whole division, as he became briskly engaged with the enemy, who tried to turn our extreme left.

At this critical moment, when the enemy had almost outflanked us on both wings, and was preparing a new attack against our centre, Major General Kearney arrived on the field of battle, and deployed by the Sudley Springs road on our right, while General Reno's troops came to our support by the Gainesville turnpike. With the consent of General Reno, I directed two regiments and one battery, under Brigadier General Stevens, to take position on the right of General Schenck—the battery on an eminence in front and centre of our line, where it did excellent work during the rest of the day, and where it relieved Captain Dilger's battery, which had held this position the whole morning. Three regiments were posted between General Milroy and General Schenck, and two others, with two mountain howitzers, were sent to the assistance of General Schurz. Scarcely were these troops in position when the contest began with renewed vigor and vehemence, the enemy attacking furiously along our whole line, from the extreme right to the extreme left. The infantry brigade of General Steinwehr, commanded by Colonel Koltes, was then sent forward to the assistance of Generals Schenck and Schurz, and one regiment was detailed for the protection of a battery posted in reserve near our centre. The troops of Brigadier General Reynolds had meanwhile (12 o'clock) taken position on our left. In order to defend our right, I sent a letter to General Kearney, saying that Longstreet was not able to bring his troops in line of battle that day, and requesting him (Kearney) to change his front to the left, and to advance, if possible, against the enemy's left flank. To assist him in this movement, I ordered two long-range rifled guns to report to him, as his own battery had remained in reserve behind his lines.

At two o'clock in the afternoon General Hooker's troops arrived on the field of battle, and were immediately ordered forward by their noble commander to participate in the battle.* One brigade, under Colonel Carr, received orders, by my request, to relieve the regiments of General Schurz's division, which had maintained their ground against repeated attacks, but were now worn out, and nearly without ammunition. Other regiments were sent forward to relieve Brigadier General Milroy, whose brigade had valiantly disputed the ground against greatly superior numbers for eight hours.

To check the enemy if he should attempt to advance, or for the purpose of preparing and supporting an attack from our side, I placed four batteries, of different commands, on a range of hills on our centre, and behind the woods, which had been the most hotly contested part of the battle-field during the day.

I had previously received a letter from Major General Pope, saying that Fitz John Porter's corps and Brigadier General King's division, numbering 20,000 men, would come in on our left. I did, therefore, not think it prudent to give the enemy time to make new arrangements, and ordered all the batteries to con-

*Hooker arrived at same time with Kearney, early in the day.—(See Heintzelman's report.)

tinue their fire, and to direct it principally against the enemy's position in the woods before our front. Some of our troops placed in front were retiring from the woods, but as the enemy, held in check by the artillery in the centre, did not venture to follow, and as at this moment new regiments of General Hooker's command arrived and were ordered forward, we maintained our position, which Generals Milroy and Schurz had occupied in the morning.

During two hours, from four to six o'clock p. m., strong cannonading and musketry continued on our centre and right, where General Kearney made a successful effort against the extreme left of the enemy's lines.

At a quarter past six o'clock Brigadier General King's division, of Major General McDowell's corps, arrived behind our front, and advanced on the Gainesville turnpike. I do not know the real result of this movement, but from the weakness of the enemy's cannonade, and the gradually decreasing musketry in the direction of General Kearney's attack, I received the impression that the enemy's resistance was broken, and that victory was on our side; and so it was. We had won the field of battle, and our army rested near the dead and wounded who had so gloriously defended the good cause of this country.

III.—*Battle of the 30th of August.*

On Saturday, the 30th of August, I was informed by Major General Pope that it was his intention to "break the enemy's left," and that I, with the first corps, should hold the centre, Major General Reno should take position on my right, and General Reynolds on my left.

The first corps took position behind Groveton, on the right of the Gainesville turnpike. My request to have two batteries in reserve behind the centre for certain emergencies—one of General Reno's and one of General Reynolds's division—was not complied with, although all my batteries were more or less worked down, several pieces unserviceable and short of ammunition, and many horses killed or disabled.* After having taken position as ordered, the corps of Major General Porter passed between the enemy and our lines, and was forming in line of battle on the open field before the first corps and that of General Reno, masking thereby our whole front. Not understanding the object of this movement, and being requested by one of the staff officers of General Porter to give my opinion in regard to the ground before us, I immediately rode over to the general (Porter) and suggested that, in accordance with the general plan, his troops should pass more to the right, join those of General Kearney on our extreme right, and direct his attack against the enemy's left flank and rear. I also informed him that there were too many troops massed in the centre, and that General Reno and myself would take care of the woods in his front.

Whilst this was going on I received repeated reports that the enemy was shifting his troops from the Gainesville turnpike to his right. I therefore ordered the 4th New York cavalry, under Lieutenant Colonel Nazer, to advance in that direction between New Market and Groveton, passing behind our left, and to scout the country as far as they could go. I also sent one regiment of General Schenck's division to the left of our position, as an outpost to observe the enemy's movements. After the lapse of about an hour I received notice that the cavalry pickets had found the enemy, and that the latter was moving against our left. I sent the messenger that brought this intelligence to General Pope's headquarters. Shortly afterwards I received an order by Colonel Ruggles, chief of staff of General Pope, to occupy the "Bald-headed hill" on my left with one brigade, which I did immediately. Meanwhile General Porter's

*General Sigel had several more batteries than any other corps, and some of them, reported to be without ammunition, I knew had been well supplied. The batteries of other corps were absolutely needed by them.

troops, who had not changed their position, advanced into the woods where we had lost a thousand men the day before. About this time on our left, where General Reynolds was posted, the musketry and cannonading began to increase. The troops of General Porter had wholly disappeared in the woods, which led me to believe that the enemy had left his position in front, and that it was the intention of General Pope to advance the first corps on the Gainesville turnpike. Suddenly heavy discharges began in front, the corps of General Porter having met the enemy who was advantageously posted behind a well-adapted breastwork—the old Manassas Gap railroad track. At the same time the enemy opened with shell and solid shot against our centre and left wing. Our batteries replied promptly and spiritedly; and from the general appearance of the battle it was evident that we had the whole army of the enemy before us.

It was now about 5 p. m., when, awaiting the further development of the battle, I received a despatch, through General McDowell, and written by General Porter, expressing his doubt as to the final result of his attack, and requesting General McDowell to "push Sigel forward." Although I had not received positive orders from General Pope, I immediotely made the necessary preparations, either to assist General Porter or to resist an attack of the enemy, should he repel General Porter and advance against my own position in the centre, by directing General Stahel to deploy his brigade in front and General Schurz to form his regiments in a line of reserve. During the execution of these movements, General Porter's troops came out of the woods in pretty good order, bringing a great number of wounded with them. In answer to my question why they were retiring after so short a time, they said that "they were out of ammunition." Expecting that the enemy would follow up this retrograde movement of a whole corps with a strong force, I kept my troops well together to meet such an event.

Thus we stood, when, suddenly, incessant volleys of musketry betrayed the enemy in great force on our left, and showed clearly his real plan of attack. To assist Colonel McLean's brigade on our left, I directed General Milroy to join his brigade with that of Colonel McLean. In executing this order, however, General Milroy directed his brigade more to the rear and left than was intended by me, so that by this disposition an interval of several hundred paces was left between these two brigades by which the enemy penetrated, attacking Colonel McLean's troops in the rear, and compelling them to change their front to the left. They thereby partially evacuated the position they had occupied on the hill. It was at this moment that General Schenck was severely wounded at the head of his troops, whom he had repeatedly led forward against the overwhelming masses of the enemy.

When this was the condition of affairs on our left, General Reynolds, who, at the beginning of the battle, had deployed his troops in front and to the left of Colonel McLean's brigade, changed his position, and withdrew his battery from a hill to the left of the Gainesville turnpike near Groveton. The enemy immediately took possession of the hill, posted a battery there, and spread his infantry out over the high and wooded ground before Colonel McLean's brigade, and on the flank and almost in rear of our centre. To dislodge the enemy from his new-gained position, I ordered forward three regiments of infantry under Colonel Koltes, who, under a terrible artillery and infantry fire, boldly advanced against the hills, but could not regain the lost ground.

In this attack I have to regret the loss of the intrepid Colonel Koltes, who was killed while executing the movement ordered. His brigade, though nearly decimated, succeeded in protecting our centre and preventing the turning of our flank.

It was now evident that, to avoid the destruction of our troops from the sweep of the enemy's batteries, and as the main attack was now on our left, I ordered General Schurz to withdraw his division from the low ground, under cover of our artillery, and take position on the hills near the stone house, one brigade to face towards the left. The brigade of General Stahel followed this movement, and formed in line of battle on our right. Immediately in front of this position, on a hill to the right (north) of the stone house, I placed a battery of the 4th regulars, which I had met on the turnpike. This battery behaved nobly, and maintained its position until the last hour. Captain Dilger's battery occupied a more advanced position near Groveton, Captain Dickman's was on our left, and Captain Schirmer's on our right, with General Stahel's brigade.

General Milroy, with his brigade, and the assistance of several additional regiments which he had brought forward, succeeded in repulsing the enemy on the left. In this gallant exploit his horse was shot under him. We maintained our second position until night had closed in upon us, when General Pope ordered a general retreat.

Following the troops of Generals Porter and McDowell, my corps crossed Young's Branch, where it remained for two hours, until the commands of Generals McDowell, Reno, and Kearney had crossed Bull Run by the ford near the stone bridge, and the whole train had passed over the bridge. It was now between 9 and 10 p. m. I then marched to the turnpike, crossed the bridge over Bull Run, and took position on the left and right of the bridge, throwing my pickets out on the other (south) side of the creek towards the battle-field. Soon afterwards an officer of General McDowell's staff directed me to fall back, as the enemy was threatening the line of retreat. It was now after midnight, when I ordered my command to continue its march towards Centreville, first destroying the bridge across Bull Run. Our rear guard was composed of part of General Schurz's division, two pieces of Captain Dilger's battery, and a detachment of Colonel Kane's Bucktail rifles, which had come up with several guns collected on their march of retreat.

I reached Centreville at daybreak on the 31st of August, my command encamping in front of, and occupying the intrenchments of, that place.

Our losses during the two days' battle, in killed, wounded, and missing, according to the official lists sent in, are 92 officers and 1,891 non-commissioned officers and privates.

To be just to the officers and soldiers under my command, I must say that they performed their duties, during the different movements and engagements of the whole campaign, with the greatest promptness, energy, and fortitude. Commanders of divisions and brigades, of regiments and batteries, and the commanders of our small cavalry force, have assisted me, under all circumstances, cheerfully and to the utmost of their ability; and so have the commanders of the two batteries of Major General Banks's corps, (Captain Romer's and Captain Hampton's,) under Major Keefer, attached to me since our arrival at Freeman's Ford.

It also affords me pleasure to mention the faithful services of the members of my staff, and of such officers as were detailed to me for special duty. To them, as well as to the officers and members of my escort, the pioneer companies, and to my scouts, I hereby express my high regard and warmest gratitude.

I have the honor to be, very respectfully, your obedient servant,

F. SIGEL,
Major General Commanding Corps.

Lieutenant Colonel CHAUNCEY MCKEEVER,
Assistant Adjutant General Defences South of the Potomac.

HEADQUARTERS ELEVENTH CORPS, ARMY OF THE POTOMAC,
Near Fort De Kalb, September 23, 1862.

COLONEL: I have the honor to submit the following report of the names of officers of this command killed, wounded, and missing in the late actions on the Rappahannock, and the battles of August 29 and 30.

	Names.	Rank.	Remarks.
FIRST DIVISION.			
First Brigade.			
8th N. York vol. inf	Wilhelm Welker	1st lieutenant	Wounded.
	William Wolf	do	Do.
45th N. York vol. inf	Jos. Spangeburg	Captain	Do.
41st N. York vol. inf	Richard Kurz	2d lieutenant	Killed.
	Otto Sibeth	Captain	Wounded.
	Charles Voelcker	do	Do.
	Charles Bang	2d lieutenant	Do.
Second Brigade.			
75th Ohio vol. inf	W. J. Ranuels	2d lieutenant	Captured at Bull Run.
73d Ohio vol. inf	Charles W. Trimble	do	Killed.
	J. C. McKell	do	Wounded.
	D. L. Greimer	do	Do.
	Samuel Fellers	1st lieutenant	Wounded and captured; since paroled.
	John T. Martin	do	Wounded and captured; since paroled.
	E. H. Miller	2d lieutenant	Wounded.
	L. H. Burkett	Captain	Mort'ly wounded; since died.
	Joshua Davis	2d lieutenant	Missing.
55th Ohio vol. inf	Daniel S. Brown	Captain	Wounded.
	Robert Bromly	1st lieutenant	Wounded, & a prisoner.
25th Ohio vol. inf	John D. Merriman	do	Wounded.
Bat. K, 1st Ohio vol. art.	H. S. Camp	do	Mort'ly wounded; since died.
THIRD DIVISION.			
First Brigade.			
	Henry Bohlen	Brig. general	Killed in action at Freeman's Ford, Aug. 22.
61st Ohio vol. inf	Henry Riff	Lieutenant	Wounded.
	James Armstrong	do	Do.
73d Pa. vol. inf	John A. Koltes	Colonel	Killed.
	Aug. Brenkner	Acting major	Do.
	Charles A. Kraft	Captain	Wounded.
	Louis Walter	do	Do.
74th Pa. vol. inf	Charles Bollstetter	do	Do.
	Gollich Hoberg	1st lieutenant	Do.
	Ferd. Heck	2d lieutenant	Do.
	Louis Fisher	do	Missing.
29th N. Y. vol. inf	Clements Loest	Colonel	Wounded.
	Charles Newhaus	Surgeon	Do.
	Fried. Zedlitz	1st lieutenant	Died at Washington.
	Fried. V. Sehleumbach	do	Missing.
	Dietrich Wulfert	2d lieutenant	Wounded.
	Albert V. Rosenburg	do	Do.
	O. V. Salin	do	Missing.
Second Brigade.			
75th Pa. vol. inf	Wm. Frolich	1st lieutenant	Killed.
	R. Theune	do	Wounded.
	Fr. Fromhagen	do	Do.

Names of officers killed, wounded, and missing, &c.—Continued.

	Names.	Rank.	Remarks.
75th Pa. vol. inf	— Schwartz	Captain	Wounded.
	Wm. Bowen	2d lieutenant	Killed.
	Richard Ledig	do	Wounded.
54th N. Y. vol. inf	E. Haberkorn	do	Killed.
	A. Beer	do	Do.
	— Wernuck	Captain	Wounded.
	— Kempe	do	Do.
	— Steinhardt	do	Do.
	Henry Brandt	Adjutant	Do.
	— Blau	1st lieutenant	Do.
	— Schirah	do	Do.
	G. Hinch	do	Do.
	— Ernemrien	Captain	Do.
58th N. Y. vol. inf	Wm. Henkel	Major	Do.
	Max Schmidt	1st lieutenant	Do.
68th N. Y. vol. inf	J. H. Kleefish	Lieut. colonel	Do.
	Ernst Donner	Captain	Do.
	John A. Koberlein	do	Do.
	Franz Buhler	do	Do.
	George G. Dalwigk	do	Do.
	Carl V. Tredell	do	Do.
	Max Amelunken	1st lieutenant	Do.
	Arnold Kummer	do	Do.
	A. Schamberg	2d lieutenant	Do.
	Aug. Von Lindstron	do	Killed.
Infantry Brigade.			
Staff	Zebulon Baird	Captain	Taken prisoner.
2d Virginia vol. inf	H. B. James	1st lieutenant	Killed.
	D. A. Jennings	2d lieutenant	Wounded.
	Thomas E. Day	do	Do.
	James Black	do	Taken prisoner.
3d Virginia vol. inf	David Gibson	Captain	Killed.
	John E. Day	1st lieutenant	Wounded; since died.
	Asa Coplin	do	Do.
	R. E. Fleming	2d lieutenant	Do.
	B. F. Lydick	do	Do.
	F. W. Thompson	Lieut. colonel	Do.
5th Virginia vol. inf	William Schilling	1st lieutenant	Do.
8th Virginia vol. inf	J. E. Curtiss	Captain	Killed.
82d Ohio vol. inf	James Cantwell	Colonel	Do.
Cavalry Brigade.			
4th N. York cavalry	James Moore	Lieutenant	Do.
	Thos. H. Phillipson	do	Wounded.
9th N. York cavalry	George C. Wooley	do	Taken prisoner.
Artillery Reserve.			
Buell's battalion	Frank Buell	Captain	Killed
			Wounded.
Detach. 1st Ind. cavalry	Harmon Miller	1st lieutenant	Do.

I am, colonel, very respectfully, your obedient servant,

F. SIGEL,
Major General Commanding.

Lieutenant Colonel C. McKEEVER,
Assistant Adjutant General.

No. 10.

LETTER OF GENERAL F. SIGEL, TRANSMITTING SUB-REPORT OF OFFICERS OF HIS COMMAND.

HEADQUARTERS ELEVENTH CORPS, ARMY OF THE POTOMAC,
Near Fort DeKalb, Virginia, September 20, 1862.

Enclosed please find the following reports:

Independent Brigade.—Brigadier General Milroy.

First Division.—First brigade, Brigadier General Stahel; second brigade, Colonel McLean; 55th Ohio volunteer infantry, Colonel Lee; 73d Ohio volunteer infantry, Colonel Smith; Captain DeBeck's battery, Lieutenant Haskin.

Second Division.—Attached to third division.

Third Division.—Second brigade, Colonel Krzyzanowski; commanding officer 54th regiment New York volunteer infantry; commanding officer 58th regiment New York volunteer infantry; commanding officer 29th regiment New York volunteer infantry; commanding officer 61st regiment Ohio volunteer infantry; commanding officer 73d regiment Pennsylvania volunteer infantry; Captain Wiedrich's battery; Captain Dilger's battery, company I, 1st Ohio volunteer artillery.

Cavalry Brigade.—Colonel Beardsley.

Commanding officer 4th New York cavalry, commanding officer 9th New York cavalry, commanding officer 6th Ohio cavalry, commanding officer 1st Maryland cavalry.

The reports of Brigadier General Schurz, commanding third division, and Colonel Schimmelpfennig, commanding first brigade, third division, and several reports of regiments and batteries not received yet, will be forwarded at once.

General Schenck being wounded, no report has yet been received from him.

I am, colonel, very respectfully, your obedient servant,

F. SIGEL,
Major General Commanding Corps.

Lieutenant Colonel C. MCKEEVER,
Assistant Adjutant General Defences South of the Potomac.

No. 11.

REPORT OF R. H. MILROY.

HEADQUARTERS INDEPENDENT BRIGADE,
Near Fort Ethan Allen, Virginia, September 12, 1862.

I have the honor to submit the following report of the movements of my command since the departure from Woodville, Virginia, on August 8, 1862:

At 9 o'clock p. m., my brigade taking the advance of the corps, started in the direction of Culpeper, arriving at the place about 5 next morning. At 5 p. m. of same day received orders to march immediately in direction of Cedar Mountain, from which direction heavy firing had been heard all the afternoon.

I again took the advance. Having marched some three miles, and finding the road blocked up by ambulances and stragglers from the battle-field, I started ahead with my cavalry detachment, (three companies of the 1st Virginia,) leaving my infantry and artillery to make the best of their way toward the front. Arriving about 8 p. m. at the front, and finding everything in confusion, I ordered my cavalry into line, under the protection of the woods nearest the enemy, and advanced alone to reconnoitre. Fifteen minutes had scarcely elapsed, when a battery of the enemy suddenly opened with great precision upon the remnant of General Banks's corps posted on my right. The enemy's fire had been directed by several large fires burning brilliantly among Banks's batteries. The result was a general stampede, artillery, cavalry, and infantry retreating in the greatest disorder. I endeavored to rally them at first without success, but finally succeeded in arresting a battery or two and some cavalry, which I brought back to their old position on the road, at the same time throwing my cavalry across on the same side. Shortly after one of Banks's batteries, having retreated to a safe position, commenced, to the left of the road and behind us, responding to the enemy's guns, the firing ceasing in about fifteen minutes.

Meanwhile, fearing that my brigade, two regiments of which had been thrown across the road to stop the terrified mass in their headlong retreat, might be delayed too long, I despatched one of my aids to hurry it forward—to push before them all of the retreating column possible. They immediately proceeded forward, and after much labor I succeeded in encamping them, near 2 a. m., in the position first selected in the evening. Having posted pickets at a suitable distance on our front, I allowed the men to rest on their arms.

Sunday, 10th.—Still holding position in advance of the corps, I threw forward a line of skirmishers, with a sufficient support, along my whole front. They found the enemy's skirmishers, supported by their whole force, strongly posted in the woods about 2,000 yards in frout of us. Here they skirmished until about noon, the enemy occasionally firing upon them by companies. Whenever this occurred I would send a few shells among them, causing their sudden withdrawal. During the afternoon my skirmishers drove the enemy from the woods, following them some three-fourths of a mile. About 4 p. m. sent out my cavalry to reconnoitre; and, if possible, to allow the ambulances to bring off some of our wounded. In this they were quite successful, bringing off about one hundred. The cavalry had in the meanwhile approached within 300 yards of the enemy's lines without drawing their fire, and having ascertained their position withdrew to our lines.

On the morning of the 11th, it being determined to take the dead and wounded from off the field, I was ordered to advance my brigade and cover the ambulances and working parties. I accordingly sent forward my three companies of cavalry, followed by my infantry. The cavalry, upon arriving at the outskirts of the wood, halted, finding ahead of them a strong cavalry force under the direction of General Bayard.

I then rode forward, followed by several ambulances, which I sent back loaded with wounded. About an hour had thus elapsed, when I was informed a flag of truce had been sent in by the enemy, and at the same time received a request from General Bayard to attend a conference with the rebel General Stuart relative to a cessation of hostilities for the purpose of attending to the dead and wounded of both parties. An armistice until 2 o'clock p. m. was finally agreed upon, but was afterwards, by mutual consent, extended to the evening.

A reconnoissance on the morning of the 12th found the enemy had withdrawn during the night in the direction of the Rapidan river. I followed as rapidly as possible as soon as this was ascertained, but only succeeded in discovering the rear guard of their cavalry in full flight. Having advanced some six miles as far as Crooked creek, and finding it impassable on account of previous heavy rains, encamped my brigade upon its banks and awaited orders.

On the morning of the 13th, finding Crooked creek and Robinson's river fordable for my cavalry and artillery, I crossed my infantry on slight bridges hastily constructed. When about 800 yards south of Robinson's river, I was obliged to halt my brigade, with the exception of cavalry, on the banks of a narrow and deep creek emptying into Robinson's river. The bottom of this creek, where it crossed the road, was composed of mud worn into deep holes, thus rendering it impassable for my artillery. In the course of two hours I had thrown across it a bridge strong enough to sustain my heaviest guns.

A party of my cavalry had in the meantime reconnoitred as far as Rapidan river, some five miles beyond us, reported a small party of the enemy on the opposite shore. Having crossed the bridge, I proceeded about a quarter of a mile to where I was ordered to halt for the day.

About 4 p. m., when I was about to post my pickets for the night, I received orders to fall back on my original position left in the morning. I accordingly withdrew my brigade, with the exception of my cavalry and a section of my battery, which I left in a favorable position.

From the evening of the 13th to the 18th remained in camp on the banks of Crooked creek. Nothing of importance occurred during the interval excepting the capture, on the 16th, of a lieutenant and three privates of the 2d Virginia while on picket by a party of rebel cavalry. At 4 p. m. of the 18th received orders to prepare to fall back as far as Sulphur Springs, the enemy being reported as advancing in great force from Richmond.

I soon had my brigade in readiness, and remained under arms until 4 a. m., when orders were received to move with my brigade in the rear, General Pope's command having required all night to withdraw.

On the 19th we marched all day, passing through Culpeper, and encamping at midnight about four miles north of that place on the Sulphur Springs road.

On the 20th at daylight resumed march toward Sulphur Springs, reaching there at 5 p. m. without any signs of the enemy in our rear.

Started on the morning of the 21st, with brigade in advance of corps, in the direction of Rappahannock station to re-enforce Banks and McDowell, who had thus far prevented the enemy from crossing the river at that point, and found a heavy artillery engagement going on. We arrived about noon, and were ordered to rest near General Pope's headquarters until a position in the field could be assigned me. About 2 p. m. I was ordered to advance toward the river and take position on the right of King's division. After advancing about a half mile, my brigade was divided, yourself, general, taking two regiments along the road, myself moving with the other two through the fields; a small squad of rebel cavalry, who had been watching our movements from the edge of the woods in front of us, fleeing at our approach.

Upon arriving at the edge of the woods I halted my column and allowed the sharpshooters and skirmishers some five minutes in advance. I then started my two regiments, crossed the woods about a quarter of a mile in width, and halted, finding ourselves on the right of the line of skirmishers then engaged, established by General Patrick, of King's division. Remaining here some two hours, the enemy making no demonstration, I fell back to the fields in the rear of the woods to rest for the night. In the meanwhile you, general, had placed my infantry and battery in position near the road on my right. Thus disposed of, we rested until the following morning.

On the morning of the 22d I was early ordered to take the advance in the direction of Freeman's Ford, about one and a half mile in front and to the right of us, where the enemy had massed the night previous and were then holding the ford. When within a quarter of a mile of the ford, in order to reconnoitre and select position, I hurried forward, accompanied by my cavalry, being screened in my approach by a long belt of pines bordering on the river. Arriving at the edge of the pines I halted my cavalry, and, accompanied by my staff, crossed the road and ascended an eminence commanding the ford. Scarcely three minutes had elapsed when the enemy opened upon me from two batteries with grape and shell. I immediately hurried my cavalry across the road to a safe position, and ordered my battery, under Captain Johnson, forward on the double quick. Too much praise cannot be awarded the captain for the promptness and skill exhibited in bringing his battery into position. In less than five minutes after receipt of the order he had his pieces in action amid a perfect shower of shot, shell, and canister from three of the rebel batteries, and in ten minutes after had silenced their heaviest battery. He continued engaging the enemy for about two hours, compelling them to constantly change the position of their guns, when his ammunition having given out, I asked for another battery. Captain De Beck's battery, of McLean's brigade, was sent me, he in turn being relieved by Captain Buell, of the reserve artillery, in about two hours. The enemy ceased firing about three o'clock p. m.

My infantry, which at the commencement of the action I had placed under cover of the woods on either flank of the battery, had suffered but little, some two killed and twelve or thirteen wounded by canister and shell.

About three p. m., wishing to ascertain the cause of the enemy's silence, I determined to cross the river, and accordingly sent for my cavalry, numbering about one hundred and fifty effective men. I then crossed the ford, sending a company of sharpshooters across and deploying them, ordering their advance up the hill occupied in the morning by the enemy's batteries; myself, with my cavalry, in the meanwhile going around by the road. Arriving at the summit of the hill, I discovered the greater part of the enemy's wagon train, accompanied by their rear guard, moving up the river in the direction of Sulphur Springs. Their cavalry, upon discovering us, gave the alarm, hurrying off their teams and stragglers in the greatest confusion. I posted a platoon of cavalry as videttes, at the same time throwing forward twenty of my sharpshooters, who commenced skirmishing with their rear guard. Being merely reconnoitring, and not having sufficient force to pursue their trains, I ordered my two remaining companies of cavalry into line under protection of the hill.

The remainder of the company of sharpshooters I deployed as skirmishers, ordering them to feel their way into the woods on my left. They had scarcely entered the woods when they met the enemy's skirmishers, and, from their number and the length of their line, I inferred that they had a large force to back them. Shortly after they opened a heavy fire to my left and rear beyond the woods I had thrown my skirmishers in, which I afterward learned was the attack of the enemy upon Bohlen's brigade, which had crossed the river below me. It now being sundown, and not being allowed to bring any force across, I returned, my brigade resting for the night without changing position.

At 7 a. m., 23d, received orders to move in the direction of Sulphur Springs, my brigade bringing up the rear of the corps. When a short distance *en route* I was directed to take a road on my left, a rougher but shorter route to the springs, the main body of the corps having continued on the main road. Upon coming into the main road again I found myself in advance of the corps.

When within a mile of the bridge across Great Run I found our cavalry in line of battle behind the woods. Upon inquiring the cause I was informed that the enemy were in force at and across the run, and had fired on them. Upon this information I passed them with my brigade, and finding the rebel guns in position across the creek, I placed my battery in a commanding position on this side and commenced shelling them, at the same time throwing my infantry into the woods, who soon found and opened a brisk fire into the rebel infantry in front of them on our side of the creek, my men being exposed from the commencement to a cross-fire of grape and canister from a masked battery across the creek. But notwithstanding all these odds, we soon forced them across the creek, and to retire for protection behind their guns. The enemy having torn up the bridge, and it now being dark, I encamped my brigade for the night a short distance back from the banks of the creek.

Next morning, 24th, a strong pioneer party having been put to work on the bridge to repair for our artillery to cross, I crossed my infantry upon the sleepers, not waiting for my cavalry or artillery. I deployed a strong skirmishing party and was soon on the track of the enemy, who had fallen back during the night to their main body which had crossed the river by the bridge at Sulphur Springs, my skirmishers advancing as far as the springs. As soon as my infantry appeared on the heights commanding the bridge across Hedgeman river, the enemy, who were in position, opened fire from the opposite shore. I sent back for my battery and returned their fire; the other batteries of the corps soon coming up, a general artillery engagement ensued, which resulted in our driving their gunners away, leaving their pieces very temptingly displayed. Wishing to take advantage of this unexpected opportunity in securing their guns, I had just crossed the bridge with one of my regiments (the 5th Virginia,) following close behind, and when nearly in reach of the prize, found myself in a hornets' nest. As if by magic, the woods and hills became alive with the enemy; the deserted batteries were suddenly manned, and a semicircle of guns nearly a mile around us commenced pouring a steady stream of shell and canister upon the bridge. I called to my regiment, which was then crossing, to retire, which it did in very good order and rapid style. Our batteries immediately responded to their fire, thus drawing their attention away from us. In a moment the air was perfectly alive with shot and shell, and I took advantage of their elevation to join my command.

At this juncture I received orders to take the advance of the corps in the direction of Waterloo bridge, six miles above Warrenton Springs. I got my brigade in motion and arrived at the bridge about 5 p. m. I placed Dickman's battery in position on a commanding eminence on the left of the road and near the bridge, immediately opening fire upon a rebel battery across the river; at the same time throwing my skirmishers down near the bridge, and along the bank, where they were soon engaging the rebel skirmishers. Thus matters stood when darkness partially put an end to the firing, but the enemy opened on us furiously several times during the night with small arms, which was promptly replied to.

On the morning of the 25th the batteries on both sides opened again and continued through the day without serious loss to us. About 3 p. m. I received orders to burn the bridge at once at all hazards, and to this end brought forward my four regiments of infantry to engage the enemy's infantry concealed in the woods near the bridge on the opposite bank.

By keeping up a steady artillery and infantry fire I succeeded in covering a party firing the bridge, which being of heavy oak, burned but slowly, and it was not till dark that the bridge was entirely consumed. We then received orders to march to Warrenton, my brigade to bring up the rear of the corps. We left about 9 p. m. and arrived at Warrenton next morning at daylight. Here we remained in camp until the morning of the 27th, when we received orders to take the advance in the direction of Gainesville.

My cavalry, upon arriving at Broad Run, within four miles of Gainesville, found the bridge on fire, and the rebel cavalry with one piece of artillery drawn up on the opposite side. Major Krepps, commanding my cavalry detachment, immediately ordered a charge, and after two successive charges succeeded in putting them to flight. By this time my infantry had arrived, and I set the pioneer corps to work repairing the bridge, which was executed with such promptness that in fifteen minutes after we were enabled to cross our artillery. Meanwhile I had pushed ahead with my cavalry and infantry in the direction of Gainesville. When within two miles of Gainesville I sent a platoon of cavalry with a regiment of infantry and a section of my battery to hold the road leading to Haymarket Station. With the rest of the brigade I continued on the main road, and upon approaching Gainesville found we had intercepted

Longstreet from joining Jackson, Ewell, and Hill, who had just passed up the railroad toward Manassas Junction.

At Gainesville we took some 200 prisoners, stragglers from Jackson's army. I here received orders to halt my brigade for the night.

Next morning, 28th, took the advance toward Manassas Junction, arriving within a mile of the junction at noon. I halted to await further orders. I accordingly turned my infantry aside into the shade of the woods, and sent my artillery ahead as far as the junction, there being no water for them nearer. Upon visiting the railroad station at the junction I found an immense amount of government stores in cars, which were yet burning, having been set on fire by the rebels the night previous, after having helped themselves to all they could carry off. At 3 p. m. I received orders to join the balance of the corps then marching in the direction of New Market. I accordingly moved across the country, and soon overtook them. After marching about an hour, skirmishing commenced in front. I was ordered to go forward and take position on Schenck's left, and pressed forward through the woods and underbrush in the direction of the rebel firing, which seemed to recede as I advanced. It finally grew dark, but I pushed forward in the direction of the firing, which had gradually grown into the thunder of a desperate battle. It becoming so dark, and the nature of the ground not admitting of my battery being pushed forward, I left it in charge of two companies of infantry, and started forward with my four regiments in the direction of the heavy firing, which suddenly ceased with great shouting, indicating, as we judged, a victory by the rebels. It being now 9 o'clock, and the darkness rendering the recognition of friend or foe impossible, I withdrew to my battery, which was on a line with the front of the corps, then fully a mile in my rear, resting my brigade here for the night.

On the following morning (the 29th) at daylight, I was ordered to proceed in search of the rebels, and had not proceeded more than 500 yards when we were greeted by a few straggling shots from the woods in front. We were now at the creek, and I had just sent forward my skirmishers when I received orders to halt, and let the men have breakfast. While they were cooking, myself, accompanied by General Schenck, rode up to the top of an eminence, some 500 yards to the front to reconnoitre. We had no sooner reached the top than we were greeted by a shower of musket-balls from the woods on our right. I immediately ordered up my battery and gave the bushwhackers a few shot and shell, which soon cleared the woods. Soon after, I discovered the enemy in great force about three-quarters of a mile in front of us, upon our right of the pike leading from Gainesville to Alexandria; I brought up my two batteries and opened upon them, causing them to fall back, I then moved forward my brigade with skirmishers deployed, and continued to advance my regiments, the enemy falling back.

General Schenck's division was off to my left, and that of General Schurz to my right. After passing a piece of woods I turned to the right, where the rebels had a battery that gave us a great deal of trouble. I brought forward one of my batteries to reply to it, and soon after heard a tremendous fire of small arms, and knew that General Schurz was hotly engaged to my right in an extensive forest. I sent two of my regiments, the 82d Ohio, Colonel Cantwell, and the 5th Virginia, Colonel Zeigler, to General Schurz's assistance. They were to attack the enemy's right flank, and I held my other two regiments in reserve for a time. The two regiments sent to Schurz were soon hotly engaged, the enemy being behind a railroad embankment, which afforded them an excellent breastwork.

The railroad had to be approached from the cleared ground on our side, through a strip of thick timber from 100 to 500 yards in width. I had intended, with the two regiments held in reserve, the 2d and 3d Virginia regiments, to charge the rebel battery, which was but a short distance from us over the top of a hill to our left; but while making my arrangements to do this, I observed that my two regiments engaged were being driven back out of the woods by the terrible fire of the rebels.

I then saw the brave Colonels Cantwell and Zeigler struggling to rally their broken regiments, on the rear of the forest out of which they had been driven, and sent two of my aids to assist them, and assure them of immediate support. They soon rallied their men and charged again and again, but were driven back each time with great loss. I then sent the 2d Virginia to their support, directing it to approach the railroad at the point on the left of my other regiments, where the woods ended, but they were met by such a destructive fire from a large rebel force, that they were soon thrown into confusion and fell back in disorder. The enemy now came on in overwhelming numbers. General Carl Schurz had been obliged to retire with his two brigades an hour before. And then the whole rebel force was turned against my brigade, and my brave lads were dashed back before the storm of bullets like chaff before the tempest.

I then ordered my reserve battery into position a short distance in the rear, and when five guns had got into position one of the wheel horses was shot dead; but I ordered it to unlimber where they were, and the six guns mowed the rebels with grape and canister with fine effect. My reserve regiment, the 3d Virginia, now opened with telling effect.

Colonel Cantwell, of the 82d Ohio, was shot through the brain and instantly killed while trying to rally his regiment during the thickest of the fight.

While the storm was raging the fiercest, General Stahel came to me and reported that he had been sent by General Schenck to support me, and inquired where he should place his brigade. I told him on my left and help support my battery. He then returned to his brigade, and, soon after being attacked from another quarter, I did not again see him during the day. I was then left wholly unsupported, except by a portion of a Pennsylvania regiment, which I found on the field and stood by me bravely during the next hour or two. I then rallied my reserved regiment and broken fragments in the woods near my battery, and sent out a strong party of skirmishers to keep the enemy at bay, while another party went forward without arms to get off as many of our dead and wounded as possible. I maintained my ground, skirmishing and occasionally firing by battalion during the greater part of the afternoon.

Toward evening General Grover came up with his New England brigade. I saw him forming a line to attack the rebel stronghold in the same place I had been all day and advised him to form line more to the left and charge bayonets on arriving at the railroad track, which his brigade executed with such telling effect as to drive the rebels in clouds before their bayonets. Meanwhile I had gathered the remnant of my brigade, ready to take advantage of any opportunity to assist him. I soon discovered a large number of rebels fleeing before the left flank of Grover's brigade. They passed over an open space some five hundred yards in width in front of my reserved regiment, which I ordered to fire on them, which they did, accelerating their speed and discomfiture so much that I ordered a charge. My regiment immediately dashed out of the woods we were in, down across the meadows in front of us after the retreating foe, but before their arriving at the other side of the meadow the retreating column received a heavy support from the railroad below them, and soon, rallying, came surging back driving before their immense columns Grover's brigade and my handful of men.

An hour before the charge I had sent one of my aids back after a fresh battery—the ammunition of both my batteries having given out—which, arriving as our boys were being driven back, I immediately ordered them into position, and commenced pouring a steady fire of grape and canister into the advancing columns of the enemy. The first discharge discomposed them a little, but the mmense surging mass behind pressed them on. I held on until they were within a hundred yards of us, and having but a handful of men to support the battery, ordered it to retire, which was executed with the loss of one gun.

I then rallied the shattered remnant of my brigade, which had been rallied by my aides and its officers, and encamped some three-quarters of a mile to the rear.

The next morning, 30th, I brought my brigade into the position assigned them, and remained in reserve until about 4 p. m., when I threw it across the road to stop the retreating masses, which had been driven back from the front.

I soon received an order to move my brigade off to the left on double quick, the enemy having massed their troops during the day in order to turn our left flank.

I formed line of battle along the road, my left resting near the edge of the woods in which the battle was raging. Soon our troops came rushing, panic-stricken, out of the woods, leaving my brigade to face the enemy, who followed the retreating masses to the edge of the woods. The road in which my brigade was formed was worn and washed from three to five feet deep, affording a splendid cover for my men. My boys opened fire on them at short range, driving the rebels back to a respectful distance. But the enemy, being constantly re-enforced from the masses in their rear, came on again and again, pouring in advance a perfect hurricane of balls, which had but little effect on my men, who were so well protected in their *road* intrenchment. But the steady fire of my brigade, together with that of a splendid brass battery on higher ground in my rear, which I ordered to fire rapidly with canister over the heads of my men, had a most withering effect upon the rebels, whose columns melted away and fast recoiled from repeated efforts to advance upon my road breastwork from the woods. But the fire of the enemy, which had affected my men so little, told with destructive results on the exposed battery in their rear, and it required a watchful effort to hold them to their effective work. My horse was shot in the head by a musket ball while in the midst of the battery cheering on the men. I got another; and soon after observing the troops on my left giving way in confusion before the rebel fire, I hastened to assist in rallying them, and while engaged in this, the battery took advantage of my absence and withdrew. I had sent one of my aides shortly before to the rear for fresh troops to support this part of our line, where the persistent efforts of the rebels showed they had determined to break through. A fine regiment of regulars was sent, which was formed in the rear of my brigade, near the position the battery had occupied. The rebels came around the forest in columns to our right and front, but the splendid firing of the regulars, with that of my brigade, thinned their ranks so rapidly that they were thrown back in confusion upon every attempt made. About this time, when the battle raged thickest, Lieutenant Estie and Lieutenant Niles, of General Schenck's staff, reported to me for duty, informing me that General Schenck had been seriously wounded, and his command thrown back from the field. Most thankfully was their valuable assistance accepted, and most gallantly and efficiently did they assist me on that most sanguine field until 8 o'clock at night, in bringing up regiments, brigades and batteries, cheering them on to action, and in rallying them when driven back before the furious fire of the enemy.

Shortly after sunset my own brigade had entirely exhausted their ammunition, and it being considerd unsafe to bring forward the ammunition wagons, where the enemy's shells were constantly flying and exploding, and the enemy having entirely ceased their efforts to break through this part of the line, and had thrown the weight of their attack still further to my left, I orderd my brigade back some one-half of a mile to replenish their ammunition boxes, and there await further orders. I remained on the field with Lieutenants Estie and Niles, my own having been sent to see to my regiments. The enemy continued their attacks upon our left until long after dark, which it required the most de termined and energetic efforts to repel. At one time, not receiving assistance from the rear, as I had a right to expect, after having sent for it, and our struggling battalions being nearly overcome by the weight and persistence of the enemy's attack, I flew back about one-half mile, to where I understood General McDowell was with a large portion of his corps. I found him and appealed to him in the most urgent manner to send a brigade forward at once to save the day, or all would be lost. He answered coldly, in substance, that it was not his business to help everybody, and he was not going to help General Sigel. I told him I was not fighting with General Sigel's corps; that my brigade had got out of ammunition some time before, and gone to the rear, and that I had been fighting with a half dozen different brigades, and that I had not inquired where or to what particular corps they belonged He inquired of one of his aides if General ——— was fighting over there on the left; he answered he thought he was. McDowell replied that he would send him help, for he was a good fellow. He then gave the order for a brigade to start, which was all I desired. I dashed in front of them, waved my sword, and cheered them forward. They raised the cheer, and came on at double quick. I soon led them to where they were most needed, and the gallant manner in which they entered the fight, and the rapidity of their fire, soon turned the tide of battle. But this gallant brigade, like many others which had preceded it, found the enemy too strong as they advanced into the forest, and was forced back by the tremendous fire that met them. But one of General Burnside's veteran brigades coming up soon after dark with a battery, again dashed back the tide of armed treason, and sent such a tempest of shot, shell, and leaden death into the dark forrest after the rebels that they did not again renew the attack.

Perhaps some mighty cheering which I got our boys to send up about that time induced the rebels to believe that we had received such re-enforcements as to make any further meddling with our lines a rather unhealthy business; feeling certain that the rebels had been completely checked and defeated in their attempts to flank us and drive us from the field, and that we could now securely hold it until morning, by which time we could rally our scattered forces, and bring up sufficient fresh troops to enable us to gain a complete victory on the morrow. I felt certain that the rebels had put forth their mightiest efforts, and were greatly cut up and crippled; I therefore determined to look up my little brigade and bring it forward into position, when we would be ready in the morning to renew the contest, and renew the great, glorious drama of the war. I left the field about 8 o'clock p. m. in possession of our gallant boys, and with Lieutenants Estie and Niles started back in the darkness, and was greatly surprised, upon coming to where I expected to find my brigade, with thousands of other troops, to find none. I kept on half a mile further, in painful, bewildering doubt and uncertainty, when I found you, general, and first learned from you, with agonizing surprise, that our whole army had been ordered to retreat back across Bull Run to Centreville.

Comment is unnecessary. I felt that all the blood, treasure, and labor of our government and people for the last year had been thrown away by that unfortunate order, and that most probably the death-knell of our glorious government had been sounded by it. The highest praise I can award to the officers and soldiers of my brigade, in all the hard service and fighting through which we have passed, is, that they have bravely, cheerfully, patiently, and nobly performed their duty. Colonels Cantwell, of the 82d Ohio, and Zeigler, of the 5th Virginia, deserve particular mention for their coolness and bravery in the long and desperate fight of the 29th with the rebels at the railroad. In the death of Colonel Cantwell the country, as well as his family, have sustained an irreparable loss. No braver man or truer patriot ever lived. He constantly studied the best interests of his soldiers and of the country, and his men loved, obeyed, and respected him as a father. Truly the loss of such an officer in these trying times is a great calamity.

I avail myself of this opportunity to return my thanks to the members of my staff—Captains Baird, Flesher, and McDonald, and Lieutenants Cravens and Hopper—for their promptness, bravery, and efficiency in the transmission and execution of orders. Captain Baird, unfortunately, in attempting to return to me on the field on the evening of the 30th, after dark, in company with one of my orderlies—Corporal Wilson, company C, 1st Virginia cavalry—took a wrong path, which led into the enemy's lines, and they were both captured, and are still prisoners. My brigade surgeon, too—Major Daniel Meeker—is always at his post, whether in field of danger, camp, or hospital. His superior science, skill, and patient industry have proved the greatest blessing to our sick and wounded soldiers.

Lists of my killed, wounded, and missing have been sent you.

I have the honor to be, very respectfully, your obedient servant,

R. H. MILROY,
Brigadier General, Commanding Independent Brigade, 1st Corps Army of Virginia.

Major T. A. MEYSENBURG,
Assistant Adjutant General.

No. 12.

REPORT OF BRIGADIER GENERAL J. STAHEL.

HEADQUARTERS OF FIRST DIVISION OF FIRST ARMY CORPS OF VIRGINIA,
Near Centreville, September 1, 1862.

SIR: I herewith have the honor to submit to you the report concerning the active participation of the 1st brigade, 1st division, at the battle on the 29th and 30th of August.

On the 28th of August, at about dark, I arrived near Robinson's farm and planted Schirmer's battery on the right near the farm, directing its fire into a wood on the right beside the road, as, at the time, heavy infantry fight took place in front of me on the Warrenton turnpike. With the increasing darkness the fire of the battery ceased, and I marched my brigade, which had been in position behind the farm, towards a hill on the left of the farm, where the brigade remained over night, extending its pickets to Young's branch. With break of day, on the 29th, I followed the 2d brigade, 1st division, marching to Dogan's farm, and took position behind the farm. I remained here but a short time, when I received the order to advance on the Warrenton turnpike beyond Groveton. Having advanced about one mile, I received the order to take position on the left of the road, resting with my right wing of the brigade on the road, and with my left wing on the 2d brigade. Here I found a number of dead and wounded soldiers from McDowell's corps from the preceding evening, and I had all the possible medical assistance bestowed upon them. Having remained here half an hour, a heavy skirmish took place to our right, and General Milroy sent to Brigadier General Schenck, commanding 1st division, for support. In order to support General Milroy, I left said position and followed the course shown to me by General Milroy's orderly. Arriving at Young's branch with my brigade, I reported myself to General Milroy and took my brigade to the left of Milroy's, along Young's branch, where I could prevent the enemy from breaking our lines, and be ready at any time to render assistance to General Milroy. Here I had but little cover for my troops and was very much exposed to the cross fire of the enemy's artillery, in consequence whereof I sustained a loss of several dead and wounded. During these proceedings one of General Stevens's batteries and two regiments were placed behind Groveton's farm to operate against the enemy's batteries. As soon as the battery commenced firing, thereby fully governing all the open ground on the right of the turnpike, and, with the assistance of the two regiments, making it impossible for the enemy to break through at this point, I received orders from General Schenck to take my brigade through a small defile to the left of the turnpike, on the left of Groveton's farm, taking position on the borders of the woods, resting my right wing on the turnpike, and the 2d brigade joining on the left. Placing the 8th and 27th regiments in front, the 45th and 41st regiments in reserve, and two pieces of the mountain howitzer battery on the left wing of my brigade, the skirmishers in front of the brigade on a small hill and in Groveton's farm. The enemy kept up a lively artillery fire upon General Stevens's battery planted on our right wing, about 200 paces to the rear, and also upon the woods occupied by us, while the enemy's skirmishers, trying to advance on the road, were warmly received by ours; and as they threw themselves in stronger force against the skirmishers of the 8th regiment, they were received on the top of the hill by a volley of the 8th regiment, whereupon they fell back and ceased firing. As the right wing seemed to have retreated, the brigade received the order at about 4 o'clock to move back slowly on the left of the road, and to take position on the chain of hills to the left of Dogan's farm. Having been here but a short time, I received further orders to encamp behind Dogan's farm; in consequence thereof, I marched there, crossing Young's branch and the turnpike, took camp behind the 2d brigade, where we remained over night.

On the 30th of August the 1st brigade remained in position in its camp, about 400 paces behind Dogan's farm, up to 1 o'clock p. m., till I received orders from Major General Sigel to take position on the crescent of the hill by the side of Dogan's farm. On the crescent itself I placed, besides two batteries already planted there, Schirmer's battery, and behind the batteries the 45th, 27th, and 8th regiments of my brigade, in the following order: adjoining the farm, the 45th; on the right of it, the 27th; and on the right of this, the 8th regiment, while the 41st regiment was posted on the left of the road. The fight began in the vicinity of Groveton's farm and to the left of it very lively; also, I saw the troops that occupied the heights to my left fall back. The 41st regiment was now ordered in support on the left wing, and later the whole of Colonel Colt's brigade. The 41st regiment was here attacked by a strong force of the enemy, defending itself with the greatest bravery, and yielded at last only to greatly superior numbers, after having already been flanked on its left, and having sustained a considerable loss of wounded and killed. Still the enemy pressed forward on our left, taking hill after hill, until he had arrived on the road leading from New Market to the Stone House.

While the enemy had taken possession of the heights opposite Dogan's farm, I received orders, through Major Meysenburg, assistant adjutant general, to take position further. In consequence thereof, I marched the 8th and 27th regiments further to their rear, and left the 45th regiment as protection to the batteries of Major General Hooker. Schirmer's battery now took position on the east side of Dogan's farm, directing its fire upon the opposite deploying column of the enemy's advance from the front.

The 45th regiment then took position between the turnpike and Dogan's farm, and has driven the enemy, who attacked from the left flank, back across Young's branch. Towards 6 o'clock the batteries left their position, while the enemy was fired upon by a battery from on the heights behind the Stone House. Now I ordered the 45th regiment back, taking the road across the heights behind the Stone House, where the 45th regiment, as also the 41st regiment have joined the brigade, where the brigade made another stand, and was shortly afterwards joined by Colonel McLean's brigade. Here I learned that General Schenck was wounded, in consequence whereof I took command of the division, transferring the command of the 1st brigade to Colonel Buschbeck. Having taken with the division a position, I ordered that all troops which came back, belonging to different commands, to rally behind the division, and reported myself to Major General Sigel, remaining with him till we arrived next morning at Centreville.

It affords me the greatest pleasure to be able to report that the regiments of the 1st brigade, as well as Schirmer's battery, under the command of First Lieutenant Bloom, on both days, fought with the greatest bravery and gallantry. To enumerate all those who distinguished themselves in the battle of the last two days is impossible, but I cannot omit to mention, with great approbation, the gallantry displayed by the following field-officers: Colonel Buschbeck, of the 27th Pennsylvania volunteers; Lieutenant Colonel Cantador, of the 27th Pennsylvania volunteers; Lieutenant Colonel Tkatislaw, commanding 45th New York State volunteers; Lieutenant Colonel Holmstedt, commanding 41st New York State volunteers; Major Von Einsiede, 41st New York State volunteers; Lieutenant Colonel Hedterich, commanding 8th New York State volunteers; Major Pokorny, 8th New York State volunteers.

I am, very respectfully, your most obedient servant,

JUL. STAHEL, *Brigadier General.*

Major T. A. Meysenburg,
Assistant Adjutant General.

No. 13.

REPORT OF COLONEL N. C. McLEAN, COMMANDING BRIGADE.

Headquarters Second Brigade, First Division.
Camp at Centreville, September 1, 1862.

General: I have the honor to report, so far as concerning the active participation of the second brigade in the battle of August 30, as follows:

The brigade had been placed in position on the evening of August 29, with the left resting on the Warrenton road, and remained there until the afternoon of August 30, when, by order, I detailed the 55th Ohio regiment to occupy a position on the left of the Warrenton road, which was pointed out to Colonel Lee by an aid, of General Sigel, the object of which was to keep up a connexion with General Reynolds on my left. A short time after this General Sigel received an order, in my presence, from General Pope, delivered by Colonel Ruggles, to place a battery with a brigade on a bald hill to my left, so as to sustain General Reynolds, and I was immediately ordered by General Sigel to that position with a battery of four pieces of artillery and the 2d brigade. The order was executed by placing the battery with the three remaining regiments of the brigade, the 73d Ohio, the 25th Ohio, and the 75th Ohio, in the position indicated, so as to sustain General Reynolds, who then with his right wing joined my left. Soon after I had taken this position, much to my surprise General Reynolds put his troops in motion and marched entirely past and across my front to the right, to what point I am not informed. Finding that this movement had entirely exposed my left flank, I immediately changed the position of my troops, and deployed in line of battle the 73d and 25th Ohio regiments, fronting the west end to the left of the battery, and the 75th and 55th Ohio, then returned from its former position, on the right of the battery; thus making my line of battle fronting the west, with the battery in the centre and two regiments on each side. I could by this time see the enemy advancing on my front and a little to the right, driving before them a regiment of zouaves. They came on rapidly, when some troops advanced to meet them from behind a hill on my right; these troops were also driven back in confusion, and as soon as they got out of the way I opened upon the enemy with the four pieces of artillery, throwing first shell, and, as they approached nearer, canister; I also commenced a heavy fire with infantry, and in a short time the enemy retreated in great confusion. During this time my attention had been called to a body of troops advancing towards my position in the rear of my left flank, and supposing them to be enemies I gave the order to turn two pieces of artillery upon them, but countermanded it upon the assurance of some one who professed to know the fact that they were our own troops, and I readily believed this as their clothing was dark, and then rested easy, thinking re-enforcements were coming to take position on my left and occupy the place vacated by General Reynolds. I then turned my exclusive attention to the enemy on my front. Soon after this a heavy force of the enemy, much superior to my own, marched out of the woods across the posititon formerly occupied by General Reynolds in front of my left flank, and swept around so as to come in heavy force both on the front and flank of my left wing. This force opened a heavy fire upon the 73d Ohio, and the next moment the troops in my rear, supposed to be friends, also opened fire with musketry and artillery. Overpowered by such superiority in numbers, after a short time the 73d and 25th fell back over the crest of the hill, but were still exposed to the fire from both columns of the enemy. I immediately, when this attack was made, gave the order to change front so as to repel it if possible, but the retreat of the battery at this moment interfered somewhat with the movement, as it passed through the 75th in its retreat. The 55th on my right flank, at the command, wheeled by battalion to the left and came up into line fronting the enemy in fine order, and the other regiments speedily formed on his left, and delivered such a heavy and continuous fire that in a short time the enemy ceased to advance and commenced to fall back; my men followed with cheers, driving the enemy back rapidly, and would have cleared them from the field but for the fact that the forces *permitted* to approach our rear had got into such a position as to rake us with grape, canister, and musketry, whilst we were attacked severely in front. Under all this, however, my brigade retained the hill until I, myself, gave the order to fall back slowly; this order was given with great reluctance, and only when my attention was called to a heavy force of the enemy approaching to attack us on our then right flank, but former front. I saw that it would but destroy my whole command to await that attack, and therefore gave the order under which we left the hill. During the course of the action General Schenck, with several regiments, came to my aid, but not until I had changed front. He greatly aided me by his gallant conduct in rallying and cheering on the men until he received the wound which drove him from the field. The loss is smaller than I supposed, under the circumstances, it could possibly be, and I will make a full return upon this point when the particulars are fully ascertained. Both officers and men, with few exceptions, behaved with great gallantry, and had such support been given me as to protect my rear from the terrible attack made upon me from that quarter, I could have continued to drive the enemy and successfully resisted his attack.

It is impossible in this report to mention the names of all those who distinguished themselves for gallantry, but I cannot refrain from noticing, with great approbation, the great coolness and gallantry displayed by the commanders of the four regiments of the brigade, Colonel Smith, 73d Ohio; Colonel Lee, 55th

Ohio; Colonel Richardson, 25th Ohio; and Major Reily, 75th Ohio, during the whole engagement. My own horse was killed under me during the hottest of the fire.

N. C. McLEAN,
Colonel Commanding 2d Brigade, 1st Division,
1st Army Corps, Army of Virginia.

Brigadier General STAHEL,
Commanding 1st Division, 1st Corps, Army of Virginia.

HEADQUARTERS SECOND BRIGADE, FIRST DIVISION,
Camp at Upton Hill, September 17, 1862.

GENERAL: I have the honor to report that late on the afternoon of the 28th of August I came up with the rear of the enemy near Bull Run. After we had reached the hill, which commanded a view of the country around, the enemy placed a battery on another hill at some distance, and appeared to be firing at some troops not in our corps. I immediately placed De Beck's battery in position on a hill to the left, and further in advance, from which we shelled the battery of the enemy until it retired. This closed the firing on our part for the night. On the next day, 29th August, we were, at an early hour, marched forward in line of battle, on the extreme left, towards the enemy, with whom we were only engaged by our skirmishers. During the whole day we were in line of battle, and often exposed to fire from the artillery of the enemy, but otherwise we were not actively engaged; our position was frequently changed; sometimes advancing, and sometimes retiring, and expecting momentarily an attack. At one time the division of General Reynolds took position on my left, and advanced a little beyond my front line; but in a short time General Meade informed me that he had placed a battery which he had been compelled to withdraw on account of the superior force in artillery which had been brought against it, and that the enemy were marching around on our left in such heavy force that he had decided to fall back immediately, and he then marched the troops which had been a little in advance on my left to some point in my rear. I reported the facts to General Schenck, and he then ordered me to fall back a short distance to another position, which was accordingly done. We remained here until near night, when we were placed in the position we occupied until the afternoon of the 30th. The particulars of the battle on that day I have already reported to you. On the night of the 29th we had an alarm which caused me to turn out the brigade and advance them in line of battle a little in advance of our camping ground, and over the crest of the hill upon which our batteries in reserve had been placed in the afternoon. After remaining under arms some two hours, we again returned to camp.

Respectfully,

N. C. McLEAN,
Colonel Commanding 2d Brigade, 1st Division.

Major General SIGEL,
Commanding 1st Army Corps.

No. 14.

REPORT OF COLONEL J. C LEE, FIFTY-FIFTH OHIO VOLUNTEERS.

HEADQUARTERS FIFTY-FIFTH REGIMENT OHIO VOL. INFANTRY,
Camp L'Anglaise, September 3, 1862.

I have, sir, in obedience to orders, to report of the 55th regiment Ohio volunteer infantry since its arrival at Rappahannock Station, 21st ultimo, as follows:

From the 21st to the 29th, inclusive, the regiment was constantly on duty with the brigade, but not actively engaged with the enemy at any time. On the 29th it was much of the day under fire of the enemy's artillery, with serious injury to no one, but with some bruises to several.

On Saturday, the 30th, about 12 m., my regiment was separated from the brigade by order of Colonel McLean, and posted as a vidette between (as I supposed) the left of General Schenck's division and the right of General Reynolds, who formed the right of General McDowell's line. My position was assigned me by a member of General Sigel's staff, with instructions as above stated. This position was to the left of Centreville pike, about one hundred rods, the brigade being close to and on the right-hand side. I found a battery on the first ridge on the left and in front of me, and a regiment of infantry to the left and rear of the battery, from me distant 50 rods, with the battalion massed in column, by division, on the eastern slope of the ridge, to protect it from the frequent solid shot of the enemy's artillery. I remained until nearly 3 o'clock p. m. The battalion of infantry then moved to the left and rear, behind the woods on the left, but without communicating with me. Almost simultaneously I saw several battalions of infantry pass by the flank eastwardly, and to the rear of my position, along the north side of this piece of woods. Musketry was also heard on the south and west side of the woods. I at once despatched Captain Gamber, with this information, to Colonel McLean, who had moved the balance of the brigade to the ridge in my rear. I also rode rapidly to the retreating forces above mentioned, but could learn nothing more than that the enemy was in the road and advancing. The balls from the enemy's musketry, yet unseen, began to fall upon us. By order, column was rapidly deployed to the left, and the battalion advanced rapidly forward toward the crest of the hill; but, at the same time, there came over the hill, and passing numerously in our front federal soldiers, driven by the advancing enemy. With this mass pressing against us it was impossible to fire, and, being wholly unsupported, the battalion was faced by the rear rank, and moved rapidly over to the ridge behind us, when we reformed on the right of the 75th, under Colonel McLean's orders. In this position we fired upon the enemy, who had fully gained the top of the ridge we had left, and from it he fell back. The enemy appearing upon our left flank, the battalion was wheeled to the left, at the same time delivering a destructive fire. An advance was made, and the enemy held at bay for some time, when he fell back, slowly at first, but soon rapidly, into the woods. *Their flag fell three times.* At this the battalion advanced with enthusiastic cheers. The colors were often pierced, but kept up and unfurled. Although the enemy had disappeared from our new front, he appeared in overwhelming numbers upon our new left and new right flanks, and with re-enforcements upon our front. Thus engaged, the fighting continued until Colonel McLean ordered a withdrawal from the field. With the colors we came off, leaving upon the field dead and wounded, and losing, as prisoners, in numbers as shown in tabular statement herewith submitted.

Of the first deployment into line, the falling back to the brigade, the reforming and the change of front, all under a murderous fire of an overwhelming force, I must say that it reflects much credit upon both men and company officers. In justice, I cannot distinguish between officers or soldiers for good behavior; all brave and true.

Owing to meagre transportation for the sick, some were picked up by the enemy in the wake of our several marches, as appears by statement herewith submitted.

I have the honor to be your most obedient servant,

J. C. LEE,
Colonel 55th Reg't Ohio Volunteer Infantry, Com'g.

Captain E. H. ALLEN,
Acting Asssitant Adjutant General.

Report of casualties in 55th regiment Ohio volunteer infantry in the battle at Bull Run, August 30, 1862.

Killed.—Private Silas P. Riley, company A; Private William F. Edwards, company F; Corporal Jacob Fetterman, company D; Corporal William Bellamy and Private Samuel McGuckin, company C; Corporal John B. Conger, Privates William H. Tallman and J. E. Case, company H; Orderly Sergeant Benjamin F. Welsh, Corporal David Gilliland, and Privates James Henry and John Sohn, company K; Private Henry Troxwell, company G; Corporal John Ostien, and Privates John Martin and David Shesely, company B.

Wounded.—Sergeant Nelson Crocket and Private William E. Sheffield, company A; Captain Daniel S. Brown, and Privates Levi Smook, John Merrar, and Wesley Lane, company F; Corporal Edward E. Shayes, and Privates William Cromwell, Carl Zenders, Jacob C. Utz, and Ed. F. Zolck, (mortally,) company D; Corporal Elisha Cole, and Privates Oscar Ramson, (since died,) Bard Randolph, Lucius Babcock, Sebastian Dohra, Oliver B. Johnson, W. W. Potter, Jesse Woodruff, and David P. Benson, company I; Sergeant John R. Lowe, Corporal David Warren, and Privates John White, Lewis Ray, Thomas J. Harris, William Coultrip, Wilbert Greene, A. Adams, and W. Conell, company C; Sergeant A. M. Ross, Corporals Dennis Spurrier and William Negele, and Privates Barney Weigle, Enoch B. Watson, and James P. Boston, company H; Privates Samuel C. Briggs, John Coupe, John W. Saltman, Ambers Rice, and Thomas E. Buckley, company E; Corporal Samuel Cooper and Privates Curtis Hoff, Henry Yager, Henry Vaughn, Levi Katterman, Charles McClary, and Thomas Casick, company K; First Lieutenant Robert Bromley, (taken prisoner,) Corporals Herman F. Neiman (left on field) and William H. Rogers, and Privates Thomas A. Longstreet, George Downs, and Valentine Denis, company G; Sergeant Evan A. Kirkwood, and Privates John Sibsell, Horner A. Durfee, Andrew Nighswander, Albert J. Maurer, John Senman, James Headley, F. N. Fell, John Wolfret, Joseph Harris, James T. Whidden, and Leonard Doke, company B.

Missing.—Privates James Carper, David Warner, and Francis Decker, company F; Corporal Cyrenus De Jean, company H; Private John Ferguson, company E; Private Harman Boucher, company K; Corporal William R. Gear and Private Benjamin Harris, company B.

Very respectfully,

J. C. LEE,
Colonel Commanding 55th Reg't Ohio Volunteer Infantry.

Statement of officers and soldiers who have fallen into the hands of the enemy from the 55th regiment Ohio volunteer infantry.

Captured and paroled.—Corporal Lyman T. Lord and Private Dexter R. Jones, company A, August 28, 1862; Corporal William R. Gear and Private Benjamin Harris, company B, August 30, 1862; Corporal Theodore Hunt, company B, September 1, 1862.

Wounded and captured.—Privates William Cromwell and Edward F. Volk, company D, August 30, 1862; Privates Thomas Buckley, Samuel C. Briggs, and John Ferguson, company E, August 30, 1862; Privates David Warner and Francis Decker, company F, August 28, 1862; First Lieutenant Robert Bromley, and Privates Thomas Longstreet and Frederick Neiman, company G, August 30, 1862.

Wounded, captured, and paroled.—Privates Samuel Camron and James Kinne, company F, captured September 1, 1862, paroled September 2, 1862; Private W. W. Potter, company I, August 30, 1862.

The above statement contains both those who were captured on the field of battle and on the march.

Very respectfully,

J. C. LEE,
Colonel 55th Reg't Ohio Volunteers, Com'g.

No. 15.

REPORT OF COLONEL ORLAND SMITH, SEVENTY-THIRD OHIO VOLUNTEERS.

HEADQUARTERS 73D OHIO VOLUNTEER INFANTRY,
Langley, Virginia, September 5, 1862.

COLONEL: I have the honor to report the part taken by the 73d Ohio volunteer infantry in the engagements of Friday and Saturday, August 29 and 30, in the neighborhood of Bull Run.

On the 29th, although not actively engaged with the enemy, the regiment was constantly on the field, and in several instances under severe artillery fire, resulting in the wounding of seven persons of my command.

The actual fighting service of the regiment during that day was confined to some slight skirmishing between companies A and B and the enemy's sharpshooters. Nevertheless, the frequent changes of position and preparations for action, continuing till a late hour at night, were fatiguing and harassing, taxing not only the patience and endurance of the men, but very frequently their courage.

I am happy to report a commendable obedience and promptness on the part of my men of all grades during the entire day, under all circumstances, whether of exposure without opportunity of replying, or of labor under privations of food and drink, without apparent results.

On the 30th our position was as a reserve, in close column of companies, on the left of the brigade. We remained in this position till the middle of the afternoon, when, in obedience to your orders, the brigade was moved to the left, the 73d being in front. I advanced to a considerable distance in the expectation of forming a junction with the forces of General Reynolds, whom I was told we were to support. Not finding any co-operating forces at the point where I had been told they were in position, I formed forward into line as rapidly as possible, and advanced one company (A) to the front, deployed as skirmishers, to observe the movements of the enemy and report. The regiment was scarcely in line before reports came from Major Hurst, on the left, that a large force of the enemy could be distinctly seen advancing on our left flank and rear. Being under the impression that we must be sustained by other forces in that direction, I could not believe it possible that a hostile force could be approaching us from that quarter with impunity, and was not convinced that they were foes till I made a personal observation, resulting in the conviction that they were not only foes, but that they were in numbers sufficient to crush us at the first onset.

I immediately despatched Adjutant B. F. Stone to advise you of the danger, and the necessity for prompt preparation to meet the emergency. On his return he reported that he had been unable to find you, but had communicated the facts to your aide, Lieutenant Morse.

In the mean time Captain Buchwalter, of company A, had reported several regiments of the enemy to be filing up a ravine, and approaching us through the woods, directly in front.

I immediately ordered the skirmishers to be recalled, and prepared to receive the approaching masses with a well-directed fire, which was done to my satisfaction. The first volley drove the enemy back, and was very destructive, as I have since learned from some of my men who visited the field on Sunday, 31st.

A devastating fire now opened from the lines of the enemy, who had already turned our flank. Our ranks were soon thinned by the overwhelming force to which we were opposed, and being too weak for further effectual resistance, no alternative was left but a retirement. This was accomplished with considerable loss, under a severe cross-fire from front, flank, and rear.

In thus falling back the regiment became somewhat scattered, but the men rallied behind a fence in the edge of the wood to which we retired, and poured a well-directed fire upon the advancing foe, retiring again, when too much exposed, to another point in rear, where they were covered by re-enforcements, which had come forward too late, however, to recover the field. Finding further effort, with my thinned ranks, useless, after having made several rallies, combining with my own forces many from other commands, whom I found isolated, I drew off to join you, which I succeeded in doing just before dark, on the ground occupied by the 1st brigade of our division.

All officers and men under my command on that day deserved and won my highest commendation for cheerful obedience and determined resistance, under the most trying circumstances. Where all did *well*, it would be useless to attempt personal distinctions.

I cannot forbear mentioning, however, the able manner in which I was sustained by Major Hurst and Adjutant Stone. The former had his horse shot under him in the early part of the action, after which he rendered efficient service on foot in rallying and steadying the men.

Company A, under command of Captain Buchwalter, and company B, under Lieutenant Kinson, are entitled to favorable mention for the skill and promptness with which they responded to the calls for skirmishers on both days. It may not be improper to mention the name of Captain Madeira, of company H, who, at great personal risk, brought off the national color, when both color bearers and the entire color-guard had fallen.

I enclose herewith a list of killed, wounded, and missing. The number, compared with the whole strength of the regiment engaged, will show a very large proportion:

The whole number taken into action was	312
Number ascertained to be killed	25
Wounded and recovered	56
Wounded prisoners paroled, 31	87
Prisoners not known to be wounded	10
Total killed, wounded, prisoners, and missing	148

Very respectfully, your obedient servant,

ORLAND SMITH,
Colonel Seventy-third Ohio Volunteer Infantry.

Colonel N. C. McLean,
Commanding 2d Brigade, 1st Division, 1st Army Corps.

List of killed, wounded, and missing, of the seventy-third regiment Ohio volunteer infantry, at the battle near Bull Run, August 29, and 30, 1862.

Killed.—Joseph Mass and Burton Crider, company A; Sergeants Charles Shepherd and B. F. Morrison, and Corporal J. H. Smith, company B; Isaac Ater, Jesse Lewis, John Godden, George Selby, Asa Harper, and Wm. Clifton, company C; Henry Lockard and John McKee, company D; Lieutenant Charles W. Trimble, Privates Thomas Biggerstaff, Henry Henson, and Marcus

Walston; Charles E. Dustin, company F; Mason Brown, company G; Wm. Robinson, company H; Sergeant A. R. Hull, John Halterman, and George A. Wilson, company I; Wm. McKinley and James Watts, company K. Total killed, so far as heard from, 25.

Wounded and recovered.—Commanding Sergeant Erskine Carson, staff; Thos. Reedy, Robert McKittrick, Thomas Clark, William Clark, Edward Sweet, and A. D. Zehrung, company A; James Lawson and Levi Russell, company B; Second Lieutenant J. C. McKell, Sergeant J. N. Hawkins, Abram Anderson, Peter Brown, Louis Nail, A. S. Watkins, and S. M. Wiley, company C; Washington Swift, Nathan McCarty, and James Chesser, company D; John Dinley, Wesley Hays, John Shoeffers, and Benjamin Sharpe, company E; Edward Welsh, Anthony Moran, James Crown, John Newman, Patrick De Lany, John Kennedy, and Patrick Hyland, company F; Second Lieutenant D. L. Greiner, Sergeant E. M. Furry, E. Welsheimer, Lewis Painter, J. B. Greiner, W. A. Detty, John Barnett, and John Weekline, company G; Second Lieutenant E. H. Miller, Wm. M. Page, B. F. Crothers, Henry Leister, J. K. Bennett, Morris Wilson, Danl. Buckley, Adam Slaughter, John Caveny, Hiram Clay, and William Kelly, company H; Captain L. H. Burkett, (mortally,) J. C. McLean, Amos Ross, and Henry Mader, company I; John Curtis and Henry Wilshire, company K. Total wounded and recovered, 56.

Wounded and paroled as prisoners.—Washington Pence, company A; Levi Miller, Jesse Rickey, and Sergeant J. H. Martin, company B; Ransom Clements, David F. Nixon, W. W. Crow, Wm. R. Farlow, and Ira W. Booten, company C; Henry Argobright and John Durham, company D; James Whalen and David Thompson, company E; Mortimer Kirkpatrick, Sergeant Wm. Barnes, Peter Donahoe, Michael Norton, and John O'Donnell, company F; Cyrus Ellis, Eli Graves, Abner De France, John P. Whellman, Isaiah Smith, and Lieut. Sam. Fellers, company G; First Lieutenant John F. Martin, and Frank Thoman, company H; Theo. Jackman and David W. Bonner, company I; Thos. McKinley, David Armstrong, and Washington Moore, company K. Total wounded prisoners paroled, 31.

Prisoners not known to be wounded.—Franklin Redd, Wm. F. Adams, and Paul Sowers, (all paroled,) company C; Frank Knighton, (paroled,) James Ray, and Wilson Smallwood, company G; Sergeant C. B. Thomson, (paroled,) company H; Anthony Palmer, Sergeant A. H. Sanders, (paroled,) William Burley, (paroled,) company K. Total known to be prisoners not wounded, 10.

Missing.—Thomas Dawson, Jos. De Haven, and Nelson Lowe, company A; Second Lieutenant Joshua Davis, John Warren, Samuel Turner, J. M. Wilson, Wm. Cline, A. S. Underwood, I. C. Fisher, and Samuel Allison, company B; Patrick Henry, company C; Amos Holdren, company D; Patrick Rogan, John McFadden, Martin Boyle, and Michael Harkins, company E; Henry Thacher, Sergeants William M. Burns and W. J. Shepherd, company G; A. M. Simmons and Wm. Dixon, (wounded,) company H; John Dye, Fordyce Wilfred, Benjamin Cooley, and Gaines Wilshire, company K. Total missing, 26.

ORLAND SMITH,

Colonel Commanding Seventy-third Ohio Volunteer Infantry.

Colonel N. C. McLEAN,

Commanding 2d Brigade, 1st Division, 1st Army Corps.

No. 16.

REPORT OF LIEUTENANT GEORGE B. HASKINS, FIRST OHIO ARTILLERY.

HEADQUARTERS BATTERY "K,"
Buffalo Fort, Virginia, September 17, 1862.

SIR: The following is a correct statement of the doings of this battery from the Rappahannock to Bull Run: Was in action near Leary's Ford, August 22, from 9 a. m. till 1 p. m., when we were relieved by Captain Weiderick's battery, and went to the rear. Staid at Leary's Ford all night, and marched from there, August 23, towards Sulphur Springs, and camped about one mile from the springs, where we remained all night. Was in action near the springs, August 24, in the morning. Marched in the evening towards Waterloo Bridge, where we remained all night. Was out of ammunition the 25th until 4 p. m., when we opened upon the enemy with two guns as they were leaving their position. Marched at 7 p. m. same day towards Warrenton, where we arrived, after marching all night, the morning of the 26th of August, and remained there all day and the night following. Marched, August 27, at 6 a. m. eight miles, towards Manassas, where we stopped all night. Marched, August 28, towards Bull Run, where we engaged the enemy from about 4 p. m. till dark, and remained in our position all night. Fighting resumed next morning, August 29, and engaged the enemy until about 11 a. m., when we ran out of ammunition, and, not being able to get more, were ordered to the rear, where we remained that and the following day, August 30, until about 5 p. m.; then were ordered to Centreville by Captain Schirmer, and started for that place at once. Lieutenant H. S. Camp was mortally wounded near Leary's Ford, August 22, and died September 15, in Washington.

GEORGE B. HASKINS,
Lieutenant Commanding Battery "K," 1st Ohio Volunteer Artillery.

Colonel McLEAN.

No. 17.

REPORT OF BRIGADIER GENERAL C. SCHURZ.

HEADQUARTERS 3D DIVISION,
Camp near Minor's Hill, September 15, 1862.

GENERAL: I have the honor to submit the following report concerning the part taken by the division under my command in the battles of the 29th and 30th of August:

On the evening of the 28th of August my division was encamped south of the turnpike leading from Centreville to Gainesville, near Mrs. Henry's farm. On the 29th, a little after 5 o'clock a. m., you ordered me to cross the turnpike, to deploy my division north of it, and to attack the forces of the enemy supposed to be concealed in the woods immediately in my front, my division forming the right wing of your army corps. In obedience to your order, I formed my division left in front, and after having forded Young's branch, deployed the 1st brigade, under Colonel Schimmelfening, on the right, and the 2d brigade, under Colonel Krzyzanowski, on the left. There was a little farm-house in front of Colonel Schimmelfening's brigade, which he was ordered to take as a point of direction, and, after having passed it, to bring his right wing a little forward, so as to execute a converging movement towards the 2d brigade, and upon the enemy's left flank. The battery of the 2d brigade, Captain Rohmes, I ordered to follow the left wing of the brigade and to take position on a rise of ground immediately on the left of a little grove, through which Colonel Krzyzanowski was to pass. The battery attached to Colonel Schimmelfening's brigade was held in reserve. As soon as the two (2) brigades, consisting of three (3) regiments each, had formed four (4) regiments in column by company in the first line, and two (2) in column doubled on the centre, in reserve behind the intervals, the skirmishers advanced rapidly a considerable distance without finding the enemy. Arrived upon open ground, behind the little patches of timber the division had passed through, I received from you the order to connect my line of skirmishers with General Milroy's, on my left. I pushed my left wing rapidly forward into the long stretch of woods before me and found myself obliged to extend my line considerably in order to establish the connexion with General Milroy, which, however, was soon effected. Hardly had this been done when the fire commenced near the point where General Milroy's right touched my left. I placed the battery of the 2d brigade upon an elevation of ground about six hundred (600) or seven hundred (700) yards behind the point where that brigade had entered the woods a little to the left, so as to protect the retreat of the regiments composing the left wing, in case they should be forced to fall back. The battery of the 1st brigade remained for the same purpose on high ground behind the woods in which Colonel Schimmelfening was engaged, covering my right. When the fire of the skirmishers had been going on a little while two (2) prisoners were brought to me, sent by Colonel Schimmelfening, who stated that there was a very large force of the enemy, Ewell's and Jackson's divisions, immediately in my front, and about the same time one of Colonel Schimmelfening's aides informed me that heavy columns of troops were seen moving on my right flank, and that it could not be distinguished whether they were Union troops or rebels. I then withdrew the reserve regiment of the 2d brigade, the 54th New York, from the woods, so as to have it at my disposal in an emergency, and ordered Colonel Schimmelfening to form one of his regiments front towards the right, and to send out skirmishers in that direction, so as to ascertain the true condition of things there. Meanwhile the fire in front had extended along the whole line and become very lively, my regiments pushing the enemy vigorously before them about one half mile. The discharges of musketry increased in rapidity and volume as we advanced, and it soon became evident that the enemy was throwing heavy masses against us. About that time General Steinwehr brought the 29th New York, under Colonel Soest, to my support, and formed it in line of battle on the edge of the roads behind a fence. I then received information that the columns which had appeared on my right, and which really seemed to have belonged to the enemy, had disappeared again in the woods without making any demonstration, and also that General Kearney's troops were coming up in my rear. Thus reassured about the safety of my right, and expecting more serious business in the centre, I sent the 54th New York forward again with the order to fill up the gap between my two brigades, occasioned by the extension of my line towards General Milroy's right. The 29th New York remained in reserve. Immediately afterwards the enemy began to press my centre so severely that it gave way, but we soon rallied it again, and after a sharp contest reoccupied the ground previously taken from the enemy. It was about 10 o'clock a. m. when an officer announced to me that General Kearney had arrived on the battle-field and desired to see me. General Kearney requested me to shorten my front and condense my line by drawing my right nearer to the left, so as to make room for him on the right. I gave my orders to Colonel Schimmelfening accordingly. A short time afterwards I discovered that two small regiments, sent to my support, had slipped in between my two brigades and were occupying part of my line in the woods. General Kearney was just moving up his troops on my right when the enemy made another furious charge upon my centre. The two regiments above mentioned, as well as the 54th New York, broke, and were thrown out of the woods in disorder, the enemy advancing rapidly and in great force to the edge of the forest. The 29th New York poured several volleys into them, checking the pursuit of the enemy only for a moment, and then fell back in good order. The moment was critical. While endeavoring to rally my men again I sent orders to the battery of the 2d brigade, which I had placed in position in the rear of my left wing, to open fire upon the enemy who threatened to come out of the woods. This was done with very good effect, and the enemy was brought to a stand almost instantaneously. Meanwhile I succeeded in forming the 54th New York again, whose commander, Lieutenant Colonel Ashby, displayed much courage and determination, and placed it *en echelon* behind the 29th New York, which advanced in splendid style upon the enemy in our centre. My extreme right, under Colonel Schimmelfening, had stood firm, with the exception of the 8th Virginia, while the extreme left, under Colonel Krzyzanowski, had contended every inch of ground against the heavy pressure of a greatly superior force. The conduct of the 75th Pennsylvania, which displayed the greatest firmness and preserved perfect order on that occasion, deploying and firing with the utmost regularity, deserves special praise.

The 29th New York and the 54th New York had just re-entered the woods when one of your aides presented to me, for perusal, a letter which you had addressed to General Kearney, requesting him to attack at once with his whole force, as the rebel general, Longstreet, who was expected to re-enforce the enemy during the day, had not yet arrived upon the battle-field, and we might hope to gain decisive advantages before his arrival. I then ordered a general advance of my whole line, which was executed with great gallantry, the enemy yielding everywhere before us. In this charge the 29th New York distinguished itself by its firmness and intrepidity. Its commander, Colonel Soest, while setting a noble example to his men, was wounded and compelled to leave the field. On my right, however, where General Kearney had taken position, all remained quiet; and it became clear to me that he had not followed your request to attack simultaneously with me. I am persuaded, if General Kearney had done at that moment what he did so gallantly late in the afternoon—that is to say, if he had thrown his column upon the enemy's left flank, enveloping the latter by a change of direction to the left—we might have succeeded in destroying the enemy's left wing, and thus gained decisive results before General Longstreet's arrival. As it was, I advanced and attacked alone. The fight came to a stand on my left, at an old railroad embankment running through the woods in a direction almost parallel to our front. From behind this cover the enemy poured a rapid and destructive fire into our infantry, who returned volley for volley. Colonel Schimmelfening's brigade, on my right, gained possession of this embankment, and advanced even beyond it, but found itself obliged, by a very severe artillery and infantry fire, to fall back. But the embankment remained in its possession.

While this was going on the battery of the 1st brigade, under Captain Hampton, was ordered to march along the outer edge of the woods in which Colonel Schimmelfening was engaged, and to take position there, in order to protect and faciltate the advance of my right; but the cross-fire of two of the enemy's batteries was so severe that Captain Hampton's battery failed, in two successive attempts, to establish itself until I sent Captain Rohmer's battery to its support, the place of the latter being filled by a battery brought from the reserve by General Steinwehr.

At this juncture you put two pieces of the mountain howitzer battery at my disposal. I ordered Major Koenig, of the 68th New York, (temporarily attached to my staff,) to bring them forward, and he succeeded in placing them into the line of skirmishers, of Colonel Krzyzanowski's brigade, in so advantageous a position that a few discharges sufficed to cause a backward movement of the enemy in front of my left. Now the whole line advanced with great alacrity, and we succeeded in driving the enemy away from his strong position, behind the embankment, when they fell into our hands on my left also.

While this was going on I heard, from time to time, very heavy firing on my left, where General Milroy stood. The sound of the musketry was swaying forward and backward, indicating that the fight was carried on with alternate success. The connexion of my left with General Milroy's right was lost, and I found my left uncovered. However, we succeeded in holding the position of the railroad embankment along my whole front, against the repeated attacks of the enemy, until about two (2) o'clock p. m., when my troops, who had started at five (5) o'clock in the morning, mostly without breakfast, had been under fire for eight (8) hours, had been decimated by enormous losses, and had exhausted nearly all their ammunition, were relieved by a number of regiments kindly sent by General ——— for that purpose. These re-enforcements arrived in my front between one and two o'clock. According to your order, I withdrew my regiments, one after another, as their places were filled by those of General Hooker. Thus the possession of that portion of the woods, which my division had taken and held, was in good order delivered to the troops that relieved me. I rallied my two brigades behind the hill on which the battery of the 2d brigade had been in position. Here the men took a new supply of ammunition, and for the first time on that day they received something to eat. From there you ordered me to take position in the woods on the right of the open ground, where we encamped for the night.

The two mountain howitzers, which had done such excellent service in the contest in the woods, I had left in position to co-operate with the troops who relieved me, and I am sorry to report that one of them was lost when these troops were temporarily driven back from the ground, the possession of which we had delivered to them.

Exhausted and worn down as my men were, my division was unable to take part in the action after two (2) o'clock p. m., nor was I called upon to do so. Heavy re-enforcements were constantly arriving and led to the front. If all these forces, instead of being frittered away in isolated efforts, had co-operated with each other at any one moment, after a common plan, the result of the day would have been far greater than the mere retaking and occupation of the ground we had already taken and occupied in the morning, and which in the afternoon was for a short time, at least, lost again.

My men, with very few exceptions, behaved well. The line my weak regiments had to take and to hold was so extensive that double the number of troops would, under ordinary circumstances, be hardly considered sufficient to perform the task. That they did perform it for many hours, without flinching, until the arrival of ample re-enforcements made their relief possible, speaks well for their courage and intrepidity.

Of those who especially distinguished themselves I have to mention the two colonels commanding brigades. Colonel Schimmelfening commanded my right wing with that cool and daring courage and that admirable judgment which he had displayed already on former occasions, and which eminently fit him for commands of great responsibility; while the gallantry with which Colonel Krzyzanowski, on the left wing, withstood and repelled the frequent and fierce assaults of the enemy, commands the highest praise. Of Colonel Soest's conspicuous bravery I have already spoken above. The members of my staff, Major Hoffman and Captain Spraul, as well as Major Koenig, of the 68th New York, temporarily attached to me, performed their dangerous and delicate duties with the greatest fearlessness and precision. Nor can I speak too highly of the valuable aid and assistance rendered to me during a part of the action by your able and excellent aide-de-camp, Captain Asmussen. There are many officers and soldiers whose conduct deserves special notice, but to whom I cannot undertake to do justice in this report. In regard to those I would respectfully refer you to the reports of the brigade and regimental commanders.

On the morning of the 30th of August you did me the honor to attach to my division Colonel Koltes's brigade, consisting of the 68th New York, the 29th New York, and the 73d Pennsylvania, together with Captain Dilger's battery. Captain Hampton's battery was placed in the reserve.

At 8 o'clock a. m. you ordered me to take position behind the woods I had occupied for the night, and while I was deploying the division I received further orders to march six or seven hundred yards to the rear and left, and to place myself behind General Schenck's division, on the open ground, not far from Dogan's farm-house, front towards Groveton. There the division remained, quietly resting on their arms, until 3 o'clock p. m. For several hours we observed distinctly thick clouds of dust at a distance in our front, indicating a movement of heavy forces of the enemy towards our left.

Our position was to be that of a general reserve. Before us we had General Fitz John Porter on our right centre and right in the woods, and General Reynolds on the heights in our front and left. If our corps was really intended to be a general reserve its position was too far advanced, for it found itself from the beginning within range of the enemy's artillery, and it was evident that if the corps in front met with any repulse we would be entangled in the fight, one brigade after another, thus losing our liberty of action and the possibility of throwing our whole power upon the decisive point.

About 3 o'clock p. m. the fire commenced in the woods occupied by General Porter, and also on our left, where General Reynolds stood. General Schenck's division was drawn forward towards Dogan's farm, and I received your order to be ready at a moment's notice. The artillery and infantry fire in our centre and left had meanwhile become quite lively. It was about 4 o'clock when you ordered me to advance towards Dogan's and to take position immediately behind General Stahel's brigade. I did so; the regiments formed in column by division right in front; Colonel Schimmelfening's brigade on the right, Koltes's on the left, and Krzyzanowski's behind the interval a little to the left. Captain Dilger's battery followed the right and took position on the crest of the hill, not far from Dogan's. The artillery fire of the enemy had now become quite severe, and our troops, densely massed upon the open ground behind Dogan's farm-house, were greatly annoyed by the shot and shell dropping among them, but remained entirely firm.

A little after 4 o'clock we saw General Porter's troops, who had been engaged in our front, leave their position and retire in the direction of the place we occupied. You ordered Colonel McLean to occupy the "bald-headed hill" in our left front, and General Stahel's forward to receive and support the retreating troops, who then passed through the intervals of my division and partly formed again behind me. About the same time, General Reynolds's troops, who had occupied the heights in our front and left, fell back, and the enemy, after having obliged them to retire, planted a battery upon the high ground abandoned by them, directly opposite us, and opened a most disagreeable fire upon my three brigades. I ordered Captain Dilger to move his battery a little to the left, and to open upon the enemy's battery above mentioned, which was done.

When Stahel's brigade had become engaged, you ordered me to send Colonel Koltes forward to the support of its left, and a few minutes afterwards, seeing Koltes hotly received and severely pressed, I ordered Colonel Krzyzanowski to ascend with his brigade the wooded hill-slopes on my left, in order to prevent Koltes from being turned on that side. This order was executed with great promptness and spirit.

But the heights on my left were soon abandoned by General Reynolds's troops, and my two brigades, Koltes and Krzyzanowski, found themselves severely pressed in front by overwhelming forces, exposed to a most destructive artillery fire and turned by the enemy in their left and rear. The contest was sharp in the extreme. The gallant Koltes died a noble death at the head of his brave regiments; Colonel Krzyzanowski, while showing his men how to face the enemy, had his horse shot under him, and the ground was soon covered with our dead and wounded. When it had become evident that we on that spot were fighting, alone and unsupported, against immensely superior numbers, you ordered me to withdraw my division and to take a position facing towards the left and front, on the next range of hills behind the stone house, which was the natural second position on this battle-field.

I gave the necessary orders at once. The regiments of Koltes's and Krzyzanowski's brigades came out of the fire in a very shattered condition. Their losses had been enormous. I had left Colonel Schimmelfening's brigade, which kept Captain Dilger's battery on my right, in reserve. They were exposed to a very heavy artillery fire, especially when the enemy had succeeded in establishing a battery of two pieces directly on our left, enfilading our whole front; but the men stood like trees until the order to retire reached them. They then fell back slowly and in good order. Captain Dilger's battery remained in position to check the pursuit of the enemy, whose infantry rushed upon him with great rapidity. He received them in two different positions, at short range, with a shower of grape shot, obliged them twice to fall back and then followed our column unmolested. His conduct cannot be praised too highly. When ascending the hill you had indicated to me as a rallying point, we found that the troops who, after the first repulse, had rallied immediately behind us, had disappeared; that the whole left wing of our army had given way, and that the enemy was rolling heavy masses of infantry after the retreating columns, towards our second position. The enemy's artillery was commanding almost the whole battle-field. Behind the ridge where I was to form again, and which was the natural position of the general reserve, I expected to find an intact reserve of several brigades ready to pounce upon the enemy as he was attempting to ascend the slopes of the range of hills we were then occupying, but nothing of the kind seemed to be there. I found Major General McDowell with his staff, and around him troops of several different corps and of all arms, in full retreat! I succeeded in inducing the captain of a battery, the name of which I do not know, to place his pieces upon the crest of a hill, and to resume the contest with the enemy's batteries immediately opposite us. My attempts to form compact bodies out of straggling soldiers met with very small success.

It was nearly 6 o'clock when you ordered me to send a brigade to the support of General Milroy, who was on our left below the farm-house used as a hospital, which two days before had been your headquarters. I brought forward Colonel Schimmelfennig's brigade, which advanced in excellent order, but did not find General Milroy, whose command had gone further to the left and rear. Colonel Schimmelfennig, however, went forward, and finding Generals Sykes and Reno near the place which had been indicated to him, formed on the right of General Sykes, ready to take part in the action whenever it should become advisable. The brigades of Colonels Krzyzanowski and Koltes had suffered so severely that I deemed it best to send them to the rear, in reserve. Only the 54th New York kept with me in order to cover Dilger's battery, which was placed on the ridge immediately commanding the Warrenton road and protecting the bridge across Young's Branch. We had been under a continual shower of shot and shell until it grew dark, when the infantry fire on our left, as well as the artillery fire of the enemy, suddenly ceased, only now and then a projectile dropping among us. The fight on our left had evidently come to a stand. It is probable that the forces of the enemy, when arriving at the foot of the heights we were occupying, were so exhausted that a vigorous offensive on our part would have had an excellent chance of success. You remember, general, that this matter was earnestly discussed among us on the battle-field. But General Pope's order to retreat, and the fact that the main body of our army was already on its way to Centreville, put an end to this question.

About 8 o'clock you ordered me to withdraw Colonel Schimmelfennig's brigade, and to march with my whole command across Young's Branch, two pieces of Captain Dilger's battery and one of my regiments forming the rear guard of the corps. For this office the 61st Ohio was selected, a regiment which, throughout the whole campaign, had exhibited the most commendable spirit. According to your order I passed the bridge across Young's Branch about 9 o'clock, and took position with your whole corps on the hilly ground between Young's Branch and Bull Run. Colonel Schimmelfennig furnished from his command the necessary guards and outposts along Young's Branch, and in the direction of the Bull Run ford.

There we remained over two hours, and after all other troops had passed Bull Run, and the road was clear of wagons for several miles, you ordered your corps to resume its march towards Centreville. We crossed the "stone bridge" between 11 and 12 o'clock. You ordered me to take position on the left of the road, front towards the creek, while General Stahel did the same on the right, throwing out our outposts on the other side of the creek, and placing Captain Dilger's two pieces so as to command the bridge. Some time afterwards one of General McDowell's officers informed you that we were threatened by the enemy on our left. About 1 o'clock a. m. you ordered your corps to resume its march. My first brigade, under Colonel Schimmelfennig, was to form the rear guard, and was instructed to destroy the bridge. Colonel Kane, of the Pennsylvania Bucktail Rifles, reported himself to you with a battalion of his men and several pieces of artillery which he had picked up on the road. The bridge was destroyed some time after 1 o'clock, and we marched towards Centreville, taking with us Colonel Kane's promiscous pieces of artillery behind the first regiment of Colonel Schimmelfennig's brigade. I rejoined you about 3 o'clock a. m., two miles from Centreville, where we bivouacked until 5. About 7 we arrived at Centreville, and, in the course of the day, a position was assigned to my command in the intrenchments.

My loss in the battles of the 29th and 30th, as will appear from the regimental reports, was extremely heavy, exceeding twenty per cent. of my whole effective force. Aside from the brave and noble Colonel Koltes, I have to deplore the death of a great many able and gallant officers. The number of "missing" was very small in proportion to the killed and wounded. Comparatively few of them have since rejoined their regiments, and the information I have received leads me to believe that a majority either remained dead on the battle-field or fell wounded into the hands of the enemy.

The commanders of my brigades and the officers of my staff behaved on all occasions, under the most trying circumstances, with their accustomed gallantry. As to the regimental officers and privates who distinguished themselves, as well as for an exact list of the killed and wounded, I beg leave to refer you to the documents accompanying this report.

I am, general, most truly, yours,

C. SCHURZ,
Brigadier General Commanding 3d Division.

Major General SIGEL,
Commanding 1st Army Corps.

No. 18.

REPORT OF COLONEL JOSEPH B. CARR, COMMANDING BRIGADE.

HEADQUARTERS THIRD BRIGADE, HOOKER'S DIVISION,
Camp near Fort Lyon, Virginia, September 6, 1862.

CAPTAIN: I have the honor to submit the following report of the part taken by my brigade in the late battles and marches:

Early on the morning of the 15th day of August I received orders to be prepared to march at daybreak, with rations provided, &c. At 8 o'clock a. m. I left camp near Harrison's Landing, and marched to within three (3) miles of the Chickahominy, where I bivouacked for the night, and on the following morning, at eleven (11) o'clock, proceeded two miles in the direction of the Chickahominy, where I remained until morning. On the 17th I crossed the Chickahominy and marched thirteen (13) miles, when I halted and bivouacked; and on the following morning, (18th,) at seven (7) o'clock, started for Williamsburg—seventeen (17) miles—which point I reached at half past one (1½) p. m., and went into camp outside the town. On the 19th, at 10.45, I broke camp and marched to within two (2) miles of Yorktown; and on the 20th, at ten (10) o'clock a. m., marched to Yorktown and went into camp outside the intrenchments. At eight (8) p. m. received orders to be prepared to embark on the steamship Baltic and steamer Vanderbilt, and at half past two (2½) all were aboard. We sailed that afternoon at six (6) o'clock. On the afternoon of the 22d the Baltic run aground, and a lighter coming up I sent off the 5th and 7th New Jersey volunteers, under command of Colonel S. H. Starr, with instructions to report at Acquia creek. On the 23d, the Baltic unable to get off, the remainder of my command with me was transferred to the steamship Cahawba. At Acquia creek I was ordered by General Hooker to proceed to Alexandria, where we arrived at six (6) o'clock. All camp equipage and baggage was discharged by 8½ p. m., and the men remained aboard during the night. On the 24th we disembarked at seven (7) a. m., and marched to the suburbs of the city and encamped. At 2½ p. m. the 115th Pennsylvania volunteers and 8th New Jersey volunteers reported, having, an hour previous, disembarked from the steamer Vanderbilt. At 3 p. m. the location of the camp was changed two miles further from the city, near the railroad. On the 26th my brigade was transported, by rail, to Warrenton Junction, (40 miles,) where we arrived at six (6) o'clock, and bivouacked. At three (3) a. m. on the morning of the 27th I received orders to be prepared to march at six (6) o'clock, and, one hour later, received orders to march at seven (7) a. m., which order was promptly carried into effect. My field and staff officers were all dismounted, in consequence of having left their horses at Alexandria, to be transported on the following day. I took up the line of march towards Manassas Junction, on line with the railroad, and after proceeding about four miles we came in sight of the enemy. My brigade being on the advance, I threw out skirmishers from the 2d New York volunteers, and formed two lines of battle. They advanced about one mile, the enemy retreating. At 2½ o'clock p. m., when within one half mile of Bristow Station, my skirmishers engaged those of the enemy. I formed line of battle with 2d New York volunteers and 5th and 8th New Jersey volunteers, and advanced through a dense wood, when the enemy made a stand. The 2d New York volunteers and 8th New Jersey volunteers were on the left of the railroad, the 5th New Jersey volunteers on the right, General Hooker taking the 6th and 7th New Jersey volunteers on the left. The 2d New York volunteers and 8th New Jersey volunteers advanced through the woods and charged the enemy, driving him about two hundred (200) yards, into a thick woods, where they again made a stand and gave battle. I sent in the 115th Pennsylvania volunteers, after an hour's fighting, to relieve the 2d New York volunteers, and they held their ground until the retreat of the enemy. After making the charge with the 2d New York and 8th New Jersey volunteers, Colonel Taylor, with the second brigade, came in and took position on my left, placing two regiments on my right, parallel to my line, to engage the enemy on the railroad. After the retreat of the enemy we formed line of battle on the right of the railroad, to support General Grover, who was then in pursuit of him. Here we remained until ordered by General Hooker to cross the creek, where we bivouacked for the night. On Thursday afternoon, August 28th, at two (2) o'clock, we were ordered to march in the direction of Manassas, but did not halt for the night until we arrived at Bull Run creek. At two (2) o'clock Friday morning, August 29, I received orders to march at three a. m. and support General Kearney, who was in pursuit of the enemy. A march of ten miles brought us to the Bull Run battle-field. About eleven (11) a. m. was ordered in position to support a battery in front of the woods, where the enemy, with General Sigel's troops, was engaged. Remaining about one hour in that position, was ordered to send in to the woods and relieve two regiments of General Sigel's corps. I sent in the 6th and 7th New Jersey volunteers. Afterwards received orders to take the balance of the brigade in the woods, which I did at about two (2) p. m. Here I at once engaged the enemy and fought him for a space of two hours, holding my position until our ammunition was all expended. About four (4) o'clock we were relieved by General Reno and Colonel Taylor, but did not reach the skirt of the woods before a retreat was made and the woods occupied by the enemy. When I arrived out of the woods I was ordered to march about half a mile to the rear and bivouac for the night. During Saturday, August 30, we remained in that position until 2 p. m., when I was ordered by General Hooker to march my brigade out on the road in pursuit of the enemy. After marching out on the road was ordered to halt and await further orders. I retained this position until four (4) p. m., and was then ordered to the front to support a battery, my brigade to constitute the second line. Here I remained, under a heavy cross-fire of the enemy, until ordered by General Hooker to march to and support a battery on the left of the field. When I reached this place I found no battery to support, but was ordered to support one in the rear and on the left, which I did. We remained there until ordered to march to the rear, in the direction of Centreville. This was about 7 p. m. We marched in perfect order, fording a stream waist deep, and arrived at Centreville at 1 o'clock a. m., where we remained until the next day, Sunday, August 31st, when we changed camp to the rear. On Monday, September 1, at 3 o'clock, received orders to march in the direction of Fairfax. At 4 p. m. took up the line of march on the centre road. When about two miles from Centreville heard firing on our right, and was ordered by General Grover to halt and form line of battle on the left of the road. I was soon after ordered to move up my line to the support of General Kearney's left. After remaining in this position about two hours, was ordered to the front, where I remained until 2 o'clock a. m. Was then ordered to take up the line of march for Fairfax, where I arrived about sunrise. Here I pitched camp and remained until 11 o'clock a. m., and then starting for Alexandria, halting for the night at about twelve (12) miles from Fairfax. Resuming the march at 6 o'clock on the following morning, I reached Fort Lyon and went into camp at 2 o'clock on the afternoon of Wednesday, September 3.

The following are the casualties in the actions of August 27th, 29th, and 30th:

Second New York volunteers.

Killed.—Corporals Oliver H. Porter, Charles Reith, Thomas B. Casey, and Frederick P. Wrigley; Privates Edward Farrell, John T. Andrews, James Taylor, John Jones, Michael Manning, Frank O'Neil, and Charles Stickney.

Wounded.—Captains John H. Quackenbush, John Maguire, and S. Lee Perkins, (since died;) First Lieutenant Francis Temple, Second Lieutenant Joseph Egolf, Second Lieutenant Cornelius Kirker; Sergeant Major Theodore Horn; First Sergeants Robert B. Dicke, George D. Smith, and Nathan F. Hodgman; Sergeants Michael Russell, William McCollough, and August Willard; Corporals Peter Robson, Joseph Homan, Lorenz Kingsby, John Rowland, Warren Harrington, Peter P. Ray, jr., George H. Pierce, Peter Bromhower, William Greenwood, William A. Gaffney, and Thomas Thrane; Privates Thomas Hines, Jacob A. Bercroft, John P. McNamara, William E. Hydom, John Lucey, John O'Brien, David Earle, Paul Manner, John Narcotte, Jacob Baker, James Duffy, James H. Flynn, Patrick Grace, Thomas Hennessey, Frank Mayatte, James Sullivan, Joseph C. Taylor, Simeon Moranville, James Beale, Henry C. Dunnell, William R. Frear, Daniel E. Gardner, James C. McGowan, James M. Sturtevant, John Finley, John Medlicott, Patrick O'Donnell, Joseph Savior, Patrick Conway, Michael Daly, William Heady, David Murray, Frederick Epting, Edward Walton, Ferdinand Wise, Frederick Wuest, and Adolphus Stande.

Missing.—Privates George Looby, Patrick Kearney, John Gormley, Michael Ryan, John A. Smith, Edward S. Wilson, John Mills, John Brinn, Henry Todt.

Fifth New Jersey volunteers.

Killed.—Captain Edward A. Acton; Second Lieutenant Frederick A. Brill; Corporal John B. Clayton; Privates John F. Lookerson and Michael Doyle, and Sergeant C. J. Boone.

Wounded.—Captains H. H. Woolsey and John Gamble; Corporals George W. Dally, John H. Van Pilt, James S. Flanigan, John Polan, and George Custis; Privates John Savage, William Petersley, John Bower, John Dennis, James Bell, William H. Flinn, Thomas Gibson, William Harris, John O'Connell, Christian Arnheiter, Edward Peel, William Heatty, Richard Gill, William Chamberlain, Augustus King, John C. Haas, William Frazer, John Buckley, John McConnell, James Greaves, William Fairhurst, William Norberry, John Gartermasker, Matthew Carney, Daniel Flanigan, James Donaldson, Thomas McBride, and Henry Rosswick.

Missing.—Lieutenant Edward P. King, Sergeant Robert Evans, and Privates Patrick McLaughlin, Emile Naugaut, Benjamin Smith, John Stryker, Richard Sibbitt, Jonathan Sibbitt, John Schornhut, John Hopple, and Charles Depsey.

Sixth New Jersey volunteers.

Killed.—First Sergeant Edward Corcoran, Sergeant Isacher Ettinger, and Privates John T. Vannote, George Higgins, William Yields, Thomas Van Brunt, Thomas Jones, William Hamlin, Benjamin F. Budd, Michael Wright, Elijah Q. Burroughs, A. C. Cornell, John Jobes, Edward Ewen, John Gaggers, Martin Marshall, James Coleman, and William Bishbring.

Wounded.—Colonel G. Mott and Major S. R. Gilkyson; First Sergeant Jonathan Maguire, Sergeants David Smith, Robert Ames, and James White; Privates John Jeffrey, Daniel Bresnahan, Samuel Applegate, Henry C. Christie, Stien E. Jamieson, William R. Morris, Johnston Lutz, James Reed, James Williams, James Quirk, George Mason, Woodward Cox, Joseph Graisberry, Job Davison, Patchie Barry, William Rianhard, Solon R. Hankinson, Robert Hancock, Isaiah Lippincott, George Jobes, Edwin Packer, William Maling, Henry Firth, Reed Price, August Secor, William Brown, John C. Whippey, William Loeb, Charles Braceland, James R. Hasted, William Hampton, Isaac T. Garton, Elias Jones, John Leo, Robert McAdoo, Michael McLaughlin, Jeremiah Price, B. F. Reeves, William V. Robinson, Isaac Warr, and Nathaniel Wilkinson.

Missing.—First Sergeant Frederick Young, and Sergeants David S. Oliphant, John E. Loeb, and William F. Goodman; Corporals Smith Applegate, Frederick Boorman, James Smith, and George Harrow; Privates Josiah Garwood, William Jemison, John Nugent, Albert B. Pryor, Michael Comer, John Evans, Henry Herrman, Nehemiah Wright, John Wagoner, Thomas Bottomly, William Groves, Levi Jess, Aaron Stone, William Bibby, Jonathan Barnes, Peter Miller, William Russell, James Sherman, Albert Woolman, Thomas Gladding, Thomas Taylor, Edward B. Hood, William Dorsey, William D. Jacob, Jacob Gilmore, James H. Webster, James W. Lewis, Watson Wertsell, John Wiley, and Wm. H. H. Lawrence.

Seven'h New Jersey volunteers.

Killed.—Captain Joseph Abbott, and Privates James Shewell and Richard Vanorden.

Wounded.—Sergeant James H. Onslow, Corporal Curtis, and Privates James McPeter, William Stevens, Andrew Kelly, Samuel Petit, Thomas Wilbravin, Henry Engle, John Corbitt, James Bennett, Thomas Mack, Patrick McEvoy, George Pritz, James Spugenbergh, Charles Johnson, Isaac Archer, and John R. Lyon.

Missing.—Assistant Surgeon Charles B. Jacques, and Privates Thomas Finning, Charles Wilson, Patrick O'Riley, Daniel Courtin, John Ryan, Patrick Corbitt, John Brady, William Willis, William Sweeney, Henry Myers, and Henry Angleman.

Eighth New Jersey volunteers.

Killed.—Captain John Yuite, Sergeant Robert Johnson, Corporal John M. Renck, and Privates William Gaysell and George Garrison.

Wounded.—Lieutenant Colonel William Ward; First Sergeant John C. Steinbar; Corporals Henry Hattman, Jacob A. Young, N. B. Clark, G. Cline, Enock Scudder, Charles Huntly, and Diltz Slack; Privates George Hopwood, William Robinson, Lawrence Healy, Christopher Farrell, Frank Crampton, Hermann Calhoun, John Kehoe, Horace B. Mackridge, William J. Lake, John T. Thompson, Francis Hackett, William Kenworth, Samuel N. Wood, Joseph Wyckoff, Arthur Nesbit, Newton Johnson, Edward Carter, D. Cooper, E. E. Wonderly, F. E. Denniss, William Donald, H. B. Graves, F. M. Harrison, J. Schultz, Thomas McSoulby, F. C. Dunker, William Donnelly, Elias Hoffman, Jabez Lee, James J. Lake, James M. Clay, John B. Stewart, Hamilton Bowlsby, William Bowlsby, John Bird, Barney Hammill, Thomas Far, Michael Harste, Charles Airy, Henry French, Napoleon Débue, John F. Cloriser, and Dennis McGowan.

One hundred and fifteenth regiment Pennsylvania volunteers.

Killed.—Corporal Boswell C. Bowie, and Privates Luther C. Neff, Frank Donelly, and Daniel Reagan.

Wounded.—Major F. A. Lancaster, Captain P. O'Murphy, Lieutenants Richard Dillon and R. L. Thompson; Corporals John Brown, Daniel Manina, A. T. McCutcheon, and Frank Spencer; Privates Michael Allen, James Burns, Samuel Rogers, William Whelan, William Fan, Michael Mulgreu, Hugh McKendrick, Isaac Weidner, John Broderick, and James Lyons.

Missing.—Corporal Charles Sweeny, and Privates James Walton, Michael Malone, John Sullivan, Michael Reardon, James Oricell, Jacob P. Wiseman, William Wood, James McCarroll, John Walls, John Linderman, and John Charlton.

RECAPITULATION.

Distribution.	Killed, wounded, and missing.						Total commissioned officers.	Total enlisted men.	Aggregate.
	Commissioned officers.	Enlisted men.	Commissioned officers.	Enlisted men.	Commissioned officers.	Enlisted men.			
2d infantry, New York volunteers....	....	11	6	55	....	9	6	75	81
5th regiment New Jersey volunteers.	2	4	2	33	1	10	5	47	52
6th regiment New Jersey volunteers.	....	18	2	50	....	38	2	106	108
7th regiment New Jersey volunteers.	1	2	....	19	1	10	2	31	33
8th regiment New Jersey volunteers.	1	4	2	52	....	....	3	56	59
115th reg't Pennsylvania volunteers.	....	4	4	14	....	12	4	30	34
	4	43	16	223	2	79	22	345	367

In conclusion, while bearing testimony to the brilliancy of the battle of Bristow Station, I am proud to record the gallant conduct rendered of the 2d New York volunteers, 5th and 8th New Jersey volunteers, and 115th Pennsylvania volunteers, (the 6th and 7th New Jersey volunteers having been detached for the time did not become engaged,) when *all* did well, it is no less a delicate than a difficult matter to make individual distinctions; still I cannot pass by so favorable and appropriate an opportunity, to mention the following officers, who particularly distinguished themselves on this occasion: Captains Park, Tibbits, Perkins, (killed,) Maquire, (wounded,) Quackenbush, (wounded,) and Hagan; and Lieutenants Savage, Temple, (wounded,) Fisher, Dickie, (wounded,) Egolf, (wounded,) and McNulty, of the 2d New York volunteers; Lieutenant Colonel Ward, 8th New Jersey volunteers; and Major Lancaster, (wounded); and Lieutenant Colonel Thompson, 115th Pennsylvania volunteers; Lieutenant Le Grand Benedict, acting assistant adjutant general, and Lieutenant George Gould, aide-de-camp.

During the desperate battle of Bull Run and, whilst under an incessant and galling fire, the following named officers won for themselves honor and distinction by gallant and meritorious conduct:

Lieutenant Colonel Small, Major Ramsey, and Captain Woolsey, (wounded,) 5th New Jersey volunteers; Colonel Mott, (wounded,) Major Gilkyson, (wounded,) Lieutenant Colonel Burling, and Captains Baker and Crawford, 6th New Jersey volunteers; Colonel Reven, 7th New Jersey volunteers; Lieutenant Colonel Ward, (wounded,) and Acting Major Juite, (killed,) 8th New Jersey volunteers; Lieutenant Le Grand Benedict, acting assistant adjutant general, and Lieutenant George Gould, aide-de-camp.

Great credit and praise are due to Chaplain Moore, 6th New Jersey volunteers, for his unceasing attentions to our wounded on the field, and also to each and every surgeon of the brigade for their faithfulness on this as well as on many other occasions.

I am proud of my brigade, and esteem it an honor of no mean order to command such a body of men and soldiers, who, not only by their gallantry on the field of battle, but also by their good conduct and strict devotion to duty in camp have reflected so much credit upon themselves, their noble division, and the States which they so faithfully represent.

I have the honor to be, very respectfully, your obedient servant,

JOS. B. CARR,
Colonel, Commanding Brigade.

Captain Jos. Dickerson,
Assistant Adjutant General.

No. 19.

REPORT OF COLONEL J. A. MUHLECK, 73d PENNSYLVANIA.

Colonel John A. Koltes, commanding brigade.

In the night from Friday to Saturday the above brigade bivouacked in the corner of a woods, in the rear and south of those woods where General Carl Schurz's division on the day before (Friday) had had a terrible encounter with the enemy, who were attacked and thrown by him, and driven at the point of the bayonet clear through the woods, over the railroad embankment.

We formed on that morning the extreme left wing of the 2d division, to which this brigade had been attached in the course of the preceding day, while the whole division was drawn up as a reserve to those troops of ours which held the battle-field over night.

At 6 o'clock a. m. on Saturday the brigade formed in "*columns of division on the centre en masse*," and soon afterwards received orders to march down to the left into the open plain field and to re-form in "columns of companies, *left* in front." Here the brigade stood in the following order: The 68th New York, under Lieutenant Colonel Kleefisch, on the *right*; the 73d Pennsylvania, Lieutenant Colonel Mühleck on the *left;* the 29th New York in the *centre*, Major Hartman commanding.

The firing up to 2 o'clock p. m. had been of little account, but soon afterwards became heavier by degrees. The enemy had crowned the plateau (a little over a mile in front of our division) with numerous batteries, and now opened a fire which now became truly terrific. General Morell's division, which was massed in front and nearest the rebel batteries, were soon forced to withdraw from the open plain and to seek shelter in the rear of the woods to their right. The enemy's firing was splendid, their range perfect. As soon as our first line had withdrawn, the rebels opened on the heavy bodies of infantry massed about 400 yards more to the rear, and of which General Schurz's division constituted a part. It was then about three o'clock p. m. Our batteries were unable to silence the enemy's raking, concentrating fire. Our loss here was heavy, (through shot and shell.)

In the meanwhile, the firing on our left (woody hills) had become extremely heavy. McDowell's troops, which had been ordered up to the extreme left of our line of battle, after a very short contest, lasting not over half an hour, were retiring from their position, abandoning the woods to the enemy, who at once poured heavy masses of infantry into them, seconded by artillery. A part of Major General Sigel's army corps (General Stahel's) had already been ordered up to the left, to re-enforce McDowell, but found themselves, on reaching the top of the hill, in front of an overpowering enemy, whom they bravely engaged. At this moment Major General Sigel, Brigadier General Schurz, commanding division, with staff, came up at full speed in front of the first brigade, and ordered its three regiments up at once to the assistance of General Stahel. I marched my regiment by the left flank, followed by the 29th New York in the centre, and 68th New York on the right. We reached the top of the hill under a terrific shower of shell, solid shot, chains, &c. I deployed at once. The enemy was right in front, advancing slowly, but steadily, in dense masses. A galling fire commenced from both sides. To our *left*, where we found the "De Kalb" regiment isolated from their brigade, a battery of some other corps d'army had been abandoned; the last named regiment, which General Stahel had wished Colonel Koltes to take under his temporary command (it being too far off from his main body) endeavored to save the cannons, but in vain. The enemy by this time had brought up, and posted near the border of the woods, (south southwest of our brigade,) two sections of artillery, which, from a distance of scarcely 200 yards, covered my own regiment, as well as the others, with a perfect shower of projectiles. It was at that supreme moment that the brave Colonel Koltes rode up to the front of his brigade, and swinging his sword high in the air, while ordering his command to take that rebel battery, that a fragment of a shell killed both horse and rider. A rush was made toward the rebel cannons; some of my men, with Second Lieutenant Kennedy, company F, reached the pieces, but were unsupported, surrounded, and the lieutenant made a prisoner, (he escaped a few moments afterwards, a man of company D, 73d Pennsylvania volunteers, killing the rebel who had made him a prisoner.) The terrain was most unfavorable for deploying, being surrounded right and left by woods, with a deep ravine in the rear, and forming a kind of clearing not more than two acres in length.

The combat here raged fierce and terrible for about half an hour, when our small regiments, exhausted and decimated and unsupported, had in their turn to fall back, though not before Colonel Koltes, who saw the enemy outflank us on the right, had given the order to fall back a little on our right and make a stand again. By this time immense forces of the enemy poured through the woods in spendid order and fighting desperately. The colors of my regiment had become rags; I had lost five of the color bearers and nearly one-half of the eight companies I brought into action, (two companies had been detailed by General —— to stop the stragglers of the corps which did retreat from the plain beneath.) My acting major, Captain A. Brückner, had fallen too; my adjutant was a prisoner; my own horse had been shot under me by four balls. We then slowly left the field, still fighting and taking along the dead body of Colonel Koltes, whom my men carried that night on muskets to Centreville, which latter place the regiment reached, rather in broken fragments, and where they rallied again on the next morning.

The loss of the 73d was very heavy; officers killed and wounded, 8; non-commissioned officers and privates killed, wounded, and missing, 138. The losses in the several regiments will be found detailed in the accompanying separate reports. Many acts of daring and heroism have been done. I will take pleasure in bringing the names of those to your knowledge in a separate report to be made out at once.

I have the honor to be, general, very respectfully, your obedient servant,

G. A. MUHLECK, *Lieutenant Colonel*
73d Pennsylvania volunteers, Commanding 1st Brigade,
3d Division, 1st Army Corps.

No. 20.

REPORT OF LIEUTENANT COLONEL S. J. McGROARTZ, SIXTY-FIRST OHIO VOLUNTEERS.

HEADQUARTERS SIXTY-FIRST OHIO VOLUNTEERS,
Camp Carl Schurz, Minor's Hill, September 13, 1863.

GENERAL: The following report would have been submitted to you sometime since in obedience to orders, but for the want of writing materials which, at the time, it was impossible to procure.

On the 24th or 25th of August I assumed command of the 61st regiment on the enemy's side of the Rappahannock, during the skirmish at Freeman's Ford. Colonel Schleich, who accompanied us across the river, was, shortly after the opening of the fight, not to be found, and the regiment being without a head was led on by Captain Koney, of General Schurz's staff, and myself. The 61st covered the retreat across the river, and being assigned a new position in anticipation of a battle, remained under arms during the night. The report of the killed and wounded has already been handed in.

On the following morning we left for White Sulphur Springs, at which place we were ordered to support a battery, (name forgotten,) and we remained about three hours under a heavy fire of the enemy's guns. We there lost two wounded and one killed, besides some missing.

At this place and during the fire I noticed the unaccountable absence of Lieutenant Rankin and Lieutenant Junkins, and Colonel Schleich was also absent from his post; also Lieutenants Hay and Givens. Major Bown, during that day, displayed remarkable coolness and energy in bringing up the rear of the regiment. We then proceeded on towards Waterloo Bridge. We were ordered out to assist Milroy's brigade in burning the bridge; at about 4 p. m. of that day attacked the enemy on the opposite side of the river to prevent the restoration of the bridge. The enemy's fire, which was very severe, both of artillery and musketry, was sustained by our men with great coolness, who delivered, in turn, their own fire with marked effect. At about 11 p. m. we were directed to cover the rear of the column. We then proceeded to Warrenton, thence to Gainesville, whence we marched to Manassas Plains, a little beyond which we bivouacked in line of battle. The men had no provision, but I had hauled some fresh beef in the ambulances, which was cooked and eaten on Thursday evening at about 11 p. m. On arriving at the ambulances, Lieutenant Biff, who was in command of a squad sent for that purpose, was told by Colonel Schleich that he should not take a God d—n bite of it, unless the regiment marched back to get it.

On the next morning, when we advanced, the 61st was posted in a wood on the right, in reserve. A few moments afterwards our skirmishers became engaged; then one and two companies, then five, then the whole regiment advanced, the 74th being on our right. We advanced about one mile and a half, pushing the enemy before us and driving them over the railroad, over which we followed them through a ravine and up to a corn-field, where we, in turn, were driven back, but rallied at the railroad, which we held until relieved at 2½ p. m. The severe firing here was very effective. At that time we understood that we were surrounded, and being ordered to make a bayonet charge, relieved ourselves from our position. We were then relieved. About one hour and a half afterwards our men were repulsed and fell back through the woods. We were again called up to form in line of battle and advance. We thereupon moved into the woods and remained all night.

On Saturday, at daybreak, we moved more towards our left and remained stationary until the firing of the afternoon began, about 4 o'clock, when we were again moved towards the centre in reserve, which position we held till near the close of the battle. We were then ordered to support Milroy's brigade. We were then placed behind Reno's division, when General Schurz ordered us quickly to retire towards Centreville. On the way down we were retained an hour or more by two of Captain Dilger's pieces which had been dismounted. Remaining near the battle-field till 11 p. m., we moved on, halting again for two hours, and thus proceeded to Centreville. There we were again formed in line of battle. Then we moved on the following evening to Fairfax, and thence to a position near the fortifications of Washington.

Through all these trials the regiment behaved with the greatest gallantry, being stimulated thereto by the bearing of Colonel Schimmelpfenning and General Schurz, in whom the men learned to repose perfect confidence.

I cannot forbear mentioning Major Bown as having been highly effective, and of all the company officers who were present. Edward H. Newcomb, quartermaster sergeant, distinguished himself by his gallant conduct, insomuch as to attract the attention of the general commanding the division on the battle-field.

The following officers were, to me, unaccountably absent since the skirmish at Freeman's Ford: Colonel N. Schleich; Lieutenants George Leininger, James H. Bird, Rankin, Junkins, Edwin Hay, McDougal, Givens; also Sergeant Major Grodinsky. I hope, general, that you will find it convenient to inquire into the reason of the absence and general conduct of the last-named officers.

Permit me to say, also, in conclusion, that of the colonel commanding the brigade and of our gallant division general, we are, one and all, justly and highly proud; and for their attention and personal example through all the scenes of those eventful days, from first to last, profoundly grateful.

I have the honor to be, very respectfully, your obedient servant,

S. J. McGROARTZ,
Lieutenant Colonel Commanding 61st Ohio.

Acting General SCHIMMELPFENNING,
Commanding 1st Brigade, 3d Division.

No. 21.

REPORT OF MAJOR F. BLESSING, SEVENTY-FOURTH PENNSYLVANIA VOLUNTEERS.

HEADQUARTERS SEVENTY-FOURTH REGIMENT PENN. VOL. INFANTRY.

Report of the battles at Manassas, Virginia, on the 29th and 30th August, 1862.

The regiment reached the heights of Manassas Plains on the 28th of August towards evening. It was ordered to reconnoitre the grounds in a direction east, but found no enemy. The skirmishers advanced through thin woods on to Young's Branch, where they halted as pickets for the night, the regiment 500 paces in their rear. At 5 o'clock a. m. August the 29th we left this place, meeting our brigade, commanded by Colonel A. Schimmelfennig, at 6 o'clock. After a rest of about fifteen minutes the regiment was ordered to take its position on the extreme right of the army corps then advancing. Under cover of skirmishers in the front and right flank we advanced in quick time over an open field until we arrived at the centre of the woods, where in an opening we halted. The skirmishers met the skirmishing line of the enemy, opened fire, and drove them from the woods. Forced by the heavy artillery fire of the enemy, we changed several times our positions. From the right flank came the report that a strong column was advancing, but that it was impossible to recognize whether friend or foe. It was afterwards ascertained to be General Kearney's corps, for our relief. The regiment was then ordered to the left, where it took its position in the general battle-line, after advancing about 400 yards under the heavy fire of the enemy, driving the latter back and out of his positions; but by the withdrawing of a regiment stationed on the left of the 74th, the enemy took advantage, and, outflanking us, we were forced back about 100 yards. Forming again in column for attack, the regiment advanced in quick time towards the enemy, who gave way until he arrived at the other side of the railroad dam. Here again flanked by the enemy, and under a galling fire of grapeshot and canister, the regiment had to leave its position, which it did by making a flank movement to the left, forcing the enemy to withdraw from the woods. We advanced over our former position, capturing an ambulance with two wounded officers, to the seam of the woods. At this point a heavy shower of grapeshot and canister pouring into us, we withdrew to the railroad dam. After resting here for about thirty minutes, we were ordered by General Schurz to support a battery on the extreme right, keeping in that position till the battery left. We then again joined our brigade. Wearied and exhausted, we camped for the night on the same ground the enemy held the night previous.

On the morning of the 30th the regiment formed in column, taking its position on the right of the centre. It was exposed all day to a tremendous shower of bomb-shell, canister, &c., but did not fall back until the order for general retreat was given. The regiment then withdrew to the left, where it took a good position, and remained until the whole army had passed. It was dark before we received the direct order from General Sigel to follow the army. We then marched to the Bull Run, and were ordered to remain there until all the wagons and ambulances had passed over the bridge. After this was done, Captain A. Mitzel, with two companies of the regiment, was ordered to destroy the bridge, which order was fulfilled with many difficulties.

The regiment again joined the army at Centreville. During these several engagements all the officers and men behaved themselves bravely and splendid, executing all orders promptly.

F. BLESSING,

Major, Com'd'g 74th Regiment Pennsylvania Volunteer Infantry.

No. 22.

REPORT OF MAJOR STEPHEN KOVACS, 54TH NEW YORK STATE VOLUNTEERS.

FIFTY-FOURTH REGIMENT NEW YORK STATE VOLUNTEERS,
Camp near Arlington Heights, September 12, 1862.

SIR: I have the honor to report that, on the 29th August, 1862, the 54th regiment New York State volunteers was drawn up in line of battle, at 6 o'clock a. m., at Manassas, and ordered for reserve by General Schurz; at 8 o'clock, by his orders, was sent to the woods to drive out the enemy, and found them in large force. The regiment instantly became engaged, and it held the woods in spite of the superior numbers until 1 o'clock, when it was relieved by another regiment. In this engagement the officers and men behaved themselves bravely, especially the 2d color-bearer, William Rauschmüller, who, seeing his comrade (the 1st color-bearer) fall, instantly seized the flag, and at the same time he cared for his wounded comrade, took him to the rear, and immediately returned again to his proper place. After this the regiment was ordered to fall back to another wood about half a mile distant, with the order to be in column by division, to be ready for any emergency, and the regiment remained under arms all night.

The 30th, the 54th regiment New York State volunteers was ordered, at 10 o'clock, to draw up in line of battle on the plains of Manassas; about 3 o'clock the enemy commenced to pour into us a terrible fire of shot and shell, and under this fire the regiment suffered very much, and stood like a wall; about 4 o'clock the regiment was ordered to advance up the hill to check the enemy, who was trying to flank our left, which was done. After this the regiment was ordered by General Krzyzanowski to be relieved. In the meantime the regiment received orders, by Major General Sigel, to hold the ditch, which was done; the commanding officer of the regiment, Lieutenant Colonel Ashby, seeing the regiment left without support, withdrew the troops slowly to the battery of Captain Dilger, reaching there at 7 o'clock p. m., and the regiment was ordered by Major General Sigel as the rear guard.

In this engagement I have the honor to mention the gallant conduct of First Lieutenant Werthheimer, who, with a small flag in his hand, advanced about 6 paces before the regiment and the regiment advanced with cheers on a double quick and fired on the enemy. I also have to mention the brave conduct of the following non-commissioned officers: Sergeant Major E. Both, Orderly Sergeant Priedle, Orderly Sergeant Ostershal, Orderly Sergeant Nelson, Sergeants Ravens, King, Steaven, Werner, Botler, Hartmann.

I am sorry to report the loss of many brave officers and men, as the original report will testify. Killed, wounded and missing—total 161 men.

I am, sir, very respectfully, your obedient servant,

STEVEN KOVACS,
Major, Commanding 54th Regiment N. Y. S. V.

General W. KRZYZANOWSKI,
Commanding 2d Brigade.

No. 23.

REPORT OF CAPTAIN F. BRAUM, 58TH NEW YORK VOLUNTEERS.

HEADQUARTERS 58TH REGIMENT NEW YORK STATE VOLUNTEERS,
Camp near Arlington Heights, September 12, 1862.

I have the honor to submit the following report:

The regiment arrived, after three days' marching from camp near Robertson river, in camp near Sulphur Springs, Virginia, on the 20th of August. The next day marched to Rappahannock Station, camped there one night, and left on the 22d for Fox Ford, on the Rappahannock river, on which place an artillery skirmish took place during the day, and that night the regiment was ordered on picket duty.

August the 23d and 24th the regiment marched down the river and passed under heavy artillery firing to Sulphur Springs, marching up the road to Warrenton. Near Waterloo, Virginia, the regiment was encamped till the 25th in the evening; to that time the regiment formed column as reserve, while a bridge was burnt down by General Milroy's forces. The same night the regiment started for Warrenton, at which place they encamped till the 27th, and left the same day, marching up the road to Gainesville 7 miles; ordered on picket duty on the right flank of the main body and went, marched the night in camp, marching 3 miles above Buckland, Virginia. The 28th instant marched through Gainesville to Manassas Plain, arrived there late in the afternoon, and took position formed in column. The 29th instant the regiment was ordered into action, and marching over a plain ground, soon was engaged with the enemy, which had taken position in the woods. The regiment held the enemy in check from 8 o'clock in the morning till 2 o'clock p. m., when the regiment was relieved. The loss of the regiment was 29 in killed, wounded and missing. The 30th August the regiment was placed in reserve during all day, heavy artillery firing was going on, and at noon the regiment was drawn into action again. Marching up a hill the regiment received a severe cross fire of artillery and sharpshooters, and had to retire; took possession of a hill on the left, and holding the enemy in check on this place till dark. The regiment's loss in this engagement was 28 killed, wounded and missing. The regiment fell back down to the Bull Run, and, after a few hours' rest, crossed over the burning bridge at midnight. Marching all night, arrived early in the morning at Centreville, Virginia, on which place the regiment was encamped under cover of the intrenchments At Centreville all property belonging to the regiment, which was taken from the train, was burnt up by higher authority.

I am, sir, very respectfully, your obedient servant,

CAPT. F. BRAUM,
Commanding 58th Regiment N. Y. S.

Major KOVACS,
Commanding 2d Brigade, 3d Division.

No. 24.

REPORT OF CAPTAIN M. WEIDRICK, COMMANDING BATTERY I, FIRST REGIMENT NEW YORK ARTILLERY.

FORT DE KALB, *September* 13, 1862.

MAJOR: In accordance to general orders of this date, I transmit you the following report.

On arriving, on the 22d of August, near Freeman's fort, I was ordered by General Schurz to advance with my battery. After advancing about a quarter of a mile, Captain Schirmer, chief of artillery, ordered me to relieve Captain De Buk's battery, which had been in action for some time. On nearing the place, I was met by Major General Sigel, who ordered me to place two ten-pound Parrott guns in a new position on a hill in some woods near the river. After posting those pieces Major General Sigel ordered me to take my other two Parrott guns to the right of Captain Buk's battery, which I did, and left my two howitzers in reserve.

The fire of the enemy was very hot where the two sections of my battery were posted.

Here we had killed and wounded as follows: Killed, Private Florian Knoch; wounded, Sergeant Jacob Bock, in the breast and foot; Sergeant Christian Stock, in the arm; Corporal John Blau, in the breast; and Private George Himmel, in the face. We also had two horses killed, and ten others rendered unfit for further service, which had to be shot. There was also, at the same time, one of our limber boxes shot in fire and exploded, but did no other damage.

August 24th we were engaged at near White Sulphur Springs, also at Waterloo Bridge. At the latter place Private George Lother was wounded. We were also engaged at the latter place August 25th, but sustained no loss. We were also engaged in the battles at Bull Run, August 29th and 30th. Went in action on the 29th at about 10 o'clock a. m., when we were ordered forward by Captain Schirmer, chief of artillery. After advancing a short distance we were met by Major General Sigel, who ordered me to take a position on the right of the road to support the infantry in case they should be driven back. After remaining in this position about half an hour, Major General Sigel came to me and ordered me ahead with the four Parrott guns to support Captain Dilger's battery; which order was executed as prompt as possible by taking a position on which the enemy had the range with one of his batteries, but in about fifteen minutes after we opened fire on it, it was silenced. We kept our position until about three o'clock in the afternoon, when our ammunition gave out, and we were obliged to retire to get a new supply. After getting the ammunition we started again to take our former position, but finding that Captain Diekman was there with his battery, I returned to where I had left my two howitzers in the forenoon. Soon after coming in action there, Lieutenant Schenkelberger had his leg shattered by a shell; also, Private William Moller, the arm; both of which had to be amputated.

After using up the remainder of our ammunition, I retired with my battery to near Major General Sigel's headquarters, where I remained during the night. On this day we had one piece dismounted, and on another the axle shot through; but I am happy to say that we brought all of the pieces out of the reach of the enemy.

August 30th, after receiving a new supply of ammunition, I was ordered, with mine and Captain Buell's battery, to report to General Schenck, who ordered me to report, with four Parrott guns, to Colonel McClean, and keep my howitzers and Captain Buell's six-pounder brass guns in reserve. We remained in a position in front of his brigade on a low hill, with the ten-pound Parrotts, until about four o'clock p. m., when at this time Colonel McClean sent me an order to follow his brigade, to take a position on a hill to the left of the road. After coming into action in a position selected by General Schenck, Major General McDowell called me to him and wanted to know what I was going to do, and forbade me to open fire for fear of injuring our own men; of which there was one battery about 500 yards in front, to our right, and some infantry a short distance in advance of that battery, to our left; one of the enemy's batteries was directly in our front, behind some woods. When, a few minutes afterwards, the aforesaid infantry was repulsed by the enemy, Major General McDowell took his infantry and artillery from our left and moved in front of my battery, towards the right flank, leaving our left, as it looked to me, uncovered. When, soon after he was gone, the enemy's infantry advanced out of some woods directly in front, where Major General McDowell stood, and attacked my battery, Colonel McClean came to our support with his brigade. The fire on both sides was very sharp, and the overwhelming numbers of the enemy forced us, after a hard contest, to fall back on another hill in our rear, where we came in position again and remained till nearly dark; and after exhausting our ammunition we fell back towards Centreville, where we arrived next morning.

Very respectfully, your obedient servant,

M. WIEDRICK,

Captain commanding Battery I, 1st regiment New York artillery.

Major MEISSENBERG,

Assistant Adjutant General.

No. 25.

REPORT OF CAPTAIN H. DILLGER, COMMANDING BATTERY I, FIRST OHIO VOLUNTEER ARTILLERY.

CAMP NEAR MINER'S HILL,

September 16, 1862.

GENERAL: Respecting the part my battery took in the late conflicts of the 29th and 30th of August, 1862, I have the honor to report the following:

On Friday, the 29th of August, the battery was ordered, under the protection of Colonel Koltes's brigade, to the support of General Schenck's division, upon the left flank of the 1st corps. I advanced to the left of the road and took position upon the outermost elevation in our front, just opposite a large battery of the enemy, which, mounting about ten guns, was posted upon the hill enclosing the valley.

After two hours' incessant firing the enemy's guns were silenced for a while, in consequence, no doubt, of the successive explosion of two of their caissons. During this pause, which was improved to prepare the battery for the continuance of the contest for the important position, opportunity was also afforded me to support the infantry on our right, that had been compelled to fall back across the railroad track, with two pieces of artillery posted on the right of my battery.

The enemy's battery, however, was not long in making its appearance again; I engaged it until Wiedrich's battery and two pieces of Dickman's battery were sent, by my request, through order of General Sigel, to my assistance, and after I had exhausted all my ammunition, of which there was not an over supply, to my relief; by this time the fire of the enemy slackened its concentration upon this position.

The loss I sustained during this engagement, which lasted four hours, was twenty-two horses, and four men slightly wounded. The damage to the guns was slight, so that they could be repaired in the evening.

On the morning of Saturday, the 30th of August, the battery was assigned to Colonel Krzyzanowski's brigade.

While the division was advancing I took position on the left of the battery that was posted upon the summit of the hill, fronting the enemy's battery which I engaged yesterday.

Being apprised by you, general, of the danger that was threatening our centre, I took the only two guns that had not been brought into position, on account of the want of room, with me, and engaged with them the battery that was in the act of flanking us from the corner of the woods.

Having remained stationary for about half an hour, I perceived one of our infantry regiments, being in full range of the enemy's guns, falling back upon the battery; I tried to bring this regiment to a stand, and to make it advance again, but the bursting of the enemy's shells in the midst of them having a demoralizing effect rendered my efforts unavailing.

Ten minutes afterwards two columns of the enemy's infantry appeared in our front, which, notwithstanding the steady firing upon them by our artillery, advanced, with sharpshooters in their front, towards the battery, compelling me to leave this position. Falling back about 100 yards, I again brought my pieces to bear upon them until they withdrew.

During my withdrawal, which was executed in a gallop, the enemy poured two volleys into me, but totally without effect.

As soon as the enemy's infantry had retired beyond the reach of my shells I again engaged the battery until one of my guns became dismounted by the demolition of an axle. As by this time all the batteries that were near me had withdrawn, I thought it my duty to do the same.

At sunset, having secured the dismounted piece below the caisson in the manner prescribed, I arrived upon the hill, in the rear from whence General Sigel directed the retreat, which I was ordered to assist in covering with two pieces of my battery. From this moment nothing more transpired that is worth alluding to.

All this day the principal movements and manœuvres of the battery (I) had been directed independent of other commands. In spite of the severe cross-fire of cannon and musketry it was subjected to on this day, we sustained no loss at all, either in men or horses, with the exception of the dismounting of one of my guns. Officers, non-commissioned officers, and cannoneers, fought with the utmost bravery and to my entire satisfaction.

I have the honor to be, general, your most obedient servant,

H. DILGER,

Captain Commanding Battery I, First Ohio Volunteer Artillery.

Brigadier General C. SCHURZ,

Commanding Third Division, First Corps d'Armée.

No. 26.

REPORT OF CAPTAIN J. N. PATTERSON, COMMANDING SECOND NEW HAMPSHIRE VOLUNTEERS.

HEADQUARTERS SECOND NEW HAMPSHIRE VOLUNTEERS,
First Brigade, Grover's Division, September 14, 1862.

SIR: In accordance with instructions, I have to report the following as the proceedings of this regiment from the date of its arrival at Alexandria, Virginia, from the vicinity of Harrison's Landing, Virginia:

This regiment left Alexandria, Virginia, by railroad, on Monday, August 25, 1862, and arrived at Warrenton Junction during the night; from thence went into camp about one mile from the point of debarkation. Subsequently we were engaged in marches and battling with the enemy until our arrival in the vicinity of Fort Lyon, Virginia, September 3, 1862.

I have here to say that I possess no data from which to compile an adequate summary of the proceedings of the regiment from the date of its march from Alexandria, but know that Colonel Marston, now absent with leave at Washington, is possessed of the required information, and desires to make the report thereon.

Very respectfully, your obedient servant,

J. N. PATTERSON,

Captain Commanding Second New Hampshire Volunteers.

Lieutenant C. H. LAWRENCE,

Acting Assistant Adjutant General.

No. 27.

REPORT OF MAJOR ROBERT L. BODINE, TWENTY-SIXTH PENNSYLVANIA VOLUNTEERS.

HEADQUARTERS 26TH REGIMENT PENNSYLVANIA VOLUNTEERS,
First Brigade, Grover's Division, September 11, 1862.

In compliance with orders from division headquarters, I have the honor to report, for the information of the colonel commanding brigade—

That the regiment now in my command landed at Alexandria on the 23d day of August, 1862, and encamped near Fort Lyon.

August 25th, left Alexandria, by rail, for Warrenton Junction.

August 27th, skirmishing at Bristol Station.

August 29th and 30th, engaged in the battles of Bull Run.

August 31st, encamped at Centreville.

September 1st, marched from Centreville.
September 2d, arrived at camp near Fort Lyon.
September 3d, arrived at our present encampment near Alexandria.

I have the honor to be, very respectfully,

ROBERT L. BODINE,
Major Commanding Twenty-sixth Pennsylvania Volunteers.

Captain LAWRENCE,
Acting Assistant Adjutant General.

No. 28.

REPORT OF COLONEL J. BEARDSLEY, COMMANDING CAVALRY BRIGADE.

HEADQUARTERS CAVALRY BRIGADE, 1ST CORPS, ARMY OF VIRGINIA,
Hall's Farm, Virginia, September 13, 1862.

GENERAL: In making out a report of the active operations of the brigade of cavalry under my command, it appears proper that I should date it back to the battle of Cedar Mountain, on the 9th day of August, although we did not come up in time to participate in the battle, yet, on the following morning, my cavalry was sent out to patrol the different thoroughfares, examine the different fords, and reconnoitre the enemy's position, and continued a series of active operations, almost without rest, up to the time we arrived in the vicinity of the Potomac, on or about the 5th day of September instant.

The horses of the command had been taxed to the utmost of their strength when we reached Warrenton Springs, on the 18th day of August. They had been almost constantly under the saddle since the battle of Cedar Mountain, having been irregularly and scantily fed upon what the barrenness of the country afforded. When the series of engagements commenced along the Rappahannock, my brigade was in constant demand, and was moved here and there, either to guard different fords or examine the country. Much of my force was, at times, detailed and placed under the different division and brigade commanders. During the engagement at Freeman's Ford I was ordered over the river with six companies of cavalry to ascertain the position of the enemy, which I was not long in doing, for upon reaching the top of the river bank they were to be seen in strong force in front and down the river on our left, which fact I reported, and soon after received orders to return. There was no time that my brigade was not in constant requisition, moving with rapidity wherever ordered. When the corps moved, my brigade invariably took the post of "rear guard" and "flankers."

On the morning after our return to near Warrenton Springs I joined General Bayard's brigade, with three regiments and two mountain howitzers, and we proceeded together to the rear of Warrenton Springs, in the direction of Waterloo Bridge, the enemy's cavalry, about one thousand strong, retiring before us.

On the afternoon of August 25, while in the vicinity of Waterloo Bridge, I received orders to occupy Warrenton Springs with such of my command as I had at my disposal. I accordingly sent a company forward to carefully reconnoitre the place, and no sooner had its advance approached the springs than it was fired upon from the houses and adjoining fields, and it was reported to me that the enemy was there in force. I reported the fact, and received orders to shell the place, which I did, after examining the woods to my right and left. The enemy being seen to cross on the burning timbers of the bridge which had been fired by our troops in the morning, and others wading, I ceased firing, and sent a small party first and then a squadron of cavalry to examine the place, and found it vacated. About this time the enemy opened with a battery from the opposite side of the river, and obtained our range. Their battery being of heavier calibre than our own, I drew back a short distance, and left pickets near the Warrenton House. The enemy then commenced shelling the place, and a shell struck the Warrenton House. The building was soon in flames, whether from our own shells or those of the enemy, I am unable to say. That night at 12 o'clock we withdrew to Warrenton village.

The next day (26th) I received orders to report with the 4th New York, 9th New York, 6th Ohio, and three companies of the Connecticut cavalry, with two pieces of artillery, to General Buford, which I did at midnight; and on the morning of the 27th I followed him in the direction of Salem, which place we reached about mid-day. Several prisoners were taken; and here it was ascertained that Longstreet, with his command, was about two miles from us, on the way up to Salem, and Jackson had passed on towards White Plains, and was en route for Thoroughfare Gap. We soon left for White Plains, picking up several stragglers from the enemy, and Salem was occupied by Longstreet's forces in a few minutes after we left, as it was ascertained by our pickets left in the rear. We turned to the right from White Plains, and struck the road leading back to Warrenton, which place we reached at 9 o'clock in the evening. The enemy was seen by our rear guard following us up to Warrenton. We guarded Warrenton that night, all other troops having left, and also guarded the road in the direction of Gainesville; and, on the 28th, brought up the rear of the army, joining the corps on the morning of the 29th. My horses were completely worn out and almost in a starving condition. All along our route, from White Plains and from Warrenton to Bull Run, they were dropping down with their riders and dying, so that when I reported to you on the morning of the 29th, most of my horses were unable to carry the rider, and had to be led. Nevertheless I selected all that could possibly be used, and placed them on duty. About mid-day on the 30th, by your directions, I placed the 4th New York cavalry on the road to the left of our position on that day, with directions to send out patrols for a mile or more to the front and left; but they had been there but a short time when they became engaged with the enemy's right. For a full report I would respectfully refer you to Lieutenant Colonel Nazer's report.

On the evening of the 30th my command remained near the battle-field, and brought up the rear of the army to Centreville the next morning.

Again a portion of my brigade brought up the rear of General Sumner's division from Fairfax on the 4th instant, a large portion having been detailed away to act with General Buford.

When a short distance from Fairfax the enemy opened upon us with two pieces of artillery stationed to our left, and as we moved our position they changed theirs, and so continued to annoy us until their cavalry were drawn into a wood, near night, for the purpose of capturing our artillery, when a brigade of infantry rose and gave them a volley, and we were no longer disturbed, until at midnight we got into a thick wood at the cross-roads this side of Vienna, when they gave us a volley and retired, killing several and wounding about twenty.

It would be difficult to enumerate all the duties which my brigade performed. It could not have done more. Without transportation, without supplies, almost constantly in the saddle day and night, frequently engaged with the enemy, they bore all without a murmur.

I remain, general, most respectfully, your obedient servant,

J. BEARDSLEY,

Colonel 9th Cavalry, Commanding Cavalry Brigade.

Major General F. SIGEL,

Commanding 1st Corps, Army of Virginia.

No. 29.

REPORTS OF COMMANDING OFFICERS OF FOURTH NEW YORK CAVALRY.

HEADQUARTERS SIXTH OHIO CAVALRY,
Hall's Farm, September 18, 1862.

ADJUTANT: Enclosed find *report* and *copy*, which I forward in the colonel's absence.

Hoping it will be satisfactory to the general,
I am, respectfully,

R. J. WRIGHT,
Adjutant Sixth Cavalry.

Assistant Adjutant General MEYSENBURG.

HEADQUARTERS FOURTH NEW YORK CAVALRY,
Camp Hall's Farm, Virginia.

COLONEL: I have the honor to report that on Saturday, the 30th August, 1862, the regiment under my command was stationed by General Sigel upon the extreme left of the army to watch a road by which re-enforcements for the enemy were expected. I remained at this point until the left wing of our army gave way and a number of shells had been thrown amongst us, when, observing a large body of the enemy's cavalry emerging from a wood with the evident intention of cutting off my command, I marched it to rejoin the army. I had proceeded but a short distance when we came upon and passed two regiments of rebel cavalry, supported by infantry, and a battery drawn up in line, under cover of the crest of a hill, preparing to charge upon General Buford's brigade, stationed on the opposite side of the hill. I informed General Buford of the enemy's whereabouts and intention, and, at his request, quickly formed my command into line behind the 1st Michigan cavalry, and with that regiment charged upon the enemy, scattering them in every direction. Reforming our lines, we engaged a fresh regiment hand to hand, but finding that we received no support from the rear, and that we were greatly outnumbered by the enemy's cavalry, also being subject to a heavy fire from their infantry, which was now advancing at double quick, we were compelled to retire. The number of men of my regiment under my command on this occasion was but 130, of these 63 are killed, wounded, and missing, besides one officer killed, Lieutenant J. Mire. Our men charged upon the enemy with sabres only, receiving, as they did so, a hot fire from their revolvers, carbines, &c.

Throughout the entire affair my command behaved with the greatest coolness and gallantry.

F. NAZER,
Lieutenant Colonel Commanding Fourth New York Cavalry.

No. 30.

REPORT OF COMMANDING OFFICER OF NINTH NEW YORK CAVALRY.

Report of the movements of the Ninth New York cavalry during the month's campaign, ending September 12, 1862.

1862.

August 18. Commencing August 18, we formed the rear guard of General Sigel's corps in its retreat from the Rapidan river.

20. Arrived at Sulphur Springs, Virginia.

1862.

August 21. Left Sulphur Springs and arrived at Freeman's Ford, where, on the 22d, we made several reconnoissances in front of the enemy.

23. Left Freeman's Ford, and formed the advanced guard to General Schenck's division. On arriving at Fayetteville, were ordered by General Schenck to make a reconnoissance to Deep creek, about two miles from Sulphur Springs. On approaching the banks of the creek, our advanced skirmishers were fired upon by a party of the enemy. An active skirmish followed, in which we silenced the enemy without suffering loss ourselves. We held our position until General Milroy's brigade came to our assistance, when a brisk fight followed.

24. We were ordered to return to Fayetteville to cover the rear of the army.

25. We were again ordered to proceed to Sulphur Springs. As we were crossing Deep creek, we were opened upon by artillery and infantry, and were obliged to retire a short distance, and proceed by another road to Warrenton.

26. We returned to Fayetteville, and escorted a portion of General Sigel's train to Warrenton.

27. We were sent with our brigade on a reconnoissance to Salem and White Plains. Our advanced skirmishers captured quite a number of prisoners.

28. We reported to General Sigel near the Bull Run battle-field.

29. We lay all day in rear of our forces, as a reserve, during the battle.

30. When the panic began we formed line in single rank, in front of our retreating forces, to check the retreat of our disorganized troops from the field.

31. We proceeded to Centreville, where we remained until the afternoon of September 1, when we were ordered to report to General Buford, at Germantown.

Sept'ber 2. We were ordered by General Buford to proceed to the incomplete railroad west of Fairfax Court-House, to cover the rear of General Sigel's corps. Our advanced skirmishers were there attacked by a party of the enemy, and in a skirmish that followed we lost two men killed and one wounded.

During the entire campaign daily detachments were made from our regiment for reconnoitring, picket, and patrol duty.

CHARLES McLEAN KNOX,
Major Commanding 9th New York Cavalry.

No. 31.

REPORT OF COMMANDING OFFICER OF SIXTH OHIO CAVALRY.

HEADQUARTERS 6TH REGIMENT OHIO VOLUNTEER CAVALRY,
Hall's Farm, D. C., September 13, 1862.

GENERAL: In obedience to general orders, this morning received, I respectfully submit the following report of the operations of the regiment under my command during the march of the army from Rapidan river:

My regiment had just returned from a reconnoissance to Stannardville, which occupied two days and nights, when we were ordered to prepare for our retrograde march with the army. We went into the saddle at 4 o'clock in the afternoon, but did not leave the camp until the afternoon of the next day, the regiment serving with the cavalry brigade, which constituted the rear guard of your corps.

We passed through Culpeper about nine o'clock at night, and about two o'clock in the morning rested a few miles from the south branch of the Rappahannock, on the road to Sulphur Springs. Our march was resumed in the morning, and we crossed the bridge on the road to the springs with the brigade before noon, and a detail from my regiment assisted in burning the bridge. We went into camp with the army at the springs about 9 p. m.

The next morning we were ordered to mount at 4 a. m., but did not move from the camp until 3 in the afternoon, when we proceeded in the rear of the corps in the direction of Rappahannock Station.

That night we halted in the middle of the camp, on the road, saddled and unfed, until 7 o'clock the next morning, when we continued our march toward Rappahannock Station.

About 9 in the morning I was directed by you to report with my regiment to General Schenck, then engaging the enemy at the north branch of the river, near its confluence with the south branch.

I found General Schenck at the extreme right of his command, near "Fant's Ford." He directed me to put my regiment in position to guard the ford and support a battery, which he shortly afterwards sent to that point.

About one o'clock in the afternoon I was directed to report to you for particular instructions, and was ordered by you to proceed with my regiment, one regiment of infantry to be furnished for the purpose by General Stahel, and one section of the mountain howitzer battery, and cross the river at Fant's Ford. The "Stone House" opposite the ford I was instructed to burn in case I should find it a protection for the enemy, whose pickets had been firing on us from the house during the morning. I was notified that a brigade would be sent across the river at the ford two miles below us. Our passage across the ford was ordered to be covered by artillery and infantry by General Stahel.

We crossed the ford, the enemy's pickets retiring before us. At the distance of a mile from the river we found, at different points, a considerable force of cavalry and some infantry, who fell back as our advance or flanking parties approached them.

Whilst across the river we found a very sharp engagement suddenly commenced below us, which we subsequently found was brought on by the brigade which crossed at the lower ford. By direction of General Stahel we recrossed the river, and encamped within gunshot of the ford for the night.

The next morning the entire corps retraced its march towards Sulphur Springs. During the march our brigade was left under my command. We reached the camping ground in the neighborhood of the springs in the evening, whilst an artillery engagement at that place was going on with great spirit. Before reaching the camp some five thousand troops, cavalry, infantry, and artillery, were crowded into a narrow space, delayed by the trains which blocked up the road, whilst the stray shot and shell falling in our midst showed we were, without the apparent knowledge of the enemy, within destructive range of his guns.

The next day we served with the brigade in reconnoitring in the neighborhood of the springs. In the afternoon four companies, of my regiment, under command of Captain Bingham, were sent back to report to General Reno, and assist in escorting his train. The remainder of the regiment proceeded with you late in the evening, as a part of your escort, towards Waterloo Bridge, and encamped some two miles from the springs.

The next morning we reached the hill a mile from the bridge, and then watched the movements of the enemy in his march from Fayetteville, some five miles distant, from daylight until noon. We then returned with the brigade to the springs, taking with us the mountain howitzers. In driving out a party of the enemy from the springs our howitzers attracted the fire from the enemy's battery across the river, whilst a shell from a howitzer set fire to the buildings at the springs, a considerable portion of which was thereby destroyed. At 10 o'clock at night, with the brigade acting as rear guard, we proceeded to Warrenton, reaching that place about 2 o'clock in the morning, resting until daylight in the street, when we went into camp.

At 4 o'clock in the afternoon I was directed, by Colonel Beardsley, to report with the brigade to General Buford, on the road to Waterloo Bridge. We encamped with him that night, and the next morning, joined by Colonel Beardsley, we accompanied General Buford and his command to Salem and White Plains. At the former place some fifty prisoners were taken, who were sent back to Warrenton, under charge of Lieutenant Wyatt, of my regiment. Here was discovered the important fact that a large force of the enemy under Jackson had passed through these villages and through Thoroughfare Gap towards Manassas Junction the day before our arrival, and that a larger force was then following him, and but a short distance from Salem.

We returned to Warrenton with the brigade, and again rested in the high road without forage for horses until daylight, the other troops of the corps having left Warrenton during the preceding day. The next morning we proceeded toward Manassas Junction.

As we approached Manassas, in the evening, we found, from heavy firing on our left, that some part of our army had engaged the enemy. We learned that you had proceeded in the direction of the battle-ground, near which we came up with the corps and remained there until morning.

Early the next morning we furnished a detail of fifty men, being nearly all that could be provided with *serviceable* horses. The regiment then went into camp near the battle-field of the 29th.

Excepting the detail already mentioned, certain aides and orderlies serving with yourself and General Steinwehr, my command was not on duty during the day, and was not again ordered out until 5 o'clock in the evening of the 30th. The whole brigade was then formed to arrest the retreat of the straggling infantry, at that time an object of great concern, occasioned, as I knew, by the sudden shifting of the line of battle from the right to the centre and left wing. Whilst my regiment was in line for this purpose, a shot fell in the ranks of company H, cutting off the fore legs of a horse. Another fell into a group of mounted men, immediately to the rear of my line, cutting off both arms of a mounted man. These shots, to my surprise, seemed to come from the extreme right of the line of battle. We were shortly afterwards ordered to withdraw, and, with the brigade conducted by Colonel Beardsley, we moved on towards Centreville with the then retreating army. We reached Centreville about midnight. The next day, Sunday, we rested, sending one company, Captain Richart, to report to your headquarters.

Monday afternoon I was ordered, with my regiment and the 9th New York and two companies of the 1st Connecticut, to report to General Buford, then on the road leading to Fairfax. A short distance from camp we found we had turned off the main road northward, and we followed in the same direction. We soon came up with the column of General Reno, whose skirmishers were there engaging the enemy then approaching the left of our line on the Centreville road, evidently for the purpose of cutting off our trains.

We passed close to Reno's column, following the course taken by General Buford. We turned the right of Reno's line when the battle was apparently hottest, a thunder-storm, in terrific fury, breaking forth at the same time. We found General Buford just at night posted on the road leading from Fairfax towards Leesburg, only a hundred yards from the Centreville pike, and apparently not more than half a mile from the battle-ground where Generals Kearney and

Stevens fell. General Buford assigned us a position near the pike, which we occupied until morning.

At daylight we found in position, on the same ground, the divisions of Majors General Hooker and Couch, and subsequently, on the Centreville road, to the left of their lines, the division of General Franklin. General Buford ordered the 9th New York on some detached duty, and left me with the 6th Ohio and two companies of the 1st Connecticut to take orders from Major General Hooker.

About four o'clock in the afternoon I was ordered by this officer to move my cavalry forward half a mile on the Leesburg road to watch the enemy, whose moving column was there visible. In the meantime his command and Franklin's were both withdrawn towards Fairfax. He then sent an order directing me to call in my pickets and return slowly to the forks of the road, and report there to General Bayard. I found General Bayard at that point with a large body of cavalry, and, by his orders, joined his column and marched to Alexandria, arriving there about daylight in the morning.

The evening of the same day I reported to you near the Chain Bridge, and by your direction went into camp at the headquarters of Colonel Beardsley, a mile above the Chain Bridge.

During this eventful march of the army our horses suffered constantly from excessive work and want of forage. No day passed in which we did not lose from one to ten from sheer exhaustion. The result is, that for our two battalions, still numbering 596 men, we need 448 horses to render my command effective.

The hard service and hard fare of my men were endured without murmuring. No enlisted man was arrested for straggling, and but two appear on the rolls of the 30th as missing. No officer of my regiment, during this fatiguing and disheartening march, absented himself from duty.

Our regimental surgeon, Dr. Finch, employed and assigned to duty in my regiment by the State of Ohio, has been serving, since the 29th ultimo, in the general hospital, and is now on duty at Alexandria. His faithful services there are entitled to especial mention.

Very respectfully, your obedient servant,

W. R. LLOYD,
Colonel Commanding 6th Ohio Volunteer Cavalry.

Major General SIGEL,
Commanding 1st Corps, Army of Virginia.

No. 32.

REPORT OF COMMANDING OFFICER OF FIRST MARYLAND CAVALRY.

HEADQUARTERS FIRST REGIMENT MARYLAND CAVALRY,
Hall's Farm, Virginia, September 17, 1862.

Pursuant to order this day received, the following report of the part taken by this command, in the recent battles on the Rappahannock and Bull Run, is respectfully forwarded:

The regiment, in common with General Sigel's corps, left Sulphur Springs on the 21st instant, under orders to proceed to Fayetteville, arriving near General Pope's headquarters at about 1 o'clock p. m. At about 3 p. m. the command moved to the right, and after remaining for some time on the right flank was bivouacked for the night, about two miles from General Pope's headquarters. During the night a portion of the command, under Major Deems, made a reconnoissance near the river bank, and were fired upon by the enemy's infantry. Early on the morning of the 22d the regiment was ordered to proceed to Freeman's Ford, near which place it remained during the day, doing duty at scouting, patrolling, &c., and bivouacking during the night. On the 23d the command returned to Sulphur Springs, arriving at that place about 3 p. m. In common with the brigade, this regiment bivouacked near Sulphur Springs; and on the morning of the 24th moved to the right, near Waterloo Bridge, discovering the enemy's pickets on the bank of the river, a short distance from the bridge. Returning to Sulphur Springs, and remaining there until about 2 p. m., when the command of General Sigel moved towards Waterloo Bridge, encamping about three miles from the bridge for the night. On the morning of the 25th moved to a piece of woods near Waterloo Bridge, and during the day did heavy duty at scouting and patrolling. About dark moved with the corps towards Warrenton, arriving at Warrenton about 8 a. m. of the morning of the 26th. The regiment remained at Warrenton until morning of the 27th, during the intervening time doing duty at scouting and reconnoitring; and on the morning of the 27th moved towards Gainesville, a portion of the regiment being in advance, and two companies acting as a rear guard. When near Gainesville the advance of General Sigel's corps fell in with the enemy, and the portion of this command that was in the advance did good service in picking up the scatterers from the enemy's force, encamping for the night near Gainesville, and proceeding on towards Manassas Junction early on the morning of the 28th instant. During the 28th the regiment was very actively engaged in scouting, flanking, and reconnoitring, and succeeded in capturing between seventy and eighty prisoners. On the afternoon of the 28th a detachment of thirty men, under the regimental adjutant, discovered, near Bull Run, a large force of confederate cavalry in line, and heavy bodies of infantry and artillery passing towards Gainesville. On reporting to a brigade general, probably General Schenck, he was ordered to advance and discover who they were. After succeeding in capturing thirty-three prisoners, fifteen of whom were abandoned afterwards, because of being closely pressed, and having no knowledge of re-enforcements coming, the squad was met by Captain Arnussen, of General Sigel's staff, with a detachment of cavalry, and ere long the corps of General Sigel moved in that direction. During Friday, the 29th, Lieutenant Colonel Wetschky, with a portion of his command, were engaged in scouting and flanking, the remainder of the command being stationed near the headquarters of General Sigel. On Friday night the regiment, which for four days had been acting in detached bodies, was again consolidated, and early on the morning of the 30th was ordered to report to Colonel Beardsley, commanding cavalry brigade. During the battle of the 30th the cavalry was held in reserve until the left wing gave way, when an effort was made by the cavalry to stop the stragglers. After remaining at this duty until orders were received from the brigade commander to form a line of battle to the right of the retreating column, scarcely had the line been formed, when a battery of the enemy commenced shelling the line. After falling behind a hill, out of range of the shell, and being ordered to remain there until receiving further orders, the regiment was left without orders until the bridge over Bull Run had been nearly destroyed, when the officer, in charge of the party who were ordered to destroy, sent a message for the cavalry to come up in great haste, that he had just discovered that they were still in the rear. After fording the stream, remained with the rear guard until arriving at near Centreville. On rejoining the cavalry brigade, which was on the 31st August, the command remained on duty at Centreville, Fairfax Court-House, and intervening points, arriving at Langley, Virginia, on the morning of the 3d September. Although from the fact of the regiment being so much scattered, it was prevented from accomplishing as much as might have been otherwise; still I feel justified in stating that the command behaved in a creditable manner.

Very respectfully, your obedient servant,

CH. WETSCHKY,
Lieutenant Colonel Commanding.

No. 33.

REPORT OF BRIGADIER GENERAL R. C. SCHENCK, (BY COLONEL CHESEBROUGH.)

WASHINGTON, D. C., *September* 17, 1862.

GENERAL: I have the honor to make the following report of the part taken by the 1st division, 1st corps, army of Virginia, in the battle of Friday, the 30th ultimo, at Bull Run:

On Thursday, the 29th ultimo, we left Buckland's Mills, passing through Gainesville, and proceeded on the Manassas Junction pike to within some four miles of that place, and then turned eastwardly, marching towards "Bull Run." The scouts in advance reported a force of the enemy, consisting of infantry and cavalry in front. We were hurried forward and formed line of battle, with our right towards Centreville. Some few shell were thrown into a clump of woods in front where the enemy were last seen, but without eliciting any response. Some two hours elapsed when heavy firing was heard on our left, which we concluded was from McDowell's corps and the enemy who had worked around from our front in that direction. We were immediately put in motion and marched on the Warrenton road, and took position for the night on a hill east of "Stone House," our right resting on the pike. On Friday morning early the engagement was commenced by General Milroy on our right, in which we soon after took part, and a rapid artillery fire ensued from both sides. For some time heavy columns of the enemy could be seen filing out of a wood in front and gradually falling back. They were within range of our guns, which were turned on them, and must have done some execution. An hour after we received the order to move one brigade by the flank to the left and advance, which was done. We here obtained a good position for artillery, and stationed De Beck's 1st Ohio battery, which did excellent service, dismounting one of the enemy's guns, blowing up a caisson, and silencing the battery. Unfortunately, however, they were poorly supplied with amunition, and soon compelled to withdraw. Our two brigades were now put in motion. General Stahel, commanding 1st brigade, marching around the right of the hill to a hollow in front, was ordered to draw up in line of battle and halt. Colonel McLean advanced around the left of the hill under cover of the woods, pressing gradually forward until he struck the turnpike at a *white house*, about one-half mile in advance of the stone house. General Milroy's brigade arrived about the same time. We here halted and sent back for General Stahel, who took the pike and soon joined us. We then formed our line of battle in the woods to the left of the pike, our right resting on the road, and then pushed on slowly. Milroy, in the meanwhile, had deployed to the right of the road, and soon became engaged with the enemy. Our division was advanced until we reached the edge of the woods and halted. In front of us was an open space (which also extended to the right of the road and to our right,) beyond which was another wood. We remained here nearly an hour, the firing in the meanwhile becoming heavy on the right. The enemy had a battery very advantageously placed on a high ridge, behind the woods in front of Milroy, on the right of the road It was admirably served, and entirely concealed. Our position becoming known, their fire was directed towards us. The general determined therefore to advance, and so pushed on across the open space in front, and took position in the woods beyond; we here discovered that we were on the battle-ground of the night before, and found the hospital of Gibbon's brigade who had engaged the enemy. The battery of the enemy still continued; we had no artillery; De Beck's and Schirmer's ammunition having given out, and Buell's battery which had reported, after a hot contest with the enemy ,(who had every advantage in position and range,) was compelled to retire. It was now determined to flank the battery and capture it, and for this purpose General Schenck ordered one of his aides to reconnoitre the position. Before he returned, however, we were requested by General Milroy to assist him, as he was very heavily pressed. General Stahel was immediately ordered to proceed with his brigade to Milroy's support. It was about this time, one or two o'clock, that a line of skirmishers were observed approaching us from the rear; they proved to be of General Reynolds's division. We communicated with General Reynolds at once, who took his position on our left, and at General Schenck suggestion he sent a battery to our right in the woods for the purpose of flanking the enemy. They secured a position and were engaged with him about an hour, but with what result we were not informed. General Reynolds now sent us word that he had dicovered the enemy bearing down upon his left in heavy columns, and that he intended to fall back to the first woods behind the cleared space, and had already put his troops in motion. We therefore accommodated ourselves to his movement. It was about this time that your order came to press towards the right. We returned answer that the enemy were in force in front of us, and that we could not do so without leaving the left much exposed. General Schenck again asked for some artillery. General Stahel's brigade that had been sent to General Milroy's assistance, having accomplished its object under a severe fire, had returned, and soon after General Stevens reported with two regiments of infantry and a battery of four twenty-pound Parrott guns. With these re-enforcements we determined to advance again and reoccupy the woods in front of the cleared space, and communicated this intention to General Reynolds. He, however, had fallen back on our left some distance to the rear; he was therefore requested to make his connexion with our left. The Parrotts, in the meanwhile, were placed in position, and under the admirable management of Lieutenant Benjanin did splendidly. Two mountain howitzers also reported, and were placed on our right in the edge of the woods, near the road, and commenced shelling the woods in front of the open space, which were now occupied by the enemy, our skirmishers having previously fallen back. The artillery fire now became very severe, and General Schenck was convinced that it was very essential that he should have another battery, and so sent me to you to get one. I arrived to find one, Captain Romer's, just starting. You also directed me to order General Schenck to fall gradually back, as he was too far forward. This he had perceived, and anticipating, fell slowly back, placing his division behind the slope of the hill, in front of the one we had occupied in the morning. Captain Romer's battery in the meanwhile had taken position in front of the white house on the right of the pike, a little in advance of the hill on which we were; Lieutenant Benjamin's battery had suffered severely, so much so, that he reported only one section fit for duty, the other having lost all its cannoneers. They were placed in position and fired one or two rounds at the woods in front of the position we had just left, more to get the range than anything else. We were now ordered to descend the hill, cross the road, and take up our position behind the house, in front of which was Captain Romer's battery. This we did deploying the brigades in line of battle, the 2d brigade in front, and the 1st brigade in the rear. We remained so during the night.

The above report is respectfully submitted, with the remark that it is made without any communication with General Schenck, he being severely wounded and prevented by his surgeon's orders from attending to any business whatever. And although fully assured that the main points are correct, there may have been some orders or movements of minor importance, which, in my position as aide, carrying orders, might not have come within my notice.

I am, general, your most obedient servant,

WM. H. CHESEBROUH,

A. D. C. and A. A. A. G., 1st Division, 1st Corps, Army of Virginia.

Major General F. SIGEL,

Commanding 1st Corps, Army of Virginia.

WASHINGTON, D. C., *September* 27, 1862.

GENERAL: I have the honor to submit a continuation of the report of the active participation of the 1st division in the battles of the 29th and 30th ultimo.

I have already stated the position taken by the division after the battle of Friday, the 29th. We remained in this position until about one o'clock p. m. of Saturday, the 30th ultimo, when we were ordered to form column by division—by battalion. This was accomplished after some difficulty, occasioned by large bodies of troops, pouring in from our rear, getting in between the brigades, and causing great confusion and much countermarching. After the movement was completed we stood as follows: to the right of the pike and to the rear of Dogan's farm; the 2d brigade in front of the 1st brigade. We remained there for some time, when you ordered us to detail one regiment to march to a point on the left of the road, for the purpose of making a connexion with General Reynolds, on our left. The 55th regiment Ohio volunteers was selected by Colonel McLean, commanding 2d brigade, and proceeded, under the direction of one of your aides, to the designated place. Soon after you ordered us to send a battery, with a brigade to support it, across and to the left of the road, to occupy a bald hill. This order was executed by sending the 2d brigade, Colonel McLean, who placed his three remaining regiments on the slope of the hill, under cover and within easy supporting distance of the battery, which was placed on the crest.

General Stahel, commanding the 1st brigade, at the same time marched forward and took position in advance of that but recently occupied by the 2d, and on either side of Dogan's house, in the following order: Schirmer's battery on the crest of the hill, joining two other batteries that were already there, with the 45th, 27th, and 8th behind it, to the right of the houses, and the 41st regiment to the left of the houses, and on the other side of the road. The 2d brigade had hardly taken their position on the bald hill when General Reynolds put his troops in motion, marching past their entire front to some point on the right or rear, thus leaving Colonel McLean on the extreme left without other support. This movement on the part of General Reynolds necessitated a change in the position of the troops, which was done by placing the battery in the centre and two regiments on either side, (the 55th regiment having rejoined the brigade,) and deploying them in line of battle, fronting west. It was at this time, while all attention was directed to the front, where General Porter was hotly engaged, that a heavy column of the enemy were seen advancing on McLean's front, driving before them a regiment of zouaves, and also repulsing some other troops who advanced to meet them from his right. Colonel McLean now opened on them with his four pieces of artillery, throwing shell, and, as they approached nearer, canister. The infantry also commenced a heavy fire, and in a short time they were compelled to retreat, which they did in great confusion. At this time a large force was seen advancing from a piece of woods to the left and rear, but they were supposed to be friends, from the fact of their clothes being dark. Soon after this another body of the enemy marched out of the woods, across the position lately occupied by General Reynolds, and commenced a heavy fire on the left flank, which was replied to with interest, and the contest became very severe. Almost at the same time those whom we had taken for our own men opened a heavy fire on our rear. General Schenck then gave the order to change front, so as to repel this attack. This manœuvre was well executed, the regiments wheeling by battalion, and coming up into line, fronting the enemy, in fine order. It was about this time that you ordered General Milroy up to the assistance of Colonel McLean, but owing to some contradictory orders only one regiment, the 5th Virginia, Colonel Zeigler, went up the hill, the others going in a different direction.

The fight now raged fiercely; but so heavy and continuous a fire was delivered by the 2d brigade that the enemy were again compelled to retire. Our men followed them closely, and would undoubtedly have driven them from the field had it not been for another force of the enemy which was seen advancing on the right flank from the point where they had first been driven back—the late front. It was about this time that General Schenck was wounded and carried off the field. He had been in the thickest of the fight, cheering and rallying the men, and at the moment he received the wound he was gallantly leading on a regiment of Pennsylvania troops to the support of McLean.

The tide of battle now turned. After fighting most successfully against superior and steadily increasing numbers without any support, and their right flank threatened, they were compelled to retire. The order was given, and they fell back across the bald hill, and, following the road towards Centreville, halted at a white house on the left of the road, a half mile from the stone house, where they commenced to reorganize.

It was about the time that the 2d brigade was retiring from the bald hill that General Stahel was ordered to send a regiment to its support. The 41st New York, and, about the same time, Colonel Koltes's brigade of General Schurz's division, followed, a short time after, by Colonel Krzyzanowski's brigade, marched up the hill; but they arrived too late to render any assistance to McLean, and, after fighting most gallantly against heavy odds, were compelled to yield. The enemy followed up their advantage vigorously, took possession of the hill, and pressed steadily on to the road. General Stahel now moved the 8th New York and 27th Pennsylvania across the heights to the right and rear of Dogan's farm, leaving the 45th New York to protect Schirmer's battery, which he placed on the hill to the rear of Dogan's house, and directed its fire on the advancing enemy. The enemy still continued to approach. The 45th now changed their position to between the pike and Dogan's house, and succeeded in checking the enemy's advance and drawing them back across the road. General Stahel then fell back, taking the road across the heights behind the stone house to a position on the left (west) of the road, and here assembled his brigade. Colonel McLean soon after reported, and then General Stahel assumed command, on hearing that General Schenck had been wounded.

I am, very respectfully, your most obedient servant,

WM. H. CHESEBROUGH,
Acting Assistant Adjutant General.

Upon mentioning to General Schenck that I had been requested to make a report of Saturday's proceedings, and while unable, in his present condition, even to revise what I have written, he yet desires me to say that he wishes to express his approbation of the coolness and bravery displayed by General Stahel, Colonel McLean, and the officers and men of their respective brigades; and also to commend Lieutenant Blume, and Lieutenant Hinchman, commander of the batteries, for the active and efficient service they performed.

Very respectfully, your obedient servant,

WM. H. CHESEBROUGH,
Aide-de-Camp and Acting Assistant Adjutant General.

WASHINGTON, D. C., *October* 20, 1862.

GENERAL: In reply to General Reynolds's letter of the 9th instant, I have the honor to make the following remarks:

I can discover but little difference between the statements of General Reynolds and my report.

He states, firstly, "that his division manœuvred on our left from early in the morning until we had gained the position alluded to on the pike, near Gibbon's battle-ground of the evening previous." This I do not attempt to deny. I merely give in my report, the time when *we* first became acquainted with his (General Reynolds's) position.

He then says that "it was here that General Schenck asked me for a battery," which agrees entirely with my report, with the exception that I did not enter so much into the details.

He then remarks that "in returning from this position to bring up the other battery and Seymour's brigade, I passed through Schenck's troops drawn up on the *right* of the woods before alluded to, in which Gibbon had been engaged." But in bringing up the battery and Seymour's brigade, he noticed that "Schenck's troops had disappeared from this position, and were nowhere in sight." In the first place, General Reynolds is incorrect in his impression of our position.

Our troops were always on the left of the pike throughout the day, except when the brigade under General Stahel was sent to Milroy's assistance.

Our position before Stahel moved was in the woods which had been occupied as a hospital by Gibbon's brigade to the left of the pike. General Stahl's right resting on the road, and Colonel McLean's brigade on his left, the woods in which Gibbon had had his principal fighting being across the pike, and to our right.

At the time that General Reynolds returned from placing the battery and Meade's brigade, it is probable that he passed through General Stahel's brigade, which was in motion and had gained the right of the pike on its way to join Milroy, and that afterwards, when General Reynolds was bringing up Ransom's battery and Seymour's brigade, they were gone, which accounts for his impression that "he was left alone;" he soon discovered his error, however, as he states in his letter, "in doing which McLean's brigade was discovered."

Colonel McLean still held his position, and was immediately moved so that his right would rest on the pike, and General Reynolds made his movement to correspond.

It was about this time that our position was changed, but not because we had ascertained that we were disconnected from the rest of Sigel's troops.

We *had been* and *were* well aware of our position.

It is true we had advanced further than was intended, being constantly urged by General Sigel to advance, and pressed towards the right, he evidently not understanding our true position. We fell back, however, on account of the information received from General Reynolds, that the enemy were bearing down on his left. General Reynolds did not communicate directly with General Schenck, as it would appear from my report, but the information was received through Colonel McLean, who told General Schenck that General Reynolds had informed him "that the enemy were bearing down, &c., and that he (Reynolds) intended to fall back, and has actually commenced the movement." Colonel McLean wished to know if he should act accordingly; General Schenck directed him to accommodate himself to General Reynolds's movement.

We retired slowly across the open space to and within the woods and halted; General Stahel rejoined us here, and General Stevens also reported with two regiments of infantry and a battery. General Stevens's force was thrown to the right of the pike, General Stahel on the left of the pike, and Colonel McLean to the left of Stahel. I here state in my report that General Schenck, on receiving these re-enforcements, determined to advance again and communicated his intention to General Reynolds. I carried this message myself, and after some difficulty found General Reynolds, and requested him to halt and form on the left of McLean. He had fallen back, however, some distance to the rear of McLean's line of battle, so much so that the enemy's skirmishers had actually flanked us, and in returning to the division I had a narrow escape from being captured. I also asked General Reynolds to ride forward to meet General Schenck, who had directed me to say that he would be at the extreme left of our line for that purpose. General Reynolds neither gave me any positive answer as to whether he would meet General Schenck, or any information as to what he intended to do. I do not know if he complied with the request to make his connexion on our left, as, on my return to General Schenck, I was immediately sent to General Sigel to represent our position, and when returning again with the order to General Schenck to retire slowly, I met the command executing the movement.

My report was intended merely as a sketch of our movements for General Sigel's information, and I endeavored throughout to be as concise as possible, and confine myself solely to the operations and movements of our division. I now submit the above statement, trusting that the explanations will be satisfactory to General Reynolds.

I am, general, very respectfully, your obedient servant,

WM. H. CHESEBROUGH,

Lieut. 11th Infantry, and A. D. C. to Major General Schenck.

Major General McDOWELL, *U. S. A., &c., &c.*

No. 34.

REPORT OF COLONEL KRZYZANOWSKI, COMMANDING SECOND BRIGADE, THIRD DIVISION.

HEADQUARTERS 2D BRIGADE, 3D DIVISION,
Near Arlington Heights, September 3, 1862.

At about half-past five o'clock a. m., on the 29th of August I received orders from General Schurz to advance with my brigade. It was done in the following order: Two regiments, in company column, left in front, and one regiment, the 54th New York volunteers, as reserve. On the right of me was Colonel Schimelpfennig with his brigade, and on the left General Milroy's brigade. A line of skirmishers having been established, we advanced towards the woods, through which the Manassas Gap railroad runs. As soon as we entered the woods I despatched my adjutant to ascertain whether the line of skirmishers was kept up on both wings, and finding such was not the case, and that I had advanced a little faster than General Milroy's and Colonel Schimelpfennig's column, I halted my skirmishers to wait until the line was re-established. However, being informed that General Milroy was advancing, I sent the 54th regiment to take position on my right wing and to try and find the lines of Colonel Schimelpfennig's skirmishers, and then I advanced, together with the former.

Scarcely had the skirmishers passed over two hundred yards when they became engaged with the enemy. For some time the firing was kept up, but our skirmishers had to yield at last to the enemy's advancing column. At this time I ordered my regiments up, and a general engagement ensued. However, I soon noticed that the 54th and 58th regiments had to fall back, owing to the furious fire of the enemy, who had evidently thrown his forces exclusively upon those two regiments. The 75th regiment Pennsylvania volunteers, which, up to this time, had not taken part in this engagement, was (at the time the 58th and 54th retired) now nobly led on, by Lieutenant Colonel Mahler, upon the right flank of the enemy, and kept him busy until I had brought the 58th at a double quick up to its previous position, when those two regiments successfully drove the enemy before them, thereby gaining the position of the Manassas Gap railroad

The 54th had meanwhile been ordered by General Schurz to take position with the 29th regiment New York State volunteers, in the interval of my brigade and that of Colonel Schimelpfennig.

At this time I observed on my right the brigade of General Roberts, to whom I explained my position, after which we advanced together a short distance; but he soon withdrew his forces, ascertaining that he got his brigade in between the column of our division. We had occupied the above-named position only a short time when the enemy again tried to force us back; but the noble conduct of my troops did not allow him to carry out his design, and he did not gain one inch of ground. We were thus enabled to secure our wounded and some of our dead, and also some of the enemy's wounded, belonging to the 10th South Carolina regiment. We held this position until two p. m., when we were relieved by a brigade of General Kearney's division, and retired about one-fourth of a mile towards our rear, where we also encamped for the night.

Most nobly did the troops behave. Amongst the officers I must mention the names of Lieutenant Colonel Mahler, 75th regiment Pennsylvania volunteers; Lieutenant Gehrke, of the same regiment, who was in command of the skirmishers; and Lieutenant W. Bowen, who was, on that day, acting adjutant of that regiment. Of the officers of the 58th regiment New York State volunteers, I have to make particular mention of the gallant conduct of Major William Henkel, who was wounded, but who remained for three hours longer on the battle-field, until his pains became too violent; also of the adjutant, Lieutenant Stoldt, of that regiment, who did valuable service with the skirmishers. Of the 54th regiment New York State volunteers, Lieutenant Colonel Ashby and Adjutant Brandt deserve great credit. The different members of my staff executed my orders promptly; Captain Theune being severely wounded while performing his duty, and Lieutenant Schmidt most gallantly cheered the men and conducted the line of skirmishers to my greatest satisfaction. Captain Maluski and Captain Weide did valuable service on that day.

On the succeeding day, August 30, at about eight a. m., I received orders to form my regiments, company column left in front. This being done, a new order directed me more towards the left, where I took position in line with the brigade of General Stahel. Here we remained until afternoon, when we were ordered up towards the stone house, where my battery took position.

I received orders to move my infantry to the right of Colonel Koltes's brigade and then to advance, which had scarcely been done when we became engaged with the enemy and kept up a brisk fire until, after the lapse of about half an hour, one of the enemy's batteries compelled us to retire towards a deep ravine just in the rear of our lines. Seeing, however, that the enemy moved towards our left, I again ordered my men up, changing my front a little towards the left, our left wing resting upon the right wing of a brigade, the name of which I was unable to ascertain. After some fifteen minutes of constant firing of our two brigades, I gave orders to my regiments to cease firing, still holding the same position, while the enemy withdrew. I then consulted with the brigade commander on my left, asking him to advance further in company with me, which he, however, refused to do.

My forces being too weak to advance alone, I remained inactive for a few minutes, until General Schurz sent orders to retire across the run and remain in reserve. I did so until 8 p. m., when a new order arrived for me to retire about one-fourth of a mile further, where nearly the whole corps was collecting. Having no special orders, I rested my men, who, after their day's work, were only glad enough to do so, until 2 a. m., 31st, at which time I was informed by a cavalry scouting party that all the troops had fallen back. I at once mounted my horse and went towards the hospital, at which place I had seen General Sigel and General Schurz at about 9 p. m. on the evening of the battle. Finding nobody besides the physicians and the wounded men there, I returned to my men, and ordered them to fall in for the purpose of marching to Centreville, whither our forces were said to have gone. I must insert here that I only had the 58th New York State volunteers and 75th Pennsylvania volunteers with me at that time, the 54th having been detailed by General Sigel late on the evening before. Arriving with my troops at the stone bridge across Bull Run, the same was in a blaze of fire, and not fit to be crossed, which circumstance compelled me to ford the river with great difficulty, as the banks are very steep. I arrived at Centreville at 6 o'clock a. m., after finding the 54th regiment encamped alongside of the road, and joined my division.

In the engagement of the 30th August the troops under my command behaved very well in general. The 75th deserves again to be especially mentioned for its bravery. Lieutenant Colonel Mahler, of the same, was wounded; also Lieutenant Ledig. Lieutenant W. Bowen, the acting adjutant, was killed, and Lieutenant Troetun. The 54th regiment suffered severely, a number of officers and men being wounded.

The gallant conduct of First Lieutenant Werthheimer, of this regiment, deserves to be noticed, who, while the enemy's batteries were pouring a perfect hail of lead into our lines, nobly grasped a guide flag, and cheered the men to follow him. Lieutenant Colonel Ashby, of this regiment, Captain Wahle, Captain Ernewein, and Adjutant Brandt, on this day, again behaved bravely. The 58th regiment was more fortunate in regard to the loss of officers, but suffered intensely in the ranks .All the officers deserve credit for their behavior on that day. As to my staff, I was as unfortunate as I was on the previous day—losing one of my aides-de-camp, Lieutenant Schmidt, who was severely wounded in the thigh. He showed great coolness and courage. The balance of my staff most promptly executed my orders. I have also to mention the gallant conduct of First Lieutenant Cheeseborough, of General Schenck's staff, whom I met on the battle-field, and who assisted me for some time. I was unfortunate enough on that day to lose my horse, which was shot under me.

Respectfully,

W. KRZYZANOWSKI,
Colonel Commanding 2d Brigade, 3d Division.

Major A. HOFFMAN,
Aide-de-camp and Acting Assistant Adjutant General.

No. 35.

REPORT OF BRIGADIER GENERAL GEORGE SYKES.

HEADQUARTERS SYKES'S DIVISION, PORTER'S ARMY CORPS,
Camp at Vanderwenker's, Virginia, September 6, 1862.

SIR: I have the honor to submit the following report: On the 27th ultimo, General F. J. Porter's army corps, of which my division forms a part, effected a junction with the army of Virginia, under General Pope.

The day following we marched to Bristow Station, on the Orange and Alexandria railroad; thence, on the 29th, to Manassas, and westwardly towards Gainesville, making a demonstration against the enemy, and exchanging a few cannon shot with him in the evening. We bivouacked for the night near Bethlehem church, on the Gainesville road, and at daylight on the 30th marched to the old battle-ground of Bull Run, arriving about 9 a. m. General Pope's army was on that ground and in its vicinity.

Two brigades of my division (1st and 2d) were thrown in advance of the Dogan house, facing to the west, their left resting on the Warrenton turnpike. The 3d brigade and my three batteries were held in reserve.

An extensive forest masked my front, and on my left, to the south of the

Warrenton turnpike, a second forest covered the country, and screened the enemy from all observation. These two forests, half a mile apart, near my advanced position, were separated by an open plain, that rose in the form of an irregular V towards a commanding crest held by the enemy.

His cannon, immediately behind this crest, overlooked my whole division, and as my troops took their place, he made good use of it.

From that time till 3 p. m. a sharp cannonade ensued, and some practice among the skirmishers. Those of the enemy were forced back into the forest, on the left of the Warrenton turnpike, and some houses and fences, previously occupied by him, were seized and held by my light troops, (3d infantry.)

Thus far we had seen none of the enemy's infantry, none of the cavalry, and only the muzzles of his cannon over the crest heretofore mentioned. We were in profound ignorance of his position, strength, or designs. About 4 p. m. I was ordered to support an attack to be made by General Butterfield. This attack was based upon the supposition that the enemy was in full retreat—so announced in the orders of General Pope. Porter's army corps was to be the pivot of operations. The troops on our right were to swing towards us, clear the enemy in front, (if there,) and then, by a joint movement with Porter, we were all to hurry him up in his retrograde movement.

The Pennsylvania reserves, under General J. F. Reynolds, had been posted on my left, south of the Warrenton pike.

Just previous to the attack these troops were withdrawn, leaving my left flank entirely uncovered, and the Warrenton road open.

Colonel Warren, 5th New York volunteers, commanding my 3d brigade, seeing the paramount necessity of holding this point, threw himself there with his brigade, the remnants of two regiments, and endeavored to fill the gap created by the removal of Reynolds.

Butterfield's attack was gallantly made, and gallantly maintained until his troops were torn to pieces. My 1st brigade, under Colonel R. C. Buchanan, United States army, moved to his aid, relieved him, and became furiously engaged. The troops on our right did not properly support this attack, in consequence of which the whole movement failed. The enemy, posted in a railroad excavation, was as secure as earthen embankments could make him, and as our troops emerged from the woods they were met by withering volleys that decimated their ranks. Their own fire was almost harmless against a sheltered foe. This advance of parts of Porter's and McDowell's army corps was on the left centre of our line.

The enemy, seeing its failure, and that our weak point lay on my left in front of Warren, poured upon his little command, under cover of the forest, a mass of infantry that enveloped—almost destroyed—him, and completely pierced our line. Out of 490 men in the 5th New York volunteers, 79 killed and 170 wounded attest the nature of this attack.

It became necessary to retire from the ground we occupied. Buchanan's and Chapman's brigades did so in columns of regiments in line of battle, under a severe artillery fire, and never wavered. Weed's, Smead's, and Randoll's batteries moved with and near them. Warren gathered the remnant of his brigade in rear of Young's Run.

I suggested to General Porter that my troops should occupy the plateau of the Henry and Robinson houses beyond Young's Run, and endeavor to hold it against the oncoming foe. Naturally, it was the strongest position on the field. He acquiesced in my suggestion, and during the movement to that point I remained with Weed's battery, that again had been brought into action near the Dogan house. After a short interval, riding rapidly towards the plateau, I learned from my adjutant general, Lieutenant Cutting, that some general officers had sent Chapman's brigade into action on the extreme left, and that the plateau was held by other troops.

Buchanan's and the remnant of Warren's brigades were then formed immediately in rear of the plateau. The enemy continuing to outflank our left, Buchanan was ordered to the support of the forces engaged in that direction, and maintained a gallant and bloody conflict with the foe until, outnumbered, outflanked, and badly crippled, I directed him to retire. Chapman, thrown in previous to Buchanan, fighting desperately for three-quarters of an hour, seriously cut up and fired into by volunteers behind him, was also ordered to retire. This was directed only after a regiment of volunteers on his right, and one on his left, had fallen back, exposing both his flanks, while a New York battery to the right of him cleared out, just when its services were most necessary. The remains of my command were then united on the plateau. My artillery joined me near this position.

Captain J. R. Smead, 5th artillery, was unfortunately killed in bringing off his guns. From the nature of the fight, he and Randoll had little opportunity to display the skill they had previously acquired in handling their batteries. Weed was in action throughout the day, and strengthened the reputation he had already acquired. He had the misfortune to lose two of his guns by the breaking of their axles. They were abandoned on the road from the battle-field to Centreville, (not taken from him by the enemy.)

After my command reunited, I received orders to move on Centreville, and reached there at midnight intact, and in excellent order.

The following morning a position was assigned me among the old rifle-pits of the rebels, which I held for 36 hours. At 1 a. m. on the 2d of September we moved to Fairfax, thence to Flint Hill, thence to our present camp.

I desire to call the attention of the major general commanding to the services of Colonels Warren, Buchanan, and Chapman, United States army, commanding brigades of my division. Their coolness, courage, and example were conspicuous. Their claim to promotion has been earned on fields of battle long prior to that of the 30th of August, 1862.

Had the efforts of these officers, those of Generals Reynolds, Reno, and Butterfield, been properly sustained, it is doubtful if the day had gone against us. Warren's command was sacrificed by the withdrawal of Reynolds's troops from my left and their non-replacement by others. The enemy masked and concealed his brigades in the forests south of the Warrenton pike. His presence was unseen and unknown until he appeared in sufficient strength to overpower the infantry opposed to him.

In fighting an offensive battle, we left behind us a position (the old battle-ground) that offered reasonable hopes of success; and in the pursuit of a supposed retreating foe, we encountered a well-posted army, flushed by victory, confident, calmly awaiting the attack he most desired.

The reports of brigade, battalion, and artillery commanders are enclosed. I respectfully refer to them for the minuter operations of the day, and cordially unite in the recommendations given in them to officers and men.

It will be seen that my troops behaved with the utmost coolness and bravery, (known to the general himself;) were exposed for many hours to a severe artillery fire, without the power of evading it; and when eventually led into battle, acted as well as troops ever do. Their conduct left me nothing to desire. It was their misfortune not to be supported, and no fault of theirs that they were compelled to join in the general retreat.

To revert to cases of individual merit: Major C. S. Lovell, 10th infantry, commanding 2d United States infantry, is particularly mentioned for his conduct on this occasion. I desire to add my personal testimony to the major's known gallantry, and to bespeak for him the advancement he so richly deserves.

All my battalion commanders were zealous, energetic, and active. They were: Major Floyd Jones, 11th infantry; Major Andrews, 17th infantry; Captains Bootes, 6th infantry, Wilkins, 3d infantry, commanding the skirmishers,

S. H. Dryer, 4th infantry, Blunt, 12th infantry, O'Connell and McKibben, 14th infantry, 1st and 2d battalions.

Colonel Bendix, 10th New York volunteers, and Captain C. Winslow, commanding 5th New York volunteers.

Lieutenant Sheridan, 3d infantry, maintained his line of skirmishers with great obstinacy, until our whole force fell back to its last position.

My personal staff—First Lieutenant Heyward Cutting, 10th United States infantry, acting assistant adjutant general, First Lieutenant George F. Ingham, 11th United States infantry, and First Lieutenant War. W. Chamberlain, 14th United States infantry, acting aides-de-camp—were under fire throughout the day, and were constantly occupied in transmitting orders to the various portions of the field. Their zeal, activity, and anxiety to do everything in their power, were always apparent.

Lieutenant Chamberlain, sent with an order to Colonel Warren, near the close of the day, is among the missing. His fate is not yet determined, but he is believed to be a prisoner, wounded, and in the hands of the enemy.

Captain Lawrence and Lieutenant Fletcher, 14th infantry, were sent with one hundred men from my command, on the 1st, to gather the wounded, and render such assistance as was possible to our people left on the field. In this distressing duty they were occupied four or five days—part of the time without food. They deserve mention for their good conduct in this connexion.

The medical officers, under Dr. Forward, United States army, were constantly engaged in their duties, and rendered all the assistance possible under the circumstances.

I append a list of casualties—the aggregate :

	Killed.	Wounded.	Missing.
Officers	7	21	3
Enlisted men	145	564	177
	152	585	180

I am, sir, respectfully, your obedient servant,

GEORGE SYKES,
Brigadier General Commanding Division.

Captain F. T. LOCKE,
Assistant Adjutant General 5th Army Corps.

No. 36.

REPORT OF COLONEL G. K. WARREN, COMMANDING THIRD BRIGADE.

HEADQUARTERS THIRD BRIGADE,
Sykes's Division, September 6, 1862.

SIR: I take leave to present herewith a sketch of the field of action of the 30th of August, as it appeared to me, with an account of what I witnessed and the part sustained by my brigade, consisting of the 5th New York volunteers, about 490 strong, and the 10th New York volunteers, about 510 strong.

Different parts of the sketch are referred to by means of the letters of the alphabet. It must be kept in mind that I make this sketch from my own points of view. The distance between the ruled lines represents 100 yards.

As a starting point, I will state the position of affairs just before the attack was made in front, by General Butterfield. His skirmishers had driven the enemy out of the woods at A, and he occupied the vicinity with his whole force. The 1st and 2d brigades of Sykes's division were between him and O. My brigade was at M, and Smead's and Randoll's batteries in the road near me. General Reynolds's division held the woods, G, with a rifled-gun battery at G. All our other forces in sight were to the right and rear of these. I knew the enemy was in the woods, and on the high ridge, from the point F all around towards our right, as far as C C, but high authority reported him retreating, and that this was only his rear guard. While General Butterfield was making his disposition to assault the enemy at C, General Reynolds's troops and rifled battery were all withdrawn from G and sent further to our left, at some point, as I, the enemy's rifled battery, at C, firing at the last of his troops making this movement. Hazlett's rifled battery was at the same time executing an order from General Porter to take up a position at G, with the other, and open on the enemy at C, so as to assist Butterfield's contemplated assault. This battery was then without support, and our whole left flank was uncovered. I immediately assumed the responsibility of occupying the place Reynolds's division had vacated, and make all the show of force I could.

For this purpose I deployed three-fifths of the 10th New York volunteers to hold the edge of the woods towards the enemy on our left, and keeping the 5th New York volunteers in reserve near H, out of view of the enemy's battery at C. Notice of this movement of mine I immediately sent, by an officer, to General Sykes or General Porter. He found the latter, who directed me to hold on, and sent me mounted orderlies to keep him informed. He was, I believe, near the point N, where Weed's battery was placed. From the point G I probably had the best view of what followed that the battle-field presented.

As soon as General Butterfield's brigade advanced up the hill there was great commotion among the rebel forces, and the whole side of the hill and edges of the woods swarmed with men before unseen. The effect was not unlike flushing a covey of quails. The enemy fell back to the line of the railroad, and took shelter on the railroad cut and behind the embankment, and lined the edges of the woods beyond. Butterfield's advance beyond the brow of the hill B was impossible, and taking his position, his troops opened fire on the enemy in front, who, from his sheltered position, returned it vigorously, while, at the same time, a battery, somewhere in the prolongation of the line E B, opened a most destructive, enfilading fire with spherical-case shot.

It became evident to me that without heavy re-enforcements General Butterfield's troops must fall back or be slaughtered, the only assistance he received being from Hazlitt's battery, which I was supporting, and Weed's, near N.

After making a most desperate and hopeless fight, General Butterfield's troops fell back, and the enemy immediately formed and advanced. Hazlitt's battery now did good execution on them, and forced one column, that advanced beyond the point of the wood at A, to fall back into it. Unwilling to retire from the position I held, which involved the withdrawal of this efficient battery and the exposure of the flanks of our retreating forces, I held on, hoping that fresh troops would be thrown forward to meet the enemy now advancing in the open fields, well knowing, however, that my position was one from which I could not retreat in the face of a superior force.

Reynolds's division, on my left, probably aware of the superior force of the enemy gathering in his front, fell back from I towards P. The enemy advanced with rapidity upon my position, with the evident intention of capturing Hazlitt's battery. The 10th New York was compelled to fall back, scarcely arriving at the position held by the 5th New York, before the enemy, and in such a manner as to almost completely prevent the 5th from firing upon them. While I was endeavoring to clear them from the front, the enemy, in force, opened fire from the woods on the rear and left flank of the 5th with most fearful effect. I then gave the order to face about and march down the hill, so as to bring the enemy all on our front, but in the roar of musketry I could only be heard a short distance. Captain Boyd, near me, repeated the command, but his men only partially obeyed it. They were unwilling to make a backward movement. He was wounded while trying to execute it. Adjutant Sovereign carried the order along the line to Captain Winslow, commanding the regiment, and to the other captains, but was killed in the act. Captain Winslow's horse was shot; Captain Lewis, acting field officer, was killed; Captain Huger was killed; Captains McConnell and Montgomery were down with wounds, and Lieutenants Raymond, Hoffman, Keyser, and Wright were wounded. Both color-bearers were shot down, and all but four of the sergeants were killed or wounded.

Before the colors and the remnant of the regiment could be extricated, 298 men of the 5th and 133 of the 10th New York were killed or wounded.

In the 10th New York, Lieutenant Hedden was killed, and Captain Dimmick, Lieutenant Deweyick, Lieutenant Mosscross, and Lieutenant Cuthane, wounded. The colors of both regiments were brought off, and the batteries we were protecting were withdrawn.

We assisted from the field 77 wounded of the 5th and 8 of the 10th. The remainder fell into the hands of the enemy. Among these were Captains Boyd, McConnell, and Montgomery, and Lieutenants Wright and Raymond, of the 5th, and Captain Dimmick, Lieutenants Mosscross and Deweyick, of the 10th. Braver men than those who fought and fell that day could not be found. It was impossible for us to do more, and, as is well known, all the efforts of our army barely checked this advance.

I submit herewith a detailed list of casualties, as accurate as circumstances will permit us to make.

Very respectfully, your obedient servant,

G. K. WARREN,

Colonel Fifth New York Volunteers, Commanding Third Brigade.

Lieutenant HEYWARD CUTTING,

Acting Aide-de-Camp and Acting Assistant Adjutant General, General Sykes's Division.

No. 37.

REPORT OF LIEUTENANT COLONEL R. C. BUCHANAN, FOURTH INFANTRY, COMMANDING BRIGADE.

HEADQUARTERS FIRST BRIGADE REGULAR INFANTRY,
Camp near Hall's Hill, Virginia, September 6, 1862.

SIR: I have the honor to submit the following report of the operations of my brigade, composed of the 3d, 4th, 1st battalion of the 12th, and 1st and 2d battalions of the 14th infantry, on the 30th ultimo, at Bull Run and in its vicinity.

At daylight on the morning of the 30th we took up our line of march from our bivouac on the Manassas and Gainesville road in the direction of Bull Run, and reached that stream about 10 a. m.; soon after which I was ordered to place my brigade in position in the field fronting the Dogan house. The 1st and 2d battalions of the 14th were deployed in a corn-field, with the 12th and 4th infantry covering them in their rear in columns of battalions, the left of our line resting on the Warrenton turnpike. The 3d was advanced to the front and right, under cover of a wood about a thousand yards distant, where it was deployed as skirmishers. About 11 a. m. the enemy commenced throwing shells into us from a battery beyond the wood in front of the 3d, killing one man and wounding several. Butterfield's brigade, which had previously been placed in position on my right, was soon advanced into the wood, and I was directed to advance the four battalions to the front and obliquely to the right, to take up a position in rear and under cover of the woods, which I did in column of battalions, left in front. As soon as notified that I was unmasked by Butterfield, I advanced the two battalions of the 14th into and through the woods to his support, and held them there until after his brigade was entirely withdrawn, when my whole column was ordered to the rear. Whilst in the woods we were under a most incessant fire of all arms, but my officers and men behaved admirably. Here it was that Captain O'Connell, of the 14th infantry, was wounded in the knee whilst commanding the 1st battalion; notwithstanding which, he continued with his command throughout the day; and Captain D. B. McKibben, 14th infantry, in the ear, whilst commanding the 2d battalion. The 3d infantry, meanwhile, had been advanced, and held possession for several hours of two houses, about a hundred and two hundred and fifty yards in front and to the left of the wood, which it held until all the troops were withdrawn from the centre. In withdrawing the 3d, the right wing united with the brigade, and the left, being across the turnpike, united with Warren's brigade, and served with it until the whole division was united on the plateau between the Henry and Robinson houses. About five p. m. the brigade was withdrawn from the wood in admirable order, moving by the fronts of battalions in column, and halted for a short time in rear of Weed's battery, on a line with the Dogan house. From this point I was ordered across the turnpike to a position on the plateau between the Henry and Robinson houses, where the brigade was deployed in line of battle, with its right resting on the Henry house. About six p. m. I was ordered to take the battalion of the 12th and 14th to a wood to our left and front, to support Meade's brigade, then severely pressed by the enemy, and almost immediately after placing these troops in position, I observed that the 3d and 4th had also been ordered up. I found the enemy in very strong force in the wood, and, during the heat of a very severe engagement, discovered that he was flanking me with large masses of troops. I immediately commenced to gain ground to my left so as to meet his movements, and held him in check for nearly an hour. But at length I found the contest too unequal; my command was being cut to pieces; the ammunition of the men nearly expended; and the enemy's masses vastly outnumbering my force, I was forced to give the order to retire. This was done in most excellent order, the men marching steadily and slowly, and I resumed my position on the plateau. Shortly after, I was ordered to retire with my brigade to Centreville, which I did, and reached that point at one o'clock at night, having the entire brigade with me in good order, and having left a few stragglers behind.

I cannot omit calling the attention of the brigadier general commanding to the firm and gallant manner in which my brigade held the enemy in check on the extreme left for such a length of time, and finally prevented his turning our flank. At one time the 3d and 4th were within thirty yards of one of his brigades, which made a flank movement to turn their left, when Captain Dryer, commanding the 4th, gave orders to fire by battalions, and poured three most destructive volleys into it before his fire could be returned. The greatest portion of my loss was at this point, and too much credit cannot be given to officers and men for their coolness and gallantry during this engagement. The 2d battalion of the 14th was under fire for the first time, and behaved admirably.

I must beg leave to call attention to Captain Wilkins, commanding 3d infantry; Captain J. B. Collins, commanding the 4th, wounded, who was succeeded in the command by Captain H. Dryer—this latter officer being especially conspicuous for his coolness and gallantry; Captain J. D. O'Connell, 14th infantry, commanding 1st battalion, severely wounded in several places, and behaving most gallantly; and Captain D. B. McKibben, 14th infantry, commanding 2d battalion 14th, who displayed conspicuous gallantry throughout.

Captain Wilkins, 3d infantry, mentions Captain Walker, acting field officer, for coolness and the prompt carrying out of his orders; Lieutenants Sheridan, Whiting, Eckert, and Penrose; Lieutenant Deare, adjutant, who rendered important services, and behaved with the same indifference to danger which has distinguished him on former occasions. Sergeant Major A. Kaisser, Sergeants Torpy, Mourton, Hopkins, Sitzinger, Smith, Hessian, Crady, Schaeffer, Morris, Hawley, Flynn, Ackland, and Scully, of the 3d infantry, and Sergeant George Lamonion, of the 12th infantry, are especially mentioned.

I would particularly mention my staff—2d Lieutenant W. H. Powell, 4th infantry, acting assistant adjutant general, and aide-de-camp 1st Lieutenant T. Van Rensselaer, 12th infantry. These officers behaved with the utmost coolness and gallantry, and carried my orders to every part of the field to which they were sent, with cheerfulness and alacrity.

My whole brigade behaved as well as I could have expected or desired, and has, I trust, earned the favorable notice of the brigadier general commanding the division.

I am, sir, respectfully, your obedient servant,

ROBERT C. BUCHANAN,
Lieutenant Colonel 4th infantry, Commanding Brigade.

First Lieutenant H. Cutting,
Acting Assistant Adjutant General, Sykes's Division.

No. 38.

REPORT OF CAPTAIN S. H. WEED, FIFTH ARTILLERY.

Camp near Rockville, Md., *September* 8, 1862.

Sir: I have the honor to submit the following report: From the 14th to the 29th ultimo, the artillery of this command were occupied in moving from Harrison's Landing to the old battle-field of Manassas, a fatiguing duty for both men and horses, but which involved no fighting.

On the 30th instant my own battery was engaged. During the day it occupied three several positions. One section—the right—was detached and posted in a corn-field to the front, about twelve hundred yards from some batteries of the enemy. It remained there doing effective service until forced to retire by a general advance of the enemy, and a falling back of our troops. About 5½ p. m. the battery took up a second position behind the house it had been in front of, and remained there engaged until nearly all the ammunition with the pieces was exhausted. The caissons were sent to the rear after the first position was abandoned. The battery left its second position about 6½ p. m. While moving off and under heavy fire, two pieces broke down, by the breaking right in two of their axles. Both these pieces were taken entirely off the field and beyond fire. It was afterward necessary to abandon them on the road. The statements of the officers who had them in charge are appended. I also transmit reports of the officers in command of the other batteries of the division. My officers and men, with scarcely an exception, behaved remarkably well. I would especially mention Lieutenants Watson and Macintire, who exhibited much coolness and gallantry during the action, and in taking off the field, under heavy fire the two broken-down guns of the battery.

My casualties were as follows:

Private Godfred Gerbiz, right hand shattered and left arm shot off.
Private Gustav Adolph, shot in the foot.

Four horses killed, two wounded and abandoned.
Two 3-inch rifled guns lost on the road to Centreville.
I am, very respectfully, your obedient servant,

STEPHEN H. WEED,
Captain 5th United States Artillery, Commanding Division.

Lieutenant HEYWARD CUTTING,
Assistant Adjutant General, Sykes's Division.

No. 39.

REPORT OF FIRST LIEUTENANT A. M. RANDOLL, FIRST ARTILLERY.

CAMP NEAR ROCKVILLE, MD., *September* 8, 1862.

SIR: I have the honor to report that when General Sykes's division advanced against the enemy, I was ordered by one of his aids (Lieutenant Ingham) to follow the movements of the second brigade of the division; but on arriving near their position, I was ordered by an aid (Lieutenant Cutting) to return to the Warrenton road, opposite the second brigade, and await further orders. I remained in that position somewhat sheltered from the view of the enemy, but exposed to a continuous and heavy fire directed at other, batteries till all the infantry on my right had retired, and Colonel Warren's brigade on my left were driven from the field. As the battery was in columns of pieces on the road commanded by the fire of the enemy, and no infantry near, it was impossible for me to open fire, so I retired, in company with Captain Smead's battery, to near the hill occupied by Captain Weed's battery, when I was ordered by an aid of General Sykes (Lieutenant Ingham) to take position on the right of the house on the hill; but when about to move to the position designated, I was ordered by General Porter to move to a hill on the left of the field, if practicable. Owing to the confusion among the ambulances, infantry, batteries, &c., which blocked the road, I was obliged to move very slowly, and on examining the hill designated, found that while moving to take position on it I would be exposed to a direct and cross fire from several of the enemy's batteries, and that the infantry and batteries which already covered the hill were retiring in confusion; so I moved to a hill directly in the rear and took position on the right of Hazlett's battery, where I remained until the final falling back of the whole army to Centreville. Although during the whole day the battery was directly under the fire of the enemy's batteries, yet at no time could I from my positions open fire on his forces without extreme danger of firing into our own troops. My loss in the action was one horse killed.

Very respectfully, your obedient servant,

A. M. RANDOLL,
First Lieutenant 1st Artillery.

Lieutenant MACINTIRE,
Adjutant, Artillery, Sykes's Division.

No. 40.

REPORT OF SECOND LIEUTENANT W. E. VAN REED, FIFTH ARTILLERY.

CAMP NEAR ROCKVILLE, MD., *September* 8, 1862.

LIEUTENANT: I have the honor to submit the following report of the movements of battery K, 5th United States artillery, since landing at Aquia Creek on 23d of August, 1862.

On the 24th the battery was ordered to join General Sykes's division, which it did on the night of the 24th, it having marched some 24 or 25 miles; passed Fredericksburg about 2 o'clock p. m.

On the 25th, moved camp about half a mile.

26th. Marched about 8 miles.

27th. Marched about 10 miles, and went into position.

28th. Marched about 9 miles.

29th. Marched to Thoroughfare Gap; passed Manassas Junction about two o'clock p. m.

30th. Marched about 6 miles and took position at Bull Run, and was ordered into a hollow to await further orders; was afterwards ordered to withdraw and take position on the hill close to a stone house, when the battery was withdrawn; and while on the road Captain Smead was killed by a shot striking him on the head. The battery then proceeded to Centreville, arriving there about two o'clock a. m. 31st. About eleven o'clock a. m. the battery was placed in a redoubt.

September 1. One section (Lieutenant Calef's) went out on a scout with Colonel Warren; returned about four p. m.

2d. About one o'clock a. m. the battery marched about 25 miles; passed through Fairfax Court-House about ten o'clock a. m.

3d. Marched to within about ten miles of Washington.

4th. Marched to Fall's farm.

6th. Marched to Tennallytown; crossed the Chain Bridge about eleven o'clock p. m.

7th. Marched to Rockville, Maryland.

Saving Captain Smead's death, no other casualty occurred in the battery.

I have the honor to be, sir, yours, &c., &c.,

WILLIAM E. VAN REED,
Second Lieutenant Commanding Battery K, 5th Artillery.

Lieutenant H. CUTTING,
Assistant Adjutant General, Sykes's Division.

No. 41.

Nominal report of casualties in Sykes's division in action of August 30, 1862.

KILLED.

Third infantry.—Privates John Mananina, company B; Benjamin F. Kellog, company C; John A. Gale, company I; Corporal Henry Loraine and Private William S. Holmes, company K. Total, 5.

Fourth infantry.—Sergeant Patrick Shannon, company G; and Private Henry Conlin, company C; Gotlieb Ott, company F. Total, 3.

Twelfth infantry.—Captain J. G. Read, company D; and Privates Frank Schipmacher, company F; Michael Cassady, company B; Ezra Carter, company D; William Deishin, company B. Total, 5.

Fourteenth infantry, first battalion.—Privates Ezra Vallene, company B; James Hart, Henry Schneider, Christian Friese, Sergeants Albertus Pierce and Thomas F. Wise, and Privates Andrew Love, James Gordon, Jackson Henion, company E; Thomas McDonald, Nicholl W. Milles, and Thomas Noonan, company G; Thomas Hannah, and David Loyall, company H. Total, 14.

Fourteenth infantry, second battalion.—Privates John Cushing, company B; John Fitzgerald and Francis Howd, company H. Total, 3.

First infantry.—Private Joseph A. McMullen.

Second infantry.—Privates William A. Nixon, company C; and William Kidd, company E. Total, 2.

Sixth infantry.—Privates John Wilson, company B; Patrick Kienan and John Mahoney, company D; Patrick Mullen and Henry Shuleg, company E; Corporal Herman Westhers, company G. Total, 6.

Tenth infantry.—Private Mathew Kelly, company G.

Eleventh infantry.—Privates James Kavanah, Andrew Selzelie, and George Lá Mountain, company A; George J. Brown, company H. Total, 4.

Seventeenth infantry.—Privates Patrick Barron, Alex. Gibb, Josiah Victory, John Flood, and Sergeant Henry Madison. Total, 5.

Fifth New York volunteers.—Captain Wilbur F. Lewis, company D; Captain George O. Hager and Adjutant Frederick W. Sovereign, company F; Corporal William B. Harrison and Privates Charles Collins, Cannin Longstaff, and ——— Soby, company B; Private Dennis G. McCauly, company C; Sergeant Joseph H. Pierce, Corporal Benjamin Berrian, and Privates W. S. Blunt and James McCarthy, company D; Corporal George W. Leavett and Privates William H. Flynn and Louis Valoux, company F; First Sergeant William M. McDowell and Privates P. H. Brady and G. W. Taylor, company G; Color Sergeant Andrew B. Allison and Privates William March and Horace E. Williams, company H; Corporal John Milliken and Private John Hannan, company I; Corporal John C. Keys and Privates James Coppers, David Davis, Francis Plumb, and Albert Silleck, company K. Total, 28.

In the number of missing in the fifth New York volunteers are three sergeants, eight corporals, and forty privates, who are known to be killed, whose names were unknown to Dr. Winslow, who visited the battle-field under a flag of truce, making the total killed 79.

Tenth New York volunteers.—Privates Harvey Compton, John C. McHale, and John Gillman, company A; Lieutenant Josiah Hedden and Corporal Fred. Bland, company C; Privates Christian Shellenbauer, company F; Frank Smith and John Will, company I. Total, 8.

Dr. Winslow also reports fifteen of the missing in the tenth New York volunteers as dead, whose names were unknown to him; making total killed 23.

Fifth United States artillery.—Captain J. R. Smead, company K.

WOUNDED.

Third infantry.—First Lieutenant George B. Eckert, company C; Second Lieutenant John Whitney, company K; Privates Thorn Smith, company B; Patrick Murphy and James Murray, company C; John Rapp, company D; James W. Pierce, company E; Samuel Ellingsworth, Richard Hazlett, and Martin Shanahan, company F; Corporal George W. Dow and Private William Taylor, company G; Corporal Jeremiah Keane and Private John Houston, company H; Privates Edward Mulholland and Harvy McDonnell, company I; William Ludwig, company K. Total, 17.

Fourth infantry.—Captain Josh. B. Collins, company D; Corporal Edward Palmer and Private Sidney Brooks, company A; Privates John Conroy, Christian Bochm, and Hubert Erne, company C; Daniel Lyons, company F; Corporal Thomas Cahill and Privates Martin Burne, John Power, 2d, John Perham, and John Russell, company H; Edward Simpson, company I; William Dowling, company K. Total, 14.

Twelfth infantry.—Sergeant ——— Erchelberger, company C; Corporal Frank Howe, Privates John Bigge, Solomon Halgreen, and Joseph Monohan, and First Sergeant August Theerman, company B; Privates John Higgins, John Kennedy, John McGuire, George F. Kinney, and Thomas Ward, company F; Corporal Bazil McKee, and Privates James Davis, John H. Bendure, Robert L. Harrison, and Leonard Sherman, company C; John Meyers, David Harrison, and John Smith, company A; Sergeant Hugh Rogers, Corporal Joseph Helvie, and

Privates Lewis Kibold, Richard Chard, John Greer, Louis Helvie, Andrew J. Kline, Abraham Kauffman, Chistopher Resling, and John Chard, company G; Martin V. James and Nathan Leach, and Corporal W. H. Nesbit, company E. Total, 32.

Fourteenth infantry, first battalion.—Captain John D. O'Connell, Corporal Jerediah L. Lyman, and Privates James Brown, Richard Byrne, Abraham Healey, Albert Kendall, Patrick Keenan, Francis Herman, Charles F. Tallcott, John Preman, Josh. Badger, John Laffin, G. L. Morrison, and James Coffey, company A; Sergeant David Parkin, and Privates G. H. Baraclough, George W. Collins, Patrick Durkin, Jeremiah Reardon, John Lavony, William Simpson, and Sylvester A. Weaver, company B; William M. Lod, Louis Blair, William Burke, William Carney, Peter Depen, Michael Gallagher, George L. Griswold, James Harwick, Lander Hotchkiss, Patrick Houston, George Howland, George R. Ives, Michael Ledwick, Henry McBride, Thomas Mitchell, Patrick Mongan, Thomas Murry, Henry Murry, Reuben G. Stevens, Erastus Woodman, and George Turner, company C; Calvin R. Porter, company D; Sergeants Joseph Bohner and Jacob Hersch, Corporal Henry Schoenewald, and Privates Walter Anderson, Edward Buston, John Killman, William Rogan, Henry Smidt, George Seeman, Philip Newmann, and Charles Lahn, company E; John Chune, John Day, Dudley Gordon, John F. Barney, William D. Boyle, Michael Brigson, Elias Griggs, John Morrison, Michael McCarus, Thomas Redman, Frederick Leidler, Eli Scron, Thomas Tully, James Townssened, and William Geiger, company F; First Sergeant Martin F. Kelly, Sergeant John Doyle, Privates Lawrence Smith, Theodore Facer, Murselis Eli, John Smith, Samuel Jamison, and Adolph Murguand, company G; Sergeants Patrick McLaughlin and John H. Beggs, Corporals James Morris and Samuel Carpenter, and Privates David R. Callen, Thomas Beardsworth, John Bennis, Edward Collins, William F. Gerald, Patrick Hart, Frank Johnston, John Murry, Robert Swindels, and George Watson, company H. Total, 92.

Fourteenth infantry, second battalion.—Captain D. B. McKibben, commanding; Captain J. J. Copinger, company A; Captain J. M. Locke and First Lieutenant J. S. Wharton, company G; Sergeant William Pierce, and Corporals Harrison Snyder and George Heves, company B; Milton Davies, company C; Privates John Bigely, Parker Colladay, John Keefer, Walter Moll, and George Seip, company A; Peter Phenis, company B; John R. Beebe, John Malley, and Samuel Miller, company C; John Fanell, company E; Jared Van Campen, John McSorley, Francis Perry, John Knopp, Henry Mason, and James Nugent, company F; John Esby, Henry Elcock, James Flanagan, Wallis Farming, Sylvester Wheeler, and Joseph Marks, company G; Arthur Cosgrove, Patrick Hefferman, and Samuel Harvey, company H; Corporal Franklin A. Brigh, company B. Total, 34.

First infantry.—Sergeant Willis B. Worth, Corporal Bernard Brady, and Privates Henry Mason, George Love, Sylvester Johnston, and Jacob Stahlman, company G. Total, 6.

Second infantry.—Privates Peter Kelly and Joel R. Dunkee, company A; and Dennis Dowell, Robert McMalley, and Louis Habermould, company B; First Sergeant James Butler, Sergeant John Murray, Corporal Ebenezer Keeler, and Privates Michael Hammill, Patrick Carroll, Thomas Fleming, Henry C. Watson, John Hirth, John Renner, William Brennan, Edmund Cook, Thomas Tracy, Homer Young, and Thomas Boboy, company C; First Sergeant Rudolph O. Theirne, and Privates James Conroy, Jacob Geiger, Owen Keely, and James Trainer, company D; Sergeant A. F. Skinner, and Privates Owen Connaghton, Terrance Carroll, William M. Corney, Michael Donnelly, Louis Jochen, Thomas Kenny, John C. Lucas, and Paul Satter, company E; Sergeant Cornelius Ryan, Corporal Francis Vausten, and Privates John Fox, Nathaniel Gordon, William A. McCoy, Christian Rapp, Thomas Scully, Henry

McGuire, and Simon Miessenback, company F; Second Lieutenant Ralph E. Ellenwood, Corporals Horace Wickham, Christopher Doyle, and Privates John Deven, Patrick Enright, Robert Flynn, Patrick Gamben, James Golden, and William Hogan, company G; Michael Heath and —— Smith, company I; Corporals William Crompton and Cornelius Daley, and Privates Gotfried Foltz, Richard Gorman, Augustus Hopke, Kasper Long, George G. Ketter, Michael McDermott, John Pearson, Alexander Shute, and Daniel Healy, company K. Total, 64.

Sixth infantry.—Corporal Owen Leonard and Privates Simon Daysers, company B; Laurence Cran and Robert Stack, company D; Corporals Edmund Healy, company E; Worden F. Logan and Privates James Fitz, company F; Michael F. Godfrey, Wm. Hartmann, Frederick Voss, and James McGuire, company G; Edward McCarthy and Wm. F. Rutherford, company H; Sergeant Thomas McGuire, Corporal Arthur Smith, and Privates John Carroll, John Cherry, Patrick H. Croley, John Fox, John Ivers, John Sullivan, John White, and Richard Willis, company I; James Brewer, James Mason, and Wm. Dougherty, company K; Second Lieutenants Charles M. Payne, company I; Jer'h B. Schindel, company E; Abram W. Brickley, company D. Total, 29.

Tenth infantry.—Private Daniel Regan, company E; Corporal G. W. Green, and Privates P. J. Boyce, P. Burke, John Schlatt, Herrmand Schuller, and Peter Sheridan, company G; David Curtling, John Sullivan, John Smith, and M. Fitzgerald, company I. Total, 11.

Eleventh infantry.—Privates Thomas Leavett, company A; Michael Harrington, Robert L. Smith, Geo. F. Winslow, and Jno. Clehane, company B; Sergeant Jno. A. Reid, company E; Privates Rudolph Dankworth, Martin Albertson, and Lorenz Lohner, company F; Sergeant Jno. McGloughlin and Private Robert Wallace, company G; Sergeants Chas. D. Brancers and Chas. Brewster, and Privates Alfred Lewis and James Doyle, company H. Total, 15.

Seventeenth infantry.—Privates William Thomas, Jno. Schaffer, and Robert Church, company A; Lawrence Connelly, Edward Shepard, Robert Ash, and John McCabe, company B; Mich'l King and Benj. F. Monroe, company C; Burns Rickman, Henry Willey, Dan'l W. Sidlinger, Wm. P. Jenkins, and Ephraim Holmes, company D; John Collins, John Madigan, Wm. Faulkner, and Ira B. Bennet, company E; Wm. Connolly, Hugh Hoyt, Wm. Martin, Mark Griffin, James Chambers, and Elbert Hewett, company F; Frank Randall, Ira J. Nichols, Joseph Henn, and Henry Levon, company G; Daniel Gaffney, Andrew Clifford, Nozaire Bodett, James Fay, John Nelson, and James Webb, company H. Total, 34.

Fifth New York volunteers.—Captain Charles S. Montgomery, company C; Captain Carlisle Boyd, company A; Captain James McConnell, company H; Second Lieutenant E. O. Wright, company D; Second Lieutenant John S. Raymond, company H; Second Lieutenant William Hoffman, company I; Second Lieutenant Henry Keyser, Sergeants Patrick Gillegan and Joseph Vail, Corporals Andrew Blair, Theodore Hart, and William J. Vethake, and Privates Charles Bonesteel, William R. Bailey, Augustus Comstock, Thomas Fox, John McPike, Gustavus Peters, Thomas Ryer, Samuel Titus, Isaac C. Thomas, and Thomas M. Wicker, company A; Sergeant H. C. Peak, Corporals Oliver J. Rodgers and H. B. Saxton, and Privates Alfred Slater, Charles Collins, Frank H. Creighton, G. F. Colwell, E. C. Ellsworth, Fred. Fowler, Henry Greenwood, Jesse C. Johnson, Robert Munnie, Joseph Robinson, C. V. Sands, Frederick G. Smart, and G. W. Taylor, company B; Sergeants —— Donohue and —— Wannemaker, Corporals C. P. Humphreys, —— Demarest, —— Reddington, and H. B. Kretzler, and Privates George Calligan, H. Chabot, J. G. Labugh, H. Loderhose, James Whytel, and James H. Tobin, company C; Sergeant John H. Reilly, Corporal G. M. Meldowney, and Privates Francis B. Bickel, Edward J. Bird, J. R. Turner, James S. Hill, Benjamin F. Pease, John Brocher, Abraham Banker, G. Daley,

Cyrus Hagadorn, Jacob Hotthaser, John Johnson, John E. Neroman, Daniel A. Shaw, and William Wildey, company D; Sergeants Joseph Gates and Goe M. Sinclair, Corporals —— Allaire, John Carroll, and John Rodgers, and Privates John Brennan, Charles Brady, George B. Burlow, James Cochran, James Connolly, Andrew Coutes, Edward Cruger, H. J. Dolson, William H. Degroot, William Davis, Jacob Hanton, F. Kimball, Joseph Leahy, Jacob Menges, George McGeehan, Charles H. Ross, T. E. Roy, and Thomas Rishton, company E; Sergeant E. W. Marsh, Corporal James H. Franklin, and Privates William F. Davidson, John Farrell, Thomas Healy, Bruno Henile, George A. Hitchcock, Nicholas Hausman, Edward McGew, James Morrissy, William M. Griffin, Samuel Parkinson, Nathaniel S. Paul, George Past, Jacob Plutch, James Riley, Charles H. Reilly, James Sherridan, Benjamin A. Sullivan, Robert Sadler, and James H. Webb, company F; Sergeants P. L. Wilson and Francis Spellman, and Privates Robert Amos, Thomas Briscoe, Leander Brown, William Cole, Peter Guiter, Dennis Gueman, John Gillen, Ignatz Entres, Enick Lawson, Michael McMahon, N. D. Rodgers, William Sheppard, George Smith, and William Wilson, company G; Corporal J. F. Boyd, and Privates Patrick Gleason, William Alexander, Frederick Bollet, James A. Cochrane, E. Engell, George Finley, Francis Killelea, Charles Sumney, William Livingston, Thomas Madden, James McLaren, William H. Roggensteen, Peter Scherer, William Walker, and William Link, company H; Color Corporal James J. Robinson, Corporal James Boyd, and Privates J. W. Almack, Edward Dillon, Charles Dawson, Moses G. Jones, Thomas Pine, Alfonso Rankin, Henry Sault, William B. Slout, Henry Simon, and Allen Wilson, company I; Sergeants Henry H. Burton and William B. Hogebrom, Corporals John H. Clayton and John Cady, and Privates Richard Ackerman, J. W. Carter, George Davison, David M. Fraleigh, John H. Haughwont, John Horgan, Thomas Herrick, John Kerrigan, J. H. Martin, F. D. Newburg, Levi P. Pond, and Charles Stuyvesant, company K. Total, 170.

Tenth New York volunteers.—Corporals Stephen C. Baker, W. A. B. Johnston, and Thomas G. Casey, and Privates Hermon Cautor, A. F. Safely, Robert E. Coffin, Auguste Lomburel, Patrick Martin, Timothy Martin, Frank M. McVeagh, and William Hall, company A; Lieutenant Thomas Culhane, Sergeant A. Alexander, Corporals Abram Merrett and Frank Salles, John Colford, and Privates Wm. Carrigan, Cornelius Callahan, James B. Hall, Thomas McQuade, and John Pickett, company B; E. Cullen and Charles Heery, company C; John Teehan, company D; Corporal E. Teal, and Privates John Gilroy and Hendrick Brum, company E; Corporal A. Smith, and Privates Thomas Sullivan J. McFarland, Michael McKean, and Thomas McEvoy, company F; Corporal John B. Adatte, and Privates Joseph Balfe, Edward Hughes, George McLeod, Napoleon Mead, J. Morris, and R. Taylor, company G; Corporals J. O. Sullivan and Thos. Holding, and Privates Peter McCann and Charles McCarthy, company H; Lieutenant Geo. M. Dewey, Sergeant William Duff, Corporals M. Keegan, Hugh Fuller, and Stephen McGarvey, and Privates John Dockham, John McClatchy, E. Morton, E. Moran, and George Kavanagh, company I; Sergeants William H. Johnson and D. H. Dougherty, Corporals George Cooper, J. Troughton, and J. D. Stevenson, and Privates Luke Higgins, P. Kiernan, C. McLaughlin, J. W. Sexton, J. Schully, William Thompson, and M. Reilly, company K. Total, 65.

Fifth United States artillery—Privates Gustav Adolph and Gottfried Gerbig, company I. Total, 2.

MISSING.

Third infantry.—Holger G. Kolaye, band; Privates David Roach, Cornelius Ryan, Patrick Oates, Joseph Morrissey, and Frederick Lund, company D; M. J. Deney, company E; Sergeant James Torpey, and Privates James Halfpenny, Peter Mallow, John McNanard, James Manghan, and Thomas Renshaw, company H; Sergeant Gustavus Gaupp, and Privates Thos. Clark, James County,

George Franz, Philip Minor, Thomas McShane, and Francis Fitzsimmons, company I; Patrick Garvey, Matthew Loven, John Lynch, John Heisler, and William Slattery, company K. Total, 25.

Fourth infantry.—William Tabb, drummer, company K.

Twelfth infantry.—Privates Robert Church and E. C. McIntyre, company A; Thomas Flanngan, company F; Joseph Higgins, drummer, company B; —— Stone, company C. Total, 5.

Fourteenth infantry, first battalion.—Privates McCabe and William Wallace, company A; Alfred D. Harkins, William J. Hutchinson, and William R. Watkins, company B; Peter G. Hackett, Charles W. Miller, George Osborne, William D. Owens, and William H. Scott, company C; Corporal William H. Reed, company D; Ferdinand Dure and Henry Krause, and Privates Nicholas Pomas, William Campbell, George Manning, and Anton Warner, company E; Alvin E. Haskins, James Ryan, musician, company F; Sergeant Rufus J. G Holmes, and Privates William H. Corp, Thomas Mulhall, and Joseph Townsend, company H. Total, 23.

Fourteenth infantry, second battalion.—Corporal James Fatzinger, and Privates Daniel Carlin, Patrick Corcaran, Edward Laughlin, Philip Lelah, John Levar, and William Ohl, company B; William H. Dayton, company C; Robert E. Croker, company E; John Newboldt, company G, and Robert H. Silvis, company H. Total, 11.

First infantry.—Privates Peter P. Morrell, James Forshee, Rufus McGuellan, and John McLaughlin, company G. Total, 4.

Second infantry.—Second Lieutenant John H. Markley, and Privates Charles Urede, William Maloney, and Edward Toomey, company F; Peter Kelly, William Martin, William Myers, and John Oberterbessing, company G. Total, 8.

Sixth infantry.—Privates John Gregan and John Casey, company D; Henry C. Bessey, company E; Robert Sorge and Hugh McIntyre, company F; Michael Gately, company I. Total, 6.

Eleventh infantry.—Privates John Healy and Oliver H. Brey, company A; Jason R. George and Alexander Hudson, company B; Abraham Walk, company C; Patrick Driscoll, company D; Augustus Fairbanks, company E; Samuel Clendaniel and Horatio Howell, company F; James P. Stanton, Adam Bowers, James Scott, and —— Flinn, company H. Total, 13.

Seventeenth infantry.—Privates George Streeter and Reuben Streeter, company A; George Roberts, company C; Joseph Martin, company F; William Gallagher, Henry Hursnon, Thomas Cogan, and Samuel Stewart, company G; George Setes, company H. Total, 9.

Fifth New York volunteers.—Corporal George Huntsman, and Privates G. Niebuhr, Henry Seely, Henry W. Stevens, and J. Thelaneus, company A; Corporals J. C. Boyd and Edward W. Lewis, and Privates Charles Ambsler, Bergen, Drummer Boyd, Privates Chrystal, Farrell, S. W. Ford, Fogarty, H. C. Gee, McLean, Musician McKenna, and Privates W. F. Wessenger, B. Powell, J. Stevenson, J. Sutherland, N. C. Warren, and John Whyte, company B; Corporal Ebenger Smith, and Privates Jonas Bryant, William Chatterton, John Gibbs, Eugene Gear, John Grogan, Henry Lespinesse, John McAnaspie, Lewis Matos, Dennis O'Brien, Thomas B. Reynolds, Washington Sofield, and Reuben W. D. Sturgis, company C; Privates Thomas H. Clarke, James P. Benham, John Hoolahan, John F. Mahon, and Joseph Tyndall, company D; Corporal John Craft, and Privates Sylvester Austin, Charles Billeter, Richard Blake, James Brady, Alfred W. Clarke, John Cassin, William Perrin, John Keer, Leon Moreon, George Mowson, George Spencer, and Peter Van Genderen, company E; Sergeant Charles B. Potter, Corporals Francis A. Morgan and William A. Wheat, and Privates Charles E. Brehen, Clinton S. Cowles, Charles E. Dennis, Edward Simmons, and David Wells, company F; Corporal John Noble, and Privates David Byrnes, John Boyle, Charles Baldwin, James Cathey, William

H. Davis, Edward Hoffman, Daniel Hogan, Victor D. Mahoney, James Martin, James Patterson, Thomas Rooney, A. J. Rodgers, James Riley, Charles Taylor, —— Van Benschoten, and R. W. Wigham, company G; William H. Ames, Francis Higgins, John Hefferman, James Kent, Dennis Lanahan, James Reynolds, James Riley, William Usher, and Henry Woodfall, company H; Samuel H. Blake, James P. Crawford, Edward Dillon, John Hearne, and John Kabb, company I; Corporal William G. Shannon, and Privates Pierce Carey, Edward Egan, John Finn, Roland Jones, and Oscar Sturgis, company K. Total, 99.

Of those ninety-nine missing, three sergeants, eight corporals, and forty privates are known to be killed, having been seen by Dr. Winslow, but did not know their names.

Tenth New York volunteers.—Sergeant Alonzo Rodgers, and Privates John Steinhauer and John Smith, company A; Captain R. A. Dimmick, and Privates John Anderson, Cornelius Lowry, George Oflying, and James Van Benschoten, company B; Nicholas Smith, A. S. Dalton, John Foley, and R. Oakley, company C; Robert Harwood and Michael J. Brady, company D; H. Mallen, company E; Lieutenant Thomas D. Mosscrop, Corporal E. A. Dubey, and Privates John Friel, E. McCabe, and John Nugent, company F; Corporal Hugh Reilly, and Privates Ben Evans, Charles Shoeck, and William Mulkey, company G; Edward French, James Smith, Charles Scott, and John Sullivan, company H; John Johnston, S. McMullins, Dennis Coleman, M. Fitzgerald, George Furnival, J. McDonald, Philip Ritter, and J. Whitwell, company I; Sergeant A. Finley, and Privates William Hook, J. Jeffries, P. Madigan, P. Ryan, and D. Sheldon, company K. Total, 42.

Of these forty-two missing, fifteen are known to be killed, having been seen by Dr. Winslow, but did not know their names.

RECAPITULATION.

Regiments.	Officers.			Enlisted men.			Total.		
	Killed.	Wounded	Missing.	Killed.	Wounded.	Missing.	Killed.	Wounded	Missing.
3d U. S. infantry	....	2	....	5	15	25	5	17	25
4th U. S. infantry	....	1	....	3	13	1	3	14	1
12th U. S. infantry	1	....	....	4	32	5	5	32	5
14th U. S. infantry, 1st batt'n.	....	1	....	14	91	23	14	92	23
14th U. S. infantry, 2d batt'n.	....	4	....	3	30	11	3	34	11
1st U. S. infantry	....	....	....	1	6	4	1	6	4
2d U. S. infantry	1	1	1	1	63	7	2	64	8
6th U. S. infantry	....	3	....	6	26	6	6	29	6
10th U. S. infantry	....	....	....	1	11	......	1	11	......
11th U. S. infantry	....	....	....	4	15	13	4	15	13
17th U. S. infantry	....	....	....	5	34	9	5	34	9
5th New York volunteers	3	7	....	76	163	48	79	170	48
10th New York volunteers	1	2	2	22	63	25	23	65	27
Battery I, 5th U. S. artillery	....	....	....	......	2	......	......	2	......
Battery K, 5th U. S. artillery	1	....	....	......	......	......	1	......	......
Totals	7	21	3	145	564	177	152	585	180

Grand total 917

No. 42.

Tabular report of casualties in Brigadier General Sykes's division in actions of August 29 and 30, 1862.

Regiments	KILLED.		WOUNDED.		MISSING.		TOTAL.		Grand total.
	Commissioned officers.	Enlisted men.	Commissioned officers.	Enlisted men.	Commissioned officers.	Enlisted men.	Commissioned officers.	Enlisted men.	
3d U. S. infantry	....	5	2	15	....	25	2	45	47
4th U. S. infantry	....	3	1	13	....	1	1	17	18
12th U. S. infantry	1	4	....	32	....	5	1	41	42
14th U. S. infantry, 1st battalion	....	14	1	91	....	23	1	128	129
14th U. S. infantry, 2d battalion	....	3	4	30	....	11	4	44	48
1st U. S. infantry	....	1	....	6	....	4	....	11	11
2d U. S. infantry	1	1	1	63	1	7	3	71	74
6th U. S. infantry	....	6	3	26	....	6	3	38	41
10th U. S. infantry	....	1	....	11	....	......	....	12	12
11th U. S. infantry	....	4	....	15	....	13	....	32	32
17th U. S. infantry	....	5	....	34	....	9	....	48	48
5th New York volunteers	3	76	7	163	....	48	10	287	297
10th New York volunteers	1	22	2	63	2	25	5	110	115
Battery I, U. S. artillery	....	......	....	2	....	......	....	2	2
Battery K, U. S. artillery	1	......	....	......	....	......	1	......	1
Totals	7	145	21	564	3	177	31	886	917

No. 43.

Nominal list of casualties in Brigadier General Morell's division, fifth army corps, Major General Fitz-John Porter commanding corps, August 29 and 30, 1862.

FIRST BRIGADE—Colonel James Barnes commanding.

Second regiment Maine volunteers.

Killed.—Lieutenant A. L. Cowan, Sergeant W. P. Holden, Corporals R. Wharton and D. B. Webber, and Privates T. Kerr and J. L. Fuleton.

Wounded.—Major D. F. Sargent, Adjutant S. P. Madgett, and Captain F. C. Foss; Sergeants A. C. Whitcomb, K. Stewart, J. M. Simpson, C. Swett, W. H. Burton, C. L. Lovejoy, J. M. Sherwood, and J. S. Nevins; Corporals W. Robbins, A. Wilson, M. D. Joy, and J. H. Sargent; Privates S. J. Rogers, W. F. Ellis, J. M. Keeve, Wm. Wilson, F. Smith, O. Templeton, F. F. Sargent, W. N. Murry, J. M. Curtis, S. J. Kenny, A. W. Strout, G. Tibbetts, William Jones, L. Gordon, D. F. Page, J. S. Knowles, L. Maddocks, William H. McKinney, S. W. Smith, H. H. Blackwell, S. B. Fowler, J. R. Veazie, William Walker, V. M. Pinkorn, F. M. Wilkins, William Mason, J. Campbell, M. Wyman, C. P. Quint, G. S. Marshall, C. Shaw, L. Trafton, B. Warner, C. Bray, H. Mitchell, J. Beckett, M. Blake, H. Wheeler, C. Moore, J. Barnold, R. W. Harreman, J. W. Carm, W. G. Libbey, A. W. Frazier, W. H. Cates, J. Smith, T. Cunningham, S. Buxton, A. Kneeland, H. W. Drinkwater, E. Carr, A. F. White, M. Keaerse, J. Corcoran, C. Cronin, D. J. Collins, and J. Morrell.

Missing.—Corporal W. A. Brown, and Privates J. Hickey, H. S. Barrett, C. F. Green, A. Tireton, A. March, A. R. Marick, F. E. Burns, A. B. Luce, H. W. Gilmore, E. C. D. West, G. W. Carlisle, L. Marol, and B. Sullivan.

Eighteenth regiment Massachusetts volunteers.

Killed.—Captain C. W. Carroll; Lieutenants W. D. Russel, P. Almy, jr., F. Fiske, and S. Kimball; Sergeants B. Shaw, J. Simmons, and J. Stringer; Corporals W. McFarlin and E. Holmes; Privates G. H. Miller, E. W. Adams, G. Kingsbury, G. Cleveland, G. P. Hero, P. Kearn, J. Conry, B. Brown, J. Higgins, P. Yurnay, J. McGowan, D. Rix, H. D. Smith, G. Y. Leonard, W. W. Randall, F. G. Smith, W. Atwood, M. Cunningham, M. Gill, M. Raymond, J. H. Maxim, D. F. Church, F. Robinson, W. Manchester, A. Stringer, J. H. Britton, J. W. Stebbins, W. Flannagan, J. Hughes, and M. O. Donnell.

Wounded.—Captain F. Weston; Lieutenants E. W. Everson, B. F. Missirvey, C. F. Pray, and L. S. Burt; Sergeants L. Littleton, H. U. Luther, B. D. Damon, B. F. Caswell, A. K. Parris, S. Hollis, and E. Howard; Corporals A. J. McDonald, C. C. Holmes, D. B. Freeman, D. Cousins, W. H. Farrington, G. H. Claflin, G. H. T. Alfred, M. Ward, W. Simpson, J Braininey, and E. N. Blake; Privates A. C. Dunham, H. H. Hosmer, J. H. Leasure, J. T. Nightingale, T. Reed, F. F. McKinney, J. Reach, J. Brown, A. F. Contrell, M. Keys, B. McKoenna, L. Pond, A. T. Williams, W. Burgess, J. Ripley, S. Barrows, D. Bickford, J. E. Eaton, C. F. Lee, J. McKillop, J. Plumby, H. A. Wilcox, A. Thomas, M. J. Shurtleff, A. J. Atwood, T. Daley, J. Gleason, W. H. Potter, P. Breason, J. G. Prince, R. Wright, E. G. Cox, J. H. Keys, M. Sperman, S. Ellis, S. Benson, H. Parmenter, C. Thayer, S. Blake, F. Denney, E. L. Perkins, W. Condon, J. J. Green, J. Wood, E. Carr, J. Jordon, H. B. Paulding, H. Jones, R. Covey, P. Mears, E. L. Thomas, S. H. Butler, P. O'Brien, A. J. White, W. A. Blake, A. F. Bates, W. Cheney, W. A. Sturdy, A. L. Bacon, E. J. Gibson, W. Q. Spear, P. Smith, H. Galligan, W. J. Barney, M. Otis, J. W. Leavitt, J. S. Robbins, W. Fuller, J. N. Parker, G. Worthen, H. Chandler, A. Ewell, A. Slumy, F. McAvoy, H. W. Pillsbury, J. W. Pickering, J. McCantry, and F. R. Kingsbury.

Missing.—Sergeant J. W. King, Corporals F. S. Churchill and S. Thomas; Privates E. C. Bacon, M. Fische, J. K. Maxim, B. F. Arnold, G. A. Ray, P. Lake, M. McCantry, H. P. Nourse, B. Sullivan, F. E. Alwood, M. Seaver, J. Elliot, W. L. Marshall, G. H. Josselyn, W. W. Bessey, G. L. Brown, S. Pierce, E. Burgess, W. Churchill, J. S. Robbins, H. Weston, D. Crouty, C. E. Morrison, G. A. Lapham, and P. Margin.

Twenty-fifth regiment New York volunteers.

Wounded.—Sergeants —— Morton and —— Faely; Privates J. Pinkerton, —— McCarrick, H. Alney, and H. Hogan.

Missing.—Corporal Hooe, and Privates Rogers, Garnurow, W. McCormick, B. McGarrey, Wilton, Selmer, King, M. Kallahan, Slatterley, M. Caffrey, Richards, and William Conriney.

Thirteenth regiment New York volunteers.

Killed.—Second Lieutenant Gotling; Sergeants J. Evans, G. H. Hill, and N. Mutz; Corporals J. Spall, S. H. Morrison, R. Ruse, J. Snyder, and T. H. Jameson; Privates G. B. Stanley, L. Kork, J. Harvey, J. Stewart, J. Ryan, H. Clark, W. H. Guilford, L. Vahn, —— Norris, J. Leitch, A. Kuhle, J. W. Whiting, M. Iraett, J. Guss, J. Kenfield, J. Benjamin, E. Galphin, J. Strout, and A. Thompson.

Wounded.—Major G. Hyland; Captains H. Geck, —— Hassler, and C. H. Savage; First Lieutenant N. J. Burmell and Second Lieutenant G. W. Kirk; Sergeants J. Spear, D. D. Stilwell, F. Mahle, E. Bicker, C. Tarcott, D. C. Jewell, C. Webb, H. M. Herrick, W. M. Martin, and J. Gilder; Corporals J. G. Wenseul, J. Cowley, J. Schider, —— Fanrull, J. Loy, and E. Jewell; Privates S. Draper, A. Kenney, J. Bollenback, J. Waevther, C. Hasenzahle, —— Campbell, W. Reynolds, W. H. Lewis, H. Tracey, H. Cusick, G. H. Huifer, William Hannis, C. Sullivan, J. Claney, L. Plews, D. Wilson, J. Jackney, F. Schlert, J. Schweir, William Portsmouth, J. White, A. Hotchkiss, S. Ralph, —— Moshier, J. S. Stater, J. Rouse, G. Hazlett, H. Morchess, A. Smith, E. Frankburg, J. Wolfe, G. F. Pickell, J. Leonard, —— Dowd, R. Price, William Gillroy, D. Deurick, E. Kochle, J. Thompson, D. Peetes, P. McGregin, William Miller, T. Robinson, H. Potter, H. C. Lauckton, M. Homplating, J. Gack, J. Kennedy, M. Sauterburn, J. Guffney, J. Bruce, William H. Jerrell, F. Robbins, W. Jurey, and L. W. Soltes.

Missing.—Privates L. Lanwold, R. Ambrose, J. Granger, G. Burdick, T. Harvey, R. C. Wood, William Rowland, E. Searle, William Billings, F. Sanders.

First regiment Michigan volunteers.

Killed.—Colonel H. S. Roberts; Captains E. Pomeroy, R. H. Alcott, C. E. Wendell, and E. F. Whittlesey; Lieutenant H. C. Arnold; Sergeants J. J. Turner and B. F. Johnston; Privates F. Cady, G. S. Little, F. D. Fowler, A. T. Engle, M. Noran, W. Wilber, F. Pugh, H. Maynard, F. Flooman, G. Muler, J. H. Almond, H. M. Withington, D. Platte, G. Language, T. Bovin, H. I. Davis, P. Miner, J. Kitrage, C. Ornley, E. M. Holt, F. Byron, G. Rowel, G. H. Tompkins, W. Murich.

Wounded.—Captain G. Hopper; Lieutenants W. Bloodgood, J. S. Hatch, and J. F. Wheaton; Second Lieutenants J. F. Wilcox and A. C. Allen; Sergeants M. Hoffman, J. Dickenson, J. E. Langley, C. H. Haydin, L. C. Randall, J. E. Lane, William L. Woodruff, F. Barney, C. Pease, and M. E. Smith; Corporals F. Man, D. Minthen, C. C. Bugley, C. O. Vibber, H. Watkins, E. Axtell, E. Leyrain, G. Beamaster, William Cole, W. F. Prince, E. Brown, G. P. West, and R. Savery; Privates J. C. Behlomen, C. Der, J. Kanouse, E. G. Rohan, H. Cook, G. H. Haviland, J. McCantry, J. R. Smith, P. Courtney, B. Kirkpatrick, S. G. Pickle, L. Turks, D. Kingston, D. S. Pierce, J. C. Cower, O. L. Gibbs, H. S. Preston, E. Keeler, L. Schnecubecker, B. Eddy, B. Path, B. A. Tucker, C. Lipscombs, P. Tuttle, J. W. Wallace, L. Spawn, J. W. Allen, J. Donnelson, D. McKane, —— Stewart, A. J. Briggs, E. Moran, J. Hauld, W. Kibber, A. F. Harris, E. F. Rogers, J. A. Miller, L. C. Wicknive, W. Baxter, G. Hillman, C. D. Paine, H. Chase, F. Moran, E. Wolfe, J. J. Welch, J. G. Villas, M. Collins, G. Casnack, H. Manchester, C. Wanderlicks, A. L. Dickenson, J. B. Marsh, O. Brotherton, L. E. Morse, O. Sanford, F. L. C. Rising, J. M. Collins, H. Putman, E. Randall, W. Collins, H. Fieze, J. Pattie, H. O. Perkins, J. Connell, T. H. Graham, L. Louva, M. G. Fisher, F. Burnuz, C. D. Hodgkins, E. Duell, E. Partridge, G. Kork, J. Dorrand, I. Lotholtz, F. Foster, P. Saugan, P. Vassan, F. Begolker, William Fryer, A. Ormsby, M. Haller, D. Vanslyke, C. W. Boncha, M. Freshetta, and William Robertson.

Missing.—Lieutenants G. C. Modyk, —— Stepper, and J. L. Garrison; Corporal —— Baumaster; Privates G. Eddy, S. Houlton, S. Bliter, H. Preston, I. Ticknor, W. Hutchinson, W. G. Fisher, P. Stapper, William M. Court, H. H. Fisher, C. Holmes, W. Fix, C. Sanderson, I. Duffy, I. Smatts, J. Depue, C. Beach, G. Moran, L. Gurnard, J. A. Woodruff, E. Davis, H. Perkins, J. M. Amesh, A. Harris, J. McViern, E. R. Wood, H. H. Cole, H. F. Manchester.

THIRD BRIGADE—Brigadier General Butterfield commanding.

Seventeenth regiment New York volunteers.

Killed.—Major T. C. Grower; Captains J. D. Blauret and James H. Demurret; Second Lieutenant James Reed; Corporals M. Welsh, John McDonald, R. W. Taylor, and W. P. Borce; Privates John Dunn, John Vogle, Manson M. Dunbar, John Hiler, Byron Meritt, Joseph Gliss, T. Connolly, Daniel Delaney, William Ives, I. Bertenshar, John Richardson, William H. Williams, and G. Gilbert.

Wounded.—Captains J. L. Burliegh, J. O. Martin, and Andrew Wilson; First Lieutenants T. V. Toley, D. Derrien, and Waldro Sprague; Second Lieutenants C. Green, and A. M. Sanford; First Sergeant M. Skully; Sergeants Thomas Beale, T. J. Waldron, John Landry, Frank Gomes, John Keynick, Theodore Miller, C. H. Pease, A. J. McCoy, James W. Money, B. C. Nodine, C. D. Immen, Thomas Claney, and Lucien Post; Corporals N. W. Miller, Cyrus Taylor, ——— Harvey, ——— Fanican, and A. F. Hisrote; Privates M. Cain, Richard Cook, H. B. Finner, Frank Garvin, Aaron R. Horton, T. H. Cauley, Peter Flood, Peter Nodiro, Joseph Kemp, J. Andrews, Peter Clark No. 1, Peter Clark No. 2, William Faulker, William Knowles, Thomas Laurence, John Kohler, Andrew Moffatt, James Becket, Garret F. Majorey, John Donahue, F. McQuade, Bernard Harrison, B. Glawson, F. Conroy, Charles Putnam, Thomas Farrell, L. Finnegan, John Cotton, John Leary, George Phillips, Charles Howell, James C. Smith, Patrick Fagan, James Phillips, John Doran, William Leaky, Benjamin J. Higgans, ——— Holmes, ——— Hagan, ——— Cashman, ——— McCoy, ——— Sesnon, ——— Jones, W. W. Ryder, A. Wesley, ——— Twiggs, William Griffin, John H. Griffin, Wm. J. Wart, William J. Hewitt, Ellis Jones, E. M. Waldron, J. N. Dines, Robert L. Sarle, F. Olmstead, James Burtley, John Bergen, A. F. Carpenter, William Lindsey, Robert McGurnney William Downing, Anson Brown, L. S. Graves, Joseph Slinot, John Monahan, John C. Sweet, Rufus Combs, Charles Crandall, J. Cunningham, Benjamin Smith, Jacob Evarts, James S. Hill, Alexander Decker, Levy J. Sweet, Charles Bills, James Conway, Henry Streamer, Tucker Martin, and Henry Schneider.

Missing.—Sergeants William Lee, Edward Farnsworth, ——— Cowan, and James Cull; Corporal ——— Burns; Private John B. Whiting, Peter Mitchell, F. Ferguson, C. Murphy, William W. Foster, John Hart, Daniel Worten, Isaac Williams, Charles Whiting, Henry Weeks, C. Niedwhishey, James Croney, Thomas Kerney, George Weston, Henry S. Hewald, William B. Hang, Frederick Panier, ——— Cook, ——— Creedon, ——— Eager, ——— Rosbach, ——— Wynkoop, J. L. Wedenburgh, William E. Worden, L. Reynolds, H. Slagle, Joseph Griggs, Joseph Paponiet, Hugh McCuffry, M. McCree, William Murray, Joseph Perott, James Scott, Robert Taylor, William H. Owens, Samuel Lawrence, Charles Nichols, Morrell Kurney, Patrick Quinn, Patrick Brown, G. W. Bullock, ——— Doane, Samuel S. Fuller, Charles Miller, James McLean, Eugene Parkhill, Emory Raynor, Daniel Sherman, Alson Peet, and Nicholas Smith; Drummer M. Kearney.

Forty-fourth regiment New York volunteers.

Killed.—Sergeant ——— Darling; Privates Eugene Walker, George Lutz, E. Frederick, and Charles Luff.

Wounded.—Captain L. S. Larabee; First Lieutenant C. W. Gibbs; Second Lieutenants E. A. Nash, J. H. Russell, and J. Hardenburgh; Sergeants S. B. Johnston, D. S. Weaver, H. A. Usher, and William H. Sentell; Corporals ——— Harris, James King, and John Downing; Privates Joseph Brandell,

Chapin Babcock, James Champlin, W. H. Cupp, James Dow, O. Horton, H. C. Hammond, George Hill, W. H. Rockwood, William Saler, William Wood, W. B. Horton, James Gould, Jacob Blackman, Peter Schafer, E. G. Stevens, Oscar Thomas, William Weaver, James W. White, M. O. McNiff, Isaac Bevier, John Shone, Nathaniel King, Darius Little, William Lavervay, S. Dearstyne, John Mitchell, William Smith, David Fikes, George Rider, James Darmas, James Dougal, George W. Webster, James B. Cass, and H. D. Buck.

Missing.—Sergeant A. G. Graves; Corporal A. J. Hood; Privates F. Burnett, A. Jennings, Hugh Galligher, H. A. Smith, M. Shaw, L. Crain, W. H. Tompkins, F. Furch, George Spry, Ira Conkling, David H. Gorden, Ralph McDougal, M S. Hill, L. D. Ladon, C. F. Balen, A. Nichols, and William Eckerson.

Eighty-third regiment Pennsylvania volunteers.

Killed.—Corporals J. H. Subburt and N. B. Smith; Privates R. Talghman, Lewis White, and E. D. Soloman.

Wounded.—Lieutenant Colonel H. J. Campbell; Captain John C. Graham; Corporal H. B. Meffert; Privates William Hibbard, G. W. Sweet, W. G. Dilley, Jas. Huffman, E. Hitchcock, S. Feathers, Jos. Goheen, James Hunter, L. Dodge, David Tuttle, S. M. Lindsey, William Kephart, Mathew Hayes, John Lillibridge, S. A. Dilley, James Hudlesen, M. A. Butterfield, William Flemming, T. E. McIntire, E. Peck, W. Dougherty, W. P. Roberts, William Lemon, L. Porter, William Bull, John Crutchlon, J. L. Dunn, Charles E. Petton, Wesley Babcock, and George Harps.

Missing.—Major W. H. Lamont; Captain D. P. Jones; Lieutenants J. Harrington, W. J. Whittick, and W. E. Bates; Sergeants R. H. Proudfit, E. J. Whittlesey, and F. C. Wittick; Corporal William Burrows; Privates J. W. Herring, George Kiddle, Comfort Hyde, I. W. Vannata, Edward Potter, George Keir, Henry Brown, David Crandle, James Weir, Richard Beet, Wilson Amon, D. Thompson, G. W. Dark, Alexander Lowry, S. Himrod, G. Kerr, H. Stafford, R. S. Vanderslice, T. G. C. Merille, James Browley, J. D. Fish, W. D. Shad, W. D. Webster, George Judd, Chester Rich, L. M. Chapin, Joseph Murray, Thos. Gillfillew, A. M. Barnet, G. W. Hazleton, William Mac, J. E. Hayes, J. H. Devoover, Willian Lyons, Archibald Browley, T. C. Godfrey, C. Swift, Buss Serone, A. McFadden, R. D. Benson, J. W. Platner, William Bushnell, Simpson Siggins, S. Butler, G. D. Judson, C. W. Stafford, J. C. Hayes, J. W. Francisco, Thomas Whitmore, John Dusties, D. Newton, R. Eckhart, William Burns, G. H. McCord, Myron Blakely, D. W. Hatch, and George Foot.

Twelfth regiment New York volunteers.

Killed.—Sergeant —— Baker, and Privates Pat Kaine, James Van Horn, Edward Hanlow, Thomas McClellen, John Deegan, W. H. Lopez, James Westlake, Peter Borglan, W. R. Wells, John Duffey, John Murphy, Thomas Wood, M. Richardson, and M. Ryan.

Wounded.—Captains William Fowler, —— Ryder, and A. J. Root; Lieutenants J. J. Beehan and J. C. Stanton; Sergeants James White, J. H. Leonard, —— Howard, —— Phillips, —— Brennan, and A. J. Nash; Corporals Charles Fenton, D. Martin, R. Herod, R. R. Wallace, Ed. Anderson, Charles Greene, James Clucy, A. Willis, H. Fitzgerald, and H. Ferguson; Privates Joel Jefferson, Chas. Elbert, Joe Denoia, Ed. Fountain, J. Downes, John McCantry, David Clark Anton Fuller, John Popple, F. Armdon, Joseph Masons, John, Flannelly, Ed. Follet, William Staunton, Garret Hicks, Charles Brown, H. Mager, J. G. Hornen, J. Wolf, William Willets, William Farlen, Joseph McAfee, Louis Paulke, John Coon, Joseph Morrell, Ed. Hodgkins, S. McCormick, Leroy Gray, Bernard Fay, F. B. Horton, George Colburn, P. Gaffrey, John McBeet, M. Kennedy, John

Love, B. Farnham, Homer Care, H. S. Neariney, E. Fitzsimmons, and Joseph Blocat.

Missing.—Lieutenant D. L. Ludden; Sergeant —— Finkington; Corporals Van Camp, —— Hitchcock, Price Germond, K. Wells, Barney Brennan, W. D. Lermon, J. Lockwood, S. Collins, Andrew Black, Thomas Ivers, George Lynch, D. H. Andrew, John Brown, Alexander Bowler, N. Kimball, James McNath, Dan. Strong, John Donaldson, and A. Whipple; Privates Peter Welsh, James Idill, John Ferguson, George W. Colwell, Henry C. Harmon, Ed. Younglove, S. Tompkins, James Butler, F. Miller, P. Mailen, John Davis, John Ivers, Daniel Kelly, William O'Brien, John Keenan, Nelson Kimball, Wallace Paige, Fred. Whiker, O. C. Hawley, H. Murray, John L. Keller, Lockhart Duff, Thomas Duke, M. Reardon, James R. Pearce, H. Smith, Thomas Slack, John King, B. J. Bennet, John Hunter, John McFadden, William Messler, N. J. Van Patten, Peter Saltler, W. Bridgeford, and H. N. Smith.

Sixteenth regiment Michigan volunteers.

Killed.—Captain R. W. Ransom; Lieutenants Michael Chittick and John Ruby; Sergeants John Copp and —— Everington; Corporals Van Vicher, D. Bradley, E. B. Coffin, and J. C. Kitchen; Privates R. Mann, R. Martinstine, Jasper Gordon, L. D. Wickham, Useb Sachairley, Ed. Smith, and John H. Johnston.

Wounded.—Captain Thos. J. Barry; Lieutenants Edward Hill and G. H. Swan; Sergeants C. Ludwig, C. E. Bowen, James Hough, T. F. Powers, John Luhman, Hanson McFarlan, and Ed. R. Tanner; Corporals C. Sherman, H. D. Filton, —— Nash, —— Richt, J. Mullenburg, Frank McGinnie, W. Quackenbush, —— Turrell, Ed. P. Strong, Jno. Van Horn, —— Stafford, and —— Steffer; Privates H. L. Davenport, Albert Doane, Cordell Greene, Francis Kinurgee, Charles Sutherby, Martin Hushman, Isaac Dodge, Emil Stoorn, —— Brown, Joseph Allen, Daniel White, H. S. Kennicott, T. Morton, Wm. Shaffer, Frank Lane, Meritt Evans, John Conquest, Philitus Barber, Aug. Grieber, Wm. Simmons, T. F. Crandell, M. L. Bagley, A. B. Toman, Chas. Wyner, Geo. W. Richards, Patrick Wyse, Jos. Snyder, Robt. Botsford, Jno. Grienther, Jno. Bigelow, James Hall, Christian Keifer, Henry W. Falcott, Owen Winn, Josiah Bond, S. K. Knight, Fred. Weidmeir, —— Van Horn, O. M. W. Greene, Henry Palmer, J. Shriver, and Wm. Munroe.

Missing.—Captain —— Lang, Sergeant George Nathan, Corporal G. R. Couden, and Privates Frank Giley, Christian Muchard, Jas. Benjamin, James Marten, John Brennan, —— Eames, Ackland McCroney, James Stewart, J. Gusenheifer, —— Whittey, Henry Prentice, Otto Schneiderwint, E. Coul.

First regiment United States sharpshooters.

Killed.—Sergeants Byron Brewer and G. C. Brown, Corporals Rudolph Semhauser and Peter Van Netten, and Private Chas. Beiler.

Wounded.—Colonel H. Berdan; Captains B. Isler and W. P. Austin; Sergeants C. N. Jacobs, J. McBain, John Coates, W. C. McLain, J. E. Nethirington, and R. W. Tyler; Corporals Norton Fitch, Theo. Shortan, Geo. Downing, H. J. Peck, and Isaac Davis; and Privates C. Armand, Charles Gameter, Geo. M. Barber, Theo. E. Gordon, N. E. Badger, Robt. Cassey, John D. Tyler, Wm. H. Lattin, Danl. Waner, Albert Bills, Thomas Hadden, P. W. Barker, J. S. Bailey, George Hartley, George Whitson, Geo. E. Whiting, S. J. Race, Wm. C. Henderson, Fred. Dittest, John Uhlrich, Orson P. Sturtevant, Saml. A. Clark, Wm. Babcock, Thos. McCall, A. C. Stannard, Wm. Close, and N. D. Wilson.

Missing.—Lieutenant C. D. McLain, Sergeant Philander Austin, and Privates L. M. McGraw, N. Wentworth, James Burns, D. C. Overton, Patrick Joyce, Dexter Field, Wm. Fisher, Jno. Nickirsgill, Jno. Tappan, F. J. Hallock, Abner Johnson, and Benj. Schaf.

Battery C, First Rhode Island artillery.

Wounded.—Privates G. H. Holden, T. H. Randall, and E. J. Leach.
Missing.—Corporal E. A. Griffiths.

No. 44.

Tabular report of casualties in Morell's division, August 29 and 30, 1862.

	KILLED.		WOUNDED.		MISSING.		TOTAL.		
	Commissioned officers.	Enlisted men.	Commissioned officers.	Enlisted men.	Commissioned officers.	Enlisted men.	Commissioned officers.	Enlisted men.	Grand total.
First Brigade.									
2d regiment Maine volunteers	1	5	3	68	....	18	4	91	95
18th reg't Massachusetts vols	3	37	5	96	....	28	8	161	169
25th reg't New York vols	....	......	....	6	....	13	....	19	19
22d reg't Massachusetts vols	....	......	....	......	....	......	....	......	......
13th reg't New York vols	1	26	6	75	....	10	7	111	118
1st reg't Michigan vols	6	26	6	106	3	30	15	162	177
	11	94	20	351	3	99	34	544	578
Second Brigade.—(Not in action.)									
Third Brigade.									
17th reg't New York vols	3	17	9	101	....	53	12	171	183
16th reg't Michigan vols	3	13	3	60	....	17	6	90	96
83d reg't Pennsylvania vols	....	5	2	34	5	61	7	100	107
44th reg't New York vols	....	5	5	42	....	19	5	66	71
12th reg't New York vols	...	15	6	57	1	64	7	136	143
	6	55	25	294	6	214	37	563	600
Berdan's U. S. sharpshooters	....	5	3	38	....	15	3	58	61
Artillery.									
Battery D, 5th U. S artillery	....	......	....	4	....	......	....	4	4
Battery C, Massachusetts	....	......	....	......	....	......	....	......	......
Battery C, Rhode Island	....	......	....	3	....	1	....	4	4
	....	......	....	7	....	1	....	8	8
Totals	17	154	48	690	9	329	74	1,173	1,247

No. 45.

REPORT OF BRIGADIER GENERAL JAMES B. RICKETTS.

HEADQUARTERS 2D DIVISION, 3D ARMY CORPS,
Hall's Hill, September 4, 1862.

COLONEL: I have the honor to submit the report of operations of my division from the 17th August, when directed by you to retire to the east side of Cedar Mountain, to this date.

On the 18th the command was ordered to retire from near Mitchell's Station, in the direction of Culpeper, and at 11 p. m. the baggage and supply trains having preceded the division, and the march much impeded by roads blocked by trains of other corps, delaying our crossing at Rappahannock Station until after sundown on the 19th.

Pursuant to orders from the major general commanding, on the 20th two regiments, 3d brigade, with a section of Mathews's Pennsylvania battery, under General Hartsuff, recrossed the river and occupied the heights commanding the ford, the rest of the brigade remaining on the north side of the river.

The 1st brigade, under General Duryee, with Leppien's Maine battery, and two sections of Mathews's Pennsylvania battery, was stationed on the heights on the north side of the river.

The 2d brigade, under General Tower, with Hall's Maine battery, stretched up the river on the right.

The 4th brigade, under Colonel Thorburn, 1st Virginia, being held in reserve. During the night a trestle bridge was constructed, and the mornmg of the 21st the remaining regiments of the 2d brigade, with Thompson's Pennsylvania battery, and the other sections of Mathews's Pennsylvania battery, crossed to the south side of the river, and skirmished with the enemy during the day.

On the 22d, Hall's Maine battery did good execution against the guns of the enemy. During the night a heavy rain swept away the trestle bridge, and endangered the railroad bridge, causing the withdrawal of the 3d brigade on the 23d, under the excellent fire from Mathews's, Thompson's, and Hall's batteries, which were then posted on the heights commanding the railroad bridge, supported by 1st brigade, and a brisk artillery fire was kept up for several hours, until ordered to destroy the bridge and retire.

I would here mention the untiring exertions of Brigadier General Hartsuff, who, although much prostrated by severe illness, continued manfully to do his duty; and also regret the severe wounding of Lieutenant Godbold, Mathews's battery, whose leg was here taken off by a shell. The destruction of the railroad bridge, and the arduous duty of protecting the rear, was intrusted to Brigadier General Tower, who performed it with admirable skill, and the night closed in a bivouac on the road towards Warrenton. On the 24th the division passed through Warrenton, and took position on the road to Sulphur Springs. On the 25th moved towards Waterloo, resting about four miles from Hedgeman's river. The 26th was occupied in a reconnoissance near the crossing at Sulphur Springs. The 27th, retired from that position to Gainesville. On the 28th, being ordered to "assist Colonel Wyndham, who, at 10.15 a. m., reported the enemy passing through Thoroughfare Gap," marched from New Baltimore through Haymarket, where the troops were relieved of their knapsacks to hasten the movement; but before reaching the gap, about 3 p. m., met Colonel Wyndham's skirmishers retiring before the enemy, already in possession. Fully realizing the importance of gaining this point, I pressed the division forward, although in a wearied condition, determined to effect the object if possible.

The road was entirely obstructed by felled timber, which delayed bringing the batteries into position; the 3d brigade in advance, then commanded by

Colonel Stiles, 83d New York, supported by the 1st and 4th brigades, the 2d brigade being held in reserve. The men moved forward gallantly, but owing to the nature of the ground, the strongest positions being already held by the enemy, we were subjected to severe loss, without any prospect of gaining the gap, although successfully maintaining our ground until dark, when I ascertained the enemy in superior force were turning both right and left, in the endeavor to surround us; then considering our position untenable, and all efforts to take the pass unavailing, I despatched two messengers to you with this report, and retired towards Gainesville for the night, where hearing from General King he was to retire at one a. m. from the pike towards Centreville, and not hearing from you, while considering the position critical, as subsequently proved, by the inquiry made by rebel officers, as to who ordered that retreat which defeated their anticipations of capturing the entire division by their overpowering numbers outflanking us. I retired by the way of Bristow, and effected a junction with the corps on the evening of the 29th, bivouacking on the field of Bull Run within range of the enemy's guns.

At sunrise on the 30th ordered by you to send two brigades to report to General Kearney, and conducted the 1st brigade, General Duryee, 4th brigade, Colonel Thorburn, which relieved a portion of General Kearney's division.

General Duryee's brigade advanced in the woods, driving the enemy along the line of the old railroad excavation, until directly under their guns, the 4th brigade a little retired on his right.

While occupying this ground General Duryee was subjected to a heavy fire of artillery and infantry, in which he received a slight wound and severe contusion from a shell, but remained at his post, animating his men, who behaved admirably. It was in this heavy fire that my aide, Captain Fisher, while with his usual zeal, acting under orders, had his horse shot under him, and was taken prisoner.

The 2d and 3d brigades, under General Tower, with the four batteries, occupied our left.

While thus disposed, received the order to "forward my division" from the right on the road leading from Sudley Springs to New Market, and follow along that road "in pursuit of the enemy." I gave this order and reported to General Heintzelman, as directed, when informed that the enemy were following up the already advanced brigade, and confident that they had no intention of retiring, so reported personally to you, and was then directed to abandon pursuit, and resume my first position, where the brigades were soon exposed to a galling cross-fire.

General Tower, commanding 2d and 3d brigades, was detached to the extreme left, with Hall's and Leppien's Maine batteries. This portion of the division most gallantly endeavored to maintain their position, suffering severely, until General Tower fell seriously wounded, and the loss of officers and men was very great.

The engagement now become general from right to left. I moved Thompson's battery to the extreme right of the line to dislodge the enemy, but was outnumbered in guns, and withdrew it to unite with Mathews's battery on the right of Stevens's division, to aid in checking the enemy's advance, which was now pushed along the front; their loss in men and horses entirely disabled these batteries, and in connexion with the casualties among the commanding officers compelled the division to retire towards night, making a desperate stand at Mrs. Carter's house, used for a hospital, which proved unavailing against the superior force.

On the 31st we remained at Centreville, supplying the exhausted division. The 4th brigade was here detached, and the commanding officer, Colonel Thorburn, being wounded, I have been unable to obtain his report, but respectfully submit the casualties in the 1st, 2nd, ad 3d brigades.

On the 1st September we took up position on the Aldie road, acting in conjunction with General Reno's division, and held this point until the 2d September, when, in compliance with orders, we fell back to Hall's Hill, near Washington.

In recapitulating the services of the brigade commanders, I would make particular mention of Brigadier General Duryee, commanding 1st brigade, for his noble conduct at Thoroughfare Gap, and his indomitable courage displayed at Bull Run while holding a trying position.

I desire to express my especial obligations to Brigadier General Tower, commanding 2d brigade, for his indefatigable zeal and valuable services on all occasions, particularly at Thoroughfare Gap, and at Bull Run, where he was detached with two brigades and their batteries, and highly distinguished himself. I commend the conduct of Colonel Root, 94th regiment New York volunteers, who, although painfully wounded at Bull Run, continued on duty.

The 3d brigade, although early deprived of their efficient commander, Brigadier General Hartsuff, behaved admirably. I particularly noticed Colonel Coulter, 11th Pennsylvania volunteers, whose regiment bore the brunt of the engagement at Thoroughfare Gap.

Colonel Thorburn, 1st Virginia, commanding 4th brigade, deserves high commendation for his valuable services—Captains Mathews's and Thompson's Pennsylvania batteries, and Captains Leppien's and Hall's Maine batteries, deserve to be mentioned, not only for their uniform attention to their duties, but for their efficiency throughout the 30th August. My thanks are due to the officers of my staff, Captain John W. Williams, assistant adjutant general, Captain W. Fisher, aide-de-camp, and Captain B. W. Richards, aide-de-camp, who severally exhibited a high degree of efficiency and personal bravery.

Surgeon N. R. Mosely, medical director, was untiring in his exertions and care of the wounded.

Major William Painter showed remarkable zeal and energy; also acting ordnance officer Lieutenant M. S. Smith, 13th Massachusetts volunteers.

Very respectfully,

JAMES B. RICKETTS,
Brigadier General Volunteers, Commanding Division.

Colonel E. SCHRIVER, *Chief of Staff.*

No. 46.

REPORT OF LIEUTENANT COLONEL WILLIAM CHAPMAN, THIRD INFANTRY.

HEADQUARTERS SECOND BRIGADE, SYKES'S DIVISION,
Camp at Hall's Farm, Virginia, September 6, 1862.

SIR: We left our position on the Gainesville road, where the division bivouacked on the night of the 29th, about a mile and a half from Manassas Junction, early on the morning of August 30; our line of march lay two miles to the left of Centreville, and was continued to Bull Run Hill. The division was then posted, about 8.30 a. m., across the Warrenton turnpike, 800 yards to the front. The 1st brigade deployed; the 2d brigade, composed of the 2d and 10th infantry, Major C. S. Lovell, 10th infantry, commanding; 6th infantry, Captain L. C. Bootes commanding; 11th infantry, Major D. L. Floyd Jones commanding; and 17th infantry, Major G. L. Andrews, 17th infantry, commanding, was formed in columns of division as a reserve in rear of the 1st. The division moved forward from this first position to support General Morell's, occupying the woods in our front. The troops of General Porter's advance were assailed on both flanks by grape and canister from the enemy's batteries. After a portion of the 1st brigade advanced into the woods, my brigade deployed its columns and formed a column of regiments in line. About 3.30 p. m., by General Porter's order, the brigade retired in admirable order to the point designated, then moved by the left flank on to the turnpike; marched on same to the summit of Bull Run Hill, the post of the commanding generals. This movement was executed with surprising order under a heavy fire of artillery, and elicited my warmest admiration. At the time of leaving our second position the enemy was massing heavy columns on our left for a flank attack. My brigade was ordered by Generals Pope, McDowell, and others to advance to our proper front, then towards the left of the position occupied by the federal forces. My arrival was most opportune; not a regiment or brigade of the immense reserve held on that field were in effective proximity to repel the advance of the enemy at the point of their approach. The 17th infantry, leading, marched to the point indicated, followed by the 11th, 6th, 2d, and 10th, and occupied the edge of the wood, through which a heavy force were advancing against us. The line was formed with the 6th infantry advanced a little way in the woods. Here, coolly and calmly, my brave troops awaited a visible evidence of the presence of the enemy, when a volley was poured into their lines, with what effect could not be seen for the cover of underbrush, &c. It was replied to by a terrific fire of musketry; the firing continued three-quarters of an hour with no material decrease on the part of the enemy. One effect of our fire was notable, the enemy was checked. A New York battery, posted on a hill towards the right and rear of my brigade, limbered to the rear and left its position at the very moment when it could have done excellent service; the enemy having disclosed itself in its front, the commanding officer may have received orders to leave; if so, they came at an unfortunate moment. The enemy's musketry was not sufficiently dangerous to drive him off, and he had the infantry support of my entire brigade. The brigade coolly delivered its fire until our loss urged a withdrawal. The enemy finding himself checked here, despatched a force further to the left, with a section of artillery, threatening our rear. The 9th New York regiment of volunteers, on the left of our line, soon retired, exclaiming "it is too hot," thus leaving our flank exposed. This also urged the withdrawal of the left. Another volunteer regiment left our right, after being engaged but a few minutes. When the 1st brigade moved up within view, I ordered the brigade to fall back; while this was being done the enemy opened on us with grape and canister, firing very rapidly; but few casualties were caused by it however. The 1st brigade advanced towards the right of the position left by us. My brigade fell back some 600 yards to Bull Run Hill, on the side towards Centreville. We rested here until orders were received, about 6.30 p. m., to march to Centreville. We reached Centreville about 11 p. m., and bivouacked for the night.

It is with the greatest pleasure I bear testimony to the splendid conduct of my command. It challenged unqualified admiration. I feel and acknowledge my indebtedness to the battalion commanders, and particularly Major Lovell, 10th infantry, commanding 2d and 10th, whose remarkable coolness in the action was encouraging and inspiriting, and whose assistance was only to be seen to be appreciated. I would recommend that his soldierly qualities be duly rewarded.

For details I respectfully refer to the battalion commanders' reports.

Loss in actions of the brigade.

2d and 10th infantry, 86; 6th infantry, 52; 11th infantry, 31; 17th infantry, 48. Total, 217.

1st Lieutenant John S. Poland, regimental quartermaster, 2d infantry, my aide-de-camp, was with me during the whole day, carrying orders under the most galling fire to every part of the field where the brigade was engaged, and was conspicuous for his gallantry.

2d Lieutenant E. E. Sellers, 10th infantry, acting assistant adjutant general, was with me during the entire day.

I would also state that I especially noticed Assistant Surgeons W. R. Ramsey and Alfred A. Woodhull, United States army, untiring in their exertions to the wounded of the brigade.

Respectfully submitted.

WILLIAM CHAPMAN,
Lieutenant Colonel 3d Infantry, Commanding Brigade.

Lieutenant HAYWARD CUTTING,
Aide-de-Camp, and Acting Assistant Adjutant General.

No. 47.

REPORT OF COLONEL WILLIAM BLAISDELL, ELEVENTH MASSACHUSETTS VOLUNTEERS.

HEADQUARTERS ELEVENTH MASSACHUSETTS VOLUNTEERS,
Camp near Alexandria, Virginia, September 14, 1862.

SIR: I have the honor to report that on the evening of August 25, 1862, this regiment left camp, near Alexandria, by the Alexandria and Orange County railroad, and arrived at Warrenton Junction at 2 a. m. August 26. At 3 p. m. same day marched to a field two miles from the Junction and encamped. August 27, at 9 a. m., marched back to Catlett's Station, met and routed the enemy after a short engagement, with the loss of one man, John V. Churchill, of company E, severely wounded by a shell while supporting a battery. August 28, marched in pursuit of the enemy and overtook them on the morning of the 29th on the old battle-field of Bull Run. After supporting several batteries the regiment was ordered to move forward and engage the enemy. At about 3 p. m., advancing about one mile to the edge of a heavy wood, then deploying and moving forward in line of battle until within range of the enemy's pickets, the line was halted, bayonets fixed. Again moving forward, driving the enemy's pickets before it, the regiment came upon and engaged a heavy line of the enemy's infantry, which was driven back and over a line of railroad, where the road-bed was ten feet high, behind which was posted another heavy line of infantry, which opened a terrific fire upon the regiment as it emerged from the woods. The 11th regiment, being the battalion of direction, was the first to reach the railroad, and of course received the heaviest of the fire. This staggered the men a little, but recovering in an instant they gave a wild hurrah and over they went, mounting the embankment, driving everything before them at the point of the bayonet. Here for two or three minutes the struggle was very severe, the combatants exchanging shots, their muskets almost muzzle to muzzle, and engaging hand to hand in deadly encounter. Private John Sawler, of company D, stove in the skull of one rebel with the butt of his musket and killed another with his bayonet. The enemy broke in confusion and ran, numbers throwing away their muskets, some fully cocked, and the owners too much frightened to fire them, the regiment pursuing them some eighty yards into the woods, where it was met by an overwhelming force in front, at the same time receiving an artillery fire which enfiladed our left and forced it to retire, leaving the dead and many of the wounded where they fell. It was near the railroad embankment that the brave Tileston, Stone, and Porter, and other gallant men, received their mortal wounds. Being thus overpowered by numerical odds, after breaking through and scattering two lines of the enemy, and compelled to evacuate the woods and enter into the open fields beyond, the enemy pursuing us hotly to the edge of the woods, I was greatly amazed to find that the regiment had been sent to engage a force of more than five times its numbers, strongly posted in thick woods and behind heavy embankments, and not a soldier to support it in case of disaster. After collecting the regiment together, and moving back to our original position, we encamped for the night. The officers and men of the regiment fought with the most desperate bravery; not a man flinched, and the losses were proportionately severe. Out of two hundred and eighty-three officers and men who participated in the fight, three officers and seven enlisted men were killed, three officers and seventy-four enlisted men were wounded, and twenty-five missing, making an aggregate of ten killed, seventy-seven wounded, and twenty-five missing, all in the space of fifteen or twenty minutes. The regiment bivouacked on the field, and the next day, after being marched from one part of the field to the other, fell back to Centreville, where it remained until September 1, 1862, whence it was marched to camp near Fort Lyon, where it arrived on the 3d of September, 1862.

Very respectfully, your obedient servant,

WILLIAM BLAISDELL,
Colonel Commanding Regiment.

Lieutenant C. H. LAWRENCE,
Acting Assistant Adjutant General, Grover's Division.

No. 48.

REPORT OF CAPTAIN W. M. GRAHAM, FIRST ARTILLERY.

CAMP AT CENTREVILLE, *September* 1, 1862.

GENERAL: I have the honor to report that my battery occupied a position on our extreme left, supported by three regiments of General Reno's brigade, on the evening of the 30th ultimo. I here fought a large force of the enemy's artillery, infantry, and cavalry, and held the position until 9 o'clock at night, when I was ordered to withdraw and take up the line of march to this point by General Gibbon, commanding the rear guard of the army. As I was unavoidably separated from your immediate command on that day by an order from Major General Heintzelman, I hope that my course may meet with your approval; and with great respect remain, general, your obedient servant,

W. M. GRAHAM,
Captain First Artillery, Commanding Battery.

General P. KEARNEY,
Commanding First Division 3d Army Corps.

No. 49.

REPORT OF CAPTAIN G. E. RANDOLPH, FIRST ARTILLERY.

EARTHWORK NEAR FAIRFAX ROAD,
September 8, 1862.

SIR: I have the honor respectfully to report that on the afternoon of September 1, I marched with the division from Alexandria in the direction of Fairfax Court-House. My first position, a temporary one, was on the left of the main road, some distance in rear of the main battle-ground of Chantilly. Afterwards, under direction of General Kearney, I took position on a knoll directly in rear of General Birney's line, and commenced a regular fire of solid shot into the woods occupied by the enemy. My position was such that I could not fire with much accuracy or effect for fear of injuring our own line of infantry, over which I was firing. What the effect of my fire was I am unable to say. My only loss was one horse killed, and my expenditure of ammunition about one hundred rounds, mostly of solid shot. By order of General Birney I withdrew my battery after dark, and after remaining in my first position several hours, marched to Fairfax Court-House, when I joined the division on the morning of the 2d.

I am, very respectfully, your obedient servant,

GEORGE E. RANDOLPH,
Captain Commanding Battery E, 1st R. I. A.

Major H. W. BREVOORT,
Assistant Adjutant General, 1st Division, 3d Corps.

No. 50.

Copies of letters from General McDowell and Lieutenant Colonel Buchanan relative to the report of Brigadier General Milroy.—(For report see No. 11.)

WASHINGTON, *October* 17, 1862.

I enclose a printed copy of Brigadier General Milroy's report of the battle of the 30th of August last, and beg to call your attention to that part of it where he speaks of asking me for re-enforcements or the day would be lost, &c. &c. I mark the portion to which I refer, as yours was the brigade which at this time was sent to re-enforce General Meade, the officer referred to by General Milroy, but whose name he does not give. I wish you would give me your recollection of the circumstances: 1st, as to the state of mind General Milroy seemed to be in, his manner, and the impression it produced at the time to which I refer; 2d, as to whether or not it was a question of my sending re-enforcements to General Sigel, and if I refused to do so; 3d, as to the part taken by General Milroy with your brigade, which he claims to have led to where they were most needed, but from which they were forced back, &c., &c.

Please return the report with your answer.

Very respectfully, yours,

IRVIN McDOWELL, *M. G.*

Colonel ROBERT C. BUCHANAN.

No. 50.

WASHINGTON, *October* 20, 1862.

GENERAL: Your note enclosing a printed copy of General Milroy's report is before me, and I will answer your questions seriatum. 1st, "As to the state of mind General Milroy seemed to be in, his manner, and the impression it produced at the time to which you refer"—that is, when he rode up and asked for re-enforcements.

Answer. General Milroy's manner was very excited, so much so as to attract the especial attention of those present, and induced many to inquire who that was that was rushing about so wildly, and what he wanted.

Second. "As to whether or not it was a question of my (your) sending re-enforcements to General Sigel, and if I (you) refused to do so?"

Answer. General Sigel's name or corps was not referred to in any way in my hearing as far as I recollect.

Third. "As to the part taken by General Milroy with your (my) brigade, which he claims to have led to where they were most needed, but from which they were forced back," &c. &c.

Answer. When re-enforcements were called for to go to the assistance of General Meade, I was ordered by General Sykes to take three of my battalions and move up to the front and left, to the point most threatened, which I did at once. I left General Milroy haranguing and gesticulating most emphatically in the same place where his conversation with you was commenced. He was calling for re-enforcements, saying that if they were sent at once the day would be ours, and that the enemy were ready to run. After I placed my three battalions in position, I moved to the right of my line, when, to my surprise, I saw, about one hundred yards to my right, the remainder of my brigade, which had been sent to the front after I left, and General Milroy was giving it some orders. I at once rode after him, and told him that those battalions belonged to my brigade of regulars, and that I could not consent to any interference with my command. He said that he did not know they were my men, did not wish to interfere with me, and only wanted to place them in the best position. I told him I was responsible for the position of my command, and did not want any assistance, either in posting or fighting it. When he left me his own brigade was not near there, and he seemed to be rushing about the field without any especial aim or object, unless it was to assist in the performance of other officers' duties wherever he could find one to listen to him. I did not lose one inch of ground after I got my brigade together, which I did immediately by moving this latter portion to the left, but held the enemy at bay for an hour; and, instead of being "forced back," I maintained my position until ordered to fall back to the position from whence we started. Had the enemy "forced" me back, in the sense of General Milroy's report, he would have obtained possession, not only of the turnpike, but of the *stone bridge*, and what would have then been the result? You are well aware—our defeat would have been disastrous.

I am, sir, respectfully, your obedient servant,

ROBERT C. BUCHANAN,
Lt. Col. 4th Inf., Commd'g 1st Brigade Reg. Inf.

Major General IRVIN McDOWELL,
U. S. Volunteers, Washington, D. C.

I return the report.

No. 51.

REPORT OF BRIGADIER GENERAL J. P. HATCH.

CAMP NEAR FREDERICK, MARYLAND,
September 13, 1862.

CAPTAIN: I have the honor to submit the following report of the movements of the 1st division, 1st corps, temporarily under my command during parts of the 29th and 30th days of August.

Late on the afternoon of the 29th ultimo I was ordered by General McDowell in person (who was at the time stationed near the stone house, on the turnpike from Gainesville to Centreville) to move the division on the Gainesville road in pursuit of the enemy, who, he informed me, were retreating.

Gibbon's brigade had been detached to support some batteries.

With the three other brigades of the division, and Garrish's battery of howitzers, I proceeded with all the speed possible, hoping, by harassing the enemy's rear, to turn their retreat into a rout.

After marching about three quarters of a mile, the 2d regiment of United States sharpshooters was deployed to the front as skirmishers, the column continuing up the road in support. The advance almost immediately became warmly engaged on the left of the road.

Two howitzers were then placed in position, one on each side of the road, and Doubleday's brigade was deployed to the front, on the left of the road, and moved up to the support of the skirmishers.

We were met by a force consisting of three brigades of infantry, one of which was posted in the woods on the left, parallel to, and about an eighth of a mile from the road. The two other brigades were drawn up in line of battle, one on each side of the road. These were, in turn, supported by a large portion of the rebel forces, estimated by a prisoner, who was taken to their rear, at about 30,000 men, drawn up in successive lines, extending a mile and a half to the rear.

Doubleday's brigade moved to the front under a very heavy fire, which they gallantly sustained; but the firing continuing very heavy, Hatch's brigade, commanded by Colonel Sullivan, was also deployed, and moved to the support of General Doubleday.

Patrick's brigade, which had been held in reserve, took up a position on the opposite side of the road, completely commanding it. The struggle, lasting some three quarters of an hour, was a desperate one, being, in many instances, a hand to hand conflict.

Night had now come on, our loss had been severe, and the enemy occupying a position in the woods on our left, which gave them a flank fire upon us, I was forced to give the order for a retreat.

The retreat was executed in good order; the attempt of the enemy to follow being defeated by a few well-directed volleys from Patrick's brigade.

On the afternoon of the 30th ultimo I was directed to report with the division to General Fitz-John Porter, who, as I was informed, would hold us, as a reserve, to support the attack on the enemy's centre.

I found General Porter's troops formed in rear of a piece of woods about one half a mile to the right of the point at which the division had been engaged the day previous.

On reporting to General Porter, and informing him of the order under which I came, he directed me to post the division on the right of his own troops, and to make the attack simultaneously with himself.

The division was drawn up in seven lines, composed as follows: 1st and 2d, Hatch's brigade; 3d and 4th, Patrick's brigade; 5th and 6th, Gibbons' brigade; 7th, Doubleday's brigade; the 2d United States sharpshooters being advanced as skirmishers in the woods.

At the word given by General Porter the division advanced, with an interval of fifty yards between the lines.

The enemy were very strongly posted behind an old disused railroad embankment where, according to their own statement, they had been awaiting us for two days.

This railroad embankment, which runs parallel to the edge of the woods where we entered in front of our right wing, bears more to the rear on reaching a piece of open ground in front of our left wing.

After passing through the woods and reaching the open space, the left wing of the first line was obliged to make a partial wheel to the right to enable them to approach the enemy. This movement was executed under a heavy fire of artillery on the left, and of musketry from the woods directly in our front.

Seeing the great disadvantages under which the 1st and 2d lines labored, the others, as they came up, were ordered to oblique more to the right, to enable them to attack the troops behind the railroad embankment, and also to get a partial flank fire upon that portion of the embankment which crosses the open field. The contest for the possession of this embankment was most desperate. The troops on both sides fought with the most determined courage, and I doubt not the conflict at this point was one of the most bloody of the whole war.

Having myself received a wound which disabled me, I was forced to leave the field before the struggle terminated.

For the details, and an account of the last of the battle, I must refer you to the reports of the brigade commander.

General Doubleday exhibited the greatest gallantry in leading on his brigade under a terrible fire, on the night of the 29th; and, with his aide-de-camp, Major U. Doubleday, and Captain E. P. Halstead, assistant adjutant general, did much, by reckless daring, towards keeping this brigade from giving way when hard pressed.

Captain Robert Chandler, assistant adjutant general, (King's staff,) and Captain J. A. Judson, assistant adjutant general, (who was taken prisoner while bearing an order on the field,) were distinguished for their good conduct on the 29th.

Lieutenant Bartlett, aide-de-camp to General King, behaved with the greatest coolness, and rendered efficient service on the 30th, bearing orders under a heavy fire.

Lieutenant James Lyon, aide-de-camp, both on the 29th and 30th of August, bore himself in the most gallant manner, and deserves, as he receives, my most heartfelt thanks.

Very respectfully, your obedient servant,

J. HATCH,
Brigadier General Volunteers.

Captain ROBERT CHANDLER,
Assistant Adjutant General.

No. 52.

REPORT OF COLONEL J. W. REVERE, SEVENTH NEW JERSEY VOLUNTEERS.

HEADQUARTERS SEVENTH REGIMENT NEW JERSEY VOLUNTEERS,
In the field, near Centreville, Virginia, August 30, 1862.

SIR: I have the honor to report that this regiment, being ordered into the woods with the sixth New Jersey volunteers, proceeding to occupy them, relieving a New York regiment of General Steinwehr's division, on the 29th instant, at 11 a. m., on the extreme right of the position of our part of the army.

Advancing about fifty yards, we encountered the enemy's pickets, and a spirited engagement ensued, with varying success; and having been relieved by the timely advance of the sixth regiment New Jersey volunteers, we drove the enemy from his position, but, having been strongly reinforced, he regained it at about 1 p. m.

The battle then re-commenced, and we held our ground, as ordered to do so, until 2.30 p. m., when our ammunition beginning to fail we were regularly relieved by the troops in reserve.

Our soldiers went into the action greatly fatigued from the hot pursuit of the enemy in the forenoon and the previous day, but fought with great courage and determination, and held their ground, until relieved, against three reliefs of the enemy in front successively.

All did well, but I particularly desire to mention a piece of notable gallantry on the part of Corporal Frederick Kock.

Sergeant Onslow, our color-bearer, having been struck down, the colors fell, and Corporal Kock seized the colors, and elevating them aloft, stuck the staff into his belt-roll, still firing his musket on the advancing enemy.

I have recommended him for promotion to a second lieutenancy for his bravery and example to the rest.

I am deeply pained to report that Captain Jos. Abbott, company E., died nobly at his post while bravely discharging his duty in the coolest manner. He is a great loss to his country and the service.

CASUALTIES.

Killed.—Captain Abbott and Private Jas. Shuvell, company E.

Wounded.—Enlisted men: Martin Haker, company A; Corporal Curtis Dangler, and Privates John McPeter and William Stevens, company C; Private Andrew Kelly, company D; Samuel Pettit, Thomas Walravin, and Henry Engle, company E; Sergeant James H. Onslow, John Corbitt, James Bennet, and John Ryon, (wounded and missing,) company F; Patrick McEvoy and George Putzle, company H; James Spangenburg, company I; John R. Lyon, company K.

Missing.—Assistant Surgeon Charles B. Jaques. He has never been reported on the morning reports, on account of not receiving the resignation of Assistant Surgeon A. Satterthwaith, now surgeon twelfth New Jersey volunteers. Enlisted men: Patrick Corbett, company F; John Brady, William Willis, and William Sweeny, company G.

Total killed commissioned officers	1
Total killed enlisted men	1
Total wounded enlisted men	16
Total missing commissioned officers	1
Total missing enlisted men	4
Aggregate killed, wounded, and missing, out of 240 who went into the fight	23

In the affair of the 30th instant our regiment was engaged, with the rest of the brigade, in supporting several batteries, and, although under the heavy fire of the enemy's batteries for several hours, during which we made several marches by the flank through their fire, I am happy to say there were no casualties to report. We retreated to Centreville the same night, reaching there at about midnight.

I am, sir, respectfully, your obedient servant,

J. W. REVERE,
Colonel Seventh Regiment New Jersey Volunteers.

Lieutenant LE GRAND BENEDICT,
Acting Assistant Adjutant General, 3d Brigade Hooker's Division.

No. 53.

REPORT OF LIEUTENANT COLONEL R. THOMPSON, ONE HUNDRED AND FIFTEENTH PENNSYLVANIA VOLUNTEERS.

HEADQUARTERS 115TH PENNSYLVANIA VOLUNTEERS,
Camp near Alexandria, September 6, 1862.

SIR: I have the honor to report, for the information of the commandant of the brigade, the part taken in the actions of the 27th, 29th, and 30th ultimo, by the one hundred and fifteenth Pensylvania volunteers, in the action of Bristow's Station:

I formed line of battle in the rear of the scene of action by order of colonel commanding, acting as a support to regiments then engaged. After remaining about fifteen minutes in my first position, was ordered to the front. I passed by the left flank along a road leading through the woods to the open ground in front. On emerging from the woods, was met by a destructive cross-fire from infantry and artillery, sustaining a serious loss in officers and men. Not having received orders as to the position to be taken, I was at a loss to know where to post my command. Finding that there was an interval to the right of the fifth New Jersey, I formed my left flank to the right flank of that regiment, closing the interval between their flank and the woods; the right wing of my command I threw into the woods to clear it from parties of the enemy then occupying it. After firing four rounds, I charged the enemy, who were posted in force behind the bed of the railroad, supported by two pieces of artillery on a height immediately in their rear. When the charge was made, the enemy fled, pursued by my regiment and the fifth New Jersey. After crossing the railroad, I rallied my command and formed line of battle in rear of the fifth New Jersey, awaiting further orders.

In the action of 29th ultimo, at Bull Run, moved into the woods with brigade, taking position assigned by commandant of the brigade, my right flank connecting with the left of the seventh New Jersey, my left flank connecting with the right of the sixth New Jersey. After I had taken my first position, which was about twenty yards in rear of the road in front of the woods, by permission of the commandant I moved my command forward to the road to support the seventh New Jersey and gain a position in which I could deliver a more effective fire upon the enemy. During the engagement my command charged across the road up to the ravine behind which the enemy were concealed. Owing to the strength of the position and weight of fire from an immense body of the enemy, were obliged to fall back to their original position, which, I am proud to record, they maintained during the engagement until relieved. During this charge I sustained a heavy loss, the amount of which it is impossible to ascertain. Many of those returned as missing met their death in this charge. After being relieved, I moved to my original position, where I encamped for the night. On the following day, 30th ultimo, my command moved with the column under the immediate supervision of the colonel commanding brigade, retired from the field at dusk, and encamped at Centreville.

While referring with just pride to the gallantry of the whole command, I would particularly request your favorable notice of the following named officers and men for coolness and exalted courage: Major F. A. Lancaster; Lieutenant R. L. Thompson, commanding company F; Lieutenant Wm. Ashe, company C; Lieutenant Rielly, commanding company E; Adjutant W. C. Ward; Captain Dunne, company B; Lieutenant Dillon, company B; Sergeant Major Connelly was particularly conspicuously for coolness and dashing conduct; the color bearer, Sergeant Hugh Barr, behaved with the greatest gallantry, bearing his colors without falter into the thickest of the fight; Sergeant Wager, of company E; and Corporal Elder, company E.

Number of officers and men engaged at Bristow Station, 204; at Bull Run, 195.

The above is respectfully submitted.

ROBERT THOMPSON,
Lieutenant Colonel 115th Pennsylvania Volunteers, Commanding.

Lieut. LE GRAND BENEDICT,
Acting Assistant Adjutant General, Patterson's brigade Hooker's division.

No. 54.

REPORT OF LIEUTENANT COLONEL G. C. BURLING, SIXTH NEW JERSEY VOLUNTEERS.

HEADQUARTERS SIXTH REGIMENT NEW JERSEY VOLUNTEERS,
Camp near Fort Lyon, Alexandria, Virginia, September 4, 1862.

SIR: I have the honor to report the following as the part taken by the 6th regiment in the battles of the 27th, 29th, and 30th of August:

On Tuesday, August 26th, in compliance with orders received from headquarters, the 6th regiment left camp near Alexandria and embarked on the cars. Arriving at Warrenton Junction we disembarked and encamped for the night.

Wednesday morning, August 27th, received orders to march with three days' rations; left camp near 7 a.m. and marched in the direction of Manassas, and when near Bristow's Station found the enemy in force. After crossing a stream the 6th and 7th regiments were temporarily detached from the brigade, by General Hooker in person. We then marched forward deploying skirmishers on our left. In a short time we met the enemy's pickets and drove them in. We were then ordered to take an advanced position on a hill to the right, in front of us, which position we gained without loss under a terrible fire of shell from the enemy. We were then ordered to relieve the 2d New York, 8th New Jersey, and 115th Pennsylvania regiments, who were engaged on the right.

Immediately on reaching our new position the enemy fled in great confusion, leaving their dead and wounded, in great numbers, on the field. We pursued them for two miles, when we encamped for the night. Thursday, August 28, pursued the enemy through the day, and encamped near Blackburn's Ford (Bull's Run) that night. Friday, August 29, left camp at 3 a.m., pursuing them through Centreville, down the Warrenton road, crossing Bull Run at 10 a. m. At 11 a. m. we formed a line of battle and advanced into the woods to relieve one of General Sigel's regiments, where we found the enemy in force behind the embankment of an old railroad; after delivering and receiving several volleys we charged and drove the enemy from his position, when he received re-enforcements and we were compelled to fall back nearly fifty yards, which position we held until we were relieved by the 2d Maryland regiment. (During this engagement Colonel G. Mott and Major S. R. Gilkyson, while gallantly encouraging their men, were wounded.) We encamped in the open field for the night. Saturday, August 30, formed a line of battle about 4 p. m., and was ordered to support batteries to the right and rear of the position we had held the day before. Through some misunderstanding, my regiment being on the right, the other regiments composing the brigade were withdrawn without my knowledge, leaving me in a very critical position.

The enemy making a charge upon the batteries in front, compelling them to fall back, I determined to resist their advance, when, to my utter astonishment, I found we were flanked right and left. I then ordered the regiment to fall back in the woods, which was done in order, and thus checked the advance of the enemy in front.

At this time, finding the flanks of the enemy rapidly closing around us, the only safety for my command was to retreat. In trying to extricate ourselves from the critical position in which we were placed my command suffered severely. I was enabled to rally my regiment on a hill in close proximity to the battle-field, under the shell of the enemy, where we remained in line of battle with several other regiments, until ordered by the ranking officer to fall back to Centreville, where I joined the brigade the following morning. We remained here until Monday afternoon, September 1, when orders were received to march with the brigade; near sunset we halted and formed a line of battle and remained in this position until daylight, when we again took up our line of march to Fairfax Court-House.

I am under obligations to Captain Baker, acting major, who rendered efficient service after Colonel G. Mott and Major S. R. Gilkyson were wounded. I must also mention Adjutant C. F. Moore, who, throughout the different engagements, displayed unusual courage, rendering efficient service.

Captains T. C. Moore, J. U. Crawford, and W. William, and Lieutenants J. Howeth, Thomas Lee, B. Coley, C. Merriam, J. W. Cogswell, J. Tallon, West Field, and Joseph C. Lee are deserving of great praise for gallantry displayed in these battles, as in former ones.

With few exceptions the non-commissioned officers and privates conducted themselves with that valor which has given our brigade and division the name which we are proud of.

It gives me pleasure to speak of the indefatigable exertions of Surgeon J. Wiley and his able assistant, B. Hendry, and also Chaplain S. T. Moore, for their care and attention to the wounded.

Herewith I enclose a list of the killed, wounded, and missing during the three days engagements.

Very respectfully, your obedient servant,

GEO. C. BURLING,
Lieutenant Colonel Commanding 6th New Jersey Volunteers.

Lieutenant LE GRAND BENEDICT,
Acting Assistant Adjutant General, 3d Brigade Hooker's Division.

HEADQUARTERS SIXTH NEW JERSEY VOLUNTEERS,
Camp near Fort Lyon, Virginia, September 4, 1862.

SIR: The following is the list of killed, wounded and missing of the sixth regiment New Jersey volunteers, in the engagements of August 27, 29, and 30.

I am unable to give the nature of the wounds received, owing to the absence of our surgeon, John Wiley, who is missing and supposed to be a prisoner.

KILLED.

August 29.—Private John Y. Vannote, company A; Private George Higgins, company C; Privates William Fields, Thomas Van Brunt, Thomas Jones, and William Hanlan, company E; Private Benjamin F. Budd, company G; Private Michael Wright, company H; Privates John Jobes and Edward Ewen, company I; First Sergeant Edward Corcoran and Private John Gaggers, company K.

August 30.—Sergeant Isachar Ettinger, company F; Private Elijah Q. Burroughs, company H; Private A. C. Cornell, company I; Privates Martin Marshall, James Coleman, and William Bisbing, company K.—18.

WOUNDED.

August 27.—Private John Jeffrey and Daniel Bresnahan, company A; Private Woodward Cox, company D.

August 29.—Privates Samuel Applegate, Henry C. Christie, Shin E. Jamison, William R. Morris, Johnston Lutz, and James Reed, company A; Sergeant David Smith and Private George Mason, company C; Private Joseph Graisberry, company D; Sergeant Robert Arnes, Privates Job Davison, Patchie Barry, and William Rianhard, company E; Private Robert Hancock and Isaiah Lippincott, company F; Privates William Maling, Henry Firth, and Reed Price, company G; Privates August Seior, William Brown, John C.

Whippey, and William Loeb, company I; Sergeant James White, Privates Charles Braceland, James R. Husted, William Hampton, Isaac T. Garton, Elias Jones, John Leo, Robert McAdoo, Michael McLaughlin, Jeremiah Price, B. F. Reeves, William V. Robinson, Isaac Warr, and Nathaniel Wilkinson, company K.

August 30.—Colonel G. Mott, musket ball through forearm and fracture of the ulna; Major S. R. Gilkyson, musket ball through thigh; Privates James Williams and James Quirk, company B; Private Solon R. Hankinson, company E; First Sergeant Jonathan Maguire, Privates George Jobes and Edwin Packer, company F.—47.

MISSING.

August 27.—Private Edward B. Hood, company I.

August 29.—Private William Bibby, company F; Private John Wiley, company K.

August 30.—Surgeon John Wiley; Sergeant David S. Oliphant, Corporal Smith Applegate, Privates Josiah Garwood, and William Jemison, company A; Private John Nugent, company B; Corporals Frederick Boorman, Albert B. Fryor, Privates Michael Corner, John Evans, Henry Herman, Nehemiah Wright, and John Wagoner, (wounded,) company C; First Sergeant Frederick Young, Privates Thomas Bottomly, William Groves, Levi Jess, and Aaron Stone, company D; Corporal James Smith, (wounded,) Privates Jonathan Barnes, Peter Miller, William Rossell, James Sherman, and Albert Woolman, company F; Corporal George Farrow, Privates Thomas Gladding, and Thomas Taylor, company G; Sergeant John E. Loeb, Privates William Dorsey, William D. Jacobs, Jacob Gilmore, James H. Webster, James W. Lewis, and Watson Wertsell, company I; Sergeant William T. Goodman, and Private William H. H. Lawrence, (wounded,) company K.—40.

Very respectfully, your obedient servant,

GEO. C. BURLING,

Lieutenant Colonel Commanding 6th New Jersey Volunteers.

No. 55.

REPORT OF CAPTAIN GEORGE HOFFMAN, EIGHTH NEW JERSEY VOLUNTEERS.

THIRD BRIGADE HOOKER'S DIVISION,
Camp 8th Regiment New Jersey Volunteers,
Near Alexandria, Virginia, September 10, 1862.

COLONEL: In compliance with orders from headquarters, issued "in accordance with circular," dated some few days since, I have the honor to submit the following report of the part this regiment acted in the recent engagements of Bristow's Station and Bull Run:

After a march of six days across the peninsula, from Harrison's Landing, Virginia, to Yorktown, the regiment embarked on board the ocean steamer, C. Vanderbilt, and after a passage of sixty hours disembarked at Alexandria. In consequence of the length of the march and the dry state of the ground, causing a continual dust, combined with great scarcity of water and the crowded condition of the ship, the men were very much exhausted, and not in a suitable condition for immediate active service. After a rest of thirty-six hours the regiment, under the command of Lieutenant Colonel Wm. Ward, was placed on the cars and proceeded to Warrenton Junction, where it bivouacked on the night of the 26th August. At daylight, on the morning of the 27th, orders were received to march with two days' rations. The line of march was taken up at sunrise. After a halt of an hour at the Junction proper the march was resumed.

At a distance of six or seven miles from the Junction, and at about 2 o'clock in the afternoon, the 2d New York regiment, composing a part of the brigade, was deployed at some distance to the front as skirmishers; after an advance of about a mile, brigade line of battle was formed, this regiment occupying the extreme left position. Arriving near Bristow's Station, the frequent fire of the skirmishers announced an enemy near. After emerging from a dense undergrowth of small pines, the enemy was discovered on the opposite side of an open field, from whence he opened a sharp fire of grape and canister from a battery stationed near the railroad. Being exposed to this fire and without cover, under orders from Lieutenant Colonel Ward, commander of the regiment, advanced in double-quick time to a small ravine, situated near the centre of the field, which afforded some protection, and from where our fire could be more effective. We immediately opened fire, which was kept up with great vigor until some twenty rounds of ammunition were expended. Our fire was directed towards the forces of the enemy which supported the battery near the railroad; it did good execution, forcing the enemy to retire from his position in the field, and seek shelter in the woods beyond. At this point the enemy were driven from their position, on the right of the railroad, by the vigorous fire and rapid charge of other regiments of the brigade; observing that they were retiring on the right, Lieutenant Colonel Ward gave the order to charge the battery on the left; the line was immediately formed, and the regiment advanced double-quick, in good order, and rapidly; so rapid was the movement that the enemy, although securing the safety of their guns, were compelled to abandon their ammunition and rammers, which were destroyed by men belonging to the regiment; some ten or twelve prisoners were captured. The engagement having been brought to an end, by the precipitate flight of the enemy from the field, we took position on ground previously occupied by the enemy on the right of the railroad, which was occupied by the regiment until near dark, when we were relieved, and proceeded to join the brigade, which had advanced in pursuit of the fleeing enemy. The further pursuit of the enemy having been abandoned for the night, the regiment, with the brigade, bivouacked for the night on the banks of a creek some two miles from the field of battle, in the enemy's direction. The loss of the regiment in this engagement was two killed and twenty-three wounded. Both officers and men deserve the highest commendation for their conduct, having behaved with the coolness and gallantry for which the regiment is distinguished.

August 28th, the regiment took up the line of march in the forenoon, passing through Manassas Junction and along the railroad to near Centreville, where it bivouacked for the night. The march was resumed very early in the morning, the 29th, halting at Centreville for a time, and arriving at Bull Run battleground at meridian, when we were immediately ordered to the front, and stacked arms in a ravine, near a dense wood, for a short rest. After a rest of an hour we advanced in line of battle into the wood, under a heavy and rapid fire from the enemy, whose exact position we were unable at the moment to discover. After a short time a large force of the enemy, consisting of a brigade, was observed passing round our left flank, when the regiment was ordered by Acting Major Fuite to retire, Colonel Ward having in the meantime been severely wounded. The enemy, in passing to the left, poured into the regiment a most galling and destructive fire, throwing it for the moment into confusion; it was, however, rallied by its few remaining officers (Acting Major Fuite being killed by a shot in the head) on the edge of the wood. Line of battle was immediately formed, our right resting on the left of the fifth. We at once became engaged, and for twenty minutes poured into the ranks of the enemy so destructive a fire as to cause him to stagger. He, however, rallied, but was again met by the same sharp fire, and the artillery, fortunately opening at this time, swept him from the flank, and the attempt to outflank us on the left was not again repeated. Our ammunition being entirely expended, we retired by the right flank for a supply, the ammunition train being to the right and rear some two hundred yards. After receiving a supply of ammunition, under orders we retired to the rear of the artillery, and bivouacked for the night. The command, during the latter part of the day, devolved upon Captain Hoffman, and he being injured from a fall, still later, the command devolved upon Captain Johnson. The loss in this day's engagement was severely felt, Acting Major Fuite being killed and Lieutenant Colonel William Ward being severely wounded; there were also thirty-three non-commissioned officers and privates killed and wounded —eight killed, twenty-five wounded Saturday morning, August 30th, Captain D. Blauvelt, jr., who had been on detached duty by order of Lieutenant Colonel Ward, joined the regiment, and, being the senior officer present, took the command in this day's engagement, which, on our part, consisted merely in supporting a battery. Our loss was one wounded by a shell, making a total loss of killed and wounded, in the different engagements, of fifty-nine.

The regiment retired with the brigade, on the night of the 30th, to Centreville, where it bivouacked, changed camp on Sunday afternoon, and proceeded on the line of march on Tuesday, reaching Fairfax Station, when it was detailed by General Grover to guard an ammunition train from that point to Alexandria, over the Annandale turnpike. The train was delivered safely into the proper hands. On Tuesday Captain Langstein, arriving in camp, assumed the command. Captain Langstein was relieved by Major Ramsey, of the 5th New Jersey volunteers, who is now in command.

I have the satisfaction of informing the colonel commanding brigade that each officer and man in the regiment has, in his proper sphere, done his duty nobly, faithfully, and in such a manner as to merit the special commendation of General Hooker, which is to me a source of great pride.

I have the honor to be, very respectfully, your obedient servant,

GEORGE HOFFMAN,
Senior Captain 8th New Jersey Volunteers.

Colonel JOSEPH B. CARR,
Commanding 3d Brigade Hooker's Division.

No. 56.

REPORT OF MAJOR G. BANKS, SIXTEENTH MASSACHUSETTS VOLUNTEERS.

The regiment left Alexandria Monday evening, August 25, by railroad, for Warrenton Junction. Arrived at Warrenton Junction on the morning of the 26th; marched about two miles, and encamped for the night. Marched from there at 10 o'clock on the morning of the 27th; had a skirmish with the enemy at Bristow Station, or Kettle Run, and encamped at the same place for the night. Started about 12 m. of the 28th for Manassas Junction; passed through Manassas Junction, and encamped near Centreville. Left camp the 29th near daybreak for Manassas, and participated in the battle in the afternoon of the same day on the old battle-ground of Bull Run. Took part in the engagement of the 30th, and left for Centreville about dusk same day. The casualties in the regiment in the battle of the 29th and 30th (principally on the 29th) were as follows:

Killed: commissioned officers, 1; enlisted men, 3. Wounded: commissioned officers, 4; enlisted men, 60. Missing: commissioned officers, 2; enlisted men, 40. Aggregate, 110.

We arrived at Centreville about 1 o'clock on the morning of the 31st, and remained in camp until about 5 p. m., when our camp was moved about half a mile towards Manassas; remained in camp last mentioned until 5 p. m. of September 1st, then started for Alexandria.

We were ordered for picket duty the same night on the battle-field of Chantilley, where Kearny's and Reno's division had been engaged with the enemy an hour previous. Left on the morning of the 2d about three o'clock, and marched about four miles beyond Fairfax Station, and encamped for the night. Left camp the morning of the 3d at daybreak, and reached Fort Lyon about 3 o'clock p. m. the same day.

GARDNER BANKS,
Major of the 16*th Massachusetts Volunteers, Commanding.*

No. 57.

REPORT OF CASUALTIES OF THE EIGHTH NEW JERSEY VOLUNTEERS.

Subjoined find the following list of names of killed and wounded of Eighth New Jersey volunteers:

Killed.—Captain John Fuite, John M. Reuck, corporal, company A; William Gaysell, private, company E; Robert Johnson, sergeant, and George Garrison, private, company H.

Wounded.—Lieutenant Colonel William Ward, John C. Steinbar, first sergeant, and George Hopwood, private, company A; William Robinson, Lawrence Healy, and Christopher Farrell, privates, Henry Huttman, corporal, and Frank Crampton, and Hermann Calhoun, privates, company B; John Kehoe, Horace B. Mockridge, William J. Lake, John J. Thompson, Francis Hackett, privates, and Jacob A. Young, corporal, company C; N. B. Clark, corporal, and William Kenworth, Samuel N. Wood, John Wyckoff, Arthur Nesbit, Newton Johnson, and Edward Carter—supposed dead, company D; G. Cline, corporal, and D. Cooper, E. E. Wonderly, F. E. Dennis, William Donald, H. B. Graves, F. M. Harrison, J. Schultz, Thomas McSoully, and F. C. Dunker, privates, company E; Enoch Scudder, corporal, and William Donnelly, Elias Hoffman, Jabez Lee, James J. Lake, James McClay, John B. Stewart, Hamilton Bowlsby, William Bowlsby, and John Bird, privates, company H; James M. Baird, and Charles Huntly, corporals, and Barney Hammell, private, company F; Thomas Far, Michael Harth, Charles Airy, and Henry French, privates, company G; Napoleon Debuc, John F. Clouser, and Dennis McGowan, privates, company I, Thomas Curlis, private, killed, and Diltz Slack, corporal, company K.

GEORGE HOFFMAN,
Senior Captain Eighth New Jersey Volunteers.

No. 58.

LIST OF CASUALTIES IN THE SECOND REGIMENT NEW YORK VOLUNTEERS.

KILLED.

August 27.—Corporal Oliver H. Porter, and Private Edward Farrell, company B; Privates John T. Andrews, and James Taylor, company C; Corporal Charles Reith, and Privates John Jones, Michael Manning, and Frank O'Niele, company D; Corporal Frederick P. Wrigley, company G; Private Charles Stickney, company K.

August 29.—Corporal Thomas B. Casey, company E.

WOUNDED.

August 27.—First Lieutenant Francis Temple, (in command of company,) and Privates Thomas Himes, Jacob A. Becroft, and John P. McNamara, company A; Corporal Peter Robson, and Privates William E. Hydorn, (since dead,) John Lucey, and John O'Brien, company B; Captain John H. Quackenbush, First Sergeant Robert B. Dickie, (acting Lieutenant,) and Privates David Earle, Paul Manner, and John Narcotte, company C; Captain John Maguire, Second Lieutenant Joseph Egolf, Sergeant Michael Russell, Corporal Lorenz Kingsley, and Privates Jacob Baker, James Duffy, James H. Flynn, Patrick Grace, Thomas Hennesy, Frank Mayatte, James Sullivan, and Joseph C. Taylor, company D; Captain S. Lee Perkins, (since dead,) and Private Simeon Moranville, company E; Corporals Warren Harrington, Peter P. Ray, jr., George H. Pierce, and Privates James Beak, Henry C. Dunnell, William R. Trear, Daniel E. Gardner, and James M. Sturtevant, company F; Second Lieutenant Cornelius Kirker, Corporal Peter Broomhower, and Privates John Finley, John Medlicott, Patrick O'Donnell, and Joseph Savior, company G; Sergeant William McCollough, (since dead,) Corporals William Greenwood, William A. Gaffney, and Privates Patrick Conway, Michael Daly, William Hadey, and David Murrey, company I; First Sergeant George D. Smith, Sergeant Augustus Willard, Corporal Thomas Thrane, and Privates Frederick Epting, Edward Walton, Ferdinand Wise, Frederick Wurst, company K.

August 29.—Corporal Joseph Homan, company C; Corporal John Rowland, and Privates Henry C. Dunnell, and James C. McGowan, company F; First Sergeant Nathan F. Hodgeman, company A; Private Adolphus Staude, company K.

August 30.—Sergeant Major Theodore Horn, company K.

MISSING.

August 29.—Private George Looby, company D; Private Patrick Kearney, company A; Private John Gormley, company B; Privates Michael Ryan, and John A. Smith, company B; Private Edward S. Wilson, company F; Privates John Mills, and John Brinn, company G; Private Henry Todt, company K.

RECAPITULATION.

Killed commissioned officers	0
Wounded commissioned officers	6
Missing commissioned officers	0
Killed enlisted men	11
Wounded enlisted men	55
Missing enlisted men	9
	81

CAMP SECOND REGIMENT NEW YORK VOLUNTEERS,
Near Alexandria, Va., September 13, 1862.

I certify that the above is a correct list of casualties in the 2d regiment New York volunteers, in the engagements of the 27th, 29th, and 30th of August, 1862.

WILLIAM A. OLMSTED,
Lieutenant Colonel 2d Infantry, New York Volunteers, Commanding.

No. 59.

REPORT OF KILLED, WOUNDED, AND MISSING, 115TH PENNSYLVANIA VOLUNTEERS IN BATTLES OF 27TH, 29TH, AND 30TH AUGUST.

STATION NEAR CAMP LYONS, VIRGINIA,
August 31, 1862.

Killed.—Corporal Roswell C. Bowie, company A; Private Frank Donnelly, company C; Privates Luther C. Neff and Daniel Regan, company E.

Wounded.—Major F. A. Lancaster, left arm shattered above elbow; Captain P. O'Murphy, flesh wound of thigh, (not dangerous,) and Private Wm. Whelan, shot through wrist, (serious,) company A; Lieutenant Richard Dillon, contused wound of hip, (by explosion of shell,) Privates Wm. Farr, shot through shoulder, and Mich'l Mulgrew, shot through hand, company B; Corporal Daniel Manine, shot through upper jaw, (dangerous,) and Private Hugh McKendrick, shot through right shoulder, (serious,) company C; Corporal John Brown, shot through left hand, (not serious,) Privates Michael Allen, shot through left shoulder, (not serious,) and James Burns, company E; Lieutenant R. L. Thompson, shot through back part of neck, (not serious,) Corporal Frank Spencer, buckshot through arm, (not serious,) Privates Isaac Weidner, shot through upper part of chest, (serious,) and John Roderick, contusion of chest by shell, (serious,) company F; Corporal A. T. McClutcheon, shot through hand, Privates Samuel Rogers, bruised thigh by bursting of shell, and James Lyons, shot through hand, (serious.)

Missing.—Privates James Walton and Michael Malone, company A; Corporal Charles Sweeney, and Privates John Sullivan, Michael Reardon, and James O'Niell, company B; Privates Jacob P. Wiseman and William Wood, company C; Private James McCarroll, company E; Private John Walls, company F; Privates John Linderman and John Charlton, company I.

T. S. BARTRAM, *Assistant Surgeon.*

No. 60.

REPORT OF CASUALTIES OF THE FIFTH NEW JERSEY VOLUNTEERS.

HEADQUARTERS 5TH NEW JERSEY VOLUNTEERS,
Camp near Alexandria, Virginia, September 5, 1862.

SIR: I have the honor to make the following report of the part taken by the regiment under my command in the action at Broad Run, August 27, 1862:

The regiment, after marching a distance of eight miles, was assigned a position on the right of the first line of the brigade, my left resting on the railroad. Advancing in this manner, I was soon entangled in a dense wood, which retarded my progress, it being almost impassable. I was obliged to halt several times and form the regiment. Skirmishers in advance reporting the enemy in my immediate vicinity, the 2d New York and 115th Pennsylvania on my left soon became engaged. Finding it impossible to push my way through the woods in anything like order, I threw one company to the left of the railroad and one across the track. These companies immediately opened a flank fire on the enemy, who were using the high embankment of the railroad as a breastwork. After a few volleys the enemy gave way, when I ordered a charge up the railroad. The regiment advanced on the double-quick, the enemy running before us at this point. I took one prisoner, who was not able to keep up with his comrades. Halting in an open field on the brow of the hill, the enemy in sight on my left and front, the regiment rested until the rest of the brigade came up. The infantry did not again become engaged. Later in the day I was ordered to picket a road two miles to the left. Whilst performing this duty the regiment captured twenty-three prisoners.

The following is a list of the casualties:

Killed.—Sergeant C. J. Boone, company B.

Wounded.—Corporal George W. Dally, company H; Private John Bower, company E; Private John Dennis, company I.

Missing.—Private Patrick McLaughlin, company H.

In this engagement the officers and men of this regiment, without any exceptions, behaved with great gallantry. All seemed to be actuated with the same spirit, and that was to fight.

I am, very respectfully, your obedient servant,

W. J. SEWELL,
Lieutenant Colonel 5th New Jersey Volunteers, Commanding Regiment.

LE GRAND BENEDICT,
Acting Assistant Adjutant General 3d Brigade.

HEADQUARTERS 5TH NEW JERSEY VOLUNTEERS,
Near Alexandria, September 5, 1862.

SIR: I have the honor to make the following report of the part taken by the regiment under my command at the battle of Bull Run, August 29, 1862:

I received orders to deploy my right wing as skirmishers in front of the brigade, in an open wood. As soon as the line advanced to where the line of another division had previously been, firing commenced on both sides, continuing up to the time the brigade was relieved.

I was soon obliged to relieve my right wing with my left wing, the former having emptied their cartridge-boxes, containing sixty rounds. The men thus relieved I posted in the rear of the line of battle to prevent stragglers from leaving the fight.

The brigade having been relieved by General Reno's brigade as I was forming the regiment, this last brigade fell back in disorder. I endeavored to stop them, but finding that the enemy were almost up to my line, deployed in the rear; and now being formed, having divided their cartridges equally, I saw that it was time for me to take care of my command. A part of the 8th New Jersey, with their colors, formed on my left. The enemy having turned the left flank of the line of battle, came out on the open field on my left, and immediately after I received their fire from the front, which I returned, driving them from our immediate vicinity and then marched to join the brigade.

The following is a list of the casualties, which are large in proportion to the number of men in the regiment. I entered the fight with 350 men:

Killed.—Captain Edward A. Acton; Lieutenant Frederick A. Brill; Corporal John B. Clayton, company K; Private John F. Loakerson, company K; Private Michael Doyle, company D.

Wounded.—Captain H. H. Woolsey, dangerously; Captain John Gamble, slightly; Corporal John H. Van Pelt; Corporal James S. Flanigan, company G; Corporal John Polan, company H; Privates James Bell, W. H. Flinn, Thomas Gibson, William Harris, and John O'Connell, company B; Privates Christian Arnbriter, Edward Peel, William Healty, and Richard Gill, company C; Private William Chamberlain, company D; Privates Augustus King and John C. Haas, company E; Private William Frazer, company F; Privates John McConnell, James Graves, William Fairhurst, and William Norberry, company

G; Privates John Gasternacker, Matthew Carney, and Daniel Flanigan, company H; Privates James Donaldson, Thomas McBride, and Henry Rosswick, company K.

Missing.—Lieutenant Edward P. Berry, assistant quartermaster; Sergeant Robert Evans, and Privates Emile Naugaret, Benjamin Smith, and John Stryker, company D; Privates Richard Sibbitt and Jonathan Sibbitt, company I; Privates John Schomhert and John Hopple, company H.

Recapitulation.—Commissioned officers: Killed, 2; wounded, 2; missing, 1; total, 5. Non-commissioned officers and privates: Killed, 3; wounded, 27; missing, 8; total, 38. Total commissioned officers, 5; non-commissioned officers and privates, 38; total—43.

In this engagement the officers and men of this regiment were continually under fire, all doing their duty nobly. Major John Ramsey and Captain Virgil M. Healey particularly distinguished themselves, leading in stragglers from different regiments, and encouraging, by their words and example, all in their immediate vicinity. Captain Acton and Lieutenant Brill killed; Captains Woolsey and Gamble wounded; Lieut. Berry missing. Their condition is the best testimonial of their gallantry.

I am, sir, very respectfully, your obedient servant,

W. J. SEWELL,
Lieutenant Colonel 5th New Jersey Volunteers, Commanding Regiment.

LE GRAND BENEDICT,
Acting Assistant Adjutant General 3d Brigade.

HEADQUARTERS FIFTH NEW JERSEY VOLUNTEERS,
Camp near Alexandria, Virginia, September 5, 1862.

SIR: I have the honor to make the following report of the part taken by the regiment under my command in the battle of Bull Run, August 30, 1862.

This regiment, having been engaged the day previous, was not brought into action, but remained under arms, with the whole division in the rear of some batteries, until late in the afternoon, when we marched towards the left, and from that point to Centreville. In marching from right to left the following casualties occurred from the shells of the enemy:

Wounded.—Corporal George Curtis, company C; Private John Savage, company B; Private William Petersly, company I.

Missing.—Charles Dempsey, company I.

I have the honor to be, very respectfully, your obedient servant,

W. J. SEWELL,
Lieutenant Colonel 5th New Jersey Volunteers,
Commanding Regiment.

LE GRAND BENEDICT,
Acting Assistant Adjutant General 3d Brigade.

No. 61.

REPORT OF CASUALTIES OF THE SEVENTH NEW JERSEY VOLUNTEERS.

List of casualties in the 7th regiment New Jersey volunteers from August 15, 1862, to September 4, 1862:

Assistant Surgeon Charles B. Jaques was left on the battle-field taking care of the wounded, August 29, 1862. He has never been reported on the morning report on account of not receiving the resignation of Assistant Surgeon A. Satterthwarth, now surgeon of the 12th New Jersey volunteers.

KILLED.

August 29.—Captain Joseph Abbott and Private James Shewell, company E.
September 1.—Richard Vanorder, (accidentally,) company C.

William Long, died of disease, September 1st.

WOUNDED.

August 27.—Private Thomas Mack, company F; Privates Charles Johnson and Isaac Archer, company K.

August 29.—Sergeant James H. Onslow, company F; Corporal Curtis Dangler, company C; Private Martin Hahn, company A; Privates John McPeter and William Stevens, company C; Private Andrew Kelly, company D; Privates Samuel Pettit, Thomas Willravin, and Henry Engle, company E; Privates John Corbitt and James Bennett, company F; Privates Patrick McEvoy and George Putzle, company H; Private James Spongenburg, company I; Private John R. Lyon, company K.

MISSING.

August 27.—Private Henry Angleman, company K.

August 29.—Privates John Ryan and Patrick Corbett, company F; Privates John Brady, William Willis, and William Sweeney, company G.

August 30.—Privates Thomas Finney, Patrick O'Reilly, Charles Wilson, and Daniel Courtin, company C; Private Henry Myers, company I.

Total commissioned officers killed	1
Total commissioned officers wounded	1
Total enlisted men killed	2
Total enlisted men died of disease	1
Total enlisted men wounded	19
Total enlisted men missing in action	10
Aggregate	34

Very respectfully, your obedient servant,

LOUIS R. FRANCINE,
Lieutenant Colonel, Commanding Regiment.

A. WITHERELL,
1*st Lieutenant company F, and Acting Adjutant.*

No. 62.

CORRESPONDENCE OF GENERALS McDOWELL AND SCHURZ.

[No. 1.]

WASHINGTON, *October* 6, 1862.

GENERAL: I notice the following in your report, as published in the Philadelphia Inquirer, of October 4th instant:

"WHAT HE EXPECTED TO FIND.

"Behind the ridge where I was to form again, and which was the natural position of the general reserve, I expected to find an intact reserve of several brigades, ready to pounce upon the enemy as he was attempting to ascend the slope of the range of hills we were then occupying; but nothing of the kind seemed to be there."

"WHAT HE DID FIND.

"I found Major General McDowell with his staff, and around him troops of several different corps—and of all arms—in full retreat, &c., &c."

As the sentence last above quoted *may* admit of two constructions, I beg to inquire if you intend to be understood as saying you found *Major General McDowell, with his staff,* "in full retreat." I send this by an officer of my staff, who will, if you please, bring me your reply.

I have the honor to be, general, very respectfully, your most obedient servant,

IRVIN McDOWELL,
Major General.

Brigadier General CARL SCHURZ,
Commanding 3d Division, &c., &c., Fairfax Court-House, Virginia.

[Answer to No. 1.]

HEADQUARTERS THIRD DIVISION, ELEVENTH CORPS,
Fairfax Court-House, October 7, 1862.

GENERAL: In reply to your note of yesterday, I beg leave to say that the language I used in my report, viz: "I found Major General McDowell with his staff, and around him troops of several corps, and of all arms, in full retreat," was not intended to convey the impression that "General McDowell and his staff were in full retreat," for such was not the case while the troops, as stated in my report, were retreating. I saw you surrounded by your officers for about half hour, near the place where I formed my division. If my memory serves me rightly, you went to the little farm house south of the road, which was then used as a hospital, and where General Pope, at the time, was said to be in consultation with several generals. If the language above quoted should have been misinterpreted by any one, I avail myself gladly of this opportunity to state its real meaning.

I am, general, very respectfully, your obedient servant,

C. SCHURZ,
Brigadier General, commanding 3d Division, 11th Corps.

Major General McDOWELL, *Washington.*

[No. 2.]

WASHINGTON, *October* 8, 1862.

GENERAL: I have the honor to acknowledge the receipt of your note of October 7, saying the language used in your report was not intended to convey the impression that Major General McDowell and staff were in full retreat, for such was not the case, &c., &c.

Will you pardon me for now troubling you further in relation to that part of your report which has been the subject of our correspondence.

The circumstances attending my meeting you; our conversation about the battery which I had posted near your troops; the instructions I gave it; the direction I took when I left you, (which was not in retreat;) my remaining near that part of the ground till dark; my posting Gibbon's brigade on that ground after yours had retired from it to Bull Run, (which brigade remained there two hours after dark, and then passed you whilst you were in bivouac near the stream,) the most of which facts could not but have been known to you, seemed to leave no other interpretation than the one you have since placed upon your report.

Yet the impression was strong in my mind, and strong to conviction on that of my friends, who did not know the facts of the case as I now give them, that in the picture you so clearly drew of what you saw when you ascended the crest, you designed that General McDowell and staff should appear as the principal group in a discreditable retreat.

This, as much from what you did not say as from what you did say. For after introducing Major General McDowell, without qualifying his presence in any way whatever as the central figure in this retreat, you left him there as if you had brought him into notice for no other purpose.

This impression was strengthened by a knowledge of your reputation as an able, clear-headed writer, having the full use of our language, and a precise knowledge of the value and force of words.

Thus it is that you have done me—unintentionally it now seems—a wrong, and I leave it to your sense of justice if that wrong should not be righted—as far as such wrongs can be righted—by a correction by you of the impression you have given in the paper in which your report was published.

I have the honor to remain, general, very respectfully, your most obedient servant,

IRVIN McDOWELL,
Major General.

Brigadier General CARL SCHURZ,
Commanding Division, &c., &c., Fairfax Court-House, Virginia.

P. S.—Permit me to correct the impression you have that I went to the little farm-house to join General Pope, "in consultation with several generals." If there was any such consultation I was and am ignorant of it. I passed by the little farm-house on my way to the left and front.

J. McD, *M. G.*

[Answer to No. 2.]

HEADQUARTERS THIRD DIVISION, ELEVENTH CORPS,
Fairfax Court-House, October 12, 1862.

GENERAL: Your favor of October 8th reached me a few moments ago. The explanation I gave you in my reply to your first letter could not leave any doubt as to my intentions. It is my desire that if there is any such doubt it shall be removed.

Before replying at length to the letter I had the honor to receive to-day, I shall endeavor to obtain whatever information I can about what my aids, and brigade, and regimental commanders saw concerning the facts in question. I shall write as soon as possible, with the understanding that my letters are your property, to be used as you may deem best. Meanwhile I beg leave to offer you the assurance that I now, as I have done hitherto on all occasions, shall use my best efforts to make the truth known, and correct error, especially if an erroneous impression should have sprung from any public expression of mine.

I have the honor to remain, general, respectfully yours,

C. SCHURZ,
Brigadier General.

Major General McDOWELL, *Washington.*

[No. 3.]

WASHINGTON, *October* 16, 1862.

GENERAL: To judge from your letter of the 12th instant, I fear I have been unfortunate in not making myself understood in my last letter.

Its object was not to trouble you and your subordinate commanders with an inquiry into any act of mine or any act of any other commander on the occasion in question. So far as I am concerned, I trust that subject will soon be disposed of by a legal court.

In your report you had expressed yourself concerning me in a way admitting two constructions. The object of my first communication was to ascertain which of the two was intended. Your answer on that point was satisfactory. The object of my last was *an appeal to your sense of justice*, to do to the public, through the newspaper in which your report was published, what you had done to me, that is, correct the impression to my prejudice, which the ambiguity of your report inevitably produced. I did not and do not now wish to go into any new discussion, and tax your time and patience by extending our correspondence beyond the simple point I have herein stated.

I have the honor to remain, general, very respectfully, your most obedient servant,

I. McDOWELL,
Major General.

Brigadier General CARL SCHURZ,
Commanding Division, &c., &c., Fairfax Court-House, Virginia.

[Answer to No. 3.]

HEADQUARTERS THIRD DIVISION, ELEVENTH CORPS,
Fairfax Court-House, October 20, 1862.

GENERAL: Your favor of the 17th instant has just reached me. You must pardon me for having delayed my answer to your letter of the 8th so long. I wanted to be positively assured of the correctness of certain impressions before writing. You are certainly right in demanding that the explanation of my report I gave you in private should be published. To this I have not the slightest objection, and I think I have already assured you of my willingness to do so; but I must confess I should never have thought that the passage in my report to which you have directed my attention could have been misinterpreted had not your first letter convinced me of the fact; nor have I to this very moment received any intimation to that effect from any other quarter. It would, therefore, seem entirely proper that my explanation should be published in connexion with your letter calling for it, and the correspondence to which it gave rise. If this meets your views, you will oblige me by sending me copies of the two letters I addressed to you, so that I may forward the whole to the New York Tribune, or you will perhaps have the kindness to send them there directly, if this should seem convenient to you. Before closing our correspondence, however, you will permit me to make a few remarks about a passage occurring in your letter of the 8th instant. You speak of circumstances attending my meeting you, our conversation about the battery you had posted near my troops, the instructions you gave it, the direction you took when you left me, (which was not in retreat,) your remaining near that part of the ground till dark, your posting Gibbon's brigade on that ground after my troops had retired from it to Bull Run, (which brigade remained there two hours after dark, and then passed us while we were in bivouac near the stream,) most of which could not but have been known to me. I am obliged to say that some of these things were unknown to me, and are somewhat in conflict with my impression. In my note of the 7th instant I stated already that I had seen you near the spot where I had met you for about half an hour, and then you went towards the farm-house on the left. From that moment I did not see you again, but it was reported to me by two of my aids, whom I had sent across Young's Branch to bring up two of my regiments, that about dusk they had seen you crossing the bridge at the head of your staff; some of your officers crying out to the retreating soldiers, who obstructed the road, "Make room for the general!" The colonel who commands my second brigade reported to me the same thing. As to Gibbon's brigade, I saw that myself, about nightfall, occupying the ground where my 1st and part of my 2d brigade had been. But from that place my troops had not "retired to Bull Run," as you suppose, but marched to the left and front, where the battle was still going on. There they remained a considerable time; it was long after dark, and the firing had ceased for a long while, when I withdrew them, by order of General Sigel. My 1st brigade formed the rear guard of General Sigel's corps, and there were no troops near us when we marched across Young's Branch and took position between it and Bull Run. So it would seem that Gibbon had either left the ground, or at least changed position, before my 1st brigade passed the creek. Colonel Schimmepenning, commander of the brigade, rode in the rear of the column and reported to me that before passing Young's Branch he had seen General Sykes, who had informed him that he (General Sykes) was to form the rear-guard of the army, that all the troops had left that part of the field, and that our column had to pass Young's Branch before him. Then, as you know, we bivouacked between Young's Branch and Bull Run for over two hours, and General Sykes passed us there. From all this I conclude that the statement, that you had posted Gibbon's brigade on that ground after my troops had retired from it to Bull Run, "rests on a mistake." These are the impressions I received from my personal observation and the reports of my officers.

Hoping that you will consider my explanation, and the manner in which, in my humble opinion, they ought to be brought before the public, satisfactory,

I remain, general, most respectfully, your obedient servant,

C. SCHURZ, *Brigadier General.*

Major General McDowell,
Washington.

No. 63.

APPENDIX "A" TO GENERAL McDOWELL'S REPORT.

WARRENTON, *Tuesday, August* 26, 1862—1.45 *a. m.*

I went on top Water Mountain yesterday afternoon, to see if anything could be seen of the enemy. The only indications I saw were his camp smokes; these extended from Sulphur Springs, back beyond Jefferson, and from Sulphur Springs up the river beyond Waterloo. I will direct Ricketts's division up the river at Sulphur Springs; but as the ground opposite the ford at this place is a low flat, extending back from the river nearly a half a mile, and closed by an amphitheatre of hills, I will, if the enemy be there in force, endeavor to occupy him by Ricketts's division while I pass King's over the river below, at the fords at Fant's or Fox's Mills. I will endeavor, as these lower fords may not be good, to get hold of part of Sigel's bridge trains, so as to make the passage as free as possible. Part of General Sigel's force, under previous orders, is passing through the town at this moment. The general himself has not come in; my aide-de-camp is searching for him in the front, with his orders.

IRVIN McDOWELL.

Major General POPE,
Warrenton Junction.

WARRENTON, *August* 26, 1862—5.30 *a. m.*

Your orders to General Sigel to force the passage of Hedgeman's river was given to him by Captain Haven a little after 2 o'clock this morning, while he was on the march from Waterloo to Warrenton. Will the failure to attack Hedgeman's river cause any modifications in the instructions to me? My divisions are on the march, as ordered.

IRVIN McDOWELL.

Major General POPE.

WARRENTON JUNCTION, *August* 26, 1862—5 *a. m.*

Please ascertain in some way whether the enemy be really in force at Waterloo Bridge. Sigel insists that he is, while Banks, who was there late yesterday afternoon, asserts positively that there was no enemy during the day there. You will easily see how important it is for us to know positively what has become of the enemy's force which was in front, and where the column has gone which took yesterday the road towards Salem. Please use every means possible to ascertain this at once. Reno will cross at Rappahannock Station and push forward a reconnoissance to Culpeper. Nothing is expected from Sigel. I wish you would send me a regiment of cavalry. I have not a mounted man here. Send one of Buford's or Bayard's.

JOHN POPE,
Major General Commanding.

General McDOWELL.

AUGUST 26, 1862.

I have just received your telegram of 5 o'clock a. m., directing me to ascertain in some way or another whether the enemy be really in force at Waterloo Bridge. My corps, as ordered, is on the march to Sulphur Springs, and I start in a few moments myself. When I get there I will endeavor to ascertain what you wish.

IRVIN McDOWELL.

Major General POPE.

WARRENTON, *August* 26, 1862.

I have just received your telegram, 8.10 o'clock a. m., informing me of the inability of Reno and Sigel to make the reconnoissances ordered at Rappahannock and Waterloo, and leaving it discretionary with me, under the circumstances, to make the reconnoissance by my whole corps at Sulphur Springs, but saying it will certainly be well for me to ascertain what there is in the direction of Waterloo Bridge and further to my right, and authorizing me to assume command of General Sigel's corps, &c. Before receiving this I had, under instructions of last night, concentrated all my command on the Sulphur Springs road to make the movement ordered at that place. General Sigel, returning from the position of Waterloo, leaves the road from that place to Warrenton but feebly held by a regiment of infantry from Reynolds, and one of cavalry from Buford. The country from Sulphur Springs, and up to and beyond Waterloo, is covered with the dust of a large moving mass. The head of my column has reached Sulphur Springs, and a brisk cannonading is now going on. I have sent out to learn where General Sigel's troops are. They were, it seems, passing through town all last night. Buford and Bayard both report their cavalry as broken down. The former says his is disorganized, the latter, that his will neither charge nor stand a charge. I had, under the discretion you gave me, decided not to throw my whole corps on to Sulphur Springs, but to place it substantially in the position indicated in general orders, and to push as strong a force as I can spare towards Waterloo; and if I can gather a force of cavalry that can perform any service, to endeavor to feel the enemy's right. If it is possible forage should be sent forward, as all our artillery and trains as well as cavalry will go. My men have two days' rations in their haversacks, and being on the march they cannot cook the three days' you desire. General Banks, I am told, is at Bealton. Sigel, I just learn, is at Warren Green hotel, by an officer just from General King. Firing is maintained by the enemy at Sulphur Springs from two four-gun batteries.

IRVIN McDOWELL.

Major General POPE.

WARRENTON, *August* 26, 1862.

I beg to inquire if it is known at army headquarters where the pontoon train of General Sigel is; and if so, to be informed thereof.

IRVIN McDOWELL,
Major General.

Major General POPE, *Warrenton Junction.*

WARRENTON, *August* 26, 1863.

General Ricketts having reported his division within two miles of Sulphur Springs, just in rear of King's, and having been on the march since early this morning from crossing over from the Waterloo road, I have, to save time, and to distribute the fatigue of marching, ordered General Reynolds's division to the Waterloo road, and Ricketts's to fall back in reserve. I have instructed King to avoid useless cannonading at Sulphur Springs. It will take till late this p. m. to get the troops into position on Waterloo road. I have written to General Sigel for a statement of the position and strength of his force, particularly his cavalry, and have sent to find General Milroy, but have not yet heard from either. Cannonading still continues at Sulphur Springs. I told King to withdraw his division out of his range.

IRVIN McDOWELL,
Major General.

Major General POPE, *Warrenton Junction.*

WARRENTON JUNCTION, *August* 26, 1862.

General King reports he has received a flag of truce from General Anderson to return a woman dressed in man's clothes, captured by them this morning. I report the circumstance as it is the first information I have of the presence of this division in our immediate front. I understand Anderson to have Huger's former division. This division, so far as I have learned, was the last of those now before us to leave Richmond, and was at Louisa Court-House when Longstreet was at Raccoon Ford. If I am right in these suppositions, it seems to strengthen the impression that I have, that the enemy's extreme right rests at Sulphur Springs. I draw another inference from this flag of truce, that there is at least a division at Sulphur Springs. It is true, these are mere inferences, and I only give them as such, for other divisions than those we have heretofore heard of may have left Richmond since our last information.

IRVIN McDOWELL,
Major General Commanding.

Major General POPE, *Warrenton Junction.*

WARRENTON, *August* 26, 1862—3.20 *p. m.*

General Sigel's bridge train has arrived. I think it may be useful. General Milroy burnt the bridge at Waterloo before he retired from that place last night, and Buford says the fords near Waterloo are bad. I have directed the available force of Sigel's cavalry, with the section of his artillery, to report to General Buford this afternoon, on the Waterloo road, with three days' cooked rations. I have directed Buford to march at dawn to-morrow towards Chester Gap, to ascertain what direction the enemy have taken on our right, whether to Rectorstown or Front Royal, through Chester Gap. He will either take the Carter Church road up the left bank of Carter run, or the road direct from this place to Chester Gap, as inquiries to be made this p. m. shall determine. However persons may have differed as to the force at Waterloo, Sulphur Springs, or elsewhere, all agree in one thing, the movement of the enemy to our right from Rappahanock to Waterloo—battalions, trains, and batteries, all have the same direction. The force of the enemy now seems to be above Sulphur Springs. In addition to Sigel's corps, now here, I beg to suggest that Hooker and Kearny be marched at once in this direction, instead of in the direction of Rappahannock Station, for whether we attack them or they attack us the contest must come off, it seems to me, as things now stand, above rather than below Sulphur Springs. If they could make a march this p. m. towards Sulphur Springs or Waterloo Bridge it would be a movement, I think, in the right direction. What is the enemy's purpose it is not easy to discover. I have thought he means to march around our right through Rectorstown to Washington; others, that he intended going down the Shenandoah, either through Chester or Thornton Gap. Either of these operations seems to me to be too hazardous for him to undertake with us in his rear and flank. Others, that it was his object to throw his trains around into the valley to draw his supplies from that direction and have his front looking to the east rather than to the north. It is also thought that whilst a portion of his force has marched up the immediate right bank of the Rappahannock, a large portion has gone through Culpeper, up the Sperryville road. No doubt these various suppositions may have occurred to you, but I have thought it not inappropriate to recapitulate them here with reference to the concentration of forces in this direction, which I have herein suggested. Cannonading still continues about the same. I have ordered Buford to send you a cavalry regiment. I cannot get hold of Bayard.

IRVIN McDOWELL,
Major General Commanding.

Major General POPE, *Warrenton Junction.*

WARRENTON JUNCTION, *August* 26, 1862—3.15 *p. m.*

Cox is not here, and will not be here to-night. What information have you received since your last telegram that makes his presence necessary with you?

JOHN POPE,
Major General Commanding.

Major General McDOWELL.

WARRENTON JUNCTION, *August* 26, 1862—7 *p. m.*

Reno marches with his whole force at daylight to-morrow morning, and will take post two miles and a half this side of Warrenton, his left on the railroad. He is directed to report to you upon his arrival and to hold himself in readiness to support you in case you need it. Cox will be pushed forward as soon as his troops arrive here, probably by to-morrow noon. Banks is at Fayetteville and will respond to any call you may make on him. Sturgis will also be pushed forward as soon as troops arrive, I hope to-morrow in the afternoon. Heintzelman's corps, not yet fully arrived, I must keep here till I hear what has become of the column moving towards Salem. Sent a cavalry regiment from Manassas to scout along the Manassas Gap railroad, as far at least as Thoroughfare Gap.

JOHN POPE,
Major General Commanding.

Major General McDOWELL.

P. S.—I have just received intelligence of the arrival of Fitz-John Porter with the regulars at Bealton.

J. P.

WARRENTON JUNCTION, *August* 26, 1862—8.50 *p. m.*

Fitz-John Porter, with Sykes's and Morell's divisions, will be within two and a half miles of Warrenton, on the Fayetteville road, to-morrow night. See if you cannot have the cross roads repaired, so that he can get from his position into the Sulphur Springs road, with his artillery, if he should be needed. I will use all efforts to have Sturgis and Cox within three miles of you to-morrow night, and have requested General Halleck to push forward Franklin at once, carrying his baggage and supplies by railroad to this point, where the Manassas Gap railroad intersects the Warrenton turnpike. From that position he can either advance to your support or prevent your right from being turned from the direction of the Manassas Gap railroad. I think our fight should be made at Warrenton, and if you can postpone it for two days everything will be right.

JOHN POPE,
Major General Commanding.

General McDOWELL.

HEADQUARTERS 3D ARMY CORPS,
Warrenton, August 26, 1862—9 *p. m.*

An intelligent negro has just come in to General Buford from White Plains and reports the advance of the enemy's column at that place. He says he saw himself at White Plains to-day at 12 o'clock two batteries of artillery, two regiments of cavalry and four regiments of infantry, and that they were marching in the direction of Thoroughfare Gap. The man's report is evidently to be relied upon, and General Buford says his statements are confirmed by his scouts, who report large trains passing up through Orleans to White Plains.

I. McDOWELL, *Major General.*

General POPE, *Warrenton Junction.*

WARRENTON, *August* 26—10 *p. m.*

One of Sigel's scouts reports that since daylight till 4 o'clock this evening there has been a continuous line of troops, although cavalry chiefly, passing forward to White Plains, where they are encamped now—Generals Jackson, Longstreet and A. P. Hill, and Stuart's cavalry. This man has the same story as to the names of the generals who are passing towards Thoroughfare. If you fear any attack in force by the enemy's coming through Thoroughfare Gap, and you should not get your force in time at Gainesville, I wish to remark that Centreville and Manassas are fortified, the former sufficiently so to offer a stout resistance, and the latter enough to aid materially raw troops. If the enemy are playing their game on us, and we can keep down the panic which their appearance is likely to create in Washington, it seems to me the advantage of position must all be on our side. I trust sufficient food and ammunition and forage may get through by to-morrow. We have wasted a good deal of artillery ammunition.

IRVIN McDOWELL.

Major General POPE,
Warrenton Junction.

WARRENTON JUNCTION, *August* 26, 1862.

As soon as Reno gets near Warrenton direct his march upon Greenwich, at which place he will take post, throwing forward four regiments of infantry and a battery to Gainesville. One mile in his rear, on the road from Weaversville to Greenwich, Kearny's division will take post to support him. In case the enemy advances this side of Thoroughfare Gap, Reno must attack and beat him. Kearny will support him. Keep your men well in hand, so that if necessary you can break up at Warrenton and march also on Thoroughfare on west side. Your trains, if you move, must take the turnpike. Send and notify Banks, if you move any part of your forces, that he may come up nearer to Warrenton. Fitz-John Porter will be near you to-morrow night. Your cavalry, or the most of it, should be well on your right or rear.

JOHN POPE,
Major General Commanding.

Major General McDOWELL.

HEADQUARTERS ARMY OF VIRGINIA,
Warrenton Junction, August 26, 1862—12 *midnight.*

General Sigel reports the enemy's rear-guard at Orlean to-night, with his main force encamped at White Plains. You will please ascertain very early in the morning whether this is so, and have the whole of your command in readiness to march. You had best ascertain it to-night. Communication has been interrupted by the enemy's cavalry near Manassas. Whether his whole force or the largest part of it, has gone round is a question which we must settle instantly, and no part of his force must march opposite to us to-night without our knowing it. I telegraphed you an hour or two ago what disposition you had made, supposing the advance through Thoroughfare Gap to be a column of not more than 10,000 or 15,000 men. If his whole force, or the largest part of it, has gone, we must know it at once. The troops here have no artillery, and if the main force of the enemy are still opposite to you, you must send forward to Greenwich, to be there to-morrow evening, two batteries of artillery, and three if you can get them, to meet Kearny. We must know at a very early hour in the morning, so as to determine our plans.

JOHN POPE,
Major General Commanding.

Major General McDowell.

HEADQUARTERS 3D ARMY CORPS,
Army of Virginia, August 27, 1862—4.30 *a. m.*

Your telegram of 12 midnight is only just received. I will endeavor to have Buford ascertain as soon as he can, and as far as he can, the extent of the enemy's movement towards White Plains. I saw General Sigel late last night and his scouts, and did not learn that the general had any other information than I gave you in my telegram of ten o'clock p. m., and he was not aware of the negro's statement which I sent you at nine o'clock p. m. Your telegram of eleven p. m. last night was received. My corps is at present posted as follows: King's division on Sulphur Springs road, one brigade near springs, Ricketts's on Waterloo road about four miles from town, Reynolds's inside and between the others.

IRVIN McDOWELL.

General Pope.

HEADQUARTERS ARMY OF VIRGINIA,
August 26, 1862—5.30 *a. m.*

I have just heard from Fitz-John Porter. He has neither wagons nor provisions, and only forty rounds of ammunition per man. The troops here have no wagons, and are very scarce of provisions. The railroad is interrupted between here and Manassas, and will require a strong force to repair it and keep it open. Meantime we shall suffer for everything. It therefore appears to me that we had best move, with our whole force, to occupy Gainesville, so as to secure our communication with Alexandria. It does not seem to me possible to hold a position so far to the front as Warrenton, while so heavy a column of the enemy is so near to our concentration—much in front of Manassas. Give me your views immediately on the subject, for we must act promptly in some way. At all events, all wagons not needed for ammunition must be got ready for an immediate movement to the rear. Let me hear from you at once.

JNO. POPE,
Major General Commanding.

General McDowell.

(No record of General McD.'s answer to this.)

WARRENTON JUNCTION,
August 27, 1862—8.30 *a. m.*

Execute the movement you suggest; but you must be careful not to let the enemy know it until the last moment. Send the trains by this way, and call Banks to you. If the movement could be made by dark it would be better. I will open the road, and join you as soon as I can. I do not know that it will be safe to wait, but you can tell better than I, as your scouts and lookouts can see the movements of the enemy. Order Banks to send his train off immediately, and also the trains you have. We must get to Gainesville to-night.

JNO. POPE,
Major General Commanding.

Major General McDOWELL.

WARRENTON, VIRGINIA,
August 27, 1862—8.45.

I have just received your telegram of 8.30 a. m. I have ordered Sigel to send immediately a strong advance from his corps to seize the position of Buckland Mills, or Broad Run, and follow immediately with his corps. Can you spare time to come to the instrument and have a conversation with me?

IRVIN McDOWELL,
Major General.

Major General POPE.

WARRENTON, AND WARRENTON JUNCTION,
August 27, 1862.

I will be in the telegraph office here the greater part of the day.

POPE.

McD.

Please let me know when the last of the wagons coming this way leave Warrenton.

POPE.

You had best load all the cars at Warrenton, and send back all the surplus stores fast as possible.

POPE.

REPLY.—I have given such orders.

I. McD.

Question. Has Reno marched to this place, or has his order been modified?
Answer. He is marching to Greenwich.
Question. Does Kearny follow him?
Answer. Yes, he will follow him; also Porter's corps are on the road.
Question. Has either Porter or Kearny any artillery?
Answer. Kearny has one battery. I presume Porter has all his artillery.
Question. I have ordered Sigel, who has a superabundance of artillery for

his infantry, to detach two batteries for Kearny, and will try and have them join him to-night. What division of force will you leave at Warrenton Junction till the baggage-wagons shall have passed?

Answer. I cannot tell yet, but one division I will leave. You need not send the three batteries till I communicate with you further. I fear they may be in some danger. Have all the stores you do not need loaded into the cars and sent down here immediately. The enemy has burned a bridge over Cedar Run. Our left wing, therefore, rests at that place until we can have the bridge repaired. Hurry up the wagons with all speed to this place.

POPE.

Send me an officer, if you have him, who knows the country between Catlett's Station and Gainesville.

Question. Had not Banks better retire by way of Warrenton Junction, preceded by his trains?

Answer. He can do so, but please send him the order from Warrenton, as he is nearer to you, and I have got no cavalry.

POPE.

Reynolds reports from Sulphur Springs that the indications are that the enemy has left that place. Sigel's advance is on march for Buckland Mills. I am anxious he should get that point, as it is of importance. Sigel thinks the enemy has passed Salem. I do not think he can yet have done it. I have this instant received the following from the signal officer on Watery Mountain:

"No sign of enemy at Jefferson; his wagons have left there. A wagon train and a line of troops northwest of this mountain moving towards Chester Gap."

Question. What became of that regiment of cavalry I directed you to send me yesterday?

POPE.

Answer. I ordered you one from Buford, because I could not get hold of Bayard. Not having heard whether he has done so, I have this morning, to make sure, ordered Bayard to send you the Maine regiment, and it marches immediately. This may result in your having two regiments.

I. McD.

Question. Have you sent the orders to Banks that I requested you to send?

Answer. Yes; to move upon Catlett's, preceded by his train.

I. McD.

WARRENTON JUNCTION—1.45 *p. m.*,
August 27, 1862.

Reno has his instructions, and is ahead of the wagon train.

JOHN POPE, *Major General Commanding*.

General McDOWELL.

WARRENTON JUNCTION—5 *p. m.*,
August 27, 1862.

I am just leaving for Bristow Station. The enemy retired from the railroad before Hooker's advance, having burned no bridges and done no damage that cannot be speedily repaired. Reno will reach Greenwich to-night. Heintzelman follows after him. Porter, with his whole corps, moves behind Heintzelman. My headquarters to-night will be with Heintzelman.

JOHN POPE.

Major General McDOWELL.

No. 64.

APPENDIX "A" TO GENERAL POPE'S REPORT.

WARRENTON—1.45 *a. m.*,
Tuesday, August 26, 1862.

I went on top Water Mountain yesterday afternoon to see if anything could be seen of the enemy. The only indications I saw were his camp smokes. These extended from Sulphur Springs back beyond Jefferson, and from Sulphur Springs up the river beyond Waterloo. I will direct Ricketts's division up the river at Sulphur Springs, but as the ground opposite the ford at this place is a low flat extending back from the river nearly half a mile, and closed by an amphitheatre of hills, I will, if the enemy be there in force, endeavor to occupy him by Ricketts's division while I pass King's over the river below, at the fords at Fant's or Fox's Mills. I will endeavor, as these lower fords may not be good, to get hold of part of Sigel's bridge trains, so as to make the passage free as possible. Part of General Sigel's force, under previous orders, is passing through the town at this moment. The general himself has not come in. My aide-de-camp is searching for him in the front with his orders.

IRVIN McDOWELL.

Major General POPE,
Warrenton Junction.

WARRENTON—5½ *a. m.*,
August 26, 1862.

Your orders to General Sigel to force the passage of Hedgeman's river was given to him by Captain Haven a little after two o'clock this morning, while he was on the march from Waterloo to Warrenton. Will the failure to attack Hedgeman's river cause any modification in the instruction to me. My divisions are on the march, as ordered.

IRVIN McDOWELL.

Major General POPE.

WARRENTON—5 *a. m.*,
August 26, 1862.

Please ascertain in some way whether the enemy be really in force at Waterloo Bridge. Sigel insists that he is, while Banks, who was there late yesterday afternoon, asserts positively that there was no enemy during the day there. You will easily see how important it is for us to know positively what has become of the enemy's force which was in front, and where the column has gone which took yesterday the road towards Salem. Please use every means possible to ascertain this at once. Reno will cross at Rappahanock Station, and push forward a reconnoissance to Culpeper. Nothing is expected from Sigel. I wish you would send me a regiment of cavalry. I have not a mounted man here. Send me one of Buford's or Bayard's.

JOHN POPE, *Major General Commanding.*

General McDOWELL.

AUGUST 26, 1862.

I have just received your telegram of 5 o'clock a. m., directing me to ascertain, in some way or another, whether the enemy be really in force at Waterloo bridge. My corps, as ordered, is on the march to Sulphur Springs, and I start in a few moments myself. When I get there I will endeavor to ascertain what you wish.

IRVIN McDOWELL.

Major General POPE.

AUGUST 26, 1862.

I have just received your telegram of 8.10 o'clock a. m., informing me of the inability of Reno and Sigel to make the reconnoissances at Rappahannock and Waterloo, and leaving it discretionary with me, under these circumstances, to make the reconnoissance by my whole corps at Sulphur Springs, but saying it will certainly be well for me to ascertain what there is in the direction of Waterloo Bridge, and further to my right, and authorizing me to assume command of General Sigel's corps, &c. Before receiving this I had, under instructions of last night, concentrated all my command on the Sulphur Springs road to make the movement ordered at that place. General Sigel returning from the position of Waterloo, leaves the road from that place to Warrenton but feebly held by a regiment of infantry from Reynolds and one of cavalry from Buford. The country between Sulphur Springs and up to and beyond Waterloo is covered with the dust of a large moving mass. The head of my column has reached Sulphur Springs, and a brisk cannonading is now going on. I have sent out to learn where General Sigel's troops are. They were, it seems, passing through town all last night. Buford and Bayard both report their cavalry as broken down. The former says his is disorganized; the latter that his will neither charge nor stand a charge. I had, under the discretion you gave me, decided not to throw my whole corps on to Sulphur Springs, but to place it substantially in the position indicated in general orders, and push as strong a force as I can spare towards Waterloo, and if I can gather a force of cavalry that can perform any service, to endeavor to feel the enemy's right, if it is possible. Forage should be sent forward, as all our artillery and trains, as well as cavalry, will go. My men have two days' rations in their haversacks, and being on the march, they cannot cook the three days' you desire. General Banks, I am told, is at Bealton. Sigel, I just learn, is at Warren Green hotel, by an officer just from General King. Firing is maintained by the enemy at Sulphur Springs from two four-gun batteries.

IRVIN McDOWELL.

Major General POPE.

WARRENTON, *August* 26, 1862.

I beg to inquire if it is known at army headquarters where the pontoon train of General Sigel is; and if so, to be informed thereof.

IRVIN McDOWELL, *Major General.*

Major General POPE, *Warrenton Junction.*

WARRENTON, *August* 26, 1862.

GENERAL: Ricketts having reported his division within two miles of Sulphur Springs, just in rear of King's, and having been on the march since early this morning, from crossing over from the Waterloo road, I have, to save time and to distribute the fatigue of marching, ordered General Reynolds's division to the Waterloo road and Ricketts to fall back in reserve. I have instructed King to avoid useless cannonading at Sulphur Springs. It will take until late this p. m. to get the troops into position on Waterloo road. I have written to General Sigel for a statement of the position and strength of his force, particularly his cavalry, and have sent to find General Milroy, but have not yet heard from either. Cannonading still continues at Sulphur Springs. I told King to withdraw his division out of his range.

IRVIN McDOWELL, *Major General.*

Major General POPE, *Warrenton Junction.*

WARRENTON, *August* 26, 1862.

General King reports that he has received a flag of truce from General Anderson to return a woman dressed in man's clothes, captured by them this morning. I report the circumstance as it is the first information that I have of the presence of this division in our immediate front. I understand Anderson to have Huger's former division. This division, so far as I have learned, was the last of those now before us to leave Richmond, and was at Louisa Court-House when Longstreet was at Raccoon Ford. If I am right in these suppositions, it seems to strengthen the impression I have that the enemy's extreme right rests at Sulphur Springs. I draw another inference from this flag of truce, that there is at least a division at Sulphur Springs. It is true these are mere inferences, and I only give them as such. For other divisions than those we have heretofore heard of may have left Richmond since our last information.

IRVIN McDOWELL,
Major General Commanding.

Major General POPE, *Warrenton Junction.*

WARRENTON, *August* 26, 1862—3.20 *p. m.*

General Sigel's bridge train has arrived. I think it may be useful. General Milroy burnt the bridge at Waterloo before he retired from that place last night, and Buford says the fords near Waterloo are bad. I have directed the available force of Sigel's cavalry, with a section of his artillery, to report to General Buford this afternoon, on the Waterloo road, with three days' cooked rations. I have directed Buford to march at dawn to-morrow towards Chester Gap to ascertain what direction the enemy have taken on our right; whether to Rectorstown or Front Royal, through Chester Gap. He will either take the Carter Church road, up the left bank of Carter Run, or the road direct from this place to Chester Gap, as inquiries to be made this p. m. shall determine. However persons may have differed as to the force at Waterloo, Sulphur Springs, or elsewhere, all agree in one thing, the movement of the enemy to our right from Rappahannock to Waterloo, battalions, trains, and batteries all have the same direction. The force of the enemy now seems to be above Sulphur Springs. In addition to Sigel's corps, now here, I beg to suggest that Hooker and Kearny be marched at once in this direction instead of in the direction of Rappahannock Station; for whether we attack them or they attack us, the contest must come off, it seems to me, as things now stand, above rather than below Sulphur Springs. If they could make a march this p. m. towards either Sulphur Springs or Waterloo Bridge it would be a movement, I think, in the right direction. What is the enemy's purpose it is not easy to discover; I have thought he means to march around our right, through Rectorstown to Washington; others, that he intended going down the Shenandoah, either through Chester or Thornton Gaps; either of these operations seems to me too hazardous for him to undertake, with us in his rear and flank; others, that it was his object to throw his trains around into the valley, to draw his supplies from that direction and have his front looking to the east rather than to the north. It is also thought that whilst a portion of his force has marched up the immediate right bank of the Rappahannock, a larger portion has gone through Culpeper, up the Sperryville road. No doubt these various suppositions may have occurred to you, but I have thought it not inappropriate to recapitulate them here, with reference to the concentration of forces in this direction which I have herein suggested. Cannonading at Sulphur Springs still continues about the same. I have ordered Buford to send you a cavalry regiment. I can't get hold of Bayard.

IRVIN McDOWELL.

Major General POPE, *Warrenton Junction.*

HEADQUARTERS THIRD ARMY CORPS,
Warrenton, August 26, 1862—9 *p. m.*

An intelligent negro has just come in to General Buford from White Plains, and reports the advance of the enemy's column at that place. He says he saw himself, at White Plains to-day at twelve o'clock, two batteries of artillery, two regiments cavalry, and four regiments infantry, and that they were marching in the direction of Thoroughfare Gap. The man's report is evidently to be relied upon, and General Buford says his statements are confirmed by his scouts, who report large trains passing up through Orleans to White Plains.

I. McDOWELL, *Major General.*

Major General POPE, *Warrenton Junction.*

WARRENTON, *August* 26—10 *p. m.*

One of Sigel's scouts reports that since daylight till four o'clock this evening there has been a continuous line of troops, although cavalry chiefly, passing forward to White Plains, where they are encamped now—Generals Jackson, Longstreet, and A. P. Hill, and Stuart's cavalry. This man has the same story as to the names of the generals who are passing towards Thoroughfare. If you fear any attack in force by the enemy's coming through Thoroughfare Gap, and you should not get your force in time at Gainesville, I wish to remark that Centreville and Manassas are fortified—the former sufficiently so to offer a stout resistance, and the latter enough to aid materially raw troops. If the enemy are playing their game on us, and we can keep down the panic which their appearance is likely to create in Washington, it seems to me the advantage of position must be all on our side. I trust sufficient food and ammunition and forage may get through by to-morrow. We have wasted a good deal of artillery ammunition.

IRVIN McDOWELL.

Major General POPE, *Warrenton Junction.*

WARRENTON JUNCTION, *August* 26, 1862.

As soon as Reno gets near Warrenton, direct his march upon Greenwich, at which place he will take post, throwing forward four regiments of infantry and a battery to Gainesville. On mile in his rear, on the road from Weaversville to Greenwich, Kearny's division will take post to support him. In case the enemy advances this side of Thoroughfare Gap, Reno must attack and beat him. Kearny will support him. Keep your men well in hand, so that if necessary you can break up at Warrenton and march also on Thoroughfare on west side. Your trains, if you move, must take the turnpike. Send and notify Banks if you move any part of your forces, that he may come up nearer to Warrenton. Fitz-John Porter will be near you to-morrow night. Your cavalry, or the most of it, should be well on your right or rear.

JOHN POPE,
Major General Commanding.

Major General McDOWELL.

P. S.—I have just received intelligence of the arrival of Fitz-John Porter, with the regulars, at Bealton.

J. P.

WARRENTON JUNCTION, *August* 26, 1862—8.50 *p. m.*

Fitz-John Porter, with Sykes's and Morell's divisions, will be within two and a half miles of Warrenton, on the Fayetteville road, to-morrow night. See if you cannot have the cross-roads repaired, so he can get from his position into the Sulphur Springs road with his artillery, if he should be needed. I will use all efforts to have Sturgis and Cox within three miles of you to-morrow night, and have requested General Halleck to push forward Franklin at once, carrying his baggage and supplies by railroad to this point, where the Manassas Gap railroad intersects the Warrenton turnpike. From that position he can either advance to your support or prevent your right from being turned from the direction of the Manassas Gap railroad. I think our fight should be made at Warrenton, and if you can postpone it for two days everything will be right

JOHN POPE,
Major General Commanding.

General McDOWELL.

WARRENTON JUNCTION, *August* 26, 1862—3.15 *p. m.*

Cox is not here, and will not be here before to-night. What information have you received, since your last telegram, that makes his presence necessary with you?

JNO. POPE,
Major General Commanding.

Major General McDOWELL.

WARRENTON JUNCTION, *August* 26, 1862—7 *p. m.*

Reno marches with his whole force at daylight to-morrow morning, and will take post two miles and a half this side of Warrenton, his left on the railroad. He is directed to report to you upon his arrival, and to hold himself in readiness to support you, in case you need it. Cox will be pushed forward as soon as his troops arrive here—probably by to-morrow noon. Banks is at Fayetteville, and will respond to any call you may make on him. Sturgis will also be pushed forward as soon as troops arrive—I hope to-morrow in the afternoon. Heintzelman's corps, not yet fully arrived, I must keep here till I hear what has become of the column moving towards Salem. Sent a cavalry regiment from Manassas to scout along the Manassas Gap railroad as far, at least, as Thoroughfare Gap.

JOHN POPE,
Major General Commanding.

Major General McDowell.

Headquarters Army of Virginia,
Warrenton Junction, August 26, 1862—12 *midnight.*

General Sigel reports the enemy's rear guard at Olean to-night, with his main force encamped at White Plains. You will please ascertain, very early in the morning, whether this is so, and have the whole of your command in readiness to march. You had best ascertain it to-night. Communication has been interrupted by the enemy's cavalry near Manassas. Whether his whole force, or the largest part of it, has gone round, is a question which we must settle instantly, and no part of his force must march opposite to us to-night without our knowing it. I telegraphed you, an hour or two ago, what disposition we had made, supposing the advance through Thoroughfare Gap to be a column of not more than 10,000 or 15,000 men. If his whole force, or the largest part of it, has gone, we must know it at once. The troops here have no artillery, and if the main force of the enemy are still opposite to you, you must send forward to Greenwich—to be there to-morrow evening—two batteries of artillery, and three, if you can get them, to meet Kearny. We must know at a very early hour in the morning, so as to determine our plans.

JOHN POPE,
Major General Commanding.

Major General McDowell.

Headquarters Third Army Corps,
Army of Virginia, August 27, 1862—4.30 *a. m.*

Your telegram of 12 midnight is only just received. I will endeavor to have Buford ascertain, as soon as he can and as far as he can, the extent of the enemy's movement toward White Plains. I saw General Sigel late last night, and his scouts, and did not learn that the general had any other information than I gave you in my telegram of 10 o'clock p. m., and he was not aware of the negro's statement which I sent you at 9 o'clock p. m. Your telegram of 11 p. m. last night was received. My corps is at present posted as follows: King's division, on Sulphur Springs road—one brigade near springs; Ricketts, on Waterloo road, about four miles from town; Reynolds, inside and between the others.

IRVIN McDOWELL.

General Pope.

HEADQUARTERS ARMY OF VIRGINIA,
August 27, 1862—5.30 *a. m.*

I have just heard from Fitz-John Porter, he has neither wagons nor provisions and only forty rounds of ammunition per man. The troops here have no wagons, and are very scarce of provisions. The railroad is interrupted between here and Manassas, and will require a strong force to repair it and keep it open; meantime we shall suffer for everything. It therefore appears to me that we had best move with our whole force to occupy Gainesville, so as to secure our communication with Alexandria. It does not seem to me as possible to hold a position so far to the front as Warrenton while so heavy a column of the enemy is so near to our concentration—much in front of Manassas. Give me your views immediately on the subject, for we must act promptly in some way. At all events, all wagons not needed for ammunition must be got ready for an immediate movement to the rear. Let me hear from you at once.

JOHN POPE,
Major General Commanding.

General McDOWELL.

No record of General McDowell's answer to this.

WARRENTON JUNCTION,
August 27, 1862—8.30 *a. m.*

Execute the movement you suggest, but you must be careful not to let the enemy know it till the last moment. Send the trains by this way, and call Banks to you. If the movement could be made by dark it would be better. I will open the road and join you as soon as I can. I do not know that it will be safe to wait; but of that you can tell better than I, as your scouts and lookouts can see the movements of the enemy. Order Banks to send his train off immediately, and also the trains you have. We must get to Gainesville to-night.

JOHN POPE,
Major General Commanding.

Major General McDOWELL.

WARRENTON, VIRGINIA,
August 27, 1862—8.45 *a. m.*

I have just received your telegram of 8.30 a. m. I have ordered Sigel to send immediately a strong advance from his corps to seize the position of Buckland Mills, on Broad Run, and follow immediately with his corps. Can you spare time to come to the instrument and have a conversation with me?

IRVIN McDOWELL,
Major General.

Major General POPE.

WARRENTON JUNCTION,
August 27, 1862—1.45 *p. m.*

Reno has his instructions and is ahead of his wagon-train.

JOHN POPE,
Major General Commanding.

General McDOWELL.

WARRENTON JUNCTION,
August 27, 1862—5 *p. m.*

I am just leaving for Bristow Station. The enemy retired from the railroad before Hooker's advance, having burnt no bridges and done no damage that cannot be speedily repaired. Reno will reach Greenwich to-night. Heintzelman follows after him. Porter, with his whole corps, moves behind Heintzelman. My headquarters to-night will be with Heintzelman.

JOHN POPE.

Major General McDOWELL.

WARRENTON AND WARRENTON JUNCTION,
August 27, 1862.

I will be in the telegraph office here the greater part of the day.

POPE.

McD.

Please let me know when the last of the wagons coming this way leave Warrenton.

POPE.

You had best load all the cars at Warrenton and send back all the surplus stores fast as possible.

POPE.

REPLY.—I have given such orders.

I. McD.

Question. Has Reno marched to this place, or has his order been modified?
Answer. He is marching to Greenwich.
Question. Does Kearny follow him?
Answer. Yes, he will follow him also. Porter's corps are on the road.
Question. Has either Porter or Kearny any artillery?
Answer. Kearny has one battery. I presume Porter has all his artillery.
Question. I have ordered Sigel, who has a superabundance of artillery for his infantry, to detach two batteries for Kearny, and will try and have them join him to-night. What division or force will you leave at Warrenton Junction till the baggage wagons shall have passed?
Answer. I cannot tell yet. But one division I will leave. You need not send the three batteries till I communicate with you further. I fear they may be in some danger. Have all the stores you do not need loaded into the cars and sent down here immediately. The enemy has burned a bridge over Cedar Run. Our left wing, therefore, rests at that place until we can have the bridge repaired. Hurry up the wagons with all speed to this place.

POPE.

Send me an officer, if you have him, who knows the country between Catlett's Station and Gainesville.

Question. Had not Banks better retire by way of Warrenton Junction, preceded by his trains?
Answer. He can do so; but please send him the order from Warrenton, as he is nearer to you and I have got no cavalry.

POPE.

Reynolds reports, from Sulphur Springs, that the indications are that the enemy has left that place. Sigel's advance is on the march for Buckland Mills. I am anxious he should get that point as it is of importance. Sigel thinks the enemy has passed Salem. I do not think he can have yet done so. I have this instant received the following from the signal officers on Watery Mountain: "No sign of enemy at Jefferson; his wagons have left there. A wagon-train and line of troops northwest of this mountain, moving towards Chester Gap."

Question. What became of that regiment of cavalry I directed you to send me yesterday?

POPE.

Answer. I ordered you one from Buford's, because I could not get hold of Bayard. Not having heard whether he has done so, I have this morning, to make sure, ordered Bayard to send you the Maine regiment, and it marches immediately. This may result in your having two regiments.

I. McD.

Question. Have you sent the orders to Banks that I requested you to send?
Answer. Yes; to move upon Catlett's, preceded by his train.

I. McD.

No. 65.

APPENDIX "B" TO GENERAL POPE'S REPORT.

Copies of such of the despatches and orders sent and received during the campaign of the army of Virginia as are referred to in the body of the report and are necessary to explain in detail the operations of the campaign.

HEADQUARTERS ARMY OF VIRGINIA,
Washington, July 18, 1862.

General orders, No. 5.]

Hereafter, as far as practicable, the troops of this command will subsist upon the country in which their operations are carried on. In all cases supplies for this purpose will be taken by the officers to whose department they properly belong, under the orders of the commanding officer of the troops for whose use they are intended. Vouchers will be given to the owners, stating on their face that they will be payable at the conclusion of the war, upon sufficient testimony being furnished that such owners have been loyal citizens of the United States since the date of the vouchers. Whenever it is known that supplies can be furnished in any district of the country where the troops are to operate, the use of trains for carrying subsistence will be dispensed with as far as possible.

By command of Major General Pope.

GEORGE D. RUGGLES,
Colonel, Assistant Adjutant General and Chief of Staff.

Official:

C. A. MORGAN,
Colonel and Aide-de-Camp.

HEADQUARTERS ARMY OF VIRGINIA,
Washington, July 18, 1862.

General orders, No. 6.]

Hereafter in any operations of the cavalry forces in this command, no supply or baggage trains of any description will be used unless so stated specially in the order for the movement. Two days' cooked rations will be carried on the persons of the men, and all villages or neighborhoods through which they pass will be laid under contribution in the manner specified by general orders No. 5, current series, from these headquarters for the subsistence of men and horses. Movements of cavalry must always be made with celerity, and no delay in such movements will be excused hereafter on any pretext. Whenever the order for the movement of any portion of this army emanates from these headquarters the time of marching, and that to be consumed in the execution of the duty, will be specifically designated, and no departure therefrom will be permitted to pass unnoticed without the gravest and most conclusive reasons.

Commanding officers will be held responsible for strict and prompt compliance with every provision of this order.

By command of Major General Pope.

GEORGE D. RUGGLES,
Colonel, Assistant Adjutant General and Chief of Staff.

Official:

D. POPE, *Captain and Aide-de-Camp.*

HDADQUARTERS ARMY OF VIRGINIA,
Washington, July 10, 1862.

General orders, No. 7.]

The people of the valley of the Shenandoah, and throughout the region of operations of this army, living along the lines of railroad and telegraph, and along the routes of travel in rear of the United States forces, are notified that they will be held responsible for any injury done to the track, line, or road, or for any attacks upon trains or straggling soldiers by bands of guerillas in their neighborhood. No privileges and immunities of warfare apply to lawless bands of individuals not forming part of the organized forces of the enemy, nor wearing the garb of soldiers, who, seeking and obtaining safety on pretext of being peaceful citizens, steal out in rear of the army, attack and murder straggling soldiers, molest trains of supplies, destroy railroads, telegraph lines, and bridges, and commit outrages disgraceful to civilized people and revolting to humanity. Evil disposed persons in rear of our armies, who do not themselves engage directly in these lawless acts, encourage them by refusing to interfere or to give any information by which such acts can be prevented or the perpetrators punished.

Safety of life and property of all persons living in rear of our advancing armies depends upon the maintenance of peace and quiet among themselves, and upon the unmolested movements through their midst of all pertaining to the military service. They are to understand distinctly that this security of travel is their only warrant of personal safety.

It is therefore ordered that wherever a railroad, wagon road, or telegraph is injured by parties of guerillas, the citizens living within five miles of the spot shall be turned out in mass to repair the damage, and shall beside pay to the United States, in money or in property, to be levied by military force, the full amount of the pay and subsistence of the whole force necessary to coerce the performance of the work during the time occupied in completing it.

If a soldier or legitimate follower of the army be fired upon from any house, the house shall be razed to the ground, and the inhabitants sent prisoners to the headquarters of this army. If such an outrage occur at any place distant from settlements, the people within five miles around shall be held accountable and made to pay an indemnity sufficient for the case.

Any persons detected in such outrages, either during the act or at any time afterward, shall be shot, without awaiting civil process. No such acts can influence the result of this war, and they can only lead to heavy afflictions to the population to no purpose.

It is therefore enjoined upon all persons, both for the security of their property and the safety of their own persons, that they act vigorously and cordially together to prevent the perpetration of such outrages.

Whilst it is the wish of the general commanding this army that all peaceably disposed persons, who remain at their homes and pursue their accustomed avocations, shall be subjected to no improper burden of war, yet their own safety must of necessity depend upon the strict preservation of peace and order among themselves, and they are to understand that nothing will deter him from enforcing promptly, and to the full extent, every provision of this order.

By command of Major General Pope.

GEORGE D. RUGGLES,
Colonel, Assistant Adjutant General and Chief of Staff.

Official:

Aide-de-Camp.

HEADQUARTERS ARMY OF VIRGINIA,
Washington, July 23, 1862.

General Orders, No. 11.]

Commanders of army corps, divisions, brigades and detached commands, will proceed immediately to arrest all disloyal male citizens within their lines, or within their reach in rear of their respective stations.

Such as are willing to take the oath of allegiance to the United States, and will furnish sufficient security for its observance, shall be permitted to remain at their homes, and pursue in good faith their accustomed avocations. Those who refuse shall be conducted south, beyond the extreme pickets of this army, and be notified that if found again anywhere within our lines, or at any point in rear, they will be considered spies, and subjected to the extreme rigor of military law.

If any person, having taken the oath of allegiance, as above specified, be found to have violated it, he shall be shot, and his property seized and applied to the public use.

All communication with any person whatever living within the lines of the enemy is positively prohibited, except through the military authorities, and in the manner specified by military law; and any person concerned in writing, or in carrying letters or messages in any other way, will be considered and treated as a spy within the lines of the United States army.

By command of Major General Pope.

GEO. D. RUGGLES,
Colonel, A. A. G. and Chief of Staff.

Official:

C. A. MORGAN,
Colonel and Aide-de-Camp.

HEADQUARTERS ARMY OF VIRGINIA,
Near Sperryville, Virginia, August 6, 1862.

General Orders, No. 18.]

Hereafter, in all marches of the army, no straggling, or lagging behind, will be allowed. Commanders of regiments will be held responsible that this order is observed, and they will march habitually in the rear of their regiments; company commanders in the rear of their respective companies.

They will suffer no man of their command to fall behind them on any excuse, except by a written permit from the medical officer of the regiment, that they are too sick to perform the march and therefore must ride in ambulances.

Medical officers will be responsible that no such written pass is improperly given.

Regimental trains will march in rear of the divisions to which the regiments belong, in the order of precedence of the regiments in that division. Brigade and division supply trains will follow in the rear of the respective army corps to which they belong.

Ambulances and ammunition wagons will follow in rear of their respective regiments, and under no consideration whatever will any wagon or other vehicle be placed in the column of march, other than as hereinbefore specified

Officers and soldiers of this army will habitually carry two days' cooked rations upon their persons, when ordered to perform a march.

It is recommended to commanders of "corps d'armée" that in all cases, when it is practicable, the shelter tents and knapsacks of the men be carried in the wagons.

At least one hundred rounds of ammunition per man will be carried habitually in the cartridge-boxes and on the persons of the men, and any captain of a company whose men at any time are deficient in this amount of ammunition will be arrested and reported to the War Department for dismissal from the service. A proper staff officer will be sent from these headquarters to inspect the troops while on the march, who will report to the major general commanding any violation of, or departure from, the provisions of this order.

Neither offi cer nor soldier will be permitted to leave his command while on the march, or enter any house without a written permit from his brigade commander. Where soldiers are obliged for necessary purposes to leave the ranks while on the march, they will turn over their muskets and accoutrements to the next man on their right, who shall carry the arms and accoutrements, and be responsible for them till the owners shall have again taken their places in the ranks.

Commanders of corps will prescribe the number of rounds of artillery ammunition to be carried with each battery; but in no case shall any battery be left with less than two hundred rounds for each gun. As good order and discipline are essential to the success of any army, a strict compliance with the provisions of this order is enjoined upon all officers and soldiers of this command, and they are expected and required to report to their superior officers every departure from them. Whilst the major general commanding the army will see to it that every soldier is kindly cared for and supplied with everything necessary for his comfort, he takes occasion to announce to the army that the severest punishment will be inflicted upon every officer and soldier who neglects his duty, and connives at or conceals any such neglect of duty or disobedience of orders on the part of any other officer or soldier. Commanders of army corps will see that this order is published, immediately after the receipt, at the head of every regiment in their command.

By command of Major General Pope.

R. O. SELFRIDGE,
Assistant Adjutant General.

Official:

Aide-de-Camp.

	Infantry.	Artillery.	Cavalry.	Total.
First army corps	10,550	948	1,730	13,208
Second army corps	13,343	1,224	4,104	18,671
Third army corps	17,604	971	2,904	21,479
	41,497	3,143	8,738	53,358
Deduct infantry brigade at Winchester		2,500		
Deduct regiment and battery at Front Royal		1,000		
Deduct cavalry unfit for service		3,000		
Total		6,500	Deduct	6,500
				46,858

I certify that this is a true copy of the consolidated morning report of the army of Virginia, dated July 31, 1862, commanded by Major General Pope.

MYER ASCH,
Captain and Aide-de-Camp.

NOTE.—Instead of 14,500 men, Banks had only about 8,000, from his report to me after the battle of Cedar Mountain.—(See correspondence on this subject with General Banks.)

UNITED STATES MILITARY TELEGRAPH,
War Department, Washington, D. C., June 30, 1862.
Middletown, June 30, 1.10 *p. m.—Time received,* 1.45 *p. m.*

[Extract.]

* * * * * * The troops forming first corps are not in good condition. They are weakened and poorly provided. The organization is not complete, and the whole cavalry force consists of not more than eight hundred (800) effective men and horses. They are scarcely sufficient for picket and patrol duty, so that I can hardly make a reconnoissance * * * * * *

F. SIGEL,
Major General Commanding.

Major General JOHN POPE.

A true copy.

T. C. H. SMITH,
Lieutenant Colonel and Aide-de-Camp.

Despatches and orders sent and received from August 8 *to August* 20, *inclusive.*

HEADQUARTERS ARMY OF VIRGINIA,
Culpeper Court-House, August 8, 1862.

One division of the enemy (Elzey's) crossed the Rapidan to-day at Barnett's Ford, about five miles west of the railroad crossing, and resting at Robertson's river. This is probably a reconnoissance in force, but it may be possibly an advance upon Culpeper. One division of McDowell's and the whole of Banks's corps are here to-night. Sigel's will be here to-morrow morning, when I shall push the enemy again behind the Rapidan and take up a strong position, as you suggest in your despatch of this date. I will be very careful that my communications with Fredericksburg are not interrupted. We captured to-day about forty prisoners from the enemy; our loss being one cavalry soldier killed and one wounded.

I have directed King to march to-morrow, and cross the Rapidan on the plank-road at Germania Mills or Ely's Ford, just below it. It is about thirty-five miles from Fredericksburg to this point.

JNO. POPE,
Major General Commanding.

Major General HALLECK, *Washington.*

A true copy.

T. C. H. SMITH,
Lieutenant Colonel and Aide-de-Camp.

HEADQUARTERS ARMY OF VIRGINIA,
Culpeper Court-House, August 8, 1862.

GENERAL: The general commanding directs me, in reply to your despatch of this date, (6.50 p. m.,) inquiring what road you shall take, to say, that you are to march direct to Culpeper Court-House by the turnpike. He is surprised that you make this inquiry, after his definite instructions of this morning. He directs that you reach this point by 12 m. to-morrow.

With great respect, general, your obedient servant,

T. C. H. SMITH,
Lieutenant Colonel and Aide-de-Camp.

Major General SIGEL,
Commanding First Army Corps.

[Received at headquarters 2d corps, August 9, 8.40 a. m.]

MADISON COURT-HOUSE, *August* 8.

All of my force is withdrawn from Madison Court-House and are in retreat towards Sperryville. The enemy is in force on both my right and left and in my rear. I may be cut off.

JOHN BUFORD, *Brigadier General.*

Major General BANKS.

Received by signal 8 a. m., Fairfax, Virginia.

A true copy.

T. C. H. SMITH,
Lieutenant Colonel and Aide-de-Camp.

HEADQUARTERS THIRD ARMY CORPS, ARMY OF VIRGINIA,
Culpeper Court-House, August 9, 1862.

GENERAL: I have just received a letter from the colonel of the Rhode Island cavalry, who says: "All is quiet in front of us. The enemy is always before my videttes; on my left there is perhaps a regiment of rebel infantry. In a word I do not believe the enemy to be in force in our front. General Bayard has just ordered me to march to repulse the enemy."

Very respectfully, general, your obedient servant,

IRVIN McDOWELL,
Major General, Commanding Third A. C. A. V.

Major General POPE.

A true copy.

T. C. H. SMITH,
Lieutenant Colonel and Aide-de-Camp.

HEADQUARTERS ARMY OF VIRGINIA, SECOND CORPS,
August 9, 1862—2.25.

General Williams's division has taken position on the right of the pike, the right on a heavy body of woods; General Augur on the left, his left resting on a mountain occupied by his skirmishers. He will soon be in position. The enemy shows his cavalry (which is strong) ostentatiously. No infantry seen, and not much artillery. Woods on left said to be full of troops. A visit to the front does not impress that the enemy intends immediate attack. He seems, however, to be taking positions.

N. P. BANKS.

Major General POPE.

A true copy.

T. C. H. SMITH,
Lieutenant Colonel and Aide-de-Camp.

HEADQUARTERS ARMY OF THE POTOMAC,
August 9, 1862—4.50.

About 4 o'clock shots were exchanged by the skirmishers. Artillery opened fire on both sides in a few minutes. One regiment of rebel infantry advancing, now deployed in front as skirmishers. I have ordered a regiment on the right, Williams's division, to meet them, and one from the left; Augur to advance on the left and in front.

N. P. BANKS.

Colonel RUGGLES, *Chief of Staff.*

5 p. m.—They are now approaching each other.

A true copy.

T. C. H. SMITH,
Lieutenant Colonel and Aide-de-Camp.

[From the War Department, August 18.]

UNITED STATES MILITARY TELEGRAPH.

I fully approve your movement. I hope to push a part of Burnside's forces to near Barnett's Ford by to-morrow night to assist you in holding that pass. Stand firm on the line till I can help you. Fight hard and aid will soon come.

H. W. HALLECK, *General-in-Chief.*

General POPE.

A true copy.

T. C. H. SMITH,
Lieutenant Colonel and Aide-de-Camp.

HEADQUARTERS ARMY OF VIRGINIA,
Rappahannock Station, August 20, 1862.

Your despatch of yesterday received last night. I shall mass my whole force along what is known as Marsh Run, about two and a half or three miles north-east of Rappahannock Ford, occupying Kelly's Ford with an advanced guard from my left; Rappahannock Ford with an advanced guard from the centre, and picketing strongly with cavalry the fords above me as far as the road from Sperryville to Warrenton. If the enemy attempt to turn my right by the way of Sulphur Springs, they will probably march direct on Warrenton, from which place a good turnpike conducts to Washington. Such a movement, however, will expose their flank and rear, and you may be sure I shall not lose the opportunity. My right will be considerably refused along the railroad, as far, at least, as Bealton Station. What relations with me will the corps of Fitz-John Porter have? I should like to know exactly. I am going out to post my command. I have heard from Reno. He crossed safely yesterday at Kelly's Ford and Barnett's Ford. The enemy so far has made no movement in advance. I think they are not yet ready, for want of transportation for supplies, to cross the Rapidan.

JNO. POPE, *Major General.*

Major General HALLECK.

A true copy.

T. C. H. SMITH,
Lieutenant Colonel and Aide-de-Camp.

Despatches and orders sent and received from August 22 *to August* 24, *inclusive.*

[Received August 21, 1862, from the War Department, Washington.]

UNITED STATES MILITARY TELEGRAPH.

I have telegraphed General Burnside to know at what hour he can re-enforce Reno. Am waiting his answer. Every effort must be made to hold the Rappahannock. Large forces will be in to-morrow.

H. W. HALLECK, *General-in-Chief.*

General POPE.

A true copy.

T. C. H. SMITH,
Lieutenant Colonel and Aide-de-Camp.

HEADQUARTERS ARMY OF VIRGINIA,
Rappahannock Station, August 21, 1862.

The enemy has made no further advance since yesterday afternoon, but his cavalry pickets are in plain view of our front. After full examination of the ground, I have determined to maintain the line of the Rappahannock instead of Marsh creek. I have, accordingly, occupied advanced and commanding positions on the south side of the river, and have three bridges, beside the fords, to connect with them. The main body of my command is posted along the north side of the river, having easy access to the front. I have masked the fords above and below me with infantry, cavalry, and artillery, and have no concern about any attack in the front, though, as previously suggested, my right can be turned at considerable distance above me. This, however, will require time, and will be, besides, a hazardous operation. We drew back behind the Rappahannock in perfect order, without leaving any article whatever.

JNO. POPE, *Major General.*

Major General HALLECK.

A true copy.

T. C. H. SMITH,
Lieutenant Colonel and Aide-de-Camp.

[From War Department, Washington, August 21, 1862.]

UNITED STATES MILITARY TELEGRAPH.

I have just sent General Burnside's reply. General Cox's forces are coming on from Parkersburg, and will be here to-morrow and the next day. Dispute every inch of ground, and fight like the devil till we can re-enforce you. Forty-eight hours more and we can make you strong enough. Don't yield an inch if you can help it.

H. W. HALLECK,
General-in-Chief.

General POPE.

A true copy.

T. C. H. SMITH,
Lieutenant Colonel and Aide-de-Camp.

HEADQUARTERS ARMY OF VIRGINIA,
Rappahannock Station, August 22, 1862—12 *m.*

Keep your cavalry scouring the woods all around you, and watching the roads, and pick up stragglers. You will keep them under guard at Catlett's Station, or use them for fatigue duty.

By order of Major General Pope.

GEORGE D. RUGGLES,
Colonel and Chief of Staff.

COMMANDING OFFICER,
Warrenton Junction.

A true copy.

T. C. H. SMITH,
Lieutenant Colonel and Aide-de-Camp.

HEADQUARTERS ARMY OF VIRGINIA,
Rappahannock Station, August 22, 1862—12 *m.*

The number of stragglers leaving this army just now, and the ease with which they escape, are becoming serious. Can they not be arrested and confined in prison at Washington, as I have not at present the means to bring them here, or to keep them when I get them?

JNO. POPE, *Major General.*

Major General HALLECK.

A true copy.

T. C. H. SMITH,
Lieutenant Colonel and Aide-de-Camp.

HEADQUARTERS ARMY OF VIRGINIA,
August 22, 1862—10.50 *a. m.*

It is very apparent that the enemy is moving with a view of turning our right He has no forces further east than Strasburg, and everything is tending up the river. I presume he will cross if possible at Sulphur Springs, on the pike to Washington. I would suggest that all the forces being sent from Fredericksburg be pushed forward immediately as far as this place, as I think there is no danger whatever on the lower fords of the Rappahannock. A captured letter from General Robert Lee to General Stewart, dated at Gordonsville, August 15, clearly indicates their movement. We had several handsome skirmishes yesterday, in one of which one of our cavalry regiments on the south side of the river charged over a regiment of rebel infantry, dispersing and driving them into the woods. Seventy head of the enemy's beef cattle and seven horses were captured. There has been heavy artillery firing all the morning, the enemy not yet having finished his preparation for attack. My whole force is massed and well in hand. We have had a great many casualties within the last two days of skirmishing and cannonading. I cannot tell how many.

JNO. POPE, *Major General.*

Major General HALLECK.

A true copy.

T. C. H. SMITH,
Lieutenant Colonel and Aide-de-Camp.

HEADQUARTERS ARMY OF VIRGINIA,
Rappahannock Station, August 22, 1862—*5 o'clock p. m.*

I think that the troops of Heintzelman and Cox had best be landed from the train at Bealton Station; Kearny on or near Licking river, say two miles southwest of Warrenton Junction. The enemy has made no attempt to-day to cross the river. His movement up towards our right seems to have been continuous all day. I have little doubt if he crosses at all it will be at Sulphur Springs. Under present circumstances I shall not attempt to prevent his crossing at Sulphur Springs, but will mass my whole force on his flank in the neighborhood of Fayetteville. By undertaking to defend the crossing at Sulphur

Springs I would much extend my lines and remove myself too far from the re-enforcements that are arriving by railroad. Before the enemy can be fairly across the river with any considerable force, I shall be strong enough to advance from Fayetteville upon his flank.

JOHN POPE, *Major General.*

Major General HALLECK.

A true copy.

T. C. H. SMITH,
Lieutenant Colonel and Aide-de-Camp.

HEADQUARTERS ARMY OF VIRGINIA,
Rappahannock Station, August 22, 1862—6.30 *o'clock p. m.*

Everything indicates clearly to me that the enemy's movement will be upon Warrenton, by way of Sulphur Springs. If I could know, with anything like certainty, by what time to expect troops that are starting from Alexandria, I could act more understandingly. I have not heard of the arrival of any of the forces from Fredericksburg at the fords below, though I have withdrawn nearly the whole of Reno's forces from Kelley's Ford. I cannot move against Sulphur Springs just now without exposing my rear to the heavy force in front of me, and having my communication with the forces coming up the Rappahannock intercepted and most likely the railroad destroyed. I think it altogether well to bring Franklin's corps to Alexandria. Lee made his headquarters at Culpeper last night. He has the whole of his army in front of me. Its numbers you can estimate as well as myself. As soon as his plans are fully developed I shall be ready to act.

JOHN POPE, *Major General.*

Major General HALLECK.

A true copy.

T. C. H. SMITH,
Lieutenant Colonel and Aide-de-Camp.

HEADQUARTERS ARMY OF VIRGINIA,
Rappahannock Station, August 22, 1862—9 *o'clock p. m.*

Scouts report a heavy force moving up across Hedgeman's river on the Sperryville and Little Washington pike towards Warrenton; also crossing at Sulphur Springs. I think a brigade should be sent to guard the railroad bridge at Cedar Run, and that Heintzelman's corps should be hurried forward with all possible despatch.

JOHN POPE, *Major General.*

Major General HALLECK.

A true copy.

T. C. H. SMITH,
Lieutenant Colonel and Aide-de-Camp.

HEADQUARTERS ARMY OF VIRGINIA,
August 22—9.15 *o'clock p. m.*

Reports from our forces near Sulphur Springs just in. Enemy was crossing river to-day at Sulphur, and on the road from Warrenton to Sperryville. He is still in heavy force at Rappahannock Ford and above, and my rear is entirely exposed if I move towards Sulphur Springs or Warrenton. I must do one of two things, either fall back and meet Heintzelman behind Cedar Run or cross the Rappahannock with my whole force and assail the enemy's flank and rear. I must do one or the other at daylight. Which shall it be? I incline to the latter, but don't wish to interfere with your plans.

JOHN POPE, *Major General.*

General HALLECK.

A true copy.

T. C. H. SMITH,
Lieutenant Colonel and Aide-de-Camp.

[Received August 22, 1862, from War Department, Washington, 22—11 p. m]

UNITED STATES MILITARY TELEGRAPH.

I think the latter of your two propositions the best. I also think you had better stop Heintzelman's corps and the troops of Sturgis and Cox as they arrive to-morrow at Warrenton Junction, instead of taking them to Bealton.

H. W. HALLECK,
General-in-Chief.

Major General POPE.

A true copy.

T. C. H. SMITH,
Lieutenant Colonel and Aide-de-Camp.

[Received August 22, 1862, from Manassas—10.40 p. m.]

UNITED STATES MILITARY TELEGRAPH.

We will continue to forward troops to Manassas unless you order otherwise, but beyond this point trains will be held to await your orders, or until further information is received.

HAUPT.

General POPE.

A true copy.

T. C. H. SMITH,
Lieutenant Colonel and Aide-de-Camp.

HEADQUARTERS ARMY OF VIRGINIA,
Rappahannock Station, August 23, 1862—2.20 *o'clock a. m.*

As nearly as I can learn the facts, the enemy's cavalry made a raid from the direction of Warrenton upon our wagon trains at Catlett's, and seem to have done some considerable damage to them through the gross carelessness of the guard, which was amply sufficient to protect them. Please hurry forward Heintzelman, as the enemy may reach Warrenton Junction before he does. Please push forward also all the troops moving up from Fredericksburg with orders to cross the Rappahannock at the various fords, and march rapidly on Strasburg. My movement will be made to-morrow as soon as I find the enemy has passed a sufficient number of his troops over the river. The troops coming up from Fredericksburg should be hastened forward with all despatch to Strasburg and Brandy Station. It will be well, also, to send with them immediately a train with bread, sugar, coffee, and salt, as our railroad communication may be unsafe for a few days.

JNO. POPE, *Major General.*

Major General HALLECK.

HEADQUARTERS FIRST CORPS,
Army of Virginia, August 23, 1862.

There is no doubt that the enemy has outflanked us, and that his army crosses near Sulphur Springs and Fox's or Lawson's Ford. I therefore must instantly beg you to send General Reno's division to Fayetteville, which will be good and necessary for all emergencies, but it should be done to-night and immediately. General Banks, instead of marching to Lawson's Ford, as directed by me, has not done it, and the enemy is therefore crossing at Fox's Ford, from which ford General Bayard retired an hour or two ago. From Fayetteville General Reno can advance to Lawson's Ford, or maintain his position until you have made your proper arrangements. It would be, according to my opinion, the best to withdraw the first corps towards Bealton, or my original position near Beverly Ford, to enable us to concentrate all our forces in a central position. General Reno would cover this movement, and we would gain one day.

I am, general, respectfully yours,

F. SIGEL,
Major General Commanding First Corps.

Major General POPE,
Commanding Army of Virginia.

A true copy.

T. C. H. SMITH,
Lieutenant Colonel and Aide-de-Camp.

HEADQUARTERS ARMY OF VIRGINIA, *August* 23, 1862.

Your despatch just received. General Buford is at Fayetteville, and will watch any movements of the enemy towards that place or towards your right. Stand firm and let the enemy develop towards Warrenton. Re-enforcements are constantly arriving in our rear. I do not wish any further extension of our lines to the right, but I desire the enemy to cross as large a force as he pleases in the direction of Warrenton. When I wish to concentrate on the railroad I will cover your movement back. Be under no concern, but keep your whole command ready to march at a moment's notice. Send word to Bayard to keep his position as far up the river as possible, and check, if you find it necessary, any attempt of the enemy to cross at Lawson's Ford.

By order of General Pope.

T. C. H. SMITH,
Lieutenant Colonel and Aide-de-Camp.

Major General SIGEL.

A true copy.

T. C. H. SMITH,
Lieutenant Colonel and Aide-de-Camp.

HEADQUARTERS ARMY OF VIRGINIA,
August 23, 1862—7.15 *o'clock a. m.*

The river has risen here six feet, and is entirely impassable at any ford. I have no doubt it is the same all the way up the river, as the main portion of the storm was above. The enemy, therefore, on this side is cut off from those on the other, and there is no fear of this position. You will accordingly march at once upon Sulphur Springs, and thence towards Waterloo Bridge, attacking and beating the enemy wherever you find him. Banks's corps and the force under General Reno will accompany and support you. McDowell with his whole corps marches direct on Warrenton, and you will be brought together in that neighborhood to-night. Move promptly up the river. The other troops will be close behind you. You ought to be in the neighborhood of Waterloo Bridge before sunset. I will accompany McDowell's corps and communicate further with you in the course of the day. You will have an effective force of 25,000 men. Leave nothing behind you.

JNO. POPE, *Major General.*

Major General SIGEL.

A true copy.

T. C. H. SMITH,
Lieutenant Colonel and Aide-de-Camp.

HEADQUARTERS ARMY OF VIRGINIA,
August 23, 1862—7.35 *o'clock a. m.*

You will accompany and support General Sigel in his forward movements towards Sulphur Springs and Waterloo Bridge. General Reno will follow you closely for the same purpose. McDowell's corps marches immediately upon Warrenton. The river has risen six feet, and is no longer passable by the enemy. His forces on this side are cut off from those on the other, and we will march against those on this side, and our whole force will unite between Warrenton and Waterloo Bridge. Call in Crawford at once, and leave nothing behind you. Follow Sigel very closely, and keep constant communication with him, as also with General Reno, in your rear. Be quick, for time is everything.

JNO. POPE, *Major General.*

Major General BANKS.

A true copy.

T. C. H. SMITH,
Lieutenant Colonel and Aide-de-Camp.

HEADQUARTERS ARMY OF VIRGINIA,
Rappahannock Station, August 23, 1862—9 *o'clock a. m.*

The heavy storm of yesterday and last night has caused the river to rise six feet. There are no longer any fords, and the bridges are carried away. I succeeded in time in withdrawing my advanced forces from the south side of the river. The movement across the river on the enemy's flank and rear is therefore impossible. The enemy's forces on this side which have crossed at Sulphur Springs and Hedgeman's River, are cut off from those on the south side. I march at once with my whole force on Sulphur Springs, Waterloo Bridge, and Warrenton, in the hope to destroy these forces before the river runs down. The rain still continues, and I think we are good for thirty-six hours. As soon as I have effected this purpose, which I hope to do by an early hour to-morrow, I shall move back, detaching a large force to reopen my communications at Catlett's, and send forward supplies. If Heintzelman and Cox move quickly, it will be easy to hold the Rappahannock, leaving the enemy much damaged by his attempt to turn our right. You may not hear from me before to-morrow night.

JNO. POPE, *Major General.*

Major General HALLECK.

A true copy.

T. C. H. SMITH,
Lieutenant Colonel and Aide-de-Camp.

HEADQUARTERS ARMY OF VIRGINIA,
August 23, 1862—11 *o'clock a. m.*

You will please, on arriving at Rappahannock Station, follow the route taken by the army corps of General McDowell, passing Brigadier General Tower, who is in command of the rear guard, and whom you will find near the railroad station. Please keep well closed, and close up to the rear of McDowell's corps. Our march is to Warrenton, about ten miles distant, which you must make to-night.

By command of General Pope, commanding army of Virginia.

T. C. H. SMITH,
Lieutenant Colonel and Aide-de-Camp.

General REYNOLDS.

A true copy.

T. C. H. SMITH,
Lieutenant Colonel and Aide-de-Camp.

HEADQUARTERS ARMY OF VIRGINIA,
Near Warrenton, August 23, 1862—10 *o'clock p. m.*

My advance entered the town about an hour ago, the enemy evacuating it on our approach. They fell back towards Hedgeman's River and Sulphur Springs. At the latter place my left was engaged about sunset, and now awaits daylight. I shall move rapidly at daylight upon Sulphur Springs and Waterloo Bridge.

If the enemy is really in large force on this side of the Rappahannock, he will be trapped, as the river is very high behind. I will communicate to-morrow.

JNO. POPE, *Major General.*

Major General HALLECK.

A true copy.

T. C. H. SMITH,
Lieutenant Colonel and Aide-de Camp.

HEADQUARTERS ARMY OF VIRGINIA,
August 24, 1862—5 *o'clock a. m.*

The advance division of McDowell's corps occupied Warrenton last night, without opposition. The head of his column was pushed just outside of town, on the road to Sulphur Springs, ready to move forward to that point, should it be necessary. I am pushing a reconnoissance towards Waterloo Bridge to see what is there. Communicate fully to me through Captain Merrill, who will hand you this note, the condition of things in front of you. Our work must be finished here to-day; we have no time to spare. Provisions will be in Warrenton this morning.

JNO. POPE, *Major General.*

Major General SIGEL, *Commanding, &c.*

A true copy.

T. C. H. SMITH,
Lieutenant Colonel and Aide-de-Camp.

[Extract. Received August 24, 1862.]

UNITED STATES MILITARY TELEGRAPH.

* * * * Thirty thousand (30,000) troops, or more, demand transportation. It is clear that the sudden demands exceed the capacity of the road. We can manage twelve thousand (12,000) troops per day, with supplies, if no accident occurs. The new troops might march, the veterans go in cars, horses driven, baggage, tents, &c., wait until they can be forwarded. Supplies take precedence.

HAUPT.

Major General POPE.

A true copy.

T. C. H. SMITH,
Lieutenant Colonel and Aide-de-Camp.

[Extract.]

UNITED STATES MILITARY TELEGRAPH,
Alexandria, August 24, 1862.

We expect to clean out all the troops now here, and all that are expected to-day. * * * * *

H. HAUPT.

Major General POPE.

A true copy.

T. C. H. SMITH,
Lieutenant Colonel and Aide-de-Camp.

HEADQUARTERS FIRST CORPS,
Near Waterloo Bridge, August 25, 1862—1.40 *p. m.*

Colonel Beardsley reports the enemy's cavalry at Sulphur Springs and the village occupied by the enemy's infantry.

Colonel Beardsley had been sent by me to Sulphur Springs with some cavalry and mountain howitzers. The main force of the enemy is advancing on this place, (Waterloo Bridge.)

General Reno should send me the 20-pounder Parrotts. I could use them here excellently.

I am, colonel, very respectfully,

F. SIGEL,
Major General Commanding First Corps.

Colonel GEORGE D. RUGGLES,
Chief of Staff.

A true copy.

T. C. H. SMITH,
Lieutenant Colonel and Aide-de-Camp.

HEADQUARTERS ARMY OF VIRGINIA,
Warrenton, August 24, 1862—3.45 *p. m.*

I arrived in Warrenton last night. The enemy had left two hours previously. Milroy's brigade, the advance of Sigel's corps, came upon the enemy late yesterday afternoon near Great River, about four miles from Warrenton Sulphur Springs, and near the mouth of it. A sharp action took place, which lasted till after dark, the enemy being driven across Great River, but destroying the bridge behind him. Early this morning General Buford reached Waterloo Bridge, which was defended by a considerable force of the enemy and one piece of artillery. He took possession of the bridge and destroyed it. Sigel's force advanced again on the left this morning, and when last heard from was pursuing the enemy in the direction of Waterloo Bridge. His column was being shelled from the opposite bank of the river, which is still too deep to be forded. The enemy has made no advance against Rappahannock Station since we left, though yesterday morning, whilst we were withdrawing our forces from the opposite side of the river, he brought forward his columns of infantry and attempted to carry the heights which we were leaving by storm. He was, however, repulsed with considerable loss. We have had a continuous engagement, principally with artillery, along the whole line of the river for eight or ten miles during the last three days. No force of the enemy has yet been able to cross, except that now enclosed by our forces between Sulphur Springs and Waterloo Bridge, which will undoubtedly be captured, unless they find some means, of which I know nothing, of escaping across the river between these places. Early to-morrow, after clearing this side of the river, I shall move back a considerable part of this force to the neighborhood of Rappahannock Station. By that time the river will doubtless be fordable again. I shall leave a corps of observation here to watch the crossings at Waterloo and Sulphur Springs. The forces arriving from Washington and Alexandria will be assembled, I think, on Licking river, between Germantown and the railroad, with a reserve for the force at Warrenton, somewhere between Warrenton Junction and this place, until you are ready to begin a forward movement. I cannot form an estimate of the forces of the enemy. He has been developed in heavy force by simultaneous reconnoissances along a line of nine miles from the railroad crossing of the Rappahannock as far, at least, as Sulphur Springs. I should like to have some idea of the forces which are coming here, and your plans of organizing them, that they may be assigned and posted in some order. Our losses during the last three days have been quite heavy; among the killed being Brigadier General Bohlen, commanding a brigade in Sigel's corps. The whole tendency of the enemy, since he appeared in front of us at Rappahannock Station, has been towards our right; but how far his movements in that direction will extend I am not yet able to say. I shall to-morrow remove my headquarters to some central point, probably Warrenton Junction.

JNO. POPE,
Major General Commanding.

Major General HALLECK,
General-in-Chief, Washington.

A true copy.

T. C. H. SMITH,
Lieutenant Colonel and Aide-de-Camp.

HEADQUARTERS ARMY OF VIRGINIA,
Warrenton, August 24, 1862.

GENERAL: To-night, or at an early hour in the morning, you will please send spies and scouts around by Front Royal to Thornton's Gap and into the valley of the Shenandoah, to ascertain whether any of the enemy's forces are moving in that direction. Send at least two or three reliable men for that purpose, and instruct them that if they find any difficulty in returning to you, they shall go into Winchester and communicate their information to General White. You will receive instructions as to your movements in the morning.

By order of General Pope.

T. C. H. SMITH,
Lieutenant Colonel and Aide-de-Camp.

Major General SIGEL, *Commanding, &c.*

A true copy.

T. C. H. SMITH,
Lieutenant Colonel and Aide-de-Camp.

HEADQUARTERS FIRST CORPS ARMY OF VIRGINIA,
Near Waterloo Bridge, Virginia, August 24, 1862.

The first corps is in bivouac at Waterloo Bridge, with the exception of an infantry brigade left at Sulphur Springs as rear guard, together with a brigade of General Banks and one of General Reno.

General Banks's corps is on the Sulphur Springs road, about four miles from the springs, and General Reno is at or near the fork of the Warrenton road.

To judge from the appearance of the camp fires and camps, I am certain that the enemy's main army is encamped on the other side of the river, perhaps two miles from the river, with the advance at Annisville and the rear opposite Sulphur Springs.

F. SIGEL,
Major General Commanding First Corps.

Colonel GEORGE D. RUGGLES,
Chief of Staff, Army of Virginia.

A true copy.

T. C. H. SMITH,
Lieutenant Colonel and Aide-de-Camp.

Despatches and orders sent and received, from August 25 to August 28, inclusive.

HEADQUARTERS ARMY OF VIRGINIA,
August 25, 1862.

Your despatch just received. Of course I shall be ready to recross the Rappahannock at a moment's notice. You will see from the positions taken that each army corps is on the best roads across the river. You wished forty-eight hours to assemble the forces from the peninsula behind the Rappahannock, and four days have passed without the enemy yet being permitted to cross. I don't think he is ready yet to do so. In ordinarily dry weather the Rappahannock can be crossed almost anywhere, and these crossing places are best protected by concentrating at central positions to strike at any force which attempts to cross. I had clearly understood that you wished to unite our whole forces before a forward movement was begun, and that I must take care to keep united with Burnside on my left, so that no movement to separate us could be made. This withdrew me lower down the Rappahannock than I wished to come. I am not acquainted with your views, as you seem to suppose, and would be glad to know them as far as my own position and operations are concerned.

I understood you clearly that at all hazards I was to prevent the enemy from passing the Rappahannock. This I have done, and shall do. I don't like to be on the defensive if I can help it, but must be so as long as I am tied to Burnside's forces, not yet wholly arrived at Fredericksburg. Please let me know, if it can be done, what is to be my own command, and if I am to act independently against the enemy. I certainly understood that as soon as the whole of our forces were concentrated you designed to take command in person, and that when everything was ready we were to move forward in concert. I judge from the tone of your despatch that you are dissatisfied with something. Unless I know what it is, of course I cannot correct it. The troops arriving here come in fragments. Am I to assign them to brigades and corps? I would suppose not, as several of the new regiments coming have been assigned to army corps directly from your office. In case I commence offensive operations, I must know what forces I am to take, and what you wish left, and what connexion must be kept up with Burnside. It has been my purpose to conform my operations to your plans, yet I was not informed when McClellan evacuated Harrison's Landing, so that I might know what to expect in that direction; and when I say these things in no complaining spirit, I think you know well that I am anxious to do everything to advance your plans of campaign. I understood that this army was to maintain the line of the Rappahannock until all the forces from the peninsula had united behind that river. I have done so. I understood distinctly that I was not to hazard anything except for this purpose, as delay was what was wanted. The enemy this morning has pushed a considerable infantry force up opposite Waterloo Bridge, and is planting batteries, and long lines of his infantry are moving up from Jeffersonville towards Sulphur Springs. His whole force, as far as can be ascertained, is massed in front of me, from railroad crossing of Rappahannock around to Waterloo Bridge, their main body being opposite Sulphur Springs.

JOHN POPE, *Major General.*

Major General HALLECK.

A true copy.

T. C. H. SMITH,
Lieutenant Colonel and Aide-de-Camp.

[Extract. Received August 26, 1862, from War Department, 11.45 a. m.]

UNITED STATES MILITARY TELEGRAPH.

Not the slightest dissatisfaction has been felt in regard to your operations on the Rappahannock. The main object has been accomplished in getting up troops from the peninsula, although they have been delayed by storms. Moreover, the telegraph has been interrupted, leaving us for a time ignorant of the progress of the evacuation. * * * * * * *

H. W. HALLECK,
General-in-Chief.

Major General POPE.

A true copy.

T. C. H. SMITH,
Lieutenant Colonel and Aide-de-Camp.

HEADQUARTERS SECOND CORPS,
August 25—11.25 *a. m.*

COLONEL: Enclosed you will please find reports by Colonel Clark, aide-de-camp, from the signal corps station, of the movements of the enemy on the south side of Hedgeman or Rappahannock river. The facts are reported as having been observed by himself, and can be relied upon as being as near the truth as the distance will permit. It seems to be apparent that the enemy is threatening or moving upon the valley of the Shenandoah, *via* Front Royal, with designs upon the Potomac, possibly beyond. Not knowing whether you have received this information, I forward it for the consideration of the commanding general.

Respectfully, &c.,

N. P. BANKS,
Major General Commanding.

Colonel RUGGLES,
Assistant Adjutant General and Chief of Staff.

A true copy.

T. C. H. SMITH,
Lieutenant Colonel and Aide-de-Camp.

WARRENTON JUNCTION,
August 25, 1862—9.30 *p. m.*

You will force the passage of the river at Waterloo Bridge to-morrow morning at daylight, and see what is in front of you. I do not believe that there is any enemy in force there, but do believe that the whole of their army has marched to the west and northwest. I am not satisfied either with your reports or your operations of to-day, and I expect to hear to-morrow, early, something much more satisfactory concerning the enemy. Send back and bring up your provision trains to your command, but no regimental trains or baggage of any description. You will consider this a positive order, to be obeyed literally. You will communicate with me by telegraph from Warrenton.

JNO. POPE,
Major General Commanding.

Major General SIGEL,
Commanding First Corps.

Send in care of General McDowell, at Warrenton.

A true copy.

T. C. H. SMITH,
Lieutenant Colonel and Aide-de-Camp.

WARRENTON JUNCTION,
August 25, 1862—9.30 *p. m.*

I believe that the whole force of the enemy has marched for the Shenandoah valley by way of Luray and Front Royal. The column which has marched to-day to Gaines's Cross-Roads has turned north, and when last seen was passing under the east base of Buck mountain towards Salem and Rectortown. I desire you, as early as possible in the morning, holding Reynolds in reserve at Warrenton or vicinity, to make a reconnoissance with your whole corps, and ascertain what is beyond the river at Sulphur Springs. There is no force of the enemy between here and Culpeper, or at Culpeper. I send you a despatch for General Sigel, which please read and send to him immediately. Communicate with me frequently by telegraph from Warrenton.

JNO. POPE,
Major General Commanding.

Major General McDOWELL, *Warrenton.*

A true copy.

T. C. H. SMITH,
Lieutenant Colonel and Aide-de-Camp.

[Received August 26, 1862, from headquarters 3d army corps, 3.30 p. m., Warrenton.]

UNITED STATES MILITARY TELEGRAPH.

General Sigel's bridge train has arrived. I think it may be useful. General Milroy burnt the bridge at Waterloo before he retired from that place last night, and Buford says the fords near Waterloo are bad. I have directed the available forces of Sigel's cavalry, with a section of his artillery, to report to General Buford this afternoon, on the Waterloo road, with three days' cooked rations. I have directed Buford to march at dawn to-morrow towards Chester Gap, to ascertain what direction the enemy has taken on our right—whether to Rectortown or Front Royal, through Chester Gap. He will either take the Carter Church road, up the left bank of Carter's Run, or the road direct from this place to Chester Gap, as inquiries to be made this afternoon shall determine. However persons may have differed as to the force at Waterloo, Sulphur Springs, or elsewhere, all agree in one thing—the movement of the enemy towards our right from Rappahannock to Waterloo. Battalions, trains, batteries—all have the same direction. The force of the enemy now seems to be above Sulphur Springs. Under these views, in addition to Sigel's corps, now here, I beg to suggest that Hooker and Kearny be marched at once in this direction, instead of the direction of Rappahannock Station; for whether we attack them or they attack us, the contest must come off, it seems to me, as things now stand, above rather than below Sulphur Springs. If they could make a march this afternoon towards either Sulphur Springs or Waterloo Bridge, it would be a movement, I think, in the right direction. What is the enemy's purpose is not easy to discover. Some have thought he means to march around our right through Rectortown to Washington; others think that he intends going down the Shenandoah, either through Thornton's or Chester Gap. Either of these operations seems to me too hazardous for him to undertake with us in his rear and flank. Others that it was his object to throw his trains around into the Valley to draw his supplies from that direction, and have his front looking to the east rather than to the north. It is also thought that whilst a portion of his force has marched up the immediate right bank of the Rappahannock, a larger portion has gone through Culpeper up the Sperryville road. No doubt these various suppositions may have occurred to you, but I have thought it not inappropriate to recapitulate them here with reference to concentrations of forces in this direction which I have herein suggested. Cannonading at Sulphur Springs still continues about the same. I have ordered Buford to send you a regiment of cavalry. I cannot get hold of Bayard.

IRVIN McDOWELL.

I have just received your telegrams of 2.20 and 3.15 p. m. I trust that Buford's reconnoissance to-morrow will obtain the information you desire concerning the movements of the enemy across the Sperryville pike, in the direction of Gaines's Cross-Roads and Salem. I also received from General Banks's signal officer the account of this movement. With reference to your inquiries as to what has occurred to make the presence of Cox here desirable, I made the suggestion, first, because in the general order issued he was ordered to join Sigel at Fayetteville. As Sigel was here, and as I understood Cox was arriving in the cars, I thought if it could be done, time would be gained by his being landed here, rather than at Warrenton Junction.

IRVIN McDOWELL,
Major General Commanding.

Major General POPE.

A true copy.

T. C. H. SMITH,
Lieutenant Colonel and Aide-de-Camp.

[Received August 26, 1862, from near Waterloo Bridge, 3.45 p. m.]

UNITED STATES MILITARY TELEGRAPH.

Trains and troops still passing over the same route. A deserter, just come in, says Longstreet's corps, embracing Anderson's, Jones's, Kemper's, Whiting's, and Evans's divisions, are located in the woods back of Waterloo Bridge. Thinks Hill's division at Jefferson; Jackson's corps somewhere above Longstreet's. He appears truthful, and I credit his story. The entire district from Jefferson to Culpeper, Sperryville, and as far as Barber's, covered with smoke and lines of dust. The deserter reports the arrival last evening of the greater portion of Longstreet's corps at its present position.

JOHN S. CLARK,
Colonel and Aide-de-Camp.

General POPE.

A true copy.

T. C. H. SMITH,
Lieutenant Colonel and Aide-de-Camp.

HEADQUARTERS THIRD CORPS,
Warrenton, August 26—9 *p. m.*

An intelligent negro has just come in to General Buford from White Plains, and reports the advance of the enemy at that place. He says he saw, himself, at White Plains, to-day at 12 o'clock, two batteries of artillery, two regiments of cavalry, four regiments of infantry, and that they were moving in the direction of Thoroughfare Gap. The man's story is evidently to be relied upon.

General Buford says his statements are confirmed by his scouts, who report large trains passing up through Orleans to White Plains.

IRVIN McDOWELL, *Major General.*

Major General POPE.

True copy.

JOHN POPE, *Major General.*

WARRENTON JUNCTION, *August* 26, 1862—8 *p. m.*

Fitz-John Porter, with Sykes's and Morell's divisions, will be within two and a half miles of Warrenton, on the Fayetteville road, to-morrow night. See if you cannot have the cross-roads repaired, so he can get from his position into the Sulphur Springs road with his artillery if he should be needed. I will use all efforts to have Sturgis and Cox within three miles of you to-morrow night, and have requested General Halleck to push forward Franklin at once, carrying his baggage and supplies by railroad to the point where the Manassas Gap railroad intersects the Warrenton turnpike. From that position he can either advance to your support or prevent your right from being turned from the direction of the Manassas Gap railroad. I think our fight should be made at Warrenton, and if you can postpone it for two days, everything will be right.

JOHN POPE,
Major General Commanding.

Major General MCDOWELL, *Warrenton.*

A true copy.

T. C. H. SMITH,
Lieutenant Colonel and Aide-de-Camp.

HEADQUARTERS ARMY OF VIRGINIA,
Warrenton Junction, August 26, 1862—8.20 *p. m.*

The major general commanding the army of Virginia directs me to send you the enclosed communications, and to request that you put a regiment on a train of cars and send it down immediately to Manassas to ascertain what has occurred, repair the telegraph wires, and protect the railroad there, till further orders.

With great respect, general, your obedient servant,

T. C. H. SMITH.
Lieutenant Colonel and Aide-de-Camp.

Major General HEINTZELMAN, *Commanding, &c.*

HEADQUARTERS ARMY OF VIRGINIA,
August 26, 1862—12 *m.*

General Sigel reports the enemy's rear guard at Orleans to-night, with his main force encamped at White Plains. You will please ascertain very early in the morning whether this is so, and have the whole of your command in readiness to march. You had best ascertain it to-night if you possibly can. Our communications have been interrupted by the enemy's cavalry near Manassas. Whether his whole force, or the larger part of it, has gone round, is a question which we must settle immediately, and no portion of his force must march opposite to us to-night without our knowing it. I telegraphed you an hour or two ago what dispositions I had made, supposing the advance through Thoroughfare to be a column of not more than ten or fifteen thousand men. If his whole force, or the larger part of it, has gone, we must know it at once.

The troops here have no artillery; and if the main forces of the enemy are still opposite to you, you must send forward to Greenwich, to be there to-morrow evening, two batteries of artillery, or three if you can get them, to meet Kearny.

We must know at a very early hour in the morning, so as to determine our plans.

JOHN POPE, *Major General.*

General McDowell.

A true copy.

T. C. H. SMITH,
Lieutenant Colonel and Aide-de-Camp.

Headquarters Army of Virginia,
Warrenton Junction, August 27, 1862.

General Orders No. —.]

The following movement of troops will be made, viz:

Major General McDowell, with his own and Sigel's corps and the division of Brigadier General Reynolds, will pursue the turnpike from Warrenton to Gainesville, so as to reach Gainesville, if possible, to-night.

The army corps of General Heintzelman, with the detachments of the ninth corps, under Major General Reno, (General Reno leading,) will take the road from Catlett's Station to Greenwich, so as to reach there to-night or early in the morning. Major General Reno will immediately communicate with Major General McDowell, and his command, as well as that of Major General Heintzelman, will support Major General McDowell in any operations against the enemy.

Major General Fitz-John Porter will remain at Warrenton Junction till he is relieved by Major General Banks, when he will immediately push forward with his corps in the direction of Greenwich and Gainesville, to assist the operations of the right wing.

Major General Banks, as soon as he arrives at Warrenton Junction, will assume the charge of the trains and cover their movement towards Manassas Junction. The trains of his own corps, under escort of two regiments of infantry and a battery of artillery, will pursue the road south of the railroad, which conducts into the rear of Manassas Junction. As soon as all the trains have passed Warrenton Junction he will take post behind Cedar Run, covering the fords and bridges of that stream, and holding his position as long as possible. He will cause all the railroad trains to be loaded with the public and private stores now here, and run them back towards Manassas Junction as far as the railroad is practicable. Wherever a bridge is burned, so as to prevent the further passage of the railroad trains, he will assemble them all as near together as possible, and protect them with his command until the bridges are rebuilt. If the enemy is too strong before him before the bridge can be repaired, he will be careful to destroy entirely the trains, locomotives, and stores, before he falls back in the direction of Manassas Junction. He is, however, to understand that he is to defend his position as long as possible, keeping himself in constant communication with Major General Porter, on his right. If any sick now in hospital at Warrenton Junction are not provided for, and able to be transported, he will have them loaded into the wagon train of his own corps, (even should this necessitate the destruction of much baggage and regimental property,) and carried to Manassas Junction. The very important duties devolving upon

Major General Banks, the major general commanding the army of Virginia feels assured will be discharged with intelligence, courage, and fidelity.

The general headquarters will be with the corps of Major General Heintzelman until further notice.

By command of Major General Pope.

GEO. D. RUGGLES,
Colonel and Chief of Staff.

A true copy.

T. C. H. SMITH,
Lieutenant Colonel and Aide-de-Camp.

HEADQUARTERS ARMY OF VIRGINIA,
Bristow Station, August 27, 1862—6.30 *p. m.*

GENERAL: The major general commanding directs that you start at one o'clock to-night and come forward with your whole corps, or such part of it as is with you, so as to be here by daylight to-morrow morning. Hooker has had a very severe action with the enemy, with a loss of about three hundred killed and wounded. The enemy has been driven back, but is retiring along the railroad. We must drive him from Manassas, and clear the country between that place and Gainesville, where McDowell is. If Morell has not joined you, send word to him to push forward immediately; also send word to Banks to hurry forward with all speed, to take your place at Warrenton Junction. It is necessary, on all accounts, that you should be here by daylight.

I send an officer with this despatch who will conduct you to this place. Be sure to send word to Banks, who is on the road from Fayetteville, probably in the direction of Bealeton. Say to Banks, also, that he had best run back the railroad trains to this side of Cedar Run. If he is not with you, write him to that effect.

By command of Major General Pope.

GEO. D. RUGGLES,
Colonel and Chief of Staff.

P. S.—If Banks is not at Warrenton Junction, leave a regiment of infantry and two pieces of artillery, as a guard, till he comes up, with instructions to follow you immediately upon his doing so. If Banks is not at the Junction, instruct Colonel Clary to run the trains back to this side of Cedar Run, and post a regiment and section of artillery with it.

By command of Major General Pope.

GEO. D. RUGGLES,
Colonel and Chief of Staff.

Major General F. J. PORTER, *Warrenton Junction.*

A true copy.

T. C. H. SMITH,
Lieutenant Colonel and Aide-de-Camp.

HEADQUARTERS, BRISTOW,
August 27, 1862—9 *o'clock p. m.*

At the very earliest blush of dawn push forward with your command with all speed to this place. You cannot be more than three or four miles distant. Jackson, A. P. Hill, and Ewell are in front of us. Hooker has had a severe fight with them to-day. McDowell marches upon Manassas Junction from Gainesville to-morrow at daybreak; Reno upon the same place at the same hour. I want you here at daydawn, if possible, and we shall bag the whole crowd. Be prompt and expeditious, and never mind wagon trains or roads till this affair is over. Lieutenant Brooks will deliver you this communication. He has one for General Reno and one for General McDowell. Please have these despatches sent forward instantly by a trusty staff officer, who will be sure to deliver them without fail; and make him bring back a receipt to you before daylight. Lieutenant Brooks will remain with you and bring you to this camp. Use the cavalry I send you, to escort your staff officer to McDowell and Reno.

JNO. POPE,
Major General Commanding.

Major General KEARNY.

A true copy.

T. C. H. SMITH,
Lieutenant Colonel and Aide-de-Camp.

HEADQUARTERS ARMY OF VIRGINIA,
Bristow Station, August 27, 1862—9 *o'clock p. m.*

At daylight to-morrow morning march rapidly on Manassas Junction with your whole force, resting your right on the Manassas Gap railroad, throwing your left well to the east. Jackson, Ewell, and A. P. Hill are between Gainesville and Manassas Junction. We had a severe fight with them to-day, driving them back several miles along the railroad. If you will march promptly and rapidly at the earliest dawn of day upon Manassas Junction, we shall bag the whole crowd. I have directed Reno to march from Greenwich at the same hour upon Manassas Junction, and Kearny, who is in his rear, to march on Bristow at daybreak. Be expeditious, and the day is our own.

JNO. POPE,
Major General Commanding.

Major General MCDOWELL.

A true copy.

T. C. H. SMITH,
Lieutenant Colonel and Aide-de-Camp.

HEADQUARTERS ARMY OF VIRGINIA,
Bristow Station, August 28, 1862—10.40 *a. m.*

GENERAL: Major General Pope directs me to say that as soon as the railroad trains and all public property shall have been safely run back from Warrenton Junction, you will move your command back to Kettle Run Bridge, where you will find the railroad obstructed and the railroad trains stopped. You will there take the same means to save the public property from attack by the enemy as directed in copy of general orders from these headquarters, sent to you yesterday through Major General Porter.

I am, general, very respectfully, your obedient servant,

GEO. D. RUGGLES,
Colonel and Chief of Staff.

Major General BANKS, *Warrenton Junction.*

A true copy.

T. C. H. SMITH,
Lieutenant Colonel and Aide-de-Camp.

HEADQUARTERS ARMY OF VIRGINIA,
Bristow Station, August 28, 1862—10.50 *a. m.*

Major General Pope directs that all the wagon trains be kept closed up and close in rear of the troops. You will accordingly give instructions to the various subordinate quartermasters, including regimental quartermasters, to keep their trains closed and immediately in rear of the troops. Please see that this order is executed.

By command of Major General Pope.

GEO. D. RUGGLES,
Colonel and Chief of Staff.

Colonel CLARY,
Chief Quartermaster, Army of Virginia.

A true copy.

T. C. H. SMITH,
Lieutenant Colonel and Aide-de-Camp.

HEADQUARTERS ARMY OF VIRGINIA,
Bristow Station, August 28, 1862—11 *a. m.*

SIR: Major General Pope directs that you take measures to hunt up the wounded of the enemy, and to provide for them the same as for our own soldiers.

I am, sir, very respectfully, your obedient servant,

GEO. D. RUGGLES,
Colonel and Chief of Staff.

Surgeon MCPARLIN,
Medical Director, Army of Virginia.

A true copy.

T. C. H. SMITH,
Lieutenant Colonel and Aide-de-Camp.

HEADQUARTERS ARMY OF VIRGINIA,
Bristow Station, August 28, 1862—11.10 *a. m.*

The major general commanding directs that one or two boxes of ammunition be thrown into every wagon that passes the railroad train where the ammunition now is, no matter to whom the wagon or wagon train belongs.

By command of Major General Pope.

GEO. D. RUGGLES,
Colonel and Chief of Staff.

Lieutenant F. J. SHUNK,
Chief of Ordnance, Army of Virginia.

A true copy.

T. C. H. SMITH,
Lieutenant Colonel and Aide-de-Camp.

HEADQUARTERS ARMY OF VIRGINIA,
Manassas Junction, August 28, 1862.

Special Orders No. —.]

The trains will come forward in the following order, viz: 1st, Heintzelman's; 2d, McDowell's; 3d, Sigel's; 4th, Porter's.

All the supply and regimental trains will be sent forward to this place as rapidly as possible, ammunition being forwarded in advance of all other supplies.

By command of Major General Pope.

GEO. D. RUGGLES,
Colonel and Chief of Staff.

A true copy.

T. C. H. SMITH,
Lieutenant Colonel and Aide-de-Camp.

HEADQUARTERS ARMY OF VIRGINIA,
Bristow Station, August 28, 1862—11.20 *a. m.*

The major general commanding directs that one or two boxes of ammunition be thrown into every wagon that passes the railroad train where the ammunition now is, no matter to whom the wagon or wagon train belongs. He also directs that the railroad trains be unloaded into the passing wagon trains in the same manner, commencing first to unload the ammunition as hereinbefore directed.

By command of Major General Pope.

GEO. D. RUGGLES,
Colonel and Chief of Staff.

Colonel CLARY,
Chief Quartermaster, Army of Virginia.

A true copy.

T. C. H. SMITH,
Lieutenant Colonel and Aide-de-Camp.

HEADQUARTERS ARMY OF VIRGINIA,
Manassas Junction, August 28, 1862—2 *p. m.*

I sent you a despatch a few minutes ago, directing you to move on Green Spring, to intercept Jackson. Since then I have received your note of this morning. I will, this evening, push forward Reno to Gainesville, and follow with Heintzelman, unless there is a large force of the enemy at Centreville, which I do not believe. Ascertain, if you can, about this. I do not wish you to carry out the order to proceed to Green Spring if you consider it too hazardous, but I will support you in any way you suggest by pushing forward from Manassas Junction across the turnpike. Jackson has a large train, which certainly should be captured. Give me your views fully; you know the country much better than I do. Come no further in this direction with your command, but call back what has advanced thus far.

JNO. POPE,
Major General Commanding.

Major General MCDOWELL.

A true copy.

T. C. H. SMITH,
Lieutenant Colonel and Aide-de-Camp.

HEADQUARTERS ARMY OF VIRGINIA,
Near Bull Run, August 28, 1862—9.50 *p. m.*

GENERAL: General McDowell has intercepted the retreat of the enemy, and is now in his front. Sigel on the right of McDowell. Unless he can escape by passes leading to the north to-night, he must be captured. I desire you to move forward at one o'clock to-night, even if you can carry with you no more than two thousand men, though I trust you will carry the larger part of your division. Pursue the turnpike from Centreville to Warrenton. The enemy is not more than three and a half miles from you. Seize any of the people of the town to guide you. Advance cautiously and drive in the enemy's pickets to-night, and at early dawn attack him vigorously. Hooker shall be close behind you. Extend your right well in the attack. Be sure to march not later than one, with all the men you can take.

JNO. POPE,
Major General Commanding.

Major General KEARNY.

A true copy.

T. C. H. SMITH,
Lieutenant Colonel and Aide-de-Camp.

HEADQUARTERS ARMY OF VIRGINIA,
Near Bull Run, August 28, 1862—10 *p. m.*

GENERAL: General McDowell has intercepted the retreat of the enemy. Sigel is immediately on his right, and I see no possibility of his escape. I have instructed Kearny to push forward cautiously at one o'clock to-night until he drives in the pickets of the enemy, and to assault him vigorously at daylight in the morning. It is of the last importance that Hooker shall march at three o'clock to-night, taking the turnpike from Centreville to Warrenton, and resting on that road one and a half mile beyond Centreville, as reserve for Kearny. Send a copy of this despatch to Hooker immediately; and I beg you particularly to see that Hooker marches at the time specified, even if he should have to do so with one-half of his men. I shall rely upon this.

JNO. POPE,
Major General Commanding.

Major General HEINTZELMAN.

Despatches and orders sent and received, from August 29 *to September* 2, *inclusive.*

HEADQUARTERS ARMY OF VIRGINIA,
Near Bull Run, August 29, 1862—3 *a. m.*

GENERAL: McDowell has intercepted the retreat of Jackson. Sigel is immediately on the right of McDowell. Kearny and Hooker march to attack the enemy's rear at early dawn. Major General Pope directs you to move upon Centreville at the first dawn of day, with your whole command, leaving your trains to follow. It is very important that you should be here at a very early hour in the morning. A severe engagement is likely to take place, and your presence is necessary.

I am, general, very respectfully, your obedient servant,

GEO. D. RUGGLES,
Colonel and Chief of Staff.

Major General PORTER.

A true copy.

T. C. H. SMITH,
Lieutenant Colonel and Aide-de-Camp.

HEADQUARTERS ARMY OF VIRGINIA,
Near Bull Run, August 29, 1862—*5 a. m.*

I sent you verbal orders by Colonel Smith last night. News from the front makes it necessary to modify them. You will accordingly move rapidly on Centreville by the road past these headquarters. Upon arriving at Centreville you will take the turnpike towards Warrenton, and push forward rapidly. You will find the whole corps of Heintzelman in front of you. Pass his stragglers, and keep well up with his command, pushing rapidly towards any firing you may hear.

JOHN POPE,
Major General Commanding.

Major General RENO.

A true copy.

T. C. H. SMITH,
Lieutenant Colonel and Aide-de-Camp.

HEADQUARTERS ARMY OF VIRGINIA,
Centreville, August 29, 1862.

You will please move forward with your joint commands towards Gainesville. I sent General Porter written orders to that effect an hour and a half ago. Heintzelman, Sigel, and Reno are moving on the Warrenton turnpike, and must now be not far from Gainesville. I desire that, as soon as communication is established between this force and your own, the whole command shall halt. It may be necessary to fall back behind Bull's Run at Centreville to-night. I presume it will be so, on account of our supplies. I have sent no orders of any description to Ricketts, and none to interfere in any way with the movements of McDowell's troops, except what I sent by his aide-de-camp last night, which were to hold his position on the Warrenton pike until the troops from here should fall on the enemy's flank and rear. I do not even know Ricketts's position, as I have not been able to find out where General McDowell was until a late hour this morning. General McDowell will take immediate steps to communicate with General Ricketts, and instruct him to rejoin the other divisions of his corps as soon as practicable.

If any considerable advantages are to be gained by departing from this order, it will not be strictly carried out. One thing must be had in view, that the troops must occupy a position from which they can reach Bull Run to-night or by morning. The indications are that the whole force of the enemy is moving in this direction at a pace that will bring them here by to-morrow night or the next day. My own headquarters will be, for the present, with Heintzelman's corps, or at this place.

JOHN POPE,
Major General Commanding.

Generals McDOWELL and PORTER.

A true copy.

SPEED BUTLER,
Colonel and Aide-de-Camp.

HEADQUARTERS IN THE FIELD,
August 29, 1862—4.30 *p. m.*

Your line of march brings you in on the enemy's right flank. I desire you to push forward into action at once on the enemy's flank, and, if possible, on his rear, keeping your right in communication with General Reynolds. The enemy is massed in the woods, but can be shelled out as soon as you can engage their flank. Keep heavy reserves and use your batteries, keeping well closed to your right all the time. In case you are obliged to fall back, do so to your right and rear, so as to keep you in close communication with the right wing.

JOHN POPE,
Major General Commanding.

Major General PORTER.

A true copy.

T. C. H. SMITH,
Lieutenant Colonel and Aide-de-Camp.

HEADQUARTERS IN THE FIELD,
August 29, 1862—5 *o'clock p. m.*

GENERAL: I would prefer that you send your trains direct to Manassas Junction and Centreville. The road is clear, and there is no difficulty about it. Send them through as soon as you can. Send back working parties to try and get the railroad in sufficiently good order, if the trains may be worked back to Bull Run. This is of the last importance, and you cannot get it done too soon. Work night and day at it.

JNO. POPE, *Major General Commanding.*

Major General BANKS.

A true copy.

T. C. H. SMITH,
Lieutenant Colonel and Aide-de-Camp.

HEADQUARTERS ARMY OF VIRGINIA,
In the field near Bull Run, August 29, 1862—8.50 *p. m.*

GENERAL: Immediately upon receipt of this order, the precise hour of receiving which you will acknowledge, you will march your command to the field of battle of to-day, and report to me in person for orders.

You are to understand that you are expected to comply strictly with this order, and to be present on the field within three hours after its reception, or after daybreak to-morrow morning.

JNO. POPE, *Major General Commanding.*

Major General F. J. PORTER.

A true copy.

T. C. H. SMITH,
Lieutenant Colonel and Aide-de-Camp.

AUGUST 29, 1862—8 *p. m.*

I have been instructed by General McClellan to inform you that he will have all the available wagons at Alexandria loaded with rations for your troops, and all of the cars, also, as soon as you will send in a cavalry escort to Alexandria as a guard to the train.

Respectfully,

W. B. FRANKLIN,
Major General Commanding Sixth Corps.

COMMANDING OFFICER *at Centreville.*

A true copy.

T. C. H. SMITH,
Lieutenant Colonel and Aide-de-Camp.

BULL RUN, *August* 30, 1862—6.30 *a. m.*

COLONEL: You will immediately send to Alexandria an officer to bring out all supplies of forage and stores (forage particularly) required for this command. The stores will be brought to Fairfax by rail, and thence by wagons to Centreville. The officer sent by you will obtain from the commanding officer at Alexandria the escort necessary to protect the train.

By command of General Pope.

GEO. D. RUGGLES,
Colonel and Chief of Staff.

Colonel CLARY,
Chief Quartermaster Army of Virginia.

A true copy.

T. C. H. SMITH,
Lieutenant Colonel and Aide-de-Camp.

HEADQUARTERS ARMY OF VIRGINIA,
Battle-field near Groveton, August 30, 1862—9 *a. m.*

Major General Pope directs that you send two hundred and fifty (250) wagons to Major General Banks, in order that he may remove his sick and public property from his present position to Centreville or vicinity.

I am, colonel, very respectfully, your obedient servant,

GEO. D. RUGGLES,
Colonel and Chief of Staff.

Colonel CLARY,
Chief Quartermaster Army of Virginia.

A true copy.

T. C. H. SMITH,
Lieutenant Colonel and Aide-de-Camp.

HEADQUARTERS ARMY OF VIRGINIA,
Near Groveton, August 30, 1862.

COLONEL: General Pope directs that all the wagons at Centreville be unloaded there and the property stored. The wagons will then be sent to Sangster's Station to haul subsistence stores from that place to Centreville.

By command of Major General Pope.

GEO. D. RUGGLES,
Colonel and Chief of Staff.

Colonel BECKWITH, *Chief of Commissary.*

A true copy.

T. C. H. SMITH,
Lieutenant Colonel and Aide-de-Camp.

HEADQUARTERS ARMY OF VIRGINIA,
August 30, 1862—6 *p. m.*

Post your command, and whatever other troops you can collect, and put them in the fortifications and other strong positions around Centreville, and hold those positions to the last extremity.

By command of General Pope.

GEO. D. RUGGLES,
Colonel and Chief of Staff.

General FRANKLIN.

A true copy.

T. C. H. SMITH,
Lieutenant Colonel and Aide-de-Camp.

AUGUST 30—6.45 *p. m.*

You will immediately put all the wagons and everything that interferes with the range of artillery from the works at Centreville a good distance to the rear, on the other side of the town, out of the range of artillery from the works.

By command of Major General Pope.

GEO. D. RUGGLES,
Colonel and Chief of Staff.

Colonel CLARY.

A true copy.

T. C. H. SMITH,
Lieutenant Colonel and Aide-de-Camp.

AUGUST 30, 1862—6.30 *p. m.*

Destroy the public property at Bristow, and fall back upon Centreville at once. Destroy all the railroad property. Your troops at Bristow will withdraw through Brentsville. Your troops at Manassas and between there and Bristow will withdraw to Centreville.

By command of Major General Pope.

GEO. D. RUGGLES,
Colonel and Chief of Staff.

General BANKS.

AUGUST 30—8 *p. m.*

GENERALS: Retire to Centreville to-night with your commands. If possible, go by the way of Sudley's Ford. General Reno commands the rear guard on the turnpike by which the balance of the army will fall back. Upon your arrival at Centreville, you will assemble your commands on the north side of that town. Early in the morning proper positions will be assigned you.

By command of Major General Pope.

GEO. D. RUGGLES,
Colonel and Chief of Staff.

General HEINTZELMAN, (to be opened and read by Generals Kearny and Hooker.)

A true copy.

T. C. H. SMITH,
Lieutenant Colonel and Aide-de-Camp.

HEADQUARTERS ARMY OF VIRGINIA,
Centreville, August 30, 1862.

Special Orders No. —.]

The prisoners of war now at this place will be sent to-morrow to Washington city, under guard of one regiment of infantry, to be furnished for this purpose by Major General McDowell.

By command of Major General Pope.

GEO. D. RUGGLES,
Colonel and Chief of Staff.

A true copy.

T. C. H. SMITH,
Lieutenant Colonel and Aide-de-Camp.

CENTREVILLE, *August* 30, 1862—9.45 *p. m.*

We have had a terrific battle again to-day. The enemy, largely re-enforced, assaulted our position early to-day. We held our ground firmly until 6 p. m., when the enemy, massing very heavy forces on our left, forced back that wing about half a mile. At dark we held that position. Under all the circumstances, both horses and men having been two days without food, and the enemy greatly outnumbering us, I thought it best to draw back to this place at dark. The movement has been made in perfect order, and without loss. The troops are in good heart, and marched off the field without the least hurry or confusion. Their conduct was very fine. The battle was most furious for hours without cessation, and the losses on both sides very heavy. The enemy is badly crippled, and we shall do well enough. Do not be uneasy. We will hold our own here. The labors and hardships of this army for two or three weeks have been beyond description. We have delayed the enemy as long as possible without losing the army. We have damaged him heavily, and I think the army entitled to the gratitude of the country. Be easy; everything will go well.

JNO. POPE.

Major General HALLECK, *General-in-Chief.*

P. S.—We have lost nothing, neither guns nor wagons.

A true copy.

T. C. H. SMITH,
Lieutenant Colonel and Aide-de-Camp.

WASHINGTON, *August* 31, 1862—11 *a. m.*

MY DEAR GENERAL: You have done nobly. Don't yield another inch if you can avoid it. All reserves are being sent forward. Couch's division goes to-day. Part of it went to Sangster's Station last night with Franklin and Sumner, who must be now with you. Can't you renew the attack? I don't write more particularly for fear despatch will not reach you. I am doing all in my power for you and your noble army. God bless you and it.

Send me news more often, if possible.

H. W. HALLECK, *General-in-Chief.*

Major General POPE.

A true copy.

——— ———,
Captain and Aide-deCamp.

[Circular.]

HEADQUARTERS ARMY OF VIRGINIA,
Camp near Centreville, August 31, 1862.

Commanders of army corps will forthwith establish suitable grand guards in front of the positions they respectively hold, and have outposts thrown forward, which shall furnish a line of sentinels covering the entire army. Those on the flanks will furnish a grand guard for the flanks. The advanced position this side of Cub Run will only be held as an outpost, and the division now there will be withdrawn.

By command of Major General Pope.

GEO. D. RUGGLES,
Colonel and Chief of Staff.

A true copy.

T. C. H. SMITH,
Lieutenant Colonel and Aide-de-Camp.

Circular to corps commanders.

HEADQUARTERS ARMY OF VIRGINIA,
Centreville, August 31, 1862—8.30 *a. m.*

GENERAL: The major general commanding the army of Virginia directs me to instruct you to take measures immediately to bring forward and distribute ammunition for your command.

1. Men should be selected to guide the wagons to the troops to be supplied, to report to Lieutenant Colonel Smith, aide-de-camp, at these headquarters.

2. A report of the amount and kind of ammunition required in your command should be made to Lieutenant Colonel Smith.

3. Empty wagons should be collected and sent to report to Lieutenant Colonel Smith.

With great respect, general, your obedient servant,

T. C. H. SMITH,
Lieutenant Colonel and Aide-de-Camp.

A true copy.

E. HAIGHT, *Captain and Aide-de-Camp.*

HEADQUARTERS ARMY OF VIRGINIA,
Centreville, August 31, 1862—10.45 *a. m.*

Our troops are all here in position, though much used up and worn out. I think it would perhaps have been greatly better if Sumner and Franklin had been here three or four days ago; but you may rely on our giving them as desperate a fight as I can force our men to stand up to.

I should like to know whether you feel secure about Washington, should this army be destroyed. I shall fight it as long as a man will stand up to the work. You must judge what is to be done, having in view the safety of the capital.

The enemy is already pushing a cavalry reconnoissance in our front at Cub Run, whether in advance of an attack to-day I do not yet know. I send you this that you may know our position and my purpose.

JOHN POPE, *Major General Commanding.*

Major General HALLECK, *General-in-Chief.*

A true copy.

T. C. H. SMITH,
Lieutenant Colonel and Aide-de-Camp

[Circular.]

HEADQUARTERS ARMY OF VIRGINIA,
Centreville, August 31, 1862.

Commanding officers of army corps will send back to Alexandria all wagons appertaining to their trains, except those absolutely necessary to haul subsistence, stores, and ammunition from Fairfax Court-House to this place for their respective corps. This movement will be under charge of Colonel Clary, chief quartermaster army of Virginia.

By command of Major General Pope.

GEO. D. RUGGLES,
Colonel and Chief of Staff

A true copy.

T. C. H. SMITH,
Lieutenant Colonel and Aide-de-Camp.

HEADQUARTERS ARMY OF VIRGINIA,
Centreville, August 31, 1862.

Special Orders No. —.]

Carroll's brigade of Ricketts's division will proceed at once to Fairfax Station and take post as a guard for commissary stores at that point. The commanding officer of these troops will report upon his arrival at Fairfax Station to Colonel E. G. Beckwith, chief commissary army of Virginia.

By command of Major General Pope.

GEO. D. RUGGLES,
Colonel and Chief of Staff.

A true copy.

T. C. H. SMITH,
Lieutenant Colonel and Aide-de-Camp.

HEADQUARTERS ARMY OF VIRGINIA,
Centreville, August 31, 1862.

SIR: Major General Pope directs you at once to send two regiments of infantry and two pieces of artillery to escort the wagon train now en route to Alexandria as far as Cloud's Mills.

I am, sir, very respectfully, your obedient servant,

GEO. D. RUGGLES,
Colonel and Chief of Staff.

COMMANDING OFFICER, *forces at Fairfax Court-House.*

A true copy.

T. C. H. SMITH,
Lieutenant Colonel and Aide-de-Camp.

CENTREVILLE, *August* 31.

DEAR GENERAL: Your despatch of 11 a. m. has been received, and I thank you for your considerate commendation. I would be glad to have it in such shape that the army might be acquainted with it. We shall fight to the last. The whole secession army engaged us yesterday. I had a letter from Lee this morning. Ewell is killed. Jackson is badly wounded, and other generals of less note wounded. The plan of the enemy will, undoubtedly, be to turn my flank. If he does so he will have his hands full. My troops are in good heart.

I need cavalry horses terribly. Send me two thousand in lots, and under strong escort. I have never yet received a single one.

JNO. POPE, *Major General.*

Major General HALLECK,
General-in-Chief.

A true copy.

T. C. H. SMITH,
Lieutenant Colonel and Aide-de-Camp.

HEADQUARTERS ARMY OF VIRGINIA,
Camp near Centreville, September 1, 1862—3 *o'clock a. m.*

The reconnoitring party of cavalry which you sent out yesterday morning under Captain Haight has, as I am informed, been captured by the enemy's cavalry. It is essential that your right be carefully watched. I desire you at daylight to push a reconnoissance of not less than one brigade, supported, if necessary, by a second, towards the north of your position, to the Little River turnpike and beyond. The direction of your reconnoissance should be as nearly due north as practicable, and should be pushed not less than five miles. It is of great importance that this reconnoissance should be made at an early hour in the morning. The orderly whom you sent to me left me without permission, so that I find it very difficult to find your headquarters. Please send him back.

JNO. POPE,
Major General Commanding.

Major General SUMNER.

A true copy.

T. C. H. SMITH,
Lieutenant Colonel and Aide-de-Camp.

HEADQUARTERS ARMY OF VIRGINIA,
Centreville, September 1, 1862.

GENERAL: The major general commanding directs me to inform you that a large supply of ammunition has arrived since yesterday, say 120 wagons, and that near the earthwork close in rear of Centreville an officer will be found charged with its distribution. The ammunition will be kept in the wagons in which it came, so as to be sent forward to the troops, to be supplied immediately when required.

With great respect, general, your obedient servant,

T. C. H. SMITH,
Lieutenant Colonel and Aide-de-Camp.

MAJOR GENERAL COMMANDING.

A true copy.

T. C. H. SMITH,
Lieutenant Colonel and Aide-de-Camp.

HEADQUARTERS ARMY OF VIRGINIA,
September 1, 1862—5.45 *a. m.*

GENERAL: The reconnoissance is only designed to ascertain whether there is any considerable movement of the enemy's infantry towards our right and rear. We have no cavalry; not a horse that can possibly perform service, and it may be necessary, in order to obtain the information I desire, to drive off the enemy's cavalry. I do not care that the brigade shall be pushed further than the Little River turnpike, whilst skirmishers are thrown still further, in order fully to ascertain whether the enemy is making any movement towards Germantown and Fairfax Court-House. I do not wish any engagement brought on at present on that ground; but where the information required shall have been obtained by the brigade, withdraw it.

JOHN POPE,
Major General Commanding.

Major General E. V. SUMNER.

A true copy.

T. C. H. SMITH,
Lieutenant Colonel and Aide-de-Camp.

HEADQUARTERS OF THE ARMY,
Washington, September 1, 1862.

Yours of last evening was received at 4 a. m. I want to issue a complimentary order, but as you are daily fighting, it could be hardly distributed. I will do so very soon.

Look out well for your right, and don't let the enemy turn it and get between you and the forts. We are strengthening the line of defence as rapidly as possible. Horses will be sent to you to-day. Send despatches to me as often as possible. I hope for an arrival of cavalry to-day.

Yours, truly,
H. W. HALLECK, *General-in-Chief.*

General POPE.

P. S.—Acknowledge hour of receipt of this.

A true copy.

T. C. H. SMITH,
Lieutenant Colonel and Aide-de-Camp.

CENTREVILLE, *September* 1—8.50 *a. m.*

All was quiet yesterday, and so far this morning. My men are resting; they need it much. Forage for our horses is being brought up. Our cavalry is completely broken down, so that there are not five horses to a company that can raise a trot. The consequence is that I am forced to keep considerable infantry along the roads in my rear to make them secure, and even then it is difficult to keep the enemy's cavalry off the roads. I shall attack again to-morrow if I can; the next day certainly. I think it my duty to call your attention to the unsoldierly and dangerous conduct of many brigade and some division commanders of the forces sent here from the peninsula. Every word, and act, and intention, is discouraging, and calculated to break down the spirits of the men and produce disaster. One commander of a corps who was ordered to march from Manassas Junction to join me near Groveton, although he was only five miles distant, failed to get up at all—worse still, fell back to Manassas without a fight, and in plain hearing, at less than three miles distance, of a furious battle which raged all day. It was only in consequence of peremptory orders that he joined me next day; one of his brigades, the brigadier general of which professed to be looking for his division, absolutely remained all day at Centreville, in plain view of the battle, and made no attempt to join. What renders the whole matter worse, these are both officers of the regular army who do not hold back from ignorance or fear. Their constant talk, indulged in publicly and in promiscuous company, is that the army of the Potomac will not fight; that they are demoralized by withdrawal from the peninsula, &c. When such example is set by officers of high rank, the influence is very bad amongst those in subordinate stations. You have hardly an idea of the demoralization among officers of high rank in the Potomac army, arising in all instances from personal feeling in relation to changes of commander-in-chief and others. These men are mere tools or parasites, but their example is producing, and must necessarily produce, very disastrous results. You should know these things, as you alone can stop it. Its source is beyond my reach, though its effects are very perceptible and very dangerous. I am endeavoring to do all I can, and will most assuredly put them where they shall fight or run away. My advice to you—I give it with freedom as I know you will not misunderstand it—is that, in view of any satisfactory results, you draw back this army to the intrenchments in front of Washington, and set to work in that secure place to reorganize and rearrange it. You may avoid great disaster by doing so. I do not consider the matter except in a purely military light, and it is bad enough and grave enough to make some action very necessary. When there is no heart in their leaders, and every disposition to hang back, much cannot be expected from the men.

Please hurry forward cavalry horses to me under strong escort. I need them badly—worse than I can tell you.

JNO. POPE, *Major General.*

Major General HALLECK, *General-in-Chief.*

A true copy.

T. C. H. SMITH,
Lieutenant Colonel and Aide-de-Camp.

HEADQUARTERS ARMY OF VIRGINIA,
Near Centreville, September 1, 1862.

GENERAL: General Pope directs you to establish your grand guards on the pike from Centreville to Warrenton. An outpost of one regiment of infantry and two pieces of artillery of Reynolds's division has been ordered to take post on the same road.

I am, general, very respectfully, your obedient servant,

GEO. D. RUGGLES,
Colonel and Chief of Staff.

Major General FRANKLIN.

A true copy.

T. C. H. SMITH,
Lieutenant Colonel and Aide-de-Camp.

HEADQUARTERS ARMY OF VIRGINIA,
Near Centreville, September 1, 1862.

General Pope directs that you furnish one regiment of infantry as an escort for a wagon train from Fairfax Court-House to Fairfax Station. Lieutenant Devens, 9th infantry, will call for the escort as he proceeds through the town.

I am, sir, very respectfully, your obedient servant,

GEO. D. RUGGLES,
Colonel and Chief of Staff.

To the officer commanding the forces around Fairfax Court-House.

A true copy.

T. C. H. SMITH,
Lieutenant Colonel and Aide-de-Camp.

HEADQUARTERS ARMY OF VIRGINIA,
Centreville, September 1, 1862—11 *o'clock a. m.*

The enemy is deploying his forces on the Little River pike, and preparing to advance by that road on Fairfax Court-House. This movement turns Centreville, and interposes between us and Washington, and will force me to attack his advance, which I shall do as soon as his movement is sufficiently developed. I have nothing like the force you undoubtedly suppose, and the fight will be necessarily desperate. I hope you will make all preparations to make a vigorous defence of the intrenchments around Washington.

JNO. POPE,
Major General Commanding,

Major General HALLECK, *Washington.*

A true copy.

T. C. H. SMITH,
Lieutenant Colonel and Aide-de-Camp.

CENTREVILLE, *September* 1, 1862—12 *m.*

You will march rapidly back to Fairfax Court-House with your whole division, assuming command of the two brigades now there, and immediately occupy Germantown with your whole force, so as to cover the turnpike from this place to Alexandria. Jackson is reported advancing on Fairfax with twenty thousand men. Move quickly.

JNO. POPE,
Major General Commanding.

Major General McDOWELL.

A true copy.

T. C. H. SMITH,
Lieutenant Colonel and Aide-de-Camp.

HEADQUARTERS ARMY OF VIRGINIA,
Centreville, September 1, 1862—1 *p. m.*

You will at once proceed to Germantown, assume command of the troops at Fairfax Court-House, together with the brigades now under command of Colonels Torbert and Hinks.

By command of Major General Pope.

GEO. D. RUGGLES,
Colonel and Chief of Staff.

Major General HOOKER.

A true copy.

T. C. H. SMITH,
Lieutenant Colonel and Aide-de-Camp.

HEADQUARTERS ARMY OF VIRGINIA,
Centreville, September 1, 1862—12.30 *p. m.*

Move your brigade at once to Germantown and join it to the one under Colonel Hinks at that place. Major General Hooker is assigned to the command of the forces arriving at Fairfax Court-House from Washington, together with those stationed at Germantown.

By command of Major General Pope.

GEO. D. RUGGLES,
Colonel and Chief of Staff.

Colonel A. T. TORBERT,
Commanding Brigade near Fairfax Court-House.

A true copy.

T. C. H. SMITH,
Lieutenant Colonel and Aide-de-Camp.

NEAR CENTREVILLE, *September* 1, 1862—4 *p. m.*

If you hear a battle raging to-night near Centreville, advance to the north, keeping your communication open with Reno and near to him, also by the right with Hooker, who will advance his left to your right.

By command of Major General Pope.

GEO. D. RUGGLES,
Colonel and Chief of Staff.

Major General McDOWELL.

A true copy.

T. C. H. SMITH,
Lieutenant Colonel and Aide-de-Camp.

HEADQUARTERS ARMY OF VIRGINIA,
Fairfax Court-House, September 1, 1862.

General Orders No. —.]

The army corps of Heintzelman, Sigel, Sumner, Porter, and Reno, as soon after daylight as possible, will begin to draw slowly to their right in the direction of Fairfax Court-House until they come closely in contact with each other. Major General Reno will follow as closely as possible the line of the old railroad now occupied by him; the others along the pike. He will notify those in his rear of his exact position and every step of his movements, and will ask support if he needs it. They will not be more than half a mile in rear of him. If any severe engagement should occur at any point of the line, the army corps commanders nearest on the right and left will immediately send forward a staff officer to report to the general commanding the troops of the attack, and to notify him that they are ready to support him if he needs it. For the present the general headquarters will be established at Fairfax Court-House.

By command of Major General Pope.

GEO. D. RUGGLES,
Colonel and Chief of Staff.

A true copy.

T. C. H. SMITH,
Lieutenant Colonel and Aide-de-Camp.

HEADQUARTERS ARMY OF VIRGINIA,
Centreville, September 1, 1862—2 *p. m.*

Send back word immediately to Alexandria to hurry up Couch's division and all other troops coming from Washington to Germantown. They must be at Germantown as early this afternoon as possible, certainly to-night. They must take up a strong position. There is no doubt the enemy is approaching you. Hold on to your position to the last. The whole army is on the move to join you.

By command of Major General Pope.

GEO. D. RUGGLES,
Colonel and Chief of Staff.

Colonel TORBERT.

A true copy.

T. C. H. SMITH,
Lieutenant Colonel and Aide-de-Camp.

FAIRFAX COURT-HOUSE, *September* 2, 1862.

As I expected, the enemy last evening attacked my right furiously in the direction of Fairfax Court-House, but were repulsed with heavy loss. Our loss was also severe, General Stevens being killed and Kearny missing. The enemy has not renewed his attack this morning, but is undoubtedly again beating around to the northeast. Your telegram of this date is just received and its provisions will be carried out at once.

JOHN POPE,
Major General Commanding.

Major General HALLECK, *Washington.*

A true copy.

T. C. H. SMITH,
Lieutenant Colonel and Aide-de-Camp.

[Circular.]

HEADQUARTERS ARMY OF VIRGINIA,
Fairfax Court-House, September 2, 1862.

The following movements of troops will be made at once in accordance with the instructions from the War Department, viz:

1. Bank's corps will march by the Braddock road and Annandale, and take post at or near Fort Worth.

2. The corps of Franklin and Hooker will pursue the Little River pike towards Alexandria.

3. Heintzelman's corps the Braddock road towards Fort Lyon.

4. McDowell's corps the road by Fall's Church, Little River and Columbia pikes towards Forts Craig and Tillinghast. The corps of Porter, Sumner, and Sigel, *via* Vienna, towards the Chain Bridge. These three latter corps will keep well closed up, and within easy supporting distance of each other.

The cavalry under General Buford will follow and cover the march of the three corps of Porter, Sumner, and Sigel, and Bayard the troops marching on the road south of it. Sumner will bring up the rear on the route he is ordered to pursue. Hooker will cover the rear on the Little River pike, and Banks the rear on the Braddock road. General Banks will call in the forces from Sangster's and Fairfax Stations, and will break up the depot at the latter place, shipping all stores by rail to Alexandria. The wagon trains, except such as are in immediate use by the corps, will pursue the Little River pike to Alexandria. The commanding officers of corps will send forward a capable officer to Alexandria to take charge of their respective trains, and will conduct them to the headquarters of their respective corps. The medical director will take immediate steps to have all the sick and wounded carried back to Alexandria. General Reno will take up the line of march immediately by the Little River turnpike to Alexandria. The commanders of these various army corps will send forward, several hours in advance, staff officers to notify General McClellan of their approach to the points which they are to occupy.

By command of Major General Pope.

GEORGE D. RUGGLES,
Colonel and Chief of Staff.

A true copy.

T. C. H. SMITH,
Lieutenant Colonel and Aide-de-Camp.

HEADQUARTERS ARMY OF VIRGINIA,
Fairfax, September 2, 1862.

The whole army is retiring in good order, without confusion or the slightest loss of property. The enemy has made no advances this morning, owing, no doubt, to his severe loss last evening. Three army corps pursue the route, *via* Vienna, to Chain Bridge, covered by all the effective cavalry; two corps by the Braddock road. These last corps are ordered to break up the depot at Fairfax Station, call in the troops from Sangster's and elsewhere on the railroad, and to move back to Alexandria. Our whole wagon train is far in advance of us, towards the same place. Our whole force is less than sixty thousand men. Everything is being safely moved back to the intrenchments. When the stragglers can be assembled our force will be largely increased. I shall leave here with the last, and encamp to-night near Ball's Cross Roads.

JNO. POPE,
Major General Commanding.

Major General HALLECK.

A true copy.

T. C. H. SMITH,
Lieutenant Colonel and Aide-de-Camp.

NEW YORK, *January* 27, 1863.

A despatch was received from Major General Banks, on the 2d of September, stating that the wagon trains in his charge had all been brought in safely—nothing lost.

T. C. H. SMITH,
Lieutenant Colonel and Aide-de-Camp.

HEADQUARTERS ARMY OF VIRGINIA,
Ball's Cross Roads, September 2, 1862—7.10 *p. m.*

I arrived here safely. Command coming in on the road without much molestation. Some artillery firing on the road, through Vienna, to Chain Bridge, but nothing of a serious character, so far as I can learn. Within an hour all the commands on the other roads will be in camp within the intrenchments—the three corps on the Vienna and Chain Bridge road by to-morrow morning. I await your orders. The enemy still continue to beat around to the north. I do not myself believe that any attack here is contemplated. The troops are very weary, but otherwise in good condition.

JNO. POPE,
Major General Commanding.

Major General HALLECK,
General-in-Chief, Washington.

www.ingramcontent.com/pod-product-compliance
Lightning Source LLC
LaVergne TN
LVHW010251110826
845151LV00004B/1441

9781425522759